AF679741

Machine Learning and Spatial Optimization

(Volume 1)

Edited by

Kanwarpreet Singh
University Centre for Research and Development (UCRD)
Chandigarh University, Mohali, Punjab
India

Arundhati
Department of Civil Engineering
Chandigarh University, Mohali, Punjab
India

Manmeet Kaur
Department of Civil Engineering
Chandigarh University, Mohali, Punjab
India

Abhishek Sharma
University Centre for Research and Development (UCRD)
Chandigarh University, Mohali, Punjab
India

Aditya Kumar Tiwary
University Centre for Research and Development (UCRD)
Chandigarh University, Mohali, Punjab
India

&

Sahil Sharma
University Centre for Research and Development (UCRD)
Chandigarh University, Mohali, Punjab
India

Machine Learning and Spatial Optimization

(Volume 1)

Editors: Kanwarpreet Singh, Arundhati, Manmeet Kaur, Abhishek Sharma,
Aditya Kumar Tiwary & Sahil Sharma

ISBN (Online): 979-8-89881-378-9

ISBN (Print): 979-8-89881-379-6

ISBN (Paperback): 979-8-89881-380-2

© 2026, Bentham Books imprint.

Published by Bentham Science Publishers Pte. Ltd. Singapore, in collaboration with Eureka Conferences, USA. All Rights Reserved.

First published in 2026.

BENTHAM SCIENCE PUBLISHERS LTD.

End User License Agreement (for non-institutional, personal use)

This is an agreement between you and Bentham Science Publishers Ltd. Please read this License Agreement carefully before using the ebook/echapter/ejournal (**"Work"**). Your use of the Work constitutes your agreement to the terms and conditions set forth in this License Agreement. If you do not agree to these terms and conditions then you should not use the Work.

Bentham Science Publishers agrees to grant you a non-exclusive, non-transferable limited license to use the Work subject to and in accordance with the following terms and conditions. This License Agreement is for non-library, personal use only. For a library / institutional / multi user license in respect of the Work, please contact: permission@benthamscience.org.

Usage Rules:

1. All rights reserved: The Work is the subject of copyright and Bentham Science Publishers either owns the Work (and the copyright in it) or is licensed to distribute the Work. You shall not copy, reproduce, modify, remove, delete, augment, add to, publish, transmit, sell, resell, create derivative works from, or in any way exploit the Work or make the Work available for others to do any of the same, in any form or by any means, in whole or in part, in each case without the prior written permission of Bentham Science Publishers, unless stated otherwise in this License Agreement.
2. You may download a copy of the Work on one occasion to one personal computer (including tablet, laptop, desktop, or other such devices). You may make one back-up copy of the Work to avoid losing it.
3. The unauthorised use or distribution of copyrighted or other proprietary content is illegal and could subject you to liability for substantial money damages. You will be liable for any damage resulting from your misuse of the Work or any violation of this License Agreement, including any infringement by you of copyrights or proprietary rights.

Disclaimer:

Bentham Science Publishers does not guarantee that the information in the Work is error-free, or warrant that it will meet your requirements or that access to the Work will be uninterrupted or error-free. The Work is provided "as is" without warranty of any kind, either express or implied or statutory, including, without limitation, implied warranties of merchantability and fitness for a particular purpose. The entire risk as to the results and performance of the Work is assumed by you. No responsibility is assumed by Bentham Science Publishers, its staff, editors and/or authors for any injury and/or damage to persons or property as a matter of products liability, negligence or otherwise, or from any use or operation of any methods, products instruction, advertisements or ideas contained in the Work.

Limitation of Liability:

In no event will Bentham Science Publishers, its staff, editors and/or authors, be liable for any damages, including, without limitation, special, incidental and/or consequential damages and/or damages for lost data and/or profits arising out of (whether directly or indirectly) the use or inability to use the Work. The entire liability of Bentham Science Publishers shall be limited to the amount actually paid by you for the Work.

General:

1. Any dispute or claim arising out of or in connection with this License Agreement or the Work (including non-contractual disputes or claims) will be governed by and construed in accordance with the laws of Singapore. Each party agrees that the courts of the state of Singapore shall have exclusive jurisdiction to settle any dispute or claim arising out of or in connection with this License Agreement or the Work (including non-contractual disputes or claims).
2. Your rights under this License Agreement will automatically terminate without notice and without the

need for a court order if at any point you breach any terms of this License Agreement. In no event will any delay or failure by Bentham Science Publishers in enforcing your compliance with this License Agreement constitute a waiver of any of its rights.

3. You acknowledge that you have read this License Agreement, and agree to be bound by its terms and conditions. To the extent that any other terms and conditions presented on any website of Bentham Science Publishers conflict with, or are inconsistent with, the terms and conditions set out in this License Agreement, you acknowledge that the terms and conditions set out in this License Agreement shall prevail.

Bentham Science Publishers Pte. Ltd.
No. 9 Raffles Place
Office No. 26-01
Singapore 048619
Singapore
Email: subscriptions@benthamscience.net

BENTHAM SCIENCE

CONTENTS

FOREWORD

The increasing severity of environmental problems facing the modern world—from the long-lasting and widespread effects of climate change and the rapid depletion of resources to the ongoing reduction in biological diversity—requires better ways of monitoring and managing the environment in more sophisticated, systematic, and holistic ways. In considering these timely issues, this book explores the essential role that spatial data can play in helping us understand and investigate them. Spatial data—the data that is somehow tied to a geographical location—are powerful tools for monitoring and assessing the environment, and therefore provide good visualizations, comparisons, and assessments of environmental patterns and processes.

This book stresses the need to develop strategies and actions to address a range of environmental issues, grounded in spatial analysis and established scientific and computational methods. From investigating some of the most serious and widespread environmental problems in the world—air pollution—to assessing the appropriate and fair management of water use, the authors in this book define interesting and useful ways that data tied to locations can show insights based on well-defined and precise frameworks in order to support evidence-based actions and policy. This shows how practitioners, researchers, and decision-makers can benefit from concrete examples. Environmental sustainability requires researchers to expand their perception of the natural world and how it can be conserved. In situations where environmental systems operate as intended, researchers and other practitioners eliminate the need to stop unsafe practices, seek to identify new pathways to environmental sustainability, and facilitate strategic alliances to operate in that manner. The case studies in this book come from diverse fields and disciplines (geography, hydrology, environmental engineering, ecology, geoscience, etc.) to identify ways to successfully utilize spatial thinking to contribute to sustainable development. The text demonstrates the necessity of collaboration, settler or stakeholder agreements, addressing issues in an ongoing manner, long-term strategic planning, and working smartly using data, data management, and technology. By identifying and sharing these ways to engage in the ongoing management of natural resources, it is hoped that the text has added value to efforts to safeguard and sustain the environment. Ultimately, it is hoped that the applications of the spatial methods and applicable models of environmental science in this text will combine to bring greater resilience, support conservation, and predictably steer communities and organizations along a healthier pathway that does not compromise the ability of other good stewards who may come after them and empowers us all to reimagine our relationship with the natural world and improve the sustainability of our resources in communion with it.

Ravi Kumar Sharma
Department of Civil Engineering
National Institute of Technology
Hamirpur, Himachal Pradesh
India

PREFACE

In the face of growing environmental degradation and increasing climate variability, the need for precise, reliable, and timely environmental monitoring has become more critical than ever before. From the melting of glaciers and rising sea levels to the intensification of droughts, floods, and wildfires, communities across the globe are experiencing the tangible impacts of ecological imbalances. This book is an earnest attempt to contribute to the global efforts aimed at understanding and mitigating these challenges through the integration of spatial data and field-based environmental monitoring techniques.

The book provides a comprehensive overview of how geospatial tools such as remote sensing, cartography, spatial mapping, and geographic information systems (GIS) can be effectively applied to study, interpret, and manage the Earth's dynamic natural processes. It highlights the role of topographic variables, land use patterns, hydrological behavior, soil characteristics, vegetation cover, and terrain features in shaping environmental outcomes. By focusing on key sectors such as water resource planning, air quality assessment, disaster preparedness, forest management, and land degradation studies, this volume offers in-depth guidance on how to use spatial analysis to inform sustainable environmental decisions.

Through its collection of thematic chapters and case studies, the book also emphasizes the importance of ground surveys, historical data, field validation, and empirical research. Each contribution reflects the interdisciplinary nature of environmental science, incorporating perspectives from geography, ecology, civil engineering, geology, and urban studies. These studies not only enhance our understanding of ecological processes but also equip policymakers, researchers, and planners with the knowledge required to develop targeted mitigation strategies. The book is intended for students, academic researchers, practitioners, and professionals involved in environmental planning, natural resource management, disaster risk reduction, and infrastructure development. It serves as both a learning resource and a technical reference for those aiming to tackle real-world environmental challenges using structured, spatially driven approaches.

Ultimately, this work aims to foster a deeper appreciation of how spatially referenced data, when combined with domain expertise and field observations, can help create more sustainable landscapes and resilient communities. We hope that the insights presented herein will stimulate further research and inspire collaborative efforts toward environmental protection and climate-sensitive development across the globe.

Kanwarpreet Singh
University Centre for Research and Development (UCRD)
Chandigarh University, Mohali, Punjab
India

Arundhati
Department of Civil Engineering
Chandigarh University, Mohali, Punjab
India

Manmeet Kaur
Department of Civil Engineering
Chandigarh University, Mohali, Punjab
India

Abhishek Sharma
University Centre for Research and Development (UCRD)
Chandigarh University, Mohali, Punjab
India

Aditya Kumar Tiwary
University Centre for Research and Development (UCRD)
Chandigarh University, Mohali, Punjab
India

&

Sahil Sharma
University Centre for Research and Development (UCRD)
Chandigarh University, Mohali, Punjab
India

List of Contributors

Amrita Chaudhary	Department of Computer Science and Engineering, Chandigarh University, Mohali, Punjab, India
Amenjor Senagah	College of Engineering, University of Liberia, Monrovia, Liberia
Ajay Kumar	Department of Civil Engineering, National Institute of Technology Delhi, New Delhi, India
Asma Heyat	Department of Civil Engineering, Jamia Millia Islamia, New Delhi, Delhi, India
Akhilesh Nautiyal	Department of Civil Engineering, National Institute of Technology (NIT) Uttarakhand, Srinagar, Uttarakhand, India Department of Electrical Engineering, National Institute of Technology (NIT) Uttarakhand, Srinagar, Uttarakhand, India
Abhishek Sharma	University Centre for Research and Development (UCRD), Chandigarh University, Mohali, Punjab, India
Aditya Kumar Tiwari	University Centre for Research and Development (UCRD), Chandigarh University, Mohali, Punjab, India
Arundhati	Department of Civil Engineering, Chandigarh University, Mohali, Punjab, India
Baldev Setia	Department of Civil Engineering, National Institute of Technology, Kurukshetra, Kurukshetra, Haryana, India
BVS Praveen	Department of Chemical Engineering, Chaitanya Bharathi Institute of Technology, Hyderabad, Telangana, India
Charnpreet Kaur	Department of Computer Science and Engineering, Chandigarh University, Mohali, Punjab, India
Chandni	School of Geography, Earth and Environmental Sciences, University of Birmingham, Birmingham, United Kingdom
Farrukh Naseem	Department of Civil Engineering, Indian Institute of Technology (Indian School of Mines) Dhanbad, Jharkhand, India
Gagandeep Singh	Department of Computer Science and Engineering, Chandigarh University, Mohali, Punjab, India
Har Amrit Singh Sandhu	Department of Civil Engineering, Punjab Engineering College (Deemed to be University), Chandigarh, India
Kanwarpreet Singh	University Centre for Research and Development (UCRD), Chandigarh University, Mohali, Punjab, India
Laxmikant Bhardwaj	Amity Institute of Environmental, Toxicology, Safety & Management (AIETSM), Amity University, Noida, Uttar Pradesh, India
Mohd. Aamir Mazhar	Department of Civil Engineering, Jamia Millia Islamia, New Delhi, Delhi, India
Mukul Bajpai	CSIR–National Institute of Science Communication and Policy Research, New Delhi, Delhi, India

Manmeet Kaur	Department of Civil Engineering, Chandigarh University, Mohali, Punjab, India
Momina	Department of Civil Engineering, Jamia Millia Islamia, New Delhi, Delhi, India
Narsimha Adimalla	School of Water Resources and Environment Engineering, East China University of Technology, Nanchang, Jiangxi, China
Puneet Kaur	Department of Computer Science and Engineering, Chandigarh University, Mohali, Punjab, India
Preety Sharma	Department of Computer Science and Engineering, Chandigarh University, Mohali, Punjab, India
Preetpal Singh	Department of Civil Engineering, Rayat Bahra University, Kharar, Punjab, India
Rakesh Choudhary	Department of Civil Engineering, National Institute of Technology Delhi, New Delhi, India
Ravinder Kumar	Department of Electrical Engineering, National Institute of Technology (NIT) Uttarakhand, Srinagar, Uttarakhand, India
Rahul Shakya	Department of Civil Engineering, Institute of Engineering and Technology Lucknow, Lucknow, Uttar Pradesh, India
Saikumar Swarnapudi	Department of Computer Science and Engineering, Chandigarh University, Mohali, Punjab, India
Shahid Ikabal	Department of Civil Engineering, Jamia Millia Islamia, New Delhi, Delhi, India Department of Chemical Engineering, Indian Institute of Technology (Indian School of Mines), Dhanbad, Jharkhand, India
Shubham Gupta	Department of Analytics and Artificial Intelligence, Center of Excellence (COE), Noblesoft Solutions Inc., San Antonio, Texas, USA
Sahil Sharma	University Centre for Research and Development (UCRD), Chandigarh University, Mohali, Punjab, India
Vanshika Bhardwaj	Department of Civil Engineering, Punjab Engineering College (Deemed to be University), Chandigarh, India

CHAPTER 1

Introduction to Environmental Monitoring

Vanshika Bhardwaj[1,*], **Har Amrit Singh Sandhu**[1] and **Baldev Setia**[2]

[1] *Department of Civil Engineering, Punjab Engineering College (Deemed to be University), Chandigarh, India*

[2] *Department of Civil Engineering, National Institute of Technology Kurukshetra, Kurukshetra, Haryana, India*

Abstract: Environmental monitoring is vital for assessing the impacts of human activities on ecosystems by systematically collecting and analyzing data on air, water, soil, and biodiversity. It provides the foundation for evidence-based policymaking and sustainable resource management, especially as global challenges like climate change, deforestation, and pollution intensify. Effective monitoring requires a multidisciplinary approach, integrating advancements in technology, spatial analysis, and data science to provide accurate and timely insights into environmental changes. One of the primary objectives of environmental monitoring is to detect and assess changes in environmental conditions over time. This includes tracking pollutants, evaluating ecosystem health, and identifying emerging risks to both natural and human systems. Advances in remote sensing, Geographic Information Systems (GIS), and the Internet of Things (IoT) have enabled global-scale data collection, improving our understanding of deforestation, glacier melting, and biodiversity loss. Furthermore, machine learning and predictive modeling enhance our ability to anticipate environmental trends and develop proactive mitigation strategies. Environmental monitoring also plays a vital role in ensuring compliance with environmental regulations and fostering accountability among governments, industries, and organizations. Despite challenges such as resource limitations and complex data interpretation, collaboration across scientific, policy, and community sectors is critical to the success of environmental monitoring initiatives, helping safeguard ecosystems and promote sustainable futures.

Keywords: Air quality, Biodiversity, Environmental monitoring, Machine learning, Remote sensing, Soil quality, Water quality.

INTRODUCTION TO ENVIRONMENTAL MONITORING

Environmental monitoring plays a pivotal role in understanding, managing, and mitigating the impacts of human activities on natural ecosystems. It encompasses

* **Corresponding author Vanshika Bhardwaj:** Department of Civil Engineering, Punjab Engineering College (Deemed to be University), Chandigarh, India; E-mail: vanshikabhardwaj.phd23civil@pec.edu.in

Kanwarpreet Singh, Arundhati, Manmeet Kaur, Abhishek Sharma, Aditya Kumar Tiwary & Sahil Sharma (Eds.)
All rights reserved-© 2026 Bentham Science Publishers

the systematic collection, analysis, and interpretation of data related to environmental parameters to assess the quality of air, water, soil, and biodiversity [1]. By providing critical insights into environmental changes and potential threats, monitoring serves as the foundation for evidence-based policymaking, sustainable resource management, and global environmental protection. The growing urgency of addressing environmental challenges such as climate change, deforestation, and pollution has significantly heightened the importance of monitoring. These challenges are complex and interlinked, often transcending geographical and political boundaries [2]. As a result, effective monitoring requires an interdisciplinary approach, leveraging advancements in technology, data science, and spatial analysis to gather accurate and comprehensive information [3].

One of the primary goals of environmental monitoring is to detect and evaluate changes in environmental conditions over time. This includes tracking pollutant levels, assessing ecosystem health, and identifying emerging trends that may pose risks to both the natural environment and human well-being [4]. For instance, monitoring air quality in urban areas can help identify sources of pollution and guide measures to improve public health. Similarly, observing water quality in rivers and lakes is essential for ensuring safe drinking water and protecting aquatic life [5]. Technological advancements have revolutionized the field of Environmental monitoring. Remote sensing, Geographic Information Systems (GIS), and the Internet of Things (IoT) have enabled real-time data collection and analysis on a global scale. These tools provide valuable insights into environmental processes, such as deforestation rates, glacier melting, and the spread of invasive species [6]. Furthermore, the integration of machine learning algorithms and predictive modeling has enhanced our ability to forecast environmental changes and develop proactive strategies to mitigate their impacts.

Another critical aspect of environmental monitoring is its role in fostering accountability and compliance with environmental regulations. Governments, industries, and organizations rely on monitoring data to demonstrate adherence to laws and standards [7]. For example, emissions monitoring ensures that industries comply with air quality regulations, while biodiversity surveys assess the effectiveness of conservation efforts. However, environmental monitoring is not without its challenges. Data collection can be resource-intensive, particularly in remote or inaccessible regions. Additionally, the interpretation of environmental data requires expertise and sophisticated analytical tools to account for variability and uncertainty [7, 8]. Collaboration among stakeholders, scientists, policymakers, industries, and communities is essential to overcome these challenges and ensure the success of monitoring programs. In summary, environmental monitoring serves as the cornerstone of efforts to understand and address the pressing environmental issues of our time. By integrating technological innovations and interdisciplinary approaches, it helps safeguard natural ecosystems, enhance environmental resilience, and build sustainable future [9].

Environmental Components of Monitoring

Environmental monitoring is an essential tool for understanding the state of our natural world and responding effectively to environmental challenges. By systematically tracking key components such as air, water, soil, biodiversity, and climate, monitoring provides critical data that supports environmental protection, public health, and sustainable development [10]. It enables early detection of pollution, assesses the effectiveness of environmental regulations, and informs policy decisions at local, national, and global levels. With the growing threats of climate change, ecosystem degradation, and resource depletion, the role of comprehensive and continuous environmental monitoring has never been more important. Strengthening monitoring systems and integrating advanced technologies such as remote sensing, GIS, and real-time sensor networks can significantly enhance our ability to protect the environment and ensure a healthy planet for future generations [11].

Air Quality Monitoring

Air quality monitoring is the process of measuring the concentration of airborne pollutants to assess the level of air contamination and its impact on human health, ecosystems, and the atmosphere. It plays a crucial role in identifying pollution sources, evaluating the effectiveness of air pollution control strategies, and ensuring compliance with national and international air quality standards. The primary pollutants typically monitored include particulate matter (PM2.5 and PM10), nitrogen dioxide (NO_2), sulfur dioxide (SO_2), carbon monoxide (CO), ozone (O_3), and volatile organic compounds (VOCs) [12]. Monitoring techniques range from fixed monitoring stations and mobile labs to advanced methods such as satellite remote sensing and low-cost sensor networks. These technologies provide both real-time and long-term data necessary for risk assessment and environmental management. For instance, the United States Environmental Protection Agency (EPA) operates the AirNow program, which provides timely air quality information to stakeholders, supporting awareness and decision-making [13]. As urbanization and industrial activities increase, particularly in developing countries, air quality monitoring becomes increasingly vital for mitigating health risks such as respiratory diseases, cardiovascular conditions, and premature mortality [12, 13].

Water Quality Monitoring

Water quality monitoring involves the systematic observation and analysis of the physical, chemical, and biological characteristics of water bodies to ensure their suitability for various uses, including drinking, irrigation, recreation, and ecosystem support [14]. Key parameters typically measured include pH, temperature, turbidity, electrical conductivity, dissolved oxygen (DO), biochemical oxygen demand (BOD), chemical oxygen demand (COD), nutrients such as nitrates and phosphates, heavy metals (*e.g.*, lead, mercury, arsenic), and microbial contaminants like *Escherichia coli*. Monitoring is carried out across different types of water sources, rivers, lakes, reservoirs, groundwater, and coastal waters using field instruments, laboratory analysis, and increasingly, remote sensing and automated sensor networks [14, 15]. The primary goals of water quality monitoring are to detect pollution, assess trends over time, support water resource management, and safeguard public health and aquatic biodiversity. Globally, initiatives such as UNEP's GEMS/Water Programme play a significant role in collecting and analyzing water quality data to inform policy and international reporting obligations [13]. Effective monitoring is crucial, especially in regions facing challenges such as rapid urbanization, agricultural runoff, industrial effluents, and climate-induced changes in hydrological cycles.

Soil Monitoring

Soil monitoring refers to the systematic assessment of soil properties and conditions to evaluate its health, fertility, and contamination levels over time. It plays a critical role in ensuring sustainable land use, maintaining agricultural productivity, preventing land degradation, and protecting environmental and public health. Key parameters typically monitored include soil pH, organic matter content, texture, moisture, nutrient concentrations (nitrogen, phosphorus, potassium), salinity, compaction, and the presence of heavy metals or pollutants. Monitoring also helps detect signs of erosion, desertification, and soil sealing due to urban expansion. Soil data is collected through field surveys, laboratory analysis, and, increasingly, remote sensing and geospatial technologies. These tools allow for large-scale assessment and real-time monitoring of soil conditions. In Europe, the European Soil Data Centre (ESDAC) provides a comprehensive platform for soil-related data and supports decision-making through harmonized methodologies and policy-relevant indicators [16]. Regular soil monitoring is essential not only for managing agricultural land but also for understanding ecosystem functions, land-use change impacts, and supporting climate change adaptation strategies, particularly in regions facing degradation risks [17].

Biodiversity Monitoring

Biodiversity monitoring is the continuous process of observing, recording, and assessing the variety and variability of living organisms and their habitats over time. It is essential for understanding the health of ecosystems, detecting changes in species populations, and guiding conservation and management strategies [16]. Key indicators include species richness, abundance, population trends, habitat integrity, and the presence of invasive or endangered species. Biodiversity monitoring can be carried out using a range of techniques, such as field surveys, remote sensing, camera traps, citizen science, and environmental DNA (eDNA) analysis. These methods allow scientists and conservationists to detect ecological disturbances caused by habitat loss, climate change, pollution, overexploitation, and invasive species. Globally, initiatives such as the Living Planet Index developed by the World Wildlife Fund (WWF) and the Zoological Society of London (ZSL) track trends in global biodiversity by analyzing thousands of vertebrate population datasets [17]. The information gathered through biodiversity monitoring is critical for evaluating progress toward international biodiversity targets, such as the Aichi Biodiversity Targets and the Kunming-Montreal Global Biodiversity Framework, and for informing policy decisions aimed at halting biodiversity loss [18].

Climate Monitoring

Climate monitoring involves the systematic observation and analysis of atmospheric, oceanic, and terrestrial variables over extended periods to detect trends, variability, and long-term changes in the Earth's climate system. It is a critical component in understanding the impacts of natural processes and anthropogenic activities, particularly the influence of greenhouse gas emissions on global warming [19]. Key parameters monitored include temperature, precipitation, humidity, atmospheric pressure, wind patterns, sea surface temperatures, ocean salinity, glacial mass balance, and sea level rise. Monitoring is conducted using a combination of ground-based observation networks, weather stations, satellites, and ocean buoys, ensuring spatial and temporal data coverage on both global and regional scales. The Global Climate Observing System (GCOS), coordinated by the World Meteorological Organization (WMO), plays a central role in maintaining the infrastructure and standards necessary for high-quality, consistent, and comprehensive climate observations. Reliable climate data is essential for developing climate models, predicting extreme weather events, informing international climate negotiations such as those under the UNFCCC, and guiding national adaptation and mitigation strategies [20].

Application of Environmental Monitoring

Environmental monitoring also plays a vital role in protecting ecosystems, ensuring public health, and guiding sustainable development. By providing accurate, real-time, and long-term data on environmental conditions, it enables early detection of ecological changes, supports informed decision-making, and ensures compliance with environmental regulations. The applications range from air and water quality management to climate change assessment, land use monitoring, and disaster risk reduction, demonstrating its significance across local, national, and global scales [21]. Advancements in sensor technology, satellite remote sensing, and data analytics have greatly enhanced our ability to monitor environmental parameters more efficiently and comprehensively [22]. Moreover, environmental monitoring supports major international initiatives such as the Sustainable Development Goals (SDGs), the Paris Agreement, and REDD+, reinforcing its role in global environmental governance. As environmental challenges continue to grow in complexity and urgency, the integration of monitoring systems with policy frameworks, community participation, and technological innovation will be key to achieving a resilient and sustainable future [23].

Air Quality Management

Air quality management refers to the systematic monitoring, regulation, and improvement of air conditions to protect human health and the environment. With increasing urbanization and industrial activities, air pollution has emerged as a major public health concern worldwide. Common pollutants such as particulate matter (PM2.5 and PM10), nitrogen dioxide (NO_2), sulfur dioxide (SO_2), carbon monoxide (CO), ozone (O_3), and volatile organic compounds (VOCs) are primarily emitted from vehicles, industrial processes, power plants, and biomass burning. These pollutants not only degrade environmental quality but also contribute to respiratory illnesses, cardiovascular diseases, and premature deaths. To effectively manage air quality, continuous monitoring is essential. This involves the use of fixed monitoring stations that provide high-precision data, mobile monitoring units for flexible assessments, satellite remote sensing for wide-scale observation, and low-cost sensor networks that enable community-level monitoring. The data collected helps governments and regulatory agencies identify pollution sources, enforce emission standards, evaluate the effectiveness of air quality policies, and issue timely health advisories to the public.

An example of effective air quality management can be seen in Delhi, India, where extensive air quality monitoring networks operated by the Central Pollution Control Board (CPCB) and Delhi Pollution Control Committee (DPCC) provide real-time data on pollution levels. These insights support the implementation of emergency measures such as the Odd-Even vehicle rationing scheme, bans on construction activities, and restrictions on firecracker use during severe pollution periods like Diwali and winter months. A notable international case is Beijing, China, which faced severe air pollution in the early 2010s. In response, the government launched the Air Pollution Prevention and Control Action Plan (2013–2017), underpinned by a comprehensive air quality monitoring system. The data enabled targeted interventions such as the replacement of coal-fired boilers, promotion of electric vehicles, and closure of polluting industries. As a result, the city achieved a significant 35% reduction in PM2.5 concentrations over the five-year period [16].

Despite its importance, air quality management faces challenges such as the high cost of establishing monitoring infrastructure, uneven distribution of monitoring stations, data accessibility issues, and limited integration of data into policymaking in many developing countries. Addressing these challenges requires stronger institutional capacity, technological innovation, and international collaboration. Air quality monitoring and management remain central to sustainable urban planning and public health protection. By leveraging accurate data and evidence-based interventions, cities across the world can mitigate the impacts of air pollution and move toward cleaner, healthier environments [24].

Water Resource Management

Water resource management involves the planning, development, distribution, and monitoring of water resources to ensure their sustainable use for domestic, agricultural, industrial, and environmental needs. As global populations grow and climate change alters hydrological cycles, efficient water management is more critical than ever. Key challenges include water scarcity, contamination of surface and groundwater sources, uneven distribution of resources, and degradation of aquatic ecosystems [25]. A core component of effective water resource management is water quality monitoring. This process assesses physical, chemical, and biological characteristics of water bodies such as rivers, lakes, aquifers, and coastal areas. Monitored parameters typically include pH, turbidity, temperature, dissolved oxygen (DO), biological oxygen demand (BOD), nutrients (nitrogen and phosphorus), heavy metals, and microbial contaminants [25]. These data help detect pollution sources, evaluate ecosystem health, and ensure compliance with water quality standards.

One prominent example is the European Union's Water Framework Directive (WFD), which mandates member states to achieve a "good" status for all water bodies through integrated water resource management and continuous monitoring

[26]. This policy framework has improved coordination between countries and promoted the use of scientific data for sustainable water governance. In developing countries, water resource management efforts have often focused on combating water pollution in rivers heavily burdened by industrial discharge, untreated sewage, and agricultural runoff. In India, the National Mission for Clean Ganga (NMCG) aims to rejuvenate the Ganga River through a multi-pronged approach involving sewage treatment infrastructure, river surface cleaning, and real-time water quality monitoring. A network of water quality monitoring stations operated by the Central Pollution Control Board (CPCB) and state agencies plays a vital role in tracking pollutant levels, identifying critical stretches, and informing restoration efforts [27].

Technological advancements have greatly enhanced water monitoring systems. Remote sensing, Geographic Information Systems (GIS), Internet of Things (IoT)-based sensors, and satellite-based monitoring now provide large-scale, near-real-time data on water availability and quality. These tools support early warning systems for floods and droughts, enable more efficient irrigation management, and help policymakers make informed decisions on water allocation and conservation strategies [26]. Despite these advancements, water resource management faces persistent challenges. Many regions lack sufficient monitoring infrastructure, data integration platforms, and skilled personnel. Additionally, water governance is often fragmented across multiple agencies, hindering coordinated action. Addressing these issues requires strong institutional frameworks, public awareness, stakeholder participation, and international cooperation. In conclusion, water resource management is essential not only for meeting current human demands but also for preserving freshwater ecosystems and ensuring long-term sustainability [27]. Through integrated monitoring and adaptive management, societies can build resilience to water-related risks and secure this vital resource for future generations.

Climate Change Assessment

Climate change assessment involves the systematic evaluation of climate-related data and trends to understand the causes, impacts, and potential responses to global warming. It draws on multidisciplinary research and long-term environmental monitoring to examine changes in temperature, precipitation patterns, sea level rise, ice sheet dynamics, and the frequency of extreme weather events [28]. These assessments are critical for identifying vulnerabilities, developing adaptation strategies, and informing climate policy at local, national, and global levels. The backbone of climate change assessment is accurate and consistent climate monitoring, which is achieved through a combination of ground-based observation networks, ocean buoys, weather stations, and satellite remote sensing [29]. Key indicators include atmospheric greenhouse gas concentrations (such as CO_2, CH_4, and N_2O), global surface temperatures, sea surface temperatures, glacier mass balance, and Arctic sea ice extent. Data from these sources are compiled and analyzed by organizations such as the Intergovernmental Panel on Climate Change (IPCC), which publishes comprehensive assessment reports every few years to guide international climate negotiations and national action plans [30].

One notable example of climate monitoring infrastructure is NASA's Earth Observing System (EOS), which uses satellites like Terra, Aqua, and Suomi NPP to collect continuous data on Earth's climate system. The Moderate Resolution Imaging Spectroradiometer (MODIS) instrument on board Terra and Aqua monitors variables such as land surface temperature, cloud cover, and vegetation health [31]. These datasets are invaluable for modeling climate scenarios, assessing ecosystem responses, and tracking long-term environmental changes. Climate change assessments have also highlighted the disproportionate impact of global warming on vulnerable communities and ecosystems. For instance, small island nations face existential threats due to rising sea levels, while sub-Saharan Africa is increasingly exposed to heatwaves, droughts, and agricultural stress. Recognizing these threats, international frameworks such as the Paris Agreement (2015) aim to limit global temperature rise to well below 2°C above pre-industrial levels, with efforts to cap it at 1.5°C [32]. Despite growing awareness, significant gaps remain in climate observation in low-income regions due to limited funding, technical capacity, and infrastructure [33]. Bridging these gaps is essential for equitable and effective climate adaptation. Moreover, integrating local knowledge systems with scientific data can enhance the relevance and applicability of assessments. In conclusion, climate change assessment is a vital tool for understanding the dynamics of Earth's climate system and for crafting informed responses to one of the most pressing challenges of our time. Continued investment in monitoring technologies, international collaboration, and capacity building will be key to enhancing our ability to predict, adapt to, and mitigate the impacts of climate change [34].

Forest and Land Use Monitoring

Forest and land use monitoring is a crucial component of environmental management that entails tracking changes in forest cover, land use patterns, and land degradation over time. It provides essential data for sustainable land management, biodiversity conservation, climate change mitigation, and policy development. Monitoring forest and land use changes helps identify deforestation, illegal logging, urban expansion, shifting cultivation, and the impacts of infrastructure development on natural ecosystems [35]. This information is vital for governments, conservationists, and planners to formulate strategies that promote ecological balance and sustainable development. Technologies such as remote sensing and Geographic Information Systems (GIS) have revolutionized forest and land monitoring by enabling large-scale, accurate, and time-efficient data collection. Satellite-based systems like Landsat, Sentinel, and MODIS are widely used to assess forest health, track land cover changes, and detect forest degradation. These datasets support initiatives such as REDD+ (Reducing Emissions from Deforestation and Forest Degradation) under the United Nations Framework Convention on Climate Change (UNFCCC), which encourages developing countries to reduce emissions through forest conservation and sustainable land management [36].

An example of large-scale monitoring is the Global Forest Watch (GFW) platform developed by the World Resources Institute (WRI). It offers real-time monitoring of forests using satellite data and cloud computing to track deforestation hotspots and provide alerts. Similarly, in Brazil, the National Institute for Space Research (INPE) operates the PRODES and DETER programs to monitor deforestation in the Amazon Rainforest, which have played an instrumental role in shaping environmental policies and enforcement actions against illegal logging. In addition to forest loss, land use monitoring also addresses land degradation, including soil erosion, desertification, and land-use conflicts. This is particularly relevant in semi-arid regions such as the Sahel in Africa and parts of South Asia, where unsustainable agricultural practices and climate variability threaten land productivity and food security [37].

Despite technological progress, challenges remain, such as cloud cover interfering with satellite imaging, the need for ground-truth validation, limited technical capacity in some countries, and difficulties in accessing high-resolution datasets. Nonetheless, the integration of advanced tools like AI-based classification [38], UAVs (drones), and mobile GIS applications continues to enhance monitoring capabilities. In conclusion, forest and land use monitoring is indispensable for protecting natural resources, supporting land-use planning, and achieving global sustainability goals. Through continuous observation and data-driven decision-making, societies can mitigate deforestation, manage land resources wisely, and build resilience against environmental degradation [39].

Disaster Risk Reduction

Disaster Risk Reduction (DRR) refers to the systematic efforts to analyze and manage the causal factors of disasters by reducing exposure to hazards, decreasing vulnerability, and enhancing preparedness, response, and recovery capabilities. With increasing frequency and intensity of natural and human-induced disasters such as floods, earthquakes, cyclones, wildfires, and industrial accidents, DRR has become a critical aspect of sustainable development and humanitarian planning. A key component of DRR is environmental monitoring, which enables the early detection and prediction of potential hazards. Technologies such as remote sensing, Geographic Information Systems (GIS), early warning systems, and real-time sensor networks are extensively used to monitor environmental parameters including rainfall intensity, river discharge, seismic activity, and land movements. These data sets support the identification of risk zones, enable timely evacuation plans, and help allocate resources during emergencies [40].

One significant international initiative in this domain is the Sendai Framework for Disaster Risk Reduction (2015–2030), adopted by the United Nations Office for Disaster Risk Reduction (UNDRR). This framework emphasizes understanding disaster risk, strengthening governance, investing in resilience, and enhancing disaster preparedness. Countries are encouraged to integrate DRR into all sectors, including urban planning, infrastructure development, education, and health services [41]. A practical example of DRR through environmental monitoring is found in Japan, which has established one of the most advanced early warning systems for earthquakes and tsunamis [41]. The Japan Meteorological Agency (JMA) utilizes a dense network of seismic sensors and ocean buoys to issue alerts within seconds of detecting seismic activity. Similarly, Bangladesh has significantly reduced cyclone-related fatalities through improved forecasting, the construction of cyclone shelters, and public awareness campaigns led by the Bangladesh Meteorological Department and international partners [42].

In addition to technology-driven approaches, community-based disaster risk management (CBDRM) plays a crucial role in enhancing local resilience. This involves training local populations in disaster preparedness, response strategies, and first aid, and encouraging the use of traditional knowledge in hazard-prone areas [43]. Integrating scientific monitoring with community action ensures a more inclusive and effective risk reduction approach. Despite significant progress, DRR efforts often face challenges such as inadequate funding, limited access to technology in low- income regions, weak institutional frameworks, and lack of public engagement. To overcome these barriers, there is a need for greater international cooperation, policy integration, capacity building, and investments in both structural and non-structural measures. In conclusion, disaster risk reduction is essential for saving lives, protecting livelihoods, and ensuring sustainable development in an increasingly unpredictable world. By combining environmental monitoring, early warning systems, governance reforms, and community participation, nations can significantly reduce the impacts of disasters and build safer, more resilient societies [44].

GLOBAL ENVIRONMENTAL ISSUES

The Earth's environment is facing unprecedented challenges due to rapid industrialization, urbanization, and human activities that have altered natural systems. These global environmental issues are complex and interrelated, affecting not only ecosystems but also human health, economic development, and societal well-being. According to the United Nations Environment Programme, the planet is undergoing critical transformations such as climate change, biodiversity loss, pollution, and land degradation at a pace and scale that threaten the stability of life-support systems. One of the most pressing concerns is climate change, driven largely by greenhouse gas emissions from fossil fuel combustion and deforestation, which has led to rising global temperatures, extreme weather events, and sea level rise [45]. Alongside this, air and water pollution continue to degrade environmental quality, causing millions of premature deaths annually and contaminating vital resources. Furthermore, deforestation and land degradation reduce the planet's ability to sustain biodiversity and regulate the climate, while the loss of biodiversity threatens the ecological balance necessary for food security, clean water, and human health [46].

Addressing these challenges requires global cooperation, sustainable policy frameworks, technological innovation, and increased environmental awareness among citizens and stakeholders. As noted by the Intergovernmental Science-Policy Platform on Biodiversity and Ecosystem Services, transformative changes are essential to safeguard nature and its contributions to humanity [47].

Climate Change

Climate change is defined as a long-term alteration of the average patterns of temperature, precipitation, wind, and other elements of the Earth's climate system. While natural factors such as volcanic activity, ocean currents, and solar radiation can contribute to climatic variations, the current trend of global climate change is primarily attributed to human activities. These include the burning of fossil fuels, deforestation, and industrial processes, which release large quantities of greenhouse gases such as carbon dioxide (CO_2), methane (CH_4), and nitrous oxide (N_2O) into the atmosphere. These gases trap heat, leading to a gradual increase in the Earth's surface temperature, a phenomenon known as the greenhouse effect. According to the Intergovernmental Panel on Climate Change [48, 49], climate change refers to a persistent change in the state of the climate that can be identified by statistical changes in the mean or variability of its properties, lasting for decades or longer. The impacts of climate change are already visible across the globe in the form of rising sea levels, melting glaciers, more frequent and intense extreme weather events, shifts in ecosystems, and threats to biodiversity. If not addressed, these changes will have profound implications for natural systems and human societies, especially in vulnerable regions [50].

Case Study: The Arctic Region

The Arctic is warming nearly four times faster than the global average, a phenomenon known as Arctic amplification. As sea ice and snow cover decrease, the darker ocean surface absorbs more heat, accelerating warming and ice melt. The Arctic Sea ice extent has declined by over 40% since 1979 during the summer months [50, 51]. This melting contributes to global sea level rise and severely disrupts ecosystems, threatening species like polar bears, walruses, and seals, which depend on ice for survival. Additionally, indigenous communities are affected by changes in hunting, fishing, and transportation routes.

Air Pollution

Air pollution refers to the presence of substances in the atmosphere, either gases, particulates, or biological molecules that are harmful or poisonous to human health, other living organisms, or the environment as a whole. These pollutants can be natural (*e.g.*, volcanic eruptions, wildfires) or anthropogenic (human-made, such as vehicle emissions and industrial discharges). According to the World Health Organization [30, 31], *Air pollution is the contamination of the indoor or outdoor environment by any chemical, physical or biological agent that modifies the natural characteristics of the atmosphere*. Common air pollutants include particulate matter (PM2.5 and PM10), nitrogen oxides (NO_X), sulfur dioxide (SO_2), carbon monoxide (CO), ozone (O_3), and volatile organic compounds (VOCs). Air pollution is a major environmental risk to human health, contributing to diseases such as stroke, heart disease, respiratory infections, and lung cancer. It also affects the climate, visibility, ecosystems, and agricultural productivity [28].

Case Study: Delhi, India

Delhi is often cited as one of the most polluted cities in the world, with air quality levels frequently breaching safe limits, particularly during winter months. The major contributors include vehicular emissions, industrial discharge, construction dust, and most significantly, crop residue burning in neighboring states such as Punjab and Haryana. In winter, atmospheric conditions such as temperature inversion trap pollutants close to the ground, exacerbating the situation. The Air Quality Index (AQI) in Delhi often falls into the "hazardous" category, prompting school closures and health advisories. According to WHO (2022), long-term exposure to Delhi's air pollution contributes to a high burden of respiratory and cardiovascular diseases among its population [48, 51].

Water Pollution and Scarcity

Water Pollution is the contamination of water bodies (such as rivers, lakes, oceans, groundwater, and aquifers) with harmful substances that degrade water quality and threaten ecosystems and human health. These pollutants may include chemicals, heavy metals, pathogens, microplastics, and excess nutrients from industrial discharge, agricultural runoff, sewage, and urban waste. Polluted water is unsafe for drinking, irrigation, or recreational use and can lead to widespread health issues such as cholera, dysentery, and other waterborne diseases [52]. Water Scarcity, on the other hand, refers to the lack of sufficient available freshwater resources to meet the demand for water within a region. It is often caused by a combination of physical water shortages (due to droughts or overuse) and economic scarcity (due to poor infrastructure or mismanagement) [53]. The United Nations defines water scarcity as a situation where water availability in a region is below 1,000 cubic meters per person per year. Water pollution exacerbates water scarcity by reducing the volume of water that is safe and usable for human and ecological needs. As freshwater sources become increasingly polluted, the burden on clean water supplies intensifies, particularly in densely populated or arid regions. Thus, pollution and scarcity are deeply interconnected and together represent a major threat to sustainable development [54].

Case Study: Flint Water Crisis, USA

One of the most alarming recent examples of water pollution is the Flint Water Crisis in Michigan, USA. In 2014, the city of Flint switched its water supply from Lake Huron (*via* Detroit) to the Flint River as a cost-cutting measure. However, the water from the Flint River was highly corrosive and was not treated properly. As a result, lead from aging pipes leached into the water supply, exposing thousands of residents, especially children, to toxic levels of lead. Symptoms included skin rashes, hair loss, and developmental issues in children. The crisis revealed systemic failures in water quality regulation, government transparency, and environmental justice [55].

Deforestation and Land Degradation

Deforestation and land degradation are two interlinked global environmental issues that significantly impact ecosystems, biodiversity, and human well-being. Deforestation refers to the large-scale removal of forest cover, often to make way for agriculture, urban development, or commercial logging. It leads to the permanent or long-term loss of forest ecosystems, reducing biodiversity and the ecological services forests provide. Closely related is the issue of land degradation, which refers to the decline in the productivity and ecological health of land caused by both natural processes and unsustainable human activities, such as deforestation, overgrazing, and improper agricultural practices [56]. The United Nations Convention to Combat Desertification describes land degradation as "the reduction or loss, in arid, semi-arid and dry sub-humid areas, of the biological or economic productivity and complexity of rain-fed cropland, irrigated cropland, or range, pasture, forest and woodlands." These processes not only diminish the ability of land to support agriculture and wildlife but also contribute to climate change through the release of stored carbon and the disruption of natural water cycles [57].

Case Study: Amazon Rainforest, Brazil

The Amazon Rainforest is the largest tropical rainforest in the world, often referred to as the "lungs of the Earth" due to its vast capacity to absorb carbon dioxide. However, it faces unprecedented threats from illegal logging, agricultural expansion (especially cattle ranching and soy farming), and infrastructure projects. According to the World Wildlife Fund [10], more than 17% of the Amazon has been lost over the past 50 years. This destruction not only endangers thousands of species but also significantly contributes to global greenhouse gas emissions. Efforts to conserve the Amazon have been hindered by weak law enforcement, economic pressures, and political disputes over land use [58].

Biodiversity Loss

Biodiversity loss refers to the significant reduction or complete disappearance of various forms of life on Earth, including species, genetic variation within species, and the variety of ecosystems. It is primarily caused by human activities such as deforestation, habitat fragmentation, pollution, overexploitation of natural resources, invasive species, and climate change. As biodiversity declines, the stability and resilience of ecosystems are compromised, leading to the collapse of essential ecosystem services such as pollination, water purification, soil fertility, and climate regulation. This loss poses a serious threat not only to wildlife but also to human health, food security, and sustainable development. Biodiversity loss involves the reduction of genetic, species, and ecosystem diversity, which affects the planet's ability to adapt to environmental changes and shocks. The Intergovernmental Science-Policy Platform on Biodiversity and Ecosystem Services highlights that around one million species are at risk of extinction, many within decades, unless urgent action is taken to halt and reverse this trend [59].

Case Study: Great Barrier Reef, Australia

The Great Barrier Reef, the world's largest coral reef system, has been severely affected by climate change, particularly by rising sea temperatures. Repeated coral bleaching events, most notably in 2016, 2017, and 2020, have led to the widespread death of corals. Bleaching occurs when corals, stressed by warmer waters, expel the symbiotic algae (zooxanthellae) that provide them with energy. Without these algae, corals turn white and often die. According to the United Nations Environment Programme [4], over 50% of shallow-water corals in the reef have died in recent decades. This biodiversity loss affects not only coral species but also the complex web of marine life that depends on the reef, including fish, sea turtles, and seabirds. The collapse of this ecosystem threatens tourism and fisheries, which are economically vital to Australia [60].

ROLE OF MACHINE LEARNING IN ENVIRONMENTAL MONITORING

Machine learning (ML) is a transformative technology within the broader field of artificial intelligence that enables computers to learn from data, identify patterns, and make predictions or decisions with minimal human intervention. Instead of being explicitly programmed for every task, ML algorithms are designed to improve automatically as they are exposed to more data over time. In the era of big data, where information is generated at an unprecedented rate, machine learning provides a robust framework for handling and interpreting complex datasets. In the context of environmental monitoring and management, machine learning has emerged as a powerful tool for addressing the growing challenges of environmental degradation, climate change, pollution, and biodiversity loss [61, 62]. Environmental data is typically vast, dynamic, and multidimensional, coming from a wide array of sources including satellite remote sensing, climate models, weather stations, sensor networks, drones, and citizen science platforms. These datasets often exhibit non-linear relationships, missing values, noise, and spatial-temporal complexity, making them difficult to analyze using traditional statistical techniques. Machine learning excels in this context by offering advanced methods to process, model, and draw meaningful insights from such data [62, 63].

One of the key strengths of ML in environmental applications is its ability to learn patterns from historical and real-time data to forecast future conditions. For instance, ML algorithms can predict air pollution levels, identify patterns of climate variability, assess water quality, classify land cover types from satellite imagery, or detect illegal deforestation in near real-time. Furthermore, deep learning, an advanced form of ML, has demonstrated exceptional capabilities in image classification, time-series analysis, and anomaly detection, which are critical in applications like flood mapping, wildfire prediction, and coral reef monitoring. ML's relevance also extends to decision support systems, where it helps governments, environmental agencies, and disaster response teams make informed choices based on accurate, up-to-date environmental information. It supports the automation of data processing pipelines, facilitates early warning systems for environmental hazards, and enables adaptive management practices based on predictive analytics [64, 65].

Moreover, as the global focus intensifies on sustainability and climate resilience, machine learning is proving to be a catalyst for innovation in Earth system science, urban planning, agriculture, and renewable energy management. Its integration with other technologies such as the Internet of Things (IoT), Geographic Information Systems (GIS), and cloud computing further enhances its potential to build smarter, data-driven environmental solutions [66, 67]. In summary, machine learning is not only relevant but essential for modern environmental monitoring and management. Its ability to handle complexity, learn from vast datasets, and provide timely insights makes it a cornerstone in the global effort to understand and mitigate environmental challenges.

Applications of Machine Learning in Environmental Monitoring

Air Quality Prediction

Air quality prediction is one of the most significant and widely applied domains of machine learning (ML) in environmental monitoring. ML models such as Random Forest (RF), Support Vector Machines (SVM), and Artificial Neural Networks (ANN) have been effectively used to forecast key pollutant concentrations, including PM2.5, PM10, NO_2, and O_3 [66, 67]. These models analyze large datasets that incorporate historical pollution levels, meteorological conditions (*e.g.*, temperature, humidity, wind speed), traffic volume, and land-use patterns to uncover complex, non-linear relationships that traditional models often fail to detect [65]. The increasing availability of real-time environmental sensors and IoT technologies enables the continuous collection of high- resolution data, which ML models can process to deliver accurate short-term and long-term forecasts. Such predictive modeling is instrumental in early warning systems, helping governments and public health agencies issue timely advisories during pollution spikes and design effective mitigation strategies [64]. Furthermore, ML supports spatial interpolation of air quality in regions lacking sensor coverage, improving the resolution and granularity of air pollution maps [20]. Cities like Beijing, Delhi, and Los Angeles have adopted ML-based air quality systems to guide decisions on traffic restrictions, industrial controls, and school closures during high-risk days. These applications illustrate the critical role of machine learning in enabling data-driven environmental governance and adaptive public health interventions in the face of worsening urban air quality [66].

Water Quality Assessment

Machine learning (ML) offers powerful tools for assessing and monitoring water quality in both natural and engineered water systems. Supervised learning algorithms such as Random Forest (RF), Support Vector Machines (SVM), Decision Trees, and Artificial Neural Networks (ANNs) can be trained on historical datasets containing physicochemical parameters such as pH, turbidity, electrical conductivity, temperature, and dissolved oxygen to predict contamination levels, classify water quality status, or detect outlier events indicating possible pollution [15, 25]. These models can be deployed in real-time to assess drinking water safety or monitor river and lake ecosystems for harmful changes. In parallel, unsupervised learning algorithms, including K- means clustering and hierarchical clustering, are used to categorize water sources based on similarities in pollution profiles. This helps identify hotspots of contamination, grouping similar catchments or aquifers for targeted intervention, and optimizing water quality monitoring networks [25]. ML also supports the integration of heterogeneous data from satellite imagery, remote sensors, and in-situ measurements, improving spatial and temporal coverage of water quality assessment. Importantly, ML-based models outperform conventional methods by effectively handling nonlinear relationships, missing data, and high-dimensional input features. In smart cities and rural water supply networks alike, these systems enhance decision support tools for resource managers and policymakers, ensuring efficient water quality governance and sustainable water resource management [14, 57].

Climate Modeling

Machine learning (ML) has become an essential tool in climate modeling by enabling scientists to better understand and predict complex interactions between atmospheric, oceanic, and terrestrial systems. Traditional physics-based climate models, while comprehensive, are computationally intensive and sometimes limited in capturing non-linear dynamics. ML, particularly deep learning approaches like convolutional neural networks (CNNs) and recurrent neural networks (RNNs), can learn intricate patterns from vast climate datasets such as temperature, pressure, sea surface temperatures, humidity, and wind patterns across spatial and temporal scales [34]. By integrating with existing climate models or acting as surrogate models,

ML contributes to downscaling global climate projections to regional levels with higher resolution and accuracy, especially for predicting temperature anomalies, rainfall variability, and extreme weather events such as hurricanes, heatwaves, and floods. Moreover, ML is used to emulate atmospheric physics, reduce uncertainties in model outputs, and analyze large-scale reanalysis datasets and satellite observations in real-time. This greatly accelerates climate simulations and enables rapid experimentation with different future emission scenarios. As climate risks grow more severe and urgent, ML provides a scalable, data-driven approach to refine predictions, guide adaptation strategies, and inform climate policy with improved foresight [26, 38].

Remote Sensing Data Interpretation

Machine learning (ML), particularly deep learning, plays a transformative role in the interpretation of remote sensing data acquired from satellites, drones, and aerial platforms. The vast amount of high-resolution imagery generated by Earth observation programs such as Landsat, Sentinel, and MODIS requires automated and intelligent techniques for effective analysis. ML models, especially Convolutional Neural Networks (CNNs), are widely used for image classification, object detection, and semantic segmentation in remote sensing tasks [7, 22]. These techniques have proven highly effective in land use and land cover (LULC) classification, vegetation health monitoring, deforestation detection, urban sprawl assessment, and disaster mapping. CNNs can learn spatial hierarchies and extract intricate features from multispectral or hyperspectral imagery, enabling accurate classification of terrain types, crop conditions, and built-up areas [68]. Additionally, ML models can detect subtle environmental changes over time by comparing temporal satellite datasets, aiding in early detection of floods, forest degradation, or drought stress. In contexts such as climate change monitoring, biodiversity mapping, and precision agriculture, ML enhances decision-making by improving the speed and accuracy of data interpretation. These capabilities are crucial for environmental managers, urban planners, and policy-makers who rely on near real-time insights for sustainable resource planning and disaster risk reduction [40].

Wildlife Monitoring and Biodiversity Assessment

Machine learning (ML) is revolutionizing wildlife monitoring and biodiversity assessment by enabling the efficient processing of large volumes of ecological data collected through camera traps, drones, acoustic sensors, and remote sensing platforms. These models automate the detection, classification, and counting of animal species in their natural habitats, significantly reducing the time and labor involved in traditional field-based methods [48]. Convolutional Neural Networks (CNNs) are especially effective in analyzing camera trap images to identify species, even under varied lighting and occlusion conditions. Similarly, bioacoustic ML models can detect and classify species-specific sounds, which is invaluable for monitoring birds, amphibians, and marine mammals [45]. ML also facilitates the tracking of animal movement, habitat use patterns, and population dynamics, which are essential for conservation planning and ecological research. For endangered species, these technologies help in early detection of population decline or changes in distribution due to threats like poaching, habitat loss, or climate change. Moreover, by integrating spatial and temporal data, ML models can map biodiversity hotspots, forecast shifts in species ranges, and support ecosystem health assessments. The automation and scalability enabled by ML not only improve accuracy but also enable continuous, real-time biodiversity monitoring across large, remote landscapes. This empowers conservationists, wildlife managers, and policymakers with actionable insights to implement targeted and timely conservation strategies [18, 36].

Disaster Prediction and Risk Assessment

ML is increasingly vital in forecasting and managing natural disasters by leveraging diverse datasets such as historical disaster records, satellite imagery, geospatial data, and real-time environmental signals (*e.g.*, rainfall, soil moisture, vegetation index). ML models, including Random Forest (RF), Support Vector Machines (SVM), and Deep Neural Networks (DNNs), can detect complex patterns and correlations among environmental variables that often precede events like landslides, floods, earthquakes, and forest fires [41, 43]. These models are widely used to generate hazard susceptibility maps, classify high-risk zones, and provide short- term predictions essential for early warning systems. For instance, in landslide-prone areas, ML integrates data on slope gradient, geology, rainfall, and land cover to predict slope failure probability with high accuracy. Similarly, flood forecasting models analyze precipitation trends, river discharge, and topography to simulate inundation extents and alert authorities in advance. Forest fire prediction systems utilize remote sensing inputs such as temperature, humidity, vegetation type, and NDVI (Normalized Difference Vegetation Index) to anticipate ignition risks and spread patterns [16]. The rapid, adaptive learning capabilities of ML enable continuous model updates as new data becomes available, enhancing resilience in dynamic, disaster-prone environments. By supporting real-time decision-making and proactive risk reduction strategies, ML-based disaster prediction tools are becoming integral to climate adaptation, emergency response planning, and safeguarding lives and infrastructure [69 - 71].

Advantages of Machine Learning over Traditional Methods

Machine learning (ML) provides advanced capabilities for processing complex, large-scale environmental data, enabling predictive modeling, pattern detection, and automated decision-making. Traditional environmental monitoring methods often rely on manual data collection, empirical models, and limited statistical analysis. In contrast, ML techniques excel in handling high-dimensional and nonlinear data, whereas traditional methods may fail to capture underlying patterns. Algorithms such as artificial neural networks and support vector machines can effectively process vast datasets and uncover intricate relationships among variables. Moreover, ML techniques are scalable and capable of automating complex tasks, reducing the need for manual intervention and enabling more timely and responsive analyses [72, 73].

Another significant advantage of ML is its ability to enhance prediction accuracy. Ensemble learning and deep learning approaches have demonstrated improved performance in environmental forecasting applications, including flood susceptibility, air quality monitoring, and climate modeling [74]. These models can be integrated with IoT devices and remote sensing platforms to support real-time environmental monitoring and to adaptively learn from streaming data. Additionally, ML algorithms enable the integration of diverse and heterogeneous data sources such as satellite imagery, sensor readings, meteorological datasets, and social media feeds, providing a more comprehensive understanding of environmental systems. ML also supports feature selection and dimensionality reduction through techniques like Principal Component Analysis (PCA) and Recursive Feature Elimination (RFE), helping researchers identify the most influential factors and improve model interpretability. These strengths collectively make machine learning a powerful and indispensable tool for modern environmental monitoring and management [75, 76].

ROLE OF SPATIAL ANALYSIS IN ENVIRONMENTAL MONITORING

Importance of Geospatial Data in Understanding Environmental Patterns

The integration of geospatial data into environmental research has fundamentally transformed how we perceive and manage natural resources. Spatial patterns and trends that were once difficult to detect can now be analyzed with high precision, enabling better forecasting and decision-making. For instance, time-series satellite imagery enables the detection of seasonal shifts in vegetation, urban encroachment into rural areas, and the progressive melting of polar ice caps. Tools such as GIS enable users to overlay multiple environmental datasets (*e.g.*, rainfall, elevation, soil type, and land use) for complex spatial analysis, such as identifying areas at risk of landslides or mapping biodiversity corridors [77, 78]. In the context of climate change, geospatial data play a pivotal role in modeling future scenarios under various emission pathways. For example, they are used to downscale global climate model outputs to regional levels, making projections more relevant for local planning. Remote sensing data from satellites such as MODIS, Sentinel, and Landsat provide essential inputs for calculating vegetation indices, surface temperatures, water levels, and snow cover parameters that are key to climate and ecosystem models [79].

Geospatial data also supports ecosystem services valuation by mapping resources like freshwater availability, carbon storage, and pollinator habitats, which are critical for sustainability assessments. In environmental justice studies, they are used to identify disparities in exposure to pollution or access to green spaces among different communities. Moreover, with the growing availability of open-source geospatial data and tools, community-based environmental monitoring and citizen science initiatives have flourished, enabling non-experts to participate in data collection, reporting, and conservation. As technology advances, the fusion of geospatial data with artificial intelligence (AI) and Internet of Things (IoT) sensors continues to improve real-time monitoring of environmental systems. This convergence enhances early warning systems for disasters, supports precision agriculture, and promotes adaptive strategies in the face of global environmental challenges [80, 81].

GIS and Remote Sensing Tools for Spatial Analysis

Geographic Information Systems (GIS) and remote sensing are essential tools in spatial analysis for environmental monitoring, natural resource management, urban planning, and disaster response. GIS is a framework for capturing, storing, analyzing, and visualizing spatial and geographic data. It allows users to overlay multiple layers of information, such as land use, soil types, hydrology, and population density, to analyze relationships, patterns, and trends across space. Remote sensing, on the other hand, involves collecting information about the Earth's surface without direct contact, typically using satellite imagery or aerial sensors. This technology provides up-to-date, large-scale environmental data, enabling the monitoring of phenomena such as deforestation, vegetation health, glacier retreat, flood mapping, and land degradation [77].

Together, GIS and remote sensing form a powerful combination: remote sensing provides raw spatial data, while GIS provides tools to process, analyze, and interpret it. For example, using Landsat or Sentinel-2 imagery in GIS software like ArcGIS or QGIS, analysts can classify land cover, track changes over time, and generate risk maps for floods, droughts, or urban sprawl. These tools also support spatial modeling, such as simulating the spread of wildfires or predicting the impact of sea-level rise on coastal areas [82]. Additionally, the integration of machine learning algorithms with GIS and remote sensing enhances classification accuracy and predictive modeling for environmental planning and policy-making. The increasing accessibility of open-source tools (*e.g.*, QGIS, Google Earth Engine) and free satellite datasets (*e.g.*, MODIS, Landsat, Sentinel) has democratized spatial analysis, allowing governments, researchers, NGOs, and even citizens to participate in sustainable land and resource management [83, 84].

Geographic Information Systems (GIS) and remote sensing technologies have become indispensable for spatial environmental analysis across various regions and ecosystems. In the Amazon Basin, for instance, researchers used multi-temporal Landsat satellite imagery in combination with Google Earth Engine and ArcGIS to monitor deforestation trends from 2000 to 2020. By analyzing the Normalized Difference Vegetation Index (NDVI), they identified critical hotspots of illegal logging and agricultural encroachment, aiding policy enforcement and conservation planning [69]. Similarly, in Jakarta, Indonesia, flood risk assessment was conducted using Sentinel-1 Synthetic Aperture Radar (SAR) data integrated with Digital Elevation Models (DEMs) and land use maps in GIS platforms. This helped city planners identify flood-prone zones and develop more effective urban drainage and disaster mitigation strategies. In Sub-Saharan Africa's Sahel region, remote sensing tools such as MODIS and spatial analysis in QGIS were used to assess drought impacts on agriculture. The Vegetation Health Index (VHI) derived from satellite data enabled early detection of vegetation stress, guiding relief agencies in allocating resources and supporting food security interventions. These case studies exemplify how the integration of geospatial tools enables timely and data-driven decision-making in environmental management worldwide [85].

In the context of flood-prone area identification, GIS-based hydrological modeling was employed in the Ganga-Brahmaputra Delta, India, using rainfall data, land cover, and digital elevation models to simulate water flow and inundation zones. This approach allowed the creation of real-time flood hazard maps, improving emergency preparedness and infrastructure planning [86 - 88]. Another innovative application occurred in the Netherlands, where LiDAR data and high-resolution topographic maps were analyzed in GIS to assess flood vulnerability under different sea-level rise scenarios. The outputs informed coastal defense and water management strategies in a country where nearly a third of the land lies below sea level. These case studies illustrate how integrated geospatial analysis offers timely, location-specific insights that guide both reactive and proactive environmental decision-making. GIS and remote sensing have been widely applied in mapping environmental transformations such as land-use change, habitat fragmentation, and flood risk zones. A notable example comes from China's Pearl River Delta, where Landsat imagery and GIS-based change detection techniques revealed rapid urban expansion and land-use conversion between 1988 and 2018, primarily from agricultural and forested lands to built-up areas. These findings provided insights for sustainable urban planning and policy formulation. In the case of habitat fragmentation, the Western Ghats in India, a global biodiversity hotspot, have been studied using high-resolution satellite data and landscape metrics in GIS to assess the impact of roads, plantations, and settlements on forest continuity. The results highlighted the urgent need for ecological corridor planning to protect endangered species [86, 89]. Regarding flood-prone area mapping, a study in Bangladesh's Brahmaputra River Basin integrated remote sensing-derived rainfall data, land elevation from DEMs, and hydrological layers within GIS to identify flood risk zones. This spatial risk analysis supported the design of community-based flood early warning systems and relocation strategies. These case studies demonstrate how geospatial tools facilitate evidence-based environmental management and planning across varied ecological and socio-economic contexts [88].

KEY MACHINE LEARNING ALGORITHMS FOR ENVIRONMENTAL DATA PROCESSING

With the increasing availability of environmental big data from satellite sensors, climate models, and ground-based monitoring stations, traditional methods of data analysis often fall short in handling the scale, heterogeneity, and complexity of these datasets. In this context, machine learning (ML) has emerged as a transformative approach, offering scalable, flexible, and accurate tools for extracting meaningful information from vast environmental datasets [62]. ML techniques are capable of modeling complex nonlinear relationships, handling noisy and incomplete data, and adapting to evolving patterns, making them particularly suitable for environmental science, where natural processes are often dynamic and interconnected [76].

Key algorithms such as Random Forests, Support Vector Machines, and Artificial Neural Networks have been widely adopted due to their robustness and predictive accuracy. For instance, Random Forests are highly effective in classification and regression tasks, making them popular in land cover mapping, soil quality assessment, and forest fire prediction [90]. Similarly, SVMs are widely used for vegetation classification and species distribution modeling due to their ability to perform well in high-dimensional spaces with limited samples. Deep learning models, especially Convolutional Neural Networks (CNNs), are revolutionizing remote sensing image interpretation, enabling automated identification of deforestation, urban expansion, and even glacier retreat with unprecedented precision. In addition, Recurrent Neural Networks (RNNs), particularly LSTM (Long Short-Term Memory) networks, are increasingly applied to time-series prediction for variables like temperature, precipitation, and flood occurrence [91, 92].

These algorithms not only improve prediction and classification accuracy but also reduce the time and cost of environmental monitoring. Furthermore, the integration of unsupervised learning methods, such as k-means clustering and principal component analysis (PCA), allows for exploratory data analysis and anomaly detection in applications like air and water quality monitoring. As climate change intensifies and environmental risks become more urgent, ML offers a path forward for data-driven environmental governance, enhancing resilience, supporting early warning systems, and guiding sustainable resource management [93, 94].

Decision Tree in Environmental Data Processing

A Decision Tree is a supervised machine learning algorithm used for classification and regression tasks. It models decisions and their possible consequences as a tree-like structure, where internal nodes represent tests on input features, branches represent outcomes of those tests, and leaf nodes represent final predictions. Its interpretability, ease of use, and ability to handle both numerical and categorical data make it highly suitable for a range of environmental applications. In environmental science, Decision Trees are particularly useful because they can handle noisy data, identify non-linear relationships, and provide clear decision rules, which are valuable for policy and management purposes [94, 95]. For instance, they have been used in:

- Predicting the air quality index (AQI) based on weather and traffic data,
- Classifying land cover types from remote sensing imagery,
- Forecasting flood risk by analyzing terrain, precipitation, and soil moisture,
- Evaluating water quality status using indicators such as pH, turbidity, and nutrient content,
- Conducting ecological risk assessment by integrating various stressors like pollution levels, proximity to industrial areas, and habitat fragmentation.

One of the main strengths of Decision Trees is their interpretability; they can provide transparent rules that are easy for stakeholders or policymakers to understand. However, they can be prone to overfitting, especially with noisy or complex datasets. This issue is often addressed using ensemble methods like Random Forests or Gradient Boosting Trees, which combine multiple decision trees to improve performance and generalization. The Decision Tree algorithm is mathematically expressed in terms of how it selects the best features to split the data at each node. The most common criteria for splitting are Information Gain (based on Entropy) as in Eq. (**1**, **2**), and Gini Impurity, as seen in Eq. (**3**) [96, 97].

1. Entropy and Information Gain (used in ID3 and C4.5 algorithms)

Entropy (H) measures the disorder or impurity in a dataset:

$$H\ (S) = -\sum_{i=1}^{n} p_i log_2(p_i) \tag{1}$$

Where:

- S is the dataset
- p_i is the proportion of instances belonging to class II
- n is the number of classes
- Information Gain (IG) is the reduction in entropy after a dataset is split on an attribute A:

$$IG(S, A) = H(S) - \sum_{v \in Values\ (A)} \frac{|S_v|}{|S|} H(S_v) \tag{2}$$

Where:

- S_v is the subset of S for which attribute A has value v.

The feature with the highest Information Gain is chosen for the split.

2. Gini Impurity (used in the CART algorithm)

The Gini Index measures the probability of misclassifying a randomly chosen element:

$$Gini\ (S) = 1 - \sum_{i=1}^{n} p_i^2 \quad \textbf{(3)}$$

The algorithm selects the feature and splits that produces the lowest weighted Gini impurity across the resulting child nodes. These mathematical formulations help the Decision Tree algorithm determine the most informative and pure splits at each level of the tree, ultimately improving classification or prediction accuracy. Decision trees have been successfully used to classify pollution levels in rivers by analyzing water quality indicators like pH, turbidity, and nutrient concentrations. Their ability to model complex, nonlinear relationships without the need for extensive data preprocessing is another advantage, making them ideal for diverse environmental datasets. However, decision trees are also sensitive to small variations in data and may suffer from overfitting, which limits their generalizability. To overcome this, ensemble methods such as Random Forests and Gradient Boosting Trees are often employed to combine multiple decision trees for improved accuracy and robustness [98, 99].

Random Forest

Random Forest is an ensemble learning algorithm that builds upon the basic structure of Decision Trees to provide improved accuracy, robustness, and generalization. It works by constructing a large number of decision trees during training and outputting the mode (for classification) or the mean (for regression) of their predictions. Each tree is trained on a random subset of the data (using bagging or bootstrap aggregation), and at each split, a random subset of features is considered. This dual randomness reduces overfitting and ensures that individual trees are less correlated, resulting in a more stable and accurate model [100]. In environmental applications, Random Forest is widely used due to its ability to handle large, high-dimensional datasets and model complex interactions among variables. It has been applied successfully in land use and land cover classification using satellite imagery, predicting air and water quality, estimating forest biomass, species distribution modeling, and flood risk mapping. Additionally, Random Forest provides feature importance scores, helping researchers identify key environmental drivers such as temperature, rainfall, or vegetation cover in ecological or climatological studies [49, 76].

Another strength of Random Forest is its resilience to noise and missing data, which is particularly valuable in environmental monitoring, where data can often be incomplete or inconsistent. However, its main limitations include reduced interpretability compared to a single decision tree and longer training times with very large datasets. Nonetheless, Random Forest remains a powerful and reliable algorithm in the environmental sciences due to its accuracy, versatility, and ease of use. The Random Forest algorithm can be mathematically described in different steps, particularly focusing on the construction of the model, prediction process, and key concepts like bootstrapping and feature randomness [81].

1. Bootstrapping (Bagging) Step

For a dataset D with N training examples, randomly sample with replacement to create B different bootstrap samples (Eq. **4**):

$$D^{(b)} = \{(x_i, y_i)\}_{i=1}^{N} \quad \textbf{(4)}$$

for b = 1, 2, ……, B

Each $D_{(b)}$ is used to train a separate decision tree T_b.

2. Tree Construction with Random Feature Selectio

At each node in the decision tree,

- Select a random subset of features $F \subseteq \{f_1, f_2, \ldots, f_d\}$ where $|F| = m \ll d$.
- Choose the feature $f^* \in F$ that gives the best split using criteria like Gini impurity or Information Gain.

The splitting continues until a stopping condition is met (*e.g.*, max depth, minimum samples per leaf).

3. Prediction Function Classification:

Classification:

The final prediction is made by majority voting across all trees (Eq. **5**):

$$\hat{y} = mode\{T_1(x), T_2(x), \ldots\ldots, T_B(x)\} \quad \textbf{(5)}$$

Regression:

The final output is the average of predictions from all trees (Eq. **6**):

$$\hat{y} = \frac{1}{B}\sum_{b=1}^{B} T_b\,(x) \quad \textbf{(6)}$$

Where:

- $T_b(x)$: prediction from the bth tree
- B: total number of trees
- x: input feature vector

4. Feature Importance (Optional):

Random Forest can also compute feature importance using the mean decrease in impurity (MDI) (Eq. **7**):

$$Importance\ (f_i) = \sum_{t \in Trees} \sum_{n \in Splites\ on\ f_i} \frac{N_n}{N} . \Delta i\ (n) \quad \textbf{(7)}$$

Where:

- N_n: number of samples reaching node n
- $\Delta i(n)$: decrease in impurity from splitting at node n

Support Vector Machine (SVM)

Support Vector Machine (SVM) is a powerful supervised learning algorithm used for both classification and regression tasks. It is particularly effective in high-dimensional spaces and is well-suited to environmental datasets where relationships between variables are often non-linear and complex. SVM works by finding the optimal hyperplane that separates data points of different classes with the maximum margin, thereby achieving better generalization on unseen data. For non-linearly separable data, SVM uses kernel functions to map inputs into higher-dimensional feature spaces where linear separation becomes possible [101].

Artificial Neural Networks (ANN)

Artificial Neural Networks (ANNs) are a class of machine learning models inspired by the structure and functioning of the human brain. They are composed of layers of interconnected nodes (neurons) that process data in a layered architecture. ANNs are particularly powerful for modeling non-linear and complex relationships in data, making them highly suitable for various environmental applications such as climate modeling, air and water quality forecasting, land cover classification, and disaster risk prediction [102, 103]. By learning from data, ANNs can uncover patterns and dependencies that are difficult to detect using traditional statistical methods. A basic ANN consists of three types of layers:

- An input layer that receives the input features.
- Hidden layer(s) which process the inputs using weights, biases, and activation functions.
- The output layer provides the final prediction.

Let's define:

- $x = (x_1, x_2, \ldots\ldots, x_n)$: input feature vector
- w_{ij}: weight from neuron i in one layer to neuron j in the next
- b_j: bias term for neuron j
- f: activation function (*e.g.*, sigmoid, ReLU, tanh)

1. Weighted Sum at Hidden Layer

For a neuron j in the hidden layer (Eq. **8**):

$$z_j = \sum_{i=1}^{n} w_{ij} x_i + b_j \tag{8}$$

2. Activation Function:

The neuron output a_j is (Eq. **9**):

$$a_j = f(z_j) \tag{9}$$

3. Output Layer:

The process is repeated in the output layer (Eq. **10**):

$$\hat{y} = f\left(\sum_{j=1}^{m} w_j a_j + b\right) \tag{10}$$

Where:

- m is the number of neurons in the hidden layer
- y^ is the predicted output (*e.g.*, class label or continuous value)

ANNs offer numerous advantages that make them particularly valuable for complex environmental modeling. One of their greatest strengths lies in their ability to model non-linear relationships between variables, which is essential in environmental systems where interactions among climate factors, land cover, and human activities are often intricate and unpredictable [104, 105]. ANNs are also highly flexible and scalable, capable of handling large datasets with many input features, including temporal and spatial data from satellite imagery, sensors, and simulations. They perform exceptionally well in tasks such as climate forecasting, air quality prediction, and land use classification. Unlike traditional models, ANNs do not require explicit feature engineering, as they can automatically learn patterns and dependencies from raw input data. Additionally, once trained, ANNs can make fast and accurate predictions, which is highly beneficial for real-time environmental monitoring and early warning systems. Their strong generalization ability makes them ideal for identifying complex trends and anomalies in diverse environmental conditions [106].

Ensemble Methods

Ensemble methods are powerful machine learning techniques that combine multiple models to produce more accurate, stable, and reliable predictions than individual models. Rather than relying on a single learner, ensemble methods pool the strengths of several models, typically called *base learners* or *weak learners,* to minimize errors caused by bias, variance, or noise. This approach is especially valuable in environmental modeling, where data can be complex, uncertain, and high-dimensional. In environmental applications such as flood forecasting, land cover classification, climate change impact modeling, and biodiversity prediction, ensemble methods help improve prediction accuracy, reduce overfitting, and increase robustness by capturing different patterns and relationships [105, 106]. The common types of Ensemble Methods are as follows:

- **Bagging (Bootstrap Aggregating):** Trains multiple models independently on randomly sampled subsets of the dataset and averages (or votes) their outputs.
- **Boosting:** Builds models sequentially, where each new model corrects the errors of the previous one.
- **Stacking (Stacked Generalization):** Combines multiple diverse models (*e.g.*, SVM, ANN, decision trees) and uses another model (meta-learner) to learn how to best combine their outputs.

Ensemble methods offer significant advantages in improving the accuracy, stability, and generalizability of machine learning models. By combining the predictions of multiple base learners, ensemble models reduce the likelihood of overfitting and help mitigate the impact of noise and variance in data. This makes them particularly useful in environmental applications where datasets are often complex, noisy, or imbalanced. For instance, methods like Random Forest and Gradient Boosting can effectively handle nonlinear relationships and high-dimensional inputs, which are common in tasks such as flood forecasting, climate modeling, and land-use classification [74, 90]. Additionally, ensemble methods are flexible; they can be applied to both regression and classification problems and often outperform single models in terms of predictive performance.

Despite their effectiveness, ensemble methods also come with certain limitations. One key drawback is their increased computational cost, as they require training multiple models rather than a single one. This can lead to longer training times and higher demands on processing power, particularly with large datasets or complex algorithms like Gradient Boosting. Another limitation is the lack of interpretability, while individual decision trees or regression models are easy to understand, ensemble models such as Random Forests and Stacking are often considered "black boxes," which may hinder their use in contexts where transparency is critical, such as environmental policy-making. Furthermore, tuning hyperparameters for ensemble models can be more complex and time-consuming, requiring careful cross-validation to avoid performance degradation [22].

Conclusion

In conclusion, the increasing availability of environmental big data, combined with the complexity of natural systems, necessitates the adoption of advanced data analysis techniques. Traditional methods are often inadequate in managing such large, heterogeneous, and dynamic datasets. Machine learning (ML) has proven to be a transformative approach, offering scalable, flexible, and accurate tools that can handle the intricate relationships and evolving patterns present in environmental data. Key ML algorithms, including Random Forests, Support Vector Machines, and deep learning models like CNNs and RNNs, have shown remarkable success in a range of environmental applications, from land cover mapping to time-series predictions. Moreover, machine learning's ability to process vast amounts of environmental data in real time offers significant advantages in addressing urgent global environmental challenges. For example, the ability to analyze large-scale datasets from satellite imagery and ground-based sensors can provide timely and actionable insights into environmental changes, such as shifts in vegetation cover, water availability, or air quality. These insights can inform policy-making, disaster response, and long-term sustainability planning. The ongoing development of ML models capable of integrating different data sources—such as remote sensing data, climate models, and socio-economic indicators—also holds great potential for creating holistic and multidimensional environmental models. In particular, the use of ML for predictive modeling in areas like climate change forecasting, natural disaster risk assessment, and ecosystem management is rapidly expanding. Models that predict temperature changes, precipitation patterns, or the likelihood of floods or droughts can help communities prepare and adapt more effectively. For instance, ML-driven models can optimize irrigation practices based on climate predictions, reducing water waste and improving crop yields. In coastal areas, ML algorithms can assess the vulnerability of ecosystems to rising sea levels, enabling the development of more targeted conservation strategies.

Furthermore, ML techniques can assist in monitoring biodiversity, enabling real-time tracking of endangered species and assessing habitat health. Algorithms like CNNs, which excel at image recognition, can process visual data from camera traps or drones to identify animal species and track their movements. This can be crucial in conservation efforts, where accurate and timely data on species populations can make the difference between successful conservation and species extinction. The integration of ML with IoT (Internet of Things) devices also enhances environmental monitoring. Sensors deployed in forests, rivers, or cities can collect real-time data on air and water quality, soil health, and wildlife activity. ML algorithms can then analyze this data to detect patterns and predict environmental events such as pollution spikes or disease outbreaks in wildlife populations. This can enable more proactive and informed responses to environmental hazards.

As machine learning techniques continue to evolve, the challenge will be ensuring the accuracy, transparency, and ethical use of these models. While ML offers powerful tools for environmental analysis, it is crucial that these models are built and applied responsibly, with proper validation and consideration of potential biases in the data. Collaboration between data scientists, environmental experts, and policymakers will be essential in ensuring that machine learning tools are used to achieve sustainable environmental management goals and to minimize unintended consequences. Ultimately, machine learning represents a paradigm shift in how environmental data is analyzed and used. By leveraging ML, we can unlock the full potential of environmental big data, making it possible to predict, monitor, and mitigate the impacts of environmental changes in ways that were previously unimaginable. This shift toward data-driven, machine learning-based environmental governance holds promise for creating more resilient ecosystems, improving resource management, and addressing the pressing challenges of climate change, pollution, and biodiversity loss.

KEY SPATIAL ANALYSIS TECHNIQUES IN ENVIRONMENTAL STUDIES

Environmental studies increasingly rely on spatial techniques to analyze, visualize, and interpret complex geographical data. These techniques are critical in addressing the dynamic nature of environmental challenges, including climate change, biodiversity loss, pollution, and land-use changes [29]. With the growing availability of spatial data from diverse sources such as satellite imagery, remote sensors, and ground-based monitoring stations, the need for robust analytical methods has intensified. Traditional environmental analysis methods often fall short in managing the scale and complexity of these datasets, leading to the adoption of advanced spatial techniques that can process and derive meaningful insights from large volumes of data [46].

Spatial analysis tools are not only integral to academic research but also play a pivotal role in policy formulation, disaster management, and environmental governance. As environmental systems are inherently interconnected and constantly evolving, spatial techniques enable the detection of trends, early warnings, and predictive modeling, fostering more adaptive and proactive management strategies. This growing reliance on spatial analysis reflects the increasing need for comprehensive, data-driven solutions to tackle global environmental challenges.

Remote Sensing

Remote Sensing is a powerful technique used to acquire information about the Earth's surface without making physical contact. It involves the use of sensors mounted on satellites, aircraft, or drones to detect and measure electromagnetic radiation reflected or emitted by objects on the Earth's surface. Remote sensing data are critical in environmental studies because they provide large-scale, continuous, and up-to-date information, which is vital for monitoring changes in land cover, climate, ecosystems, and natural resources [7, 68, 77, 107].

Key Concepts in Remote Sensing

1. **Electromagnetic Spectrum**: Remote sensing relies on the interaction of electromagnetic radiation (EMR) with the Earth's surface. The EMR spectrum includes visible light, infrared, microwave, and radio waves, each of which provides different types of information depending on the wavelength. Sensors can detect specific wavelengths to analyze various surface features, such as vegetation, water, or urban areas [108].
   - **Visible and Near-Infrared (VNIR)**: These wavelengths are commonly used

for land cover classification, vegetation health, and mapping soil moisture.

   - **Thermal Infrared (TIR)**: Thermal infrared sensors are used to measure surface temperatures and detect heat anomalies, such as fires or geothermal activity.
   - **Microwave and Radar**: Radar sensors (*e.g.*, Synthetic Aperture Radar, or SAR) can penetrate cloud cover and are useful for mapping topography, vegetation structure, and water surface conditions.
2. **Platforms**: Remote sensing data can be collected from various platforms, including:
   - **Satellites**: Provide global coverage and are widely used for large-scale environmental monitoring. Examples include Landsat, MODIS, and Sentinel satellites.
   - **Aerial Platforms (Drones and Aircraft)**: Offer higher spatial resolution and are ideal for localized studies. Drones are increasingly used for high-precision mapping and monitoring.
   - **Ground-Based Sensors**: These sensors provide in-situ data that can be integrated with remote sensing data for enhanced analysis.

Applications of Remote Sensing in Environmental Studies

Remote sensing plays a pivotal role in environmental studies by providing consistent, large-scale, and long-term observations of Earth's surface and atmosphere. One of its primary applications is in monitoring Land Use and Land Cover Change, where satellite imagery, particularly from the Landsat program, enables the detection of urban expansion, deforestation, agricultural shifts, and wetland degradation. It also serves as a critical tool for Vegetation and Ecosystem Monitoring, with vegetation indices like the Normalized Difference Vegetation Index (NDVI) being widely used to assess plant health, productivity, and responses to stressors such as droughts and pest outbreaks [69]. In Water Resource Management, remote sensing allows for the monitoring of freshwater bodies, providing insights into changes in water levels, quality, and ecosystem health in rivers, lakes, and reservoirs. Furthermore, remote sensing contributes significantly to Climate Change Monitoring by supplying key data on variables such as land surface temperature, ice sheet dynamics, and sea-level rise, which are essential for modeling and assessing the impacts of climate change on both ecosystems and human societies. It also plays a crucial role in Disaster Management, enabling real-time tracking of natural disasters like floods, wildfires, hurricanes, and earthquakes, which aids in damage assessment and the coordination of emergency responses [14, 25]. Lastly, remote sensing supports Biodiversity Conservation by identifying critical habitats, monitoring species distribution, and evaluating habitat degradation, thus aiding in the development and implementation of effective conservation strategies. Through these diverse applications, remote sensing proves to be an indispensable technology in advancing our understanding and management of the environment.

Advantages of Remote Sensing

Remote sensing offers numerous advantages that make it a vital tool in environmental studies. One of its key strengths is its large-scale coverage, which enables monitoring of extensive, often inaccessible areas such as dense forests, vast oceans, and remote terrain, thereby providing data across broad spatial scales. Its repeatability is another significant benefit, as satellite and aerial imagery can be captured at regular intervals, enabling the tracking of environmental changes over time—such as deforestation, glacier retreat, or urban expansion. Remote sensing is also highly cost-effective, minimizing the need for frequent and expensive field surveys while allowing for continuous and systematic data collection. Furthermore, the timeliness of remote sensing data, which can be obtained in near real-time, makes it exceptionally useful for applications such as disaster response, monitoring rapidly changing environmental phenomena, and supporting early warning systems [109, 110].

Challenges and Limitations of Remote Sensing

Interpreting remote sensing data presents several challenges that require careful consideration. Firstly, data interpretation demands specialized expertise, as surface features may appear similar across different spectral bands, making it difficult to accurately differentiate between certain land covers or environmental conditions. Additionally, cloud cover and adverse weather conditions pose significant limitations for satellite-based optical remote sensing, as they can obscure the Earth's surface and hinder the consistent acquisition of clear images [111]. Another key limitation is spatial resolution; while remote sensing offers valuable broad-scale insights, the resolution of some sensors may not be sufficient for applications that require fine detail, such as precise urban planning or localized ecological assessments. These challenges highlight the importance of selecting appropriate sensors, employing advanced image processing techniques, and integrating ground-truthing methods to enhance the reliability and applicability of remote sensing data in environmental studies.

Remote sensing has become an indispensable tool in environmental studies, providing comprehensive, timely, and large-scale data that enhances our understanding of the Earth's systems. By monitoring land cover, vegetation, water resources, and climate change, remote sensing supports sustainable resource management, conservation, and disaster response efforts. As technology continues to advance, the use of remote sensing in environmental monitoring will become even more critical in addressing the global environmental challenges of the 21st century [86, 112].

Geographic Information Systems (GIS)

Geographic Information Systems (GIS) are a powerful tool that allows for the collection, management, analysis, and visualization of spatial and geographic data. GIS integrates hardware, software, and data to enable the capture, manipulation, and display of geographically referenced information. In the context of environmental studies, GIS is instrumental in analyzing spatial patterns, modeling complex environmental processes, and supporting decision-making in areas such as land management, resource allocation, conservation, and disaster response [86].

Key Components of GIS

1. **Hardware**: The physical devices required to operate GIS, including computers, GPS units, and remote sensing equipment.
2. **Software**: GIS software provides the tools to process, analyze, and visualize spatial data. Popular GIS software includes ArcGIS, QGIS, and GRASS GIS, which offer a range of tools for mapping, spatial analysis, and geospatial modeling.
3. **Data**: Spatial data are the foundation of GIS. These can include vector data (points, lines, and polygons) representing features such as roads, rivers, and land parcels, or raster data (gridded data) that represent continuous phenomena such as elevation or temperature.
4. **People**: GIS analysts and decision-makers who use GIS tools to interpret data and make informed decisions.

Advantages of GIS in Environmental Studies

GIS play a crucial role in environmental studies by enabling advanced spatial analysis, data integration, visualization, and decision support. Through spatial analysis, GIS allows researchers to examine relationships such as proximity, adjacency, and connectivity, which are essential for understanding complex environmental processes and interactions [108]. GIS can integrate diverse datasets including satellite imagery, ground survey data, and socio-economic information into a unified analytical framework, offering a holistic view of environmental issues. In addition, GIS enhances data interpretation through the creation of maps, 3D models, and visualizations that make complex spatial data more accessible and comprehensible. These capabilities collectively empower policymakers, environmental managers, and planners by providing detailed, accurate, and timely spatial information to support informed decision-making in areas such as land use planning, resource management, and conservation strategies [109].

Challenges and Limitations of GIS

The effectiveness of Geographic Information Systems (GIS) in environmental studies is closely tied to the quality, resolution, and availability of spatial data. In many regions, especially in developing or remote areas, accurate and up-to-date data may be scarce or difficult to obtain, limiting the reliability of analyses and decision-making. Additionally, while GIS offers powerful tools for spatial analysis and modeling, interpreting the results often requires a deep understanding of both the technology and the specific environmental context being studied. This complexity can present challenges for users who lack technical expertise. Moreover, the cost and accessibility of GIS software can be a barrier; high-end proprietary GIS platforms may be expensive and require specialized training. However, the emergence of open-source alternatives like QGIS has significantly improved accessibility, enabling broader use of GIS in academic research, policy planning, and community-based environmental monitoring [7, 111].

GIS has revolutionized environmental studies by providing a versatile platform for spatial data analysis and decision-making. Its applications span a wide range of fields, from conservation and land-use planning to disaster management and climate change modeling. As environmental challenges become more complex, GIS will continue to play a pivotal role in helping researchers, policymakers, and conservationists make data-driven decisions that support sustainable management of natural resources.

Spatial Interpolation

Spatial Interpolation is a geostatistical technique used to estimate the values of a spatially continuous phenomenon at unmeasured locations based on observed data from surrounding locations. This technique is crucial in environmental studies where data points are limited or unevenly distributed, such as in soil quality monitoring, precipitation forecasting, or air pollution mapping. By using spatial interpolation methods, researchers can create continuous surfaces that represent the variation of environmental variables across a geographic area, which is important for modeling, decision-making, and resource management [55].

Applications of Spatial Interpolation in Environmental Studies

Spatial interpolation plays a vital role across various environmental and geoscientific applications. In climate and weather modeling, it is widely used to estimate variables such as temperature, precipitation, and wind speed across a region using data from a limited number of weather stations. This process enables the creation of weather maps, regional climate predictions, and climate models. In soil science, spatial interpolation helps map soil properties like pH, nutrient content, and organic matter, which are essential for precision agriculture, sustainable land management, and environmental monitoring [113]. For air quality and pollution mapping, interpolation techniques are employed to estimate pollutant concentrations—such as CO_2 and particulate matter in areas where monitoring stations are sparse, facilitating comprehensive air quality assessments and pollution control strategies. In hydrological modeling, spatial interpolation is used to estimate parameters like river discharge, groundwater levels, and rainfall distribution in regions with uneven data availability, thereby supporting flood prediction, watershed management, and hydrological simulations. Additionally, biodiversity and habitat mapping rely on interpolation to estimate the distribution of species and ecosystems across large landscapes, which is critical for conservation efforts, monitoring habitat degradation, and identifying biodiversity hotspots.

Advantages of Spatial Interpolation

Spatial interpolation offers several key advantages that make it invaluable for environmental analysis and decision-making. One of its primary benefits is data completeness; interpolation techniques enable the estimation of values at unsampled locations, thereby creating a continuous surface for analysis even when data points are sparse or irregularly distributed. This ensures a more comprehensive understanding of spatial phenomena. Another major advantage is cost and time efficiency. Since collecting remote sensing or field data across vast areas can be both expensive and time-consuming, interpolation allows researchers and practitioners to maximize the utility of existing datasets to generate meaningful insights over larger regions. Additionally, spatial interpolation offers flexibility, as different methods such as Kriging, Inverse Distance Weighting (IDW), or spline interpolation can be chosen based on the nature of the data and specific research goals. This adaptability makes it suitable for addressing a wide range of environmental challenges, from air quality assessments to agricultural planning [114, 115].

Limitations of Spatial Interpolation

Despite its advantages, spatial interpolation has several limitations that can affect the accuracy and reliability of its results. One major limitation lies in the assumptions of spatial continuity. Most interpolation methods are based on the premise that geographically closer points are more similar than those farther apart. However, this assumption may not hold true in regions with high spatial variability or abrupt changes, potentially leading to misleading estimates. Another critical factor is data quality; the effectiveness of interpolation is highly dependent on the accuracy and distribution of the input data. Poor-quality measurements or unevenly spaced sampling points can result in biased or inaccurate predictions. Additionally, edge effects pose a common challenge in spatial interpolation. At the boundaries of the study area, fewer surrounding data points are available to inform the estimation, often resulting in less reliable outputs. These limitations highlight the need for careful consideration when applying interpolation techniques, especially in complex or data-scarce environments.

Spatial interpolation is a powerful tool in environmental studies that enables researchers and practitioners to estimate values at unsampled locations, providing continuous surfaces for analysis. Its applications span various fields such as climate modeling, soil science, hydrology, and biodiversity conservation. However, the choice of interpolation method must be carefully considered based on the data characteristics and the specific research objectives to ensure accurate and reliable results [116].

Buffer Analysis

Buffer Analysis is a spatial analysis technique used in Geographic Information Systems (GIS) to create a zone around a specific geographic feature (*e.g.*, point, line, or polygon). This zone, called a "buffer," is defined by a specific distance from the feature and can be used to analyze spatial relationships and proximity between different features within the buffer zone. Buffer analysis is widely used in environmental studies, urban planning, resource management, and infrastructure development, as it helps assess areas affected by certain phenomena or conditions [107, 112].

Applications of Buffer Analysis in Environmental Studies

1. Environmental Protection and Conservation:

Buffer zones play a crucial role in various environmental management and planning efforts by defining areas of influence or protection around specific features. In the context of protected areas, buffer zones are established around national parks, wildlife reserves, and other conservation sites to safeguard sensitive ecosystems from external pressures [117]. These zones help limit human activities such as agriculture, construction, or urban expansion, thereby reducing disturbances to wildlife and preserving biodiversity. In pollution impact assessments, buffer zones are used to evaluate the potential reach and influence of pollutants originating from sources like industrial facilities, waste disposal sites, or major roadways. For instance, creating a buffer around a factory can help assess the potential risk of air or groundwater contamination in nearby residential areas or natural water sources. By delineating these zones, planners and environmentalists can make informed decisions to mitigate negative impacts and ensure sustainable development [22].

2. Urban Planning and Infrastructure Development:

Buffer zones are integral to zoning and land use planning, helping to delineate areas for specific purposes such as residential, commercial, or industrial use while protecting environmentally sensitive or incompatible zones from adverse development. By establishing clear boundaries, buffer zones ensure that land use is strategically organized to minimize conflicts and promote sustainable growth. In infrastructure planning, buffer zones are particularly useful for assessing the impact of transportation networks, such as roads, railways, and pipelines. These buffers help identify areas affected by factors like noise pollution, air quality degradation, and safety hazards. For example, creating a buffer around a proposed highway can aid in evaluating its potential effects on nearby communities, agricultural lands, or natural ecosystems. Such analyses enable planners to implement mitigation measures and make more informed decisions that balance development with environmental and social considerations.

3. Wildlife and Habitat Conservation:

Buffer zones are essential tools in wildlife conservation, particularly for protecting wildlife corridors and mitigating habitat fragmentation. Buffers established around wildlife corridors help shield these critical passageways from human disturbance, allowing animals to move safely between habitats for feeding, breeding, and seasonal migration. This protection is vital for maintaining healthy populations and reducing the risk of roadkill, poaching, or other human-related threats [118]. Additionally, buffer zones play a key role in addressing habitat fragmentation by preserving ecological connectivity. When natural habitats are divided by roads, agriculture, or urban development, buffers around key areas such as breeding grounds or migratory routes help maintain the movement and interaction of species across the landscape. For instance, creating buffer zones around the migratory paths of endangered species ensures these routes remain intact and free from disruptive development, thereby supporting long-term biodiversity and ecosystem resilience [48, 59].

4. Water Resource Management:

Riparian buffer zones and floodplain buffers are critical components of sustainable land and water management. Riparian buffer zones, which are established along rivers, lakes, and wetlands, serve to protect water quality by filtering pollutants, trapping sediment, and reducing nutrient runoff from nearby agricultural or urban areas. These buffers also help prevent soil erosion and provide habitat for a diverse range of plant and animal species, thereby preserving local biodiversity. For example, maintaining buffer zones along streams can significantly reduce the impact of agricultural runoff and sedimentation on aquatic ecosystems. Similarly, in floodplain management, buffer zones are used to regulate development in areas prone to flooding. By restricting construction and other high-risk activities within designated buffer areas, the potential damage from flood events can be minimized, protecting both human settlements and the natural landscape. Establishing such buffers not only enhances public safety but also maintains the ecological functions of floodplains, such as water storage and habitat provision [38, 52].

5. Disaster Risk Assessment and Emergency Management:

Buffer zones are essential for managing natural hazard risks and enhancing disaster preparedness. In hazard zones, buffers are used to delineate areas vulnerable to events such as flooding, wildfires, earthquakes, and landslides. These designated zones support emergency planning by identifying high-risk areas, guiding evacuation route design, and informing the placement of emergency services. For example, establishing buffer zones around earthquake fault lines or flood-prone regions helps planners and responders prepare for potential disasters and implement timely evacuation or mitigation measures. In wildfire-prone areas, buffer zones play a critical role in assessing fire risk and preventing the spread of wildfires to residential or ecologically sensitive regions [70]. By analyzing potential fire behavior within these buffers, authorities can develop more effective firebreaks, manage vegetation, and implement land-use regulations to reduce fire hazards and protect both human life and the environment.

6. Agriculture and Forestry:

In agriculture and forest management, buffer zones are vital for promoting environmental protection and sustainable practices. Buffer zones for pesticide application are established around farmlands to prevent the drift of harmful chemicals into adjacent ecosystems, water bodies, or residential areas. These zones act as protective barriers, reducing the risk of contamination and safeguarding biodiversity and public health. For example, creating buffer zones around agricultural fields can help shield nearby forests, rivers, or communities from the adverse effects of pesticide exposure. In forest management, buffer zones are used to protect ecologically sensitive areas, regulate logging activities, and manage fire risks [49, 76]. By setting up buffers around forested regions, authorities can preserve wildlife habitats, maintain ecosystem integrity, and implement fire control strategies that minimize the risk of wildfires spreading to or from forested zones. These practices contribute to the long-term sustainability and resilience of both agricultural and forested landscapes.

Advantages of Buffer Analysis

Buffer analysis offers several advantages that make it a widely used tool in environmental and urban planning. One of its key strengths is its simplicity and versatility simplicity and versatility; it provides a straightforward method for assessing spatial relationships and proximity, applicable across a range of contexts from conservation planning to infrastructure development. Buffer analysis also supports informed decision-making by offering clear, visual representations of areas influenced by specific phenomena or land-use activities. These visual tools help planners, policymakers, and stakeholders better understand the spatial impacts of proposed developments or environmental threats. Additionally, buffer creation is cost-effective and computationally efficient. With the help of Geographic Information Systems, buffer zones can be generated quickly and easily, allowing for timely analysis and response in planning and management processes.

Limitations of Buffer Analysis

Buffer analysis, as commonly applied in geographic information systems (GIS), often relies on several assumptions that may not always reflect the complexity of real-world conditions. One such assumption is the uniform distance around a feature, which implies that the impact or influence of a feature extends evenly in all directions. However, this assumption can be unrealistic, especially in cases where environmental factors, such as elevation gradients or varying land use, cause spatial variations that are not accounted for by a uniform buffer. Additionally, buffer analysis may fail to consider spatial heterogeneity, overlooking how environmental or social factors influence the impact of the feature beyond the defined buffer zone. This limitation becomes especially apparent when local variations in the surrounding landscape or community characteristics are crucial to understanding the true effects of the feature. Furthermore, buffer zones themselves are often an oversimplification, representing generalized areas that do not fully capture the complexity of spatial interactions or the potential impacts that may occur in more dynamic, real-world settings. Therefore, while buffer analysis provides a useful tool for certain applications, it is important to recognize its limitations when applied to complex spatial problems.

Buffer analysis is a valuable tool in GIS for studying spatial relationships, assessing environmental risks, and supporting land-use planning, conservation efforts, and resource management. By defining zones around key features, buffer analysis helps evaluate the potential impact of human activities and natural phenomena on surrounding areas. Despite its simplicity, buffer analysis provides critical insights into environmental protection, urban planning, and disaster risk management, although it should be used alongside other spatial analysis techniques to address more complex issues [119, 120].

Multicriteria Decision Analysis (MCDA)

Multicriteria Decision Analysis (MCDA) is a decision-making tool that helps evaluate and compare multiple alternatives based on several criteria. This technique is widely used in environmental studies, urban planning, resource management, and many other fields where decisions need to be made considering multiple, often conflicting, criteria. MCDA provides a structured approach to making decisions that take into account diverse factors, helping decision-makers prioritize options, balance trade-offs, and reach the most appropriate and feasible solution.

Key Concepts of MCDA

1. **Alternatives**: These are the different options or scenarios under evaluation in the decision-making process. For example, in environmental management, alternatives might include different land use plans, site selections for a new infrastructure project, or strategies for conservation.
2. **Criteria**: These are the factors or attributes that are important for making the decision. Each criterion represents a dimension of the problem, such as cost, environmental impact, social benefits, or economic feasibility. Criteria can be qualitative or quantitative, and they are often weighted based on their relative importance.
3. **Weights**: In MCDA, criteria are typically assigned weights to indicate their

relative importance in the decision-making process. These weights reflect the preferences or priorities of stakeholders involved in the decision. They help decision-makers balance trade-offs between different criteria.

4. **Performance Scores**: For each alternative, a performance score is calculated for each criterion. These scores can be based on data, expert judgment, or a combination of both. A performance score indicates how effectively an alternative satisfies a given criterion.
5. **Aggregation**: The final step in MCDA involves aggregating the weighted performance scores across all criteria to generate an overall score for each alternative. Various methods can be used for aggregation, depending on the specific MCDA technique being applied (*e.g.*, weighted sum model, analytical hierarchy process).

MCDA Methods

There are several methods for conducting MCDA, each with its own approach to evaluating and aggregating alternatives:

Weighted Sum Model (WSM):

The Weighted Sum Model (WSM) is a decision-making technique in which each alternative is assessed based on various criteria. For each criterion, a performance score is assigned to every alternative, and these scores are then multiplied by the corresponding weights of the criteria, which represent their relative importance. The weighted scores are summed to produce an overall score for each alternative, enabling a direct comparison of their overall performance. This method is widely used due to its simplicity and effectiveness, particularly when the criteria are comparable and can be measured on the same scale. Its straightforward nature makes it a popular choice for decision-making, especially when multiple alternatives need to be evaluated across several criteria. However, that all criteria are both quantifiable and comparable to ensure that the results provide meaningful insights.

Analytical Hierarchy Process (AHP):

The Analytical Hierarchy Process (AHP) is a more sophisticated Multi-Criteria Decision Analysis (MCDA) method that involves performing pairwise comparisons between alternatives and criteria. This method relies on hierarchical decomposition, breaking down the decision problem into a tree structure that includes criteria and sub-criteria. AHP allows for the calculation of the relative importance of each criterion and alternative by conducting a series of pairwise comparisons, usually on a scale from 1 (indicating equal importance) to 9 (that one is extremely more important than the other). This process helps to structure complex decision-making situations where judgments are subjective and difficult to quantify. AHP is particularly useful in cases where multiple criteria are involved, helping decision- makers understand how alternatives compare relative to each other across these criteria. The method uses matrix algebra and eigenvalue computation to derive the relative weights of the criteria and the performance scores for each alternative, allowing for a more precise and systematic comparison of alternatives [121, 122].

Applications of MCDA in Environmental Studies

1. **Land Use Planning**: MCDA is frequently used in land use planning to assess different land management strategies, such as urban development, agriculture, or conservation. Criteria might include economic feasibility, environmental impact, and social benefits.
2. **Environmental Impact Assessment (EIA)**: MCDA helps determine the most sustainable and least harmful development options by evaluating the potential impacts on air quality, biodiversity, water resources, and human health.
3. **Water Resource Management**: MCDA can aid in water resource allocation decisions by evaluating alternative water supply and conservation options based on factors such as cost, efficiency, environmental sustainability, and social equity.
4. **Renewable Energy Planning**: In the context of renewable energy, MCDA is used to assess different energy production technologies (*e.g.*, solar, wind, hydro) based on criteria such as efficiency, cost, environmental impact, and scalability.
5. **Climate Change Adaptation**: MCDA supports decision-making in climate change adaptation by evaluating different strategies (*e.g.*, flood protection measures, drought management) based on effectiveness, cost, and social acceptance.
6. **Conservation and Biodiversity Protection**: MCDA helps prioritize conservation actions, such as the establishment of protected areas or wildlife corridors, by considering factors like biodiversity value, threats, and feasibility.

Advantages of MCDA

MCDA offers several advantages that make it a powerful tool in decision-making. One key benefit is its structured approach, which provides a systematic and transparent framework for evaluating multiple criteria. This helps decision-makers understand the trade-offs between alternatives and justify their final choices, ensuring that decisions are well-grounded and rational. Additionally, MCDA is highly flexible, as it can accommodate both quantitative and qualitative criteria, which makes it applicable across a wide range of decision-making scenarios, from economic analyses to environmental assessments [123]. It also fosters the inclusion of multiple stakeholders by integrating their preferences and values into the decision-making process, which is crucial when dealing with complex, multifaceted issues like environmental management. Moreover, MCDA can combine quantitative data, such as economic costs or environmental impacts, with qualitative data, such as stakeholder opinions or social acceptability, enabling a holistic view of the alternatives being considered. This versatility makes MCDA a comprehensive tool for making informed and balanced decisions across various domains [121, 124].

Limitations of MCDA

While MCDA (Multi-Criteria Decision Analysis) offers many benefits, it also presents some challenges that must be considered. One of the main drawbacks is subjectivity, as the selection of criteria, assignment of weights, and performance scoring often rely on subjective judgment. If these aspects are not handled carefully, they can introduce bias into the decision-making process, leading to skewed results. Another limitation is the high data requirement of MCDA, as it demands reliable and comprehensive data for each alternative and criterion [121]. Unfortunately, such data may not always be available, particularly in complex or emerging fields where information is scarce. Additionally, complexity can be a significant issue, especially when a large number of criteria and alternatives are involved. Without the appropriate tools and expertise, implementing MCDA can become cumbersome and challenging. Lastly, MCDA can be sensitive to weights, meaning that the results can change dramatically with small alterations in the assigned weight values. This sensitivity underscores the importance of carefully considering how weights are determined, as even minor changes can affect the rankings of alternatives. These limitations highlight the need for thoughtful application and caution when using MCDA for decision-making [125].

MCDA is a powerful tool for making complex decisions in environmental studies and many other fields. By allowing decision-makers to evaluate alternatives based on multiple criteria, MCDA provides a transparent and structured approach to managing trade-offs and selecting the most balanced solution. However, its effectiveness depends on the careful selection of criteria, accurate data, and appropriate aggregation methods to ensure valid and reliable results [125].

CONCLUSION

Spatial techniques have become essential tools in environmental studies, offering powerful methods for analyzing, visualizing, and interpreting complex geographical and environmental data. These techniques, including Geographic Information Systems (GIS), Remote Sensing, Spatial Interpolation, Buffer Analysis, and Multicriteria Decision Analysis (MCDA), provide the necessary framework to understand spatial patterns, trends, and relationships within the environment. GIS plays a central role by integrating diverse datasets, enabling researchers to map, analyze, and model environmental processes. Remote sensing, with its ability to capture data over large areas and at regular intervals, offers invaluable insights into land cover changes, deforestation, water quality, and urban expansion. Spatial interpolation techniques allow for accurate prediction and estimation of environmental variables in areas with sparse data, while buffer analysis helps assess impacts within specific distances from features such as roads, rivers, or protected areas.

Moreover, MCDA enhances decision-making by evaluating multiple, often conflicting, criteria and offering a structured approach to selecting the most suitable alternatives in environmental management. Whether in land use planning, water resource management, or climate change adaptation, these spatial techniques support more informed and sustainable decisions by incorporating various spatial, environmental, and social factors. In conclusion, the integration and application of these spatial techniques are crucial for effective environmental monitoring, management, and policy development. They facilitate a deeper understanding of the dynamics of environmental systems and enable more precise, data-driven decision-making. As environmental challenges become increasingly complex, the continued advancement and application of spatial technologies will be key to promoting sustainable development and mitigating environmental risks.

LIST OF ABBREVIATIONS

AI	Artificial Intelligence
ANN	Artificial Neural Network
BOD	Biochemical Oxygen Demand
CO	Carbon Monoxide
COD	Chemical Oxygen Demand
DO	Dissolved Oxygen
GIS	Geographic Information Systems
IoT	Internet of Things
ML	Machine Learning

MODIS Moderate Resolution Imaging Spectroradiometer

NO_2 Nitrogen Dioxide

O_3 Ozone

PM2.5 Particulate Matter 2.5 microns

PM10 Particulate Matter 10 microns

RF Random Forest

SAR Synthetic Aperture Radar

SO_2 Sulfur Dioxide

SVM Support Vector Machine

VOCs Volatile Organic Compounds

REFERENCES

[1] D.B. Olawade, O.Z. Wada, A.O. Ige, B.I. Egbewole, A. Olojo, and B.I. Oladapo, "Artificial intelligence in environmental monitoring: Advancements, challenges, and future directions", *Hyg. Environ. Health Adv.,* vol. 12, p. 100114, 2024. [http://dx.doi.org/10.1016/j.heha.2024.100114]

[2] J. Awewomom, F. Dzeble, Y. D. Takyi, W. B. Ashie, E. N. Y. O. Ettey, P. E. Afua, L. N. A. Sackey, F. Opoku, and O. Akoto, "Addressing global environmental pollution using environmental control techniques: A focus on environmental policy and preventive environmental management," *Discov. Environ.*, vol. 2, no. 1, p. 8, 2024. [http://dx.doi.org/10.1007/S44274-024-00033-5]

[3] T.T. Nguyen, U. Grote, F. Neubacher, D.B. Rahut, M.H. Do, and G.P. Paudel, "Security risks from climate change and environmental degradation: implications for sustainable land use transformation in the Global South", *Curr. Opin. Environ. Sustain.,* vol. 63, p. 101322, 2023. [http://dx.doi.org/10.1016/j.cosust.2023.101322]

[4] M.A. Butt, G.S. Voronkov, E.P. Grakhova, R.V. Kutluyarov, N.L. Kazanskiy, and S.N. Khonina, "Environmental monitoring: A comprehensive review on optical waveguide and fiber-based sensors", *Biosensors (Basel),* vol. 12, no. 11, p. 1038, 2022. [http://dx.doi.org/10.3390/bios12111038] [PMID: 36421155]

[5] Y. Li, B. Chen, S. Yang, Z. Jiao, M. Zhang, Y. Yang, and Y. Gao, "Advances in environmental pollutant detection techniques: Enhancing public health monitoring and risk assessment", *Environ. Int.,* vol. 197, p. 109365, 2025. [http://dx.doi.org/10.1016/j.envint.2025.109365] [PMID: 40101528]

[6] E. Alotaibi, and N. Nassif, "Artificial intelligence in environmental monitoring: in-depth analysis", *Discov. Artif. Intell.,,* vol. 4, no. 1, p. 84, 2024. [http://dx.doi.org/10.1007/s44163-024-00198-1]

[7] "Remote sensing and satellite technology for green sustainability," TraceX Technologies, [Online]. Available from: https://tracextech.com/remote-sensing-and-satellite-technology-for-environmental-monitoring/

[8] B. Katie, "Internet of Things (IoT) for Environmental Monitoring", *Int. J. Comput. Eng.,,* vol. 6, no. 3, pp. 29-42, 2024. [http://dx.doi.org/10.47941/ijce.2139]

[9] R. Willow, A. Ella, and A. Abbas, "The role of AI in climate change mitigation and environmental monitoring," *Atmospheric Sciences: Climate Change & Geoscience*, Nov. 2023. Available from: https://www.researchgate.net/publication/377762233_The_Role_of_AI_in_Climate_Change_Mitigatio

n_and_Environmental_Monitoring

[10] A.G. Abo-Khalil, "Integrating sustainability into higher education challenges and opportunities for universities worldwide", *Heliyon,* vol. 10, no. 9, p. e29946, 2024. [http://dx.doi.org/10.1016/j.heliyon.2024.e29946] [PMID: 38707336]

[11] B.J. Singh, A. Chakraborty, and R. Sehgal, "A systematic review of industrial wastewater management: Evaluating challenges and enablers", *J. Environ. Manage.,* vol. 348, p. 119230, 2023. [http://dx.doi.org/10.1016/j.jenvman.2023.119230] [PMID: 37832302]

[12] Y. Li, K. I. Hoi, K. M. Mok, and K. V. Yuen, "Emerging air quality monitoring methods," in *Air Quality Monitoring and Advanced Bayesian Modeling.* Amsterdam, Netherlands: Elsevier, 2023, pp. 105–172. [http://dx.doi.org/10.1016/B978-0-323-90266-3.00005-4]

[13] T. Seesaard, K. Kamjornkittikoon, and C. Wongchoosuk, "A comprehensive review on advancements in sensors for air pollution applications", *Sci. Total Environ.,* vol. 951, p. 175696, 2024. [http://dx.doi.org/10.1016/j.scitotenv.2024.175696] [PMID: 39197792]

[14] K Vatitsi, S Siachalou, D Latinopoulos, I Kagalou, CS Akratos, and G Mallinis, "Monitoring water quality parameters in small rivers using SuperDove imagery", *Water,* vol. 16, no. 5, pp. 758-758, 2024. [http://dx.doi.org/10.3390/W16050758]

[15] United States Environmental Protection Agency, Office of Water, "Chapter 5: Water quality conditions," in *National Water Quality Inventory: Report to Congress*, Washington, DC, USA: U.S. EPA.

[16] P. Panagos, M. Van Liedekerke, A. Jones, and L. Montanarella, "European soil data centre: Response to european policy support and public data requirements", *Land Use Policy,* vol. 29, no. 2, pp. 329-338, 2012. [http://dx.doi.org/10.1016/j.landusepol.2011.07.003]

[17] A. Ebenstein, M. Fan, M. Greenstone, G. He, and M. Zhou, "New evidence on the impact of sustained exposure to air pollution on life expectancy from China's Huai River Policy", *Proc. Natl. Acad. Sci. USA,* vol. 114, no. 39, pp. 10384-10389, 2017. [http://dx.doi.org/10.1073/pnas.1616784114] [PMID: 28893980]

[18] C. Maney, D. Guaras, J. Harrison, A. Guizar-Coutiño, M.B.J. Harfoot, S.L.L. Hill, N.D. Burgess, and W. Sutherland, "National commitments to aichi targets and their implications for monitoring the kunming-montreal global biodiversity framework", *npj Biodiversity,* vol. 3, no. 1, p. 6, 2024. [http://dx.doi.org/10.1038/s44185-024-00039-5] [PMID: 39242842]

[19] H.D. Guo, L. Zhang, and L.W. Zhu, "Earth observation big data for climate change research", *Adv. Clim. Chang. Res.,* vol. 6, no. 2, pp. 108-117, 2015. [http://dx.doi.org/10.1016/j.accre.2015.09.007]

[20] S. Bolan, L.P. Padhye, T. Jasemizad, M. Govarthanan, N. Karmegam, H. Wijesekara, D. Amarasiri, D. Hou, P. Zhou, B.K. Biswal, R. Balasubramanian, H. Wang, K.H.M. Siddique, J. Rinklebe, M.B. Kirkham, and N. Bolan, "Impacts of climate change on the fate of contaminants through extreme weather events", *Sci. Total Environ.,* vol. 909, p. 168388, 2024. [http://dx.doi.org/10.1016/j.scitotenv.2023.168388] [PMID: 37956854]

[21] M. Puig, and R.M. Darbra, "Innovations and insights in environmental monitoring and assessment in port areas", *Curr. Opin. Environ. Sustain.,* vol. 70, p. 101472, 2024. [http://dx.doi.org/10.1016/j.cosust.2024.101472]

[22] J. Wang, J. Zhen, W. Hu, S. Chen, I. Lizaga, M. Zeraatpisheh, and X. Yang, "Remote sensing of soil degradation: Progress and perspective", *Int. Soil Water Conserv. Res.,* vol. 11, no. 3, pp. 429-454, 2023. [http://dx.doi.org/10.1016/j.iswcr.2023.03.002]

[23] R Avtar, "Remote sensing for international peace and security: Its role and implications", *Remote Sensing,* vol. 13, no. 3, pp. 439-439, 2021.
[http://dx.doi.org/10.3390/RS13030439]

[24] J. Burston, "Closing the air quality gap: Why national monitoring needs global funding," Clean Air Fund, 2024. Available: https://www.cleanairfund.org/news-item/closing-the-air-quality-gap/

[25] W.J. Cosgrove, and D.P. Loucks, "Water management: Current and future challenges and research directions", *Water Resour. Res.,* vol. 51, no. 6, pp. 4823-4839, 2015.
[http://dx.doi.org/10.1002/2014WR016869]

[26] N. Voulvoulis, K.D. Arpon, and T. Giakoumis, "The EU water framework directive: From great expectations to problems with implementation", *Sci. Total Environ.,* vol. 575, pp. 358-366, 2017.
[http://dx.doi.org/10.1016/j.scitotenv.2016.09.228] [PMID: 27744201]

[27] E. Undeman, H. Josefsson, M. Ågerstrand, A. Sobek, and A. Nilsson, "The potential of the EU water framework directive for reducing emissions of pollutants is limited: a case study on river basin specific pollutants in Swedish environmental permitting processes", *Environ. Sci. Eur.,* vol. 34, no. 1, p. 123, 2022.
[http://dx.doi.org/10.1186/s12302-022-00705-0]

[28] Institute of Medicine, *Global Climate Change and Extreme Weather Events: Understanding the Contributions to Infectious Disease Emergence: Workshop Summary.* Washington, DC, USA: National Academies Press, 2008. [Online]. Available: https://www.nationalacademies.org/read/12435/chapter/1
[http://dx.doi.org/10.17226/12435]

[29] A.T. Asresu, E. Furlan, F. Horneman, F. Zennaro, N.D. Nguyen, S. Torresan, A. Critto, and A. Marcomini, "A systematic review of climate change impacts on water quality in transitional environments from a multi-hazard perspective", *Estuar. Coast. Shelf Sci.,* vol. 317, p. 109194, 2025.
[http://dx.doi.org/10.1016/j.ecss.2025.109194]

[30] Y. Malhi, J. Franklin, N. Seddon, M. Solan, M. G. Turner, C. B. Field, and N. Knowlton, "Climate change and ecosystems: threats, opportunities and solutions," *Philos. Trans. R. Soc. Lond. B Biol. Sci.,* vol. 375, no. 1794, 2020.
[http://dx.doi.org/10.1098/rstb.2019.0104]

[31] V.V. Salomonson, W. Barnes, J. Xiong, S. Kempler, and E. Masuoka, "An overview of the earth observing system MODIS instrument and associated data systems performance", In: *Proc. IEEE Int. Geosci. Remote Sens. Symp. (IGARSS)* vol. 2. Toronto, ON, Canada, 2002, pp. 1174-1176.
[http://dx.doi.org/10.1109/IGARSS.2002.1025812]

[32] X. Xiong, A. Angal, T. Chang, K. Chiang, N. Lei, Y. Li, J. Sun, K. Twedt, and A. Wu, "MODIS and VIIRS calibration and characterization in support of producing long-term high-quality data products," *Remote Sens*., vol. 12, no. 19, p. 3167, 2020.
[http://dx.doi.org/10.3390/RS12193167]

[33] OECD, "Scaling up adaptation finance in developing countries," *Green Finance and Investment*, Nov., 2023.
[http://dx.doi.org/10.1787/b0878862-en]

[34] A. Azhoni, S. Jude, and I. Holman, "Adapting to climate change by water management organisations: Enablers and barriers", *J. Hydrol. (Amst.),* vol. 559, pp. 736-748, 2018.
[http://dx.doi.org/10.1016/j.jhydrol.2018.02.047]

[35] R. Karki, S. Bhatta, and S. Pandey, "Impact of forest cover and land use change on tree species diversity and carbon stocks in shivapuri nagarjun national park, nepal", *Discover Environment,* vol. 3, no. 1, p. 24, 2025.
[http://dx.doi.org/10.1007/s44274-025-00205-x]

[36] L. Wang, F. Wei, T. Tagesson, Z. Fang, and J.C. Svenning, "Transforming forest management through

rewilding: Enhancing biodiversity, resilience, and biosphere sustainability under global change", *One Earth,* vol. 8, no. 3, p. 101195, 2025.
[http://dx.doi.org/10.1016/j.oneear.2025.101195]

[37] Hadi, A Krasovskii, V Maus, P Yowargana, S Pietsch, and M Rautiainen, "Monitoring deforestation in rainforests using satellite data: A pilot study from Kalimantan, Indonesia", *Forests,* vol. 9, no. 7, pp. 389-389, 2018.
[http://dx.doi.org/10.3390/F9070389]

[38] S. Kumar, S. Imen, V.K. Sridharan, A. Gupta, W. McDonald, J.J. Ramirez-Avila, O.I. Abdul-Aziz, R. Talchabhadel, H. Gao, N.W.T. Quinn, W.J. Weiss, T. Poulose, S.S. Palmate, C.M. Lee, and L. Baskaran, "Perceived barriers and advances in integrating earth observations with water resources modeling", *Remote Sens. Appl. Soc. Environ.,* vol. 33, p. 101119, 2024.
[http://dx.doi.org/10.1016/j.rsase.2023.101119]

[39] AYA Abdelmajeed, and R Juszczak, "Challenges and limitations of remote sensing applications in northern peatlands: Present and future prospects", *Remote Sensing,* vol. 16, no. 3, pp. 591-591, 2024.
[http://dx.doi.org/10.3390/RS16030591]

[40] United Nations Office for Disaster Risk Reduction (UNDRR), "Disaster risk reduction and disaster risk management," [Online]. Available: https://www.preventionweb.net/understanding-disaste--risk/ky-concepts/disaster-risk-reduction-disaster-risk-management

[41] United Nations Office for Disaster Risk Reduction (UNDRR), "Reading the Sendai Framework for Disaster Risk Reduction 2015–2030," [Online]. Available: https://www.preventionweb.net/drr

[42] M. Hoshiba and T. Ozaki, "Earthquake early warning and tsunami warning of the Japan Meteorological Agency, and their performance in the 2011 off the Pacific Coast of Tohoku earthquake (Mw 9.0)," in *Early Warning for Geological Disasters*, Berlin, Germany: Springer, 2014, pp. 1–28.
[http://dx.doi.org/10.1007/978-3-642-12233-0_1]

[43] D. Van Niekerk, L. D. Nemakonde, L. Kruger, and K. Forbes-Genade, "Community-based disaster risk management," in *Handbook of Disaster Research*, H. Rodríguez, W. Donner, and J. Trainor, eds., *Handbooks of Sociology and Social Research*, Cham, Switzerland: Springer, 2018, pp. 411–429.
[http://dx.doi.org/10.1007/978-3-319-63254-4_20]

[44] K. Shrestha, *Community based approach in disaster management: A study of disaster management committees in Chitwan District*, M.S. thesis, Human and Natural Resources Studies, Kathmandu University, Nepal, Nov. 2023.
[http://dx.doi.org/10.13140/RG.2.2.25501.93920]

[45] United Nations, "*Biodiversity: our strongest natural defense against climate change*", [Online]. Available: https://www.un.org/en/climatechange/science/climate-issues/biodiversity. Accessed: Apr. 8, 2026

[46] E. W. Chu and J. R. Karr, "*Environmental impact: concept, consequences, measurement,*" in Reference Module in Life Sciences, 2016.
[http://dx.doi.org/10.1016/B978-0-12-809633-8.02380-3]

[47] K. Afifa, K. Arshad, N. Hussain, M.H. Ashraf, and M.Z. Saleem, "Air pollution and climate change as grand challenges to sustainability", *Sci. Total Environ.,* vol. 928, p. 172370, 2024.
[http://dx.doi.org/10.1016/j.scitotenv.2024.172370] [PMID: 38604367]

[48] G. Carlos, A. Velmurugan, B.A. Jerard, R. Karthick, and I. Jaisankar, "Biodiversity of polynesian islands: Distribution and threat from climate change", *Biodivers. Clim. Change Adapt. Trop. Isl.,* no. Jan, pp. 105-125, 2008.
[http://dx.doi.org/10.1016/B978-0-12-813064-3.00004-1]

[49] S.S. Verma, "Developing adaptive capability of agricultural societies in the context of climate change", *Climate Change and Agricultural Ecosystems: Current Challenges and Adaptation.* K. K. Choudhary, A. Kumar, and A. K. Singh, eds., pp. 433–445, 2019.
[http://dx.doi.org/10.1016/B978-0-12-816483-9.00014-1]

[50] National Geographic, "*Earth's changing climate*", [Online]. Available: https://education.nationalgeographic.org/resource/earths-changing-climate/. Accessed: Apr. 8, 2026.

[51] Business Standard, "*Why Delhi-NCR struggles with severe air pollution every winter*", [Online]. Available: https://www.business-standard.com/india-news/explained-why-delhi-ncr-struggl-s-with-severe-air-pollution-every-winter-124111501328_1.html. Accessed: Apr. 8, 2026.

[52] L. Lin, H. Yang, and X. Xu, "Effects of water pollution on human health and disease heterogeneity: A review", *Front. Environ. Sci.,* vol. 10, p. 880246, 2022. [http://dx.doi.org/10.3389/fenvs.2022.880246]

[53] L.M. Bexfield, P.L. Toccalino, K. Belitz, W.T. Foreman, and E.T. Furlong, "Hormones and pharmaceuticals in groundwater used as a source of drinking water across the United States", *Environ. Sci. Technol.,* vol. 53, no. 6, pp. 2950-2960, 2019. [http://dx.doi.org/10.1021/acs.est.8b05592] [PMID: 30834750]

[54] M. Asif, F. Hai, J. Kang, J. Van de Merwe, F. Leusch, K. Yamamoto, W. Price, and L. Nghiem, "Degradation of trace organic contaminants by a membrane distillation—enzymatic bioreactor", *Appl. Sci. (Basel),* vol. 7, no. 9, p. 879, 2017. [http://dx.doi.org/10.3390/app7090879]

[55] M. Hanna-Attisha, J. LaChance, R.C. Sadler, and A. Champney Schnepp, "Elevated blood lead levels in children associated with the flint drinking water crisis: A spatial analysis of risk and public health response", *Am. J. Public Health,* vol. 106, no. 2, pp. 283-290, 2016. [http://dx.doi.org/10.2105/AJPH.2015.303003] [PMID: 26691115]

[56] World Wide Fund for Nature, "*Deforestation and forest degradation*", [Online]. Available: https://www.worldwildlife.org/threats/deforestation-and-forest-degradation. Accessed: Apr. 8, 2026.

[57] R.K. Mishra, S.S. Mentha, Y. Misra, and N. Dwivedi, "Emerging pollutants of severe environmental concern in water and wastewater: A comprehensive review on current developments and future research", *Water-Energy Nexus,* vol. 6, pp. 74-95, 2023. [http://dx.doi.org/10.1016/j.wen.2023.08.002]

[58] B. Hosen, "Exploring the ecological consequences of deforestation in tropical rainforests", *Environ. Ecosyst. Sci.,,* vol. 7, no. 2, pp. 112-121, 2023. [http://dx.doi.org/10.26480/ees.02.2023.112.121]

[59] U. Nations, "Biodiversity - our strongest natural defense against climate change | United Nations", Available from: https://www.un.org/en/climatechange/science/climate-issues/biodiversity

[60] B.J. Henley, H.V. McGregor, A.D. King, O. Hoegh-Guldberg, A.K. Arzey, D.J. Karoly, J.M. Lough, T.M. DeCarlo, and B.K. Linsley, "Highest ocean heat in four centuries places Great Barrier Reef in danger", *Nature,* vol. 632, no. 8024, pp. 320-326, 2024. [http://dx.doi.org/10.1038/s41586-024-07672-x] [PMID: 39112620]

[61] M. Hino, E. Benami, and N. Brooks, "Machine learning for environmental monitoring", *Nat. Sustain.,* vol. 1, no. 10, pp. 583-588, 2018. [http://dx.doi.org/10.1038/s41893-018-0142-9]

[62] S. Shalu and G. Singh, "Environmental monitoring with machine learning," *EPRA International Journal of Multidisciplinary Research (IJMR)*, no. May, pp. 208–212, 2023. [http://dx.doi.org/10.36713/epra13330]

[63] M. S. Binetti, C. Massarelli, and V. F. Uricchio, "Machine learning in geosciences: A review of complex environmental monitoring applications," *Mach. Learn. Knowl. Extract*, vol. 6, no. 2, pp. 1263–1280, 2024. [http://dx.doi.org/10.3390/make6020059]

[64] S. Subramaniam, N. Raju, A. Ganesan, N. Rajavel, M. Chenniappan, C. Prakash, A. Pramanik, A. K. Basak, and S. Dixit, "Artificial intelligence technologies for forecasting air pollution and human health: A narrative review", *Sustainability,* vol. 14, no. 16, 2022.

[http://dx.doi.org/10.3390/SU14169951]

[65] Y. Zhou, X. Zhao, K.P. Lin, C.H. Wang, and L. Li, "A Gaussian process mixture model-based hard-cut iterative learning algorithm for air quality prediction", *Appl. Soft Comput.,* vol. 85, p. 105789, 2019.
[http://dx.doi.org/10.1016/j.asoc.2019.105789]

[66] K. Aayush, D. Vishal, N. Hammad, and K.S. Manu, "Application of Artificial Intelligence in Curbing Air Pollution: The Case of India", *Asian Journal of Management,* vol. 11, no. 3, p. 285, 2020.
[http://dx.doi.org/10.5958/2321-5763.2020.00044.X]

[67] P. Mannucci, and M. Franchini, "Health effects of ambient air pollution in developing countries", *Int. J. Environ. Res. Public Health,* vol. 14, no. 9, p. 1048, 2017.
[http://dx.doi.org/10.3390/ijerph14091048] [PMID: 28895888]

[68] H Li, J Cui, X Zhang, Y Han, and L Cao, "Dimensionality reduction and classification of hyperspectral remote sensing image feature extraction", *Remote Sensing,* vol. 14, no. 18, pp. 4579-4579, 2022.
[http://dx.doi.org/10.3390/RS14184579]

[69] M. Aghababaei, A. Ebrahimi, A.A. Naghipour, E. Asadi, and J. Verrelst, "Vegetation types mapping using multi-temporal landsat images in the google earth engine platform", *Remote Sens. (Basel),* vol. 13, no. 22, p. 4683, 2021.
[http://dx.doi.org/10.3390/rs13224683] [PMID: 36082003]

[70] A. Akhyar, M. A. Zulkifley, J. Lee, T. Song, J. Han, C. Cho, S. Hyun, Y. Son, and B-W. Hong, "Deep artificial intelligence applications for natural disaster management systems: A methodological review", *Ecol. Indic.,* vol. 163, p. 112067, 2024.
[http://dx.doi.org/10.1016/j.ecolind.2024.112067]

[71] H. Wang, G. Barone, and A. Smith, "Current and future role of data fusion and machine learning in infrastructure health monitoring", *Struct. Infrastruct. Eng.*. vol. 19, no. 13, pp. 1853–1882, 2023.
[http://dx.doi.org/10.1080/15732479.2023.2165118]

[72] I.H. Sarker, "Machine learning: Algorithms, real-world applications and research directions", *SN Comput. Sci.,* vol. 2, no. 3, p. 160, 2021.
[http://dx.doi.org/10.1007/s42979-021-00592-x] [PMID: 33778771]

[73] M. Apriani, S.K. Wijaya, and Daryono, "Earthquake Magnitude Estimation Based on Machine Learning: Application to Earthquake Early Warning System", *J. Phys. Conf. Ser.,* vol. 1951, no. 1, p. 012057, 2021.
[http://dx.doi.org/10.1088/1742-6596/1951/1/012057]

[74] L. Breiman, "Random Forests", *Mach. Learn.,* vol. 45, no. 1, pp. 5-32, 2001.
[http://dx.doi.org/10.1023/A:1010933404324]

[75] D.W. Aha, D. Kibler, and M.K. Albert, "Instance-based learning algorithms", *Mach. Learn.,* vol. 6, no. 1, pp. 37-66, 1991.
[http://dx.doi.org/10.1023/A:1022689900470]

[76] F. Balducci, D. Impedovo, and G. Pirlo, "Machine learning applications on agricultural datasets for smart farm enhancement", *Machines,* vol. 6, no. 3, p. 38, 2018.
[http://dx.doi.org/10.3390/machines6030038]

[77] T. Akinboyewa, Z. Li, H. Ning, and M. N. Lessani, "GIS Copilot: towards an autonomous GIS agent for spatial analysis," *Int. J. Digit. Earth*, vol. 18, no. 1, 2025.
[http://dx.doi.org/10.1080/17538947.2025.2497489]

[78] G. Mai, Y. Xie, X. Jia, N. Lao, J. Rao, Q. Zhu, Z. Liu, Y-Y. Chiang, and J. Jiao, "Towards the next generation of Geospatial Artificial Intelligence", *Int. J. Appl. Earth Obs. Geoinf.,* vol. 136, p. 104368, 2025.
[http://dx.doi.org/10.1016/j.jag.2025.104368]

[79] R. Bommasani, D. A. Hudson, E. Adeli, R. Altman, S. Arora, S. von Arx, M. S. Bernstein, J. Bohg, A. Bosselut, E. Brunskill, E. Brynjolfsson, S. Buch, D. Card, R. Castellon, N. Chatterji, A. Chen, K. Creel, J. Q. Davis, D. Demszky, C. Donahue, M. Doumbouya, E. Durmus, S. Ermon, J. Etchemendy, K. Ethayarajh, L. Fei-Fei, C. Finn, T. Gale, L. Gillespie, K. Goel, N. Goodman, S. Grossman, N. Guha, T. Hashimoto, P. Henderson, J. Hewitt, D. E. Ho, J. Hong, K. Hsu, J. Huang, T. Icard, S. Jain, D. Jurafsky, P. Kalluri, S. Karamcheti, G. Keeling, F. Khani, O. Khattab, P. W. Koh, M. Krass, R. Krishna, R. Kuditipudi, A. Kumar, F. Ladhak, M. Lee, T. Lee, J. Leskovec, I. Levent, X. L. Li, X. Li, T. Ma, A. Malik, C. D. Manning, S. Mirchandani, E. Mitchell, Z. Munyikwa, S. Nair, A. Narayan, D. Narayanan, B. Newman, A. Nie, J. C. Niebles, H. Nilforoshan, J. Nyarko, G. Ogut, L. Orr, I. Papadimitriou, J. S. Park, C. Piech, E. Portelance, C. Potts, A. Raghunathan, R. Reich, H. Ren, F. Rong, Y. Roohani, C. Ruiz, J. Ryan, C. Ré, D. Sadigh, S. Sagawa, K. Santhanam, A. Shih, K. Srinivasan, A. Tamkin, R. Taori, A. W. Thomas, F. Tramèr, R. E. Wang, W. Wang, B. Wu, J. Wu, Y. Wu, S. M. Xie, M. Yasunaga, J. You, M. Zaharia, M. Zhang, T. Zhang, X. Zhang, Y. Zhang, L. Zheng, and P. Liang, "On the opportunities and risks of foundation models," *arXiv preprint arXiv:2108.07258*, 2021.

[80] R.P. Shete, A.M. Bongale, and D. Dharrao, "IoT-enabled effective real-time water quality monitoring method for aquaculture", *MethodsX,* vol. 13, p. 102906, 2024. [http://dx.doi.org/10.1016/j.mex.2024.102906] [PMID: 39263361]

[81] "IoT-based real-time soil health monitoring system for precision agriculture," ResearchGate. [Online]. Available: https://www.researchgate.net/publication/382295328_IoTBased_Real_Time_Soil_Health_Monitoring_System_for_Precision_Agriculture

[82] S Sharma, "Remote sensing and GIS in natural resource management: Comparing tools and emphasizing the importance of in-situ data", *Remote Sensing,* vol. 16, no. 22, 2024. [http://dx.doi.org/10.3390/RS16224161]

[83] M. Wang, M. Wander, S. Mueller, N. Martin, and J.B. Dunn, "Evaluation of survey and remote sensing data products used to estimate land use change in the United States: Evolving issues and emerging opportunities", *Environ. Sci. Policy,* vol. 129, pp. 68-78, 2022. [http://dx.doi.org/10.1016/j.envsci.2021.12.021]

[84] P.J. Verkerk, R. Costanza, L. Hetemäki, I. Kubiszewski, P. Leskinen, G.J. Nabuurs, J. Potočnik, and M. Palahí, "Climate-Smart Forestry: the missing link", *For. Policy Econ.,* vol. 115, p. 102164, 2020. [http://dx.doi.org/10.1016/j.forpol.2020.102164]

[85] D. Stampoulis, H.G. Damavandi, D. Boscovic, and J. Sabo, "Using satellite remote sensing and machine learning techniques towards precipitation prediction and vegetation classification", *J. Environ. Inform.,* vol. 37, no. 1, pp. 1-15, 2020. [http://dx.doi.org/10.3808/jei.202000427]

[86] M. Avand, H. Moradi, and M.R. lasboyee, "Using machine learning models, remote sensing, and GIS to investigate the effects of changing climates and land uses on flood probability", *J. Hydrol. (Amst.),* vol. 595, p. 125663, 2021. [http://dx.doi.org/10.1016/j.jhydrol.2020.125663]

[87] S. Aakre, I. Banaszak, R. Mechler, D. Rübbelke, A. Wreford, and H. Kalirai, "Financial adaptation to disaster risk in the European Union", *Mitig. Adapt. Strategies Glob. Change,* vol. 15, no. 7, pp. 721-736, 2010. [http://dx.doi.org/10.1007/s11027-010-9232-3]

[88] K.M. Ang, E.K. Seow, P.S. Fam, and L.H. Cheng, "Classification of edible bird's nest samples using a logistic regression model through the mineral ratio approach", *Food Control,* vol. 137, p. 108921, 2022. [http://dx.doi.org/10.1016/j.foodcont.2022.108921]

[89] A. Ahmadalipour, and H. Moradkhani, "A data-driven analysis of flash flood hazard, fatalities, and damages over the CONUS during 1996–2017", *J. Hydrol. (Amst.),* vol. 578, p. 124106, 2019.

[http://dx.doi.org/10.1016/j.jhydrol.2019.124106]

[90] C.I. Allen Akselrud, "Random forest regression models in ecology: Accounting for messy biological data and producing predictions with uncertainty", *Fish. Res.,* vol. 280, p. 107161, 2024. [http://dx.doi.org/10.1016/j.fishres.2024.107161]

[91] Y. LeCun, Y. Bengio, and G. Hinton, "Deep learning", *Nature,* vol. 521, no. 7553, pp. 436-444, 2015. [http://dx.doi.org/10.1038/nature14539] [PMID: 26017442]

[92] J. Schmidhuber, "Deep learning in neural networks: An overview", *Neural Netw.,* vol. 61, pp. 85-117, 2015. [http://dx.doi.org/10.1016/j.neunet.2014.09.003] [PMID: 25462637]

[93] A. Krizhevsky, I. Sutskever, and G. E. Hinton, "ImageNet classification with deep convolutional neural networks," in *Advances in Neural Information Processing Systems*, vol. 25, 2012. [http://dx.doi.org/10.1145/3065386]

[94] Z. Pei, A.M. Rojas-Arevalo, F.J. de Haan, N. Lipovetzky, and E.A. Moallemi, "Reinforcement learning for decision-making under deep uncertainty", *J. Environ. Manage.,* vol. 359, p. 120968, 2024. [http://dx.doi.org/10.1016/j.jenvman.2024.120968] [PMID: 38703643]

[95] M Chapman, L Xu, M Lapeyrolerie, and C Boettiger, "Bridging adaptive management and reinforcement learning for more robust decisions", *Philos. Trans. R. Soc. B: Biol. Sci.,* vol. 378, no. 1881, 2023. [http://dx.doi.org/10.1098/RSTB.2022.0195]

[96] A. Chinnaraju, "Explainable AI (XAI) for trustworthy and transparent decision-making: A theoretical framework for AI interpretability", *World J. Adv. Eng. Technol. Sci.,,* vol. 14, no. 3, pp. 170-207, 2025. [http://dx.doi.org/10.30574/wjaets.2025.14.3.0106]

[97] AnalytixLabs, "Decision tree algorithm in machine learning: Advantages, disadvantages, and limitations," AnalytixLabs. [Online]. Available: https://www.analytixlabs.co.in/blog/decision-tre--algorithm/

[98] I.D. Mienye, and N. Jere, "A Survey of Decision Trees: Concepts, Algorithms, and Applications", *IEEE Access,* vol. 12, pp. 86716-86727, 2024. [http://dx.doi.org/10.1109/ACCESS.2024.3416838]

[99] H. Singh, "Splitting decision trees with Gini impurity," Analytics Vidhya, 2025. [Online]. Available: https://www.analyticsvidhya.com/articles/gini-impurity/

[100] M. Belgiu, and L. Drăguţ, "Random forest in remote sensing: A review of applications and future directions", *ISPRS Journal of Photogrammetry and Remote Sensing,* pp. 24-31, 2016. [http://dx.doi.org/10.1016/j.isprsjprs.2016.01.011]

[101] A. Cutler, D.R. Cutler, and J.R. Stevens, Random forests. In: *Ensemble machine learning,* Springer, Z.-H. Zhou, G. Brown, and T. Dietterich, Eds. Boston, MA, pp. 157-175, 2012. [http://dx.doi.org/10.1007/978-1-4419-9326-7_5]

[102] D Koldasbayeva, P Tregubova, M Gasanov, A Zaytsev, A Petrovskaia, and E Burnaev, "Challenges in data-driven geospatial modeling for environmental research and practice", *Nature Communications,* vol. 15, no. 1, pp. 1-16, 2024. [http://dx.doi.org/10.1038/s41467-024-55240-8]

[103] A. Aghajanyan, S. Gupta, and L. Zettlemoyer, "Intrinsic dimensionality explains the effectiveness of language model fine-tuning", In: *Proc. Annu. Meeting Assoc. Comput. Linguistics*, 2021, pp. 7319-7328. [http://dx.doi.org/10.18653/v1/2021.acl-long.568]

[104] S. Kollmannsberger, D. D'Angella, M. Jokeit, and L. Herrmann, "Neural Networks", *Studies in Computational Intelligence,* vol. 977, pp. 19-45, 2021. [http://dx.doi.org/10.1007/978-3-030-76587-3_3]

[105] A. V. Joshi, "Perceptron and neural networks," in Machine Learning and Artificial Intelligence, J. Smith and R. Kumar, Eds. Springer, 2023, pp. 57–72.
[http://dx.doi.org/10.1007/978-3-031-12282-8_6]

[106] O.A. Montesinos López, A. Montesinos López, and J. Crossa, "Fundamentals of Artificial Neural Networks and Deep Learning", In: *Multivariate Statistical Machine Learning Methods for Genomic Prediction* Springer, 2022, pp. 379-425.
[http://dx.doi.org/10.1007/978-3-030-89010-0_10]

[107] N.I. Saikh, and P. Mondal, "GIS-based machine learning algorithm for flood susceptibility analysis in the Pagla river basin, Eastern India", *Nat. Hazards Rev.,* vol. 3, no. 3, pp. 420-436, 2023.
[http://dx.doi.org/10.1016/j.nhres.2023.05.004]

[108] J. B. Campbell, R. H. Wynne, and V. A. Thomas, Introduction to Remote Sensing, 6th ed. New York, NY: Guilford Press, 2022.

[109] R. A. Schowengerdt, "The nature of remote sensing," in *Remote Sensing*, 3rd ed., Academic Press, 2007, pp. 1–44.
[http://dx.doi.org/10.1016/B978-012369407-2/50004-8]

[110] J.G. Masek, D.J. Hayes, M. Joseph Hughes, S.P. Healey, and D.P. Turner, "The role of remote sensing in process-scaling studies of managed forest ecosystems", *For. Ecol. Manage.,* vol. 355, pp. 109-123, 2015.
[http://dx.doi.org/10.1016/j.foreco.2015.05.032]

[111] SkyWatch, “Advantages and disadvantages of remote sensing,” 2025. [Online]. Available: https://skywatch.com/advantages-and-disadvantages-of-remote-sesing-understanding-th--limits-of-a-powerful-technology

[112] M. P. Punia, “Interaction of EMR with surface and atmosphere,” in *Remote sensing, GIS and GPS*, e-book, Simple Book Publishing, 2024. [Online]. Available: https://ebooks.inflibnet.ac.in/geop10/chapter/interaction-of-emr-with-surface-and-atmosphere/

[113] A.M. Helmi, M. Elgamal, M.I. Farouk, M.S. Abdelhamed, and B.T. Essawy, "Evaluation of geospatial interpolation techniques for enhancing spatiotemporal rainfall distribution and filling data gaps in asir region, Saudi Arabia", *Sustainability (Basel),* vol. 15, no. 18, p. 14028, 2023.
[http://dx.doi.org/10.3390/su151814028]

[114] J. Mallick, S. Talukdar, M. Alsubih, R. Salam, M. Ahmed, N.B. Kahla, and M. Shamimuzzaman, "Analysing the trend of rainfall in Asir region of Saudi Arabia using the family of Mann-Kendall tests, innovative trend analysis, and detrended fluctuation analysis", *Theor. Appl. Climatol.,* vol. 143, pp. 823-841, 2021.
[http://dx.doi.org/10.1007/s00704-020-03448-1]

[115] M.Y.A. Khan, M. ElKashouty, A.M. Subyani, F. Tian, and W. Gusti, "GIS and RS intelligence in delineating the groundwater potential zones in Arid Regions: a case study of southern Aseer, southwestern Saudi Arabia", *Appl. Water Sci.,* vol. 12, no. 1, p. 3, 2022.
[http://dx.doi.org/10.1007/s13201-021-01535-w]

[116] L.A. Sanabria, X. Qin, J. Li, R.P. Cechet, and C. Lucas, "Spatial interpolation of McArthur’s Forest Fire Danger Index across Australia: Observational study", *Environ. Model. Softw.,* vol. 50, pp. 37-50, 2013.
[http://dx.doi.org/10.1016/j.envsoft.2013.08.012]

[117] D. Tuia, B. Kellenberger, S. Beery, B.R. Costelloe, S. Zuffi, B. Risse, A. Mathis, M.W. Mathis, F. van Langevelde, T. Burghardt, R. Kays, H. Klinck, M. Wikelski, I.D. Couzin, G. van Horn, M.C. Crofoot, C.V. Stewart, and T. Berger-Wolf, "Perspectives in machine learning for wildlife conservation", *Nat. Commun.,* vol. 13, no. 1, p. 792, 2022.
[http://dx.doi.org/10.1038/s41467-022-27980-y] [PMID: 35140206]

[118] S. Jotikapukkana, Å. Berg, and A. Pattanavibool, "Wildlife and human use of buffer-zone areas in a

wildlife sanctuary", *Wildl. Res.,* vol. 37, no. 6, pp. 466-474, 2010.
[http://dx.doi.org/10.1071/WR09132]

[119] M. Ergen, "Using the buffer zone method to measure the accessibility of the green areas in Tokat, Turkey," in *Landscape Architecture-Processes and Practices Towards Sustainable Development*, L. Loures and M. Ergen, Eds. IntechOpen, 2021.
[http://dx.doi.org/10.5772/intechopen.92744]

[120] M.M. Nizamani, Q. Zhang, G. Muhae-Ud-Din, M. Awais, M. Qayyum, M. Farhan, M. Jabran, and Y. Wang, "Application of GIS and remote-sensing technology in ecosystem services and biodiversity conservation", *Deep learning for multimedia processing applications,* no. Dec, pp. 284-321, 2023.
[http://dx.doi.org/10.1201/9781032646268-12]

[121] S. Greco, B. Matarazzo, and R. Słowiński, "Decision rule approach," in *Multiple criteria decision analysis: State of the art surveys*, S. Greco, M. Ehrgott, and J. R. Figueira, Eds., Int. Ser. Oper. Res. Manage. Sci., vol. 233, Springer, 2016, pp. 497–552.
[http://dx.doi.org/10.1007/978-1-4939-3094-4_13]

[122] M. Herva, and E. Roca, "Review of combined approaches and multi-criteria analysis for corporate environmental evaluation", *J. Clean. Prod.,* vol. 39, pp. 355-371, 2013.
[http://dx.doi.org/10.1016/j.jclepro.2012.07.058]

[123] G. Ferla, B. Mura, S. Falasco, P. Caputo, and A. Matarazzo, "Multi-Criteria Decision Analysis (MCDA) for sustainability assessment in food sector. A systematic literature review on methods, indicators and tools", *Sci. Total Environ.,* vol. 946, p. 174235, 2024.
[http://dx.doi.org/10.1016/j.scitotenv.2024.174235] [PMID: 38944301]

[124] D. Aidonis, D. Folinas, C. Achillas, D. Triantafyllou, and G. Malindretos, "Multi-criteria evaluation of sustainable supply chains in the agrifood sector", *Int. J. Sustain. Agric. Manag. Inform.,* vol. 1, no. 2, pp. 106-119, 2015.
[http://dx.doi.org/10.1504/IJSAMI.2015.070747]

[125] A. Kandakoglu, A. Frini, and S. Ben Amor, "Multicriteria decision making for sustainable development: A systematic review", *J. Multi-Criteria Decis. Anal.,* vol. 26, no. 5-6, pp. 202-251, 2019.
[http://dx.doi.org/10.1002/mcda.1682]

CHAPTER 2

Application of Machine Learning in Environmental Monitoring

Charnpreet Kaur[1,*], Saikumar Swarnapudi[1], Amrita Chaudhary[1], Puneet Kaur[1], Preety Sharma[1] and **Chandni[2]**

[1] *Department of Computer Science and Engineering, Chandigarh University, Mohali, Punjab, India*

[2] *School of Geography, Earth and Environmental Sciences, University of Birmingham, Birmingham, United Kingdom*

Abstract: Environmental monitoring has undergone a transformative shift with the integration of Machine Learning (ML), enabling data-driven insights into complex ecological systems. This chapter provides a comprehensive exploration of supervised, unsupervised, and reinforcement learning techniques applied across key environmental domains, including pollution monitoring, climate modeling, biodiversity conservation, and ecosystem management. Traditional mechanistic models, while interpretable, often struggle with the non-linear, high-dimensional, and spatiotemporal nature of environmental data. In contrast, ML excels in pattern recognition, predictive modeling, and real-time decision-making, making it indispensable for modern environmental science. This chapter discusses the theoretical foundations of ML in environmental contexts, emphasizing the role of neural networks (CNNs, LSTMs), decision trees, random forests, and support vector machines (SVMs) in handling diverse datasets. Deep learning proves particularly effective for remote sensing and high-dimensional data, while ensemble methods like random forests demonstrate robustness in heterogeneous environmental datasets. Additionally, clustering and dimensionality reduction techniques (*e.g.*, PCA, t-SNE) help uncover hidden patterns in ecological data. Emerging trends such as federated learning, physics-informed ML, and edge computing are revolutionizing environmental monitoring by improving scalability, privacy, and real-time processing. However, challenges persist, including data scarcity, computational costs, model interpretability, and ethical concerns. We analyze these limitations and propose mitigation strategies, such as hybrid modeling, transfer learning, and explainable AI (XAI) techniques, to enhance reliability and transparency. This chapter serves as a practical guide for researchers and policymakers, offering performance benchmarks, case studies, and implementation frameworks to optimize ML applications in environmental science. By bridging the gap between AI advancements and ecological sustainability, we pave the way for intelligent, adaptive, and ethical environmental monitoring systems.

[*] **Corresponding author Charnpreet Kaur:** Department of Computer Science and Engineering, Chandigarh University, Mohali, Punjab, India; E-mail: vanshikabhardwaj.phd23civil@pec.edu.in

Kanwarpreet Singh, Arundhati, Manmeet Kaur, Abhishek Sharma, Aditya Kumar Tiwary & Sahil Sharma (Eds.)
All rights reserved-© 2026 Bentham Science Publishers

Keywords: Machine learning (ML), Environmental monitoring, Deep learning, Neural networks, Climate modeling, Biodiversity conservation, Remote sensing, IoT sensors, Air quality prediction.

INTRODUCTION

Environmental science has traditionally relied on mechanistic models based on physical, chemical, and biological principles to interpret intricate environmental processes [1]. However, the unprecedented scale, complexity, and speed of environmental data collected through remote sensing, monitoring networks, citizen science, and laboratory experiments present both opportunities and challenges for conventional analysis [2]. Environmental system complexity characterized by non-linear relationships, feedback processes, spatiotemporal heterogeneity, and multi-scale linkages often exceeds the capabilities of traditional statistical and process-based models [3]. Machine learning (ML) offers a transformative methodology for environmental science by automating pattern detection, relationship extraction, and insight generation from large, unstructured datasets without requiring explicit programming of underlying processes [4] This shift from traditional modelling to ML represents a paradigm shift, enabling researchers to derive knowledge from datasets of previously unmanageable scale and complexity [5]. Table **1** contrasts traditional process-based models with machine learning approaches, highlighting differences in modeling approach, scalability, interpretability, data requirements, and adaptability. Traditional models rely on predefined equations, while ML excels in handling large, noisy datasets but often lacks interpretability.

Table 1. Comparison between traditional modeling and machine learning in environmental science.

Aspect	Traditional Process Based Models	Machine Learning Models	References
Modelling Approach	Based on pre-defined physical, chemical, and biological equations	Data-driven, finds patterns and correlations in data	[6]
Scalability	Limited by computational complexity	Highly scalable with large datasets	[7, 8]
Interpretability	Clear understanding of system behaviour	Often considered a "black box"	[9, 10]
Data Requirements	Requires high-quality input parameters	Can work with large and noisy datasets	[10, 11]
Adaptability	Struggles with complex, high-dimensional data	Adapts well to large, multisource datasets	[9, 12]

Machine learning (ML) has transformed environmental monitoring by offering automated means of statistical assessment, prediction, and decision-making [13]. With the mounting availability of environmental data from sensors, satellites, and other assets, ML methodologies allow real-time assessment and prediction of pollution levels, climate change, and catastrophe probability management [14]. These strategies provide the extraction of valuable information from extensive amounts of environmental data, assisting scientists and policymakers in well-informed decisions [15]. The ML conceptual framework in environmental monitoring illustrates how environmental data from multiple assets of ML models are handled for prediction and assessment. This results in actionable knowledge that encompasses pollution levels and weather forecasting. Data preprocessing, functional engineering, model training, and testing constitute the central additives of this framework [16].

OVERVIEW OF MACHINE LEARNING

ML consists of three major types: supervised, unsupervised, and reinforcement learning, each suited to specific environmental tasks. Fig. (**1**) provides an insight into the machine learning framework for environmental monitoring. The integration of machine learning (ML) algorithms into environmental studies has revolutionized the analysis of complex ecological data, the prediction of environmental changes, and the development of sustainable solutions. The exponential growth in environmental data, driven by advances in remote sensing, IoT sensors, and climate modeling, has necessitated the use of sophisticated computational techniques for effective analysis and decision-making. Among the plethora of ML techniques, algorithms such as Neural Networks, Decision Trees, Random Forests, and Support Vector Machines (SVMs) have been prominently utilized [17]. The escalating complexity of environmental data necessitates advanced analytical methods beyond traditional statistical approaches. Machine Learning (ML) provides robust tools capable of uncovering intricate patterns and making accurate predictions, thereby enhancing decision-making in environmental conservation and policy formulation. Applications range from climate change forecasting to deforestation detection, demonstrating ML's transformative impact on environmental problem-solving. Environmental datasets, often sourced from remote sensing, Internet of Things (IoT) devices, and field surveys, require sophisticated techniques for trend analysis, anomaly detection, and the generation of actionable insights [18]. This paper explores the pivotal role of ML algorithms in addressing environmental challenges, compares their effectiveness and applicability across contexts, and highlights real-world applications.

- **Supervised Learning:** Employs labeled records to train models, projecting input capabilities to recognized outputs. Common programs include climate forecasting and air quality forecasting [19].

- **Unsupervised Learning:** Finds patterns within unlabeled facts, useful in clustering and anomaly detection for environmental datasets. Examples include species class and land cover segmentation [20].

- **Reinforcement Learning:** Optimizes motion based on comments from the environment, often carried out in aid control and power optimization [21].

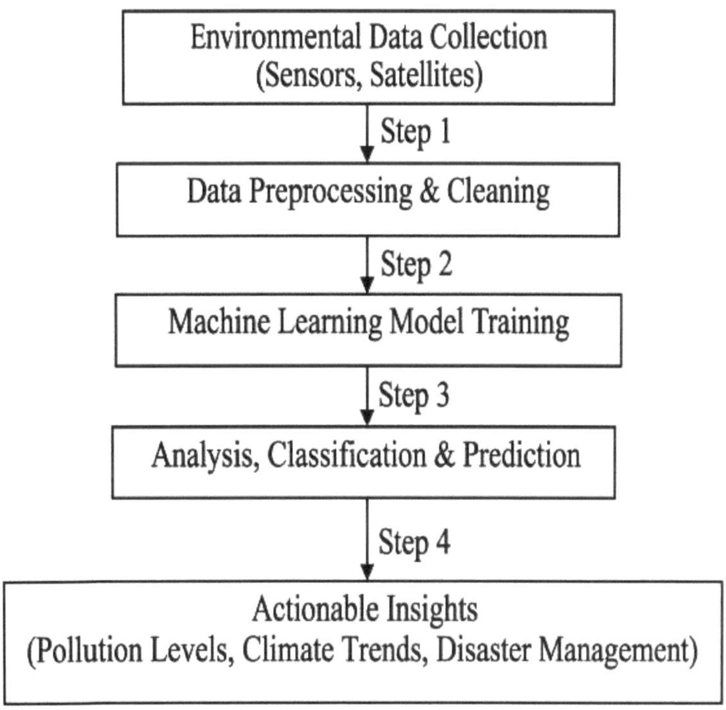

Fig. (1). Machine learning framework for environmental monitoring.

Table **2** summarizes the strengths and limitations of different ML paradigms in environmental applications, helping practitioners choose the right approach based on data availability and problem type. Supervised learning is best suited for tasks involving pollution identification, while Unsupervised learning is defined by the identification of hiddennvironmental patterns [22].

Table 2. Comparison of ML techniques.

Machine Learning Paradigm	Key Environmental Applications	Data Requirements	Typical Output	References
Supervised Learning	Species distribution modeling, Land cover classification, Air quality prediction	Labeled historical data with features and outcomes.	Predictive models for classification or regression.	[23, 24]
Unsupervised Learning	Ecosystem type identification, Environmental pattern discovery, Anomaly detection in monitoring data	Unlabeled feature data without explicit outcome variables.	Clusters, reduced-dimension representations, outlier detection	[25]
Reinforcement Learning	Resource management, Conservation planning, Adaptive sampling strategies	Environment with definable states, actions, and rewards.	Optimal policy for decision-making under uncertainty	[26, 27]

Supervised Learning in Environmental Monitoring

Supervised learning models are widely used in environmental prediction and classification [16]. This process involves a set of facts, building a school of models, efforts, and predictions of pollutants, weather modeling, and environmental prediction classes [17].

Linear Regression Equation (Supervised Learning): $y = wx + b$ [28]

Unsupervised Learning in Environmental Monitoring

Unsupervised learning helps discover hidden patterns in environmental data [20]. Better approaches, such as self-organizing maps (SOMs) and principal component analysis (PCA), improve data interpretation [10].

K-Means Clustering Objective Function: $J = \Sigma \|x_j - c_i\|^2$ [29]

Fig. (**2**) highlights the flow chart of the training dataset of supervised learning and the training dataset of unsupervised learning.

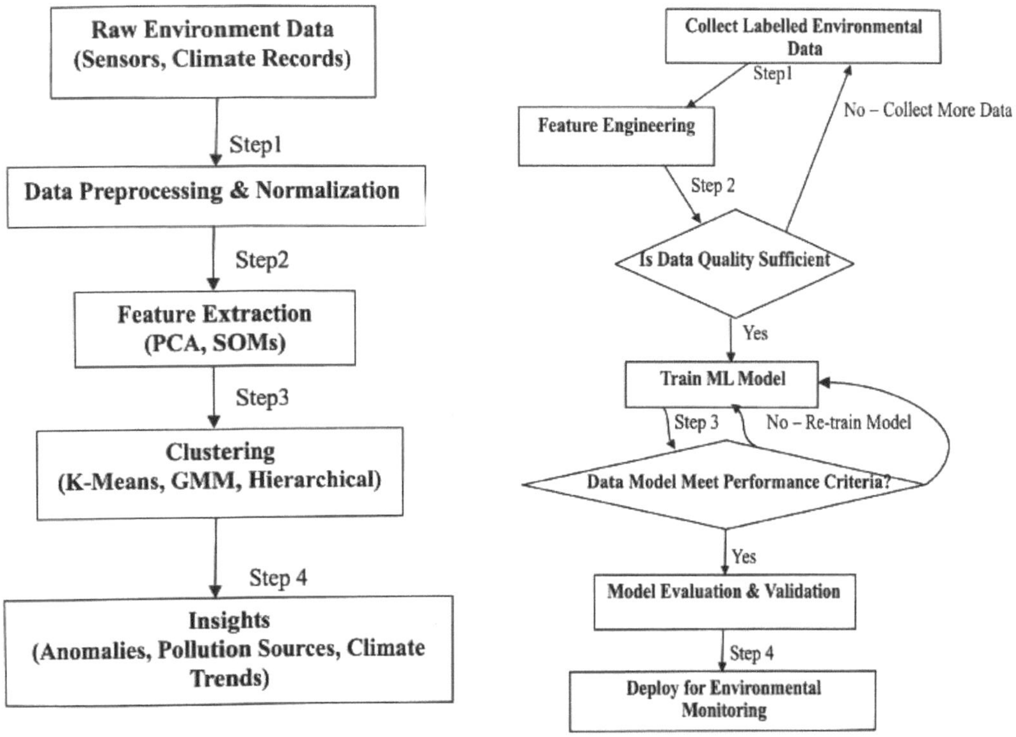

Fig. (2). Flow Chart of (a) Training dataset of Supervised Learning (b) Training dataset of unsupervised learning.

Reinforcement Learning in Environmental Monitoring

Reinforcement learning is used in adaptive systems for autonomous monitoring and resource optimization. Reinforcement learning vendors interact with the world to maximize actions that are entirely based on rewards. It is widely utilized in applications that include power efficiency management, adaptive environmental monitoring, and self-sufficient catastrophe response structures. Guidelines are nuanced for the application of deep reinforcement learning methods, including Q-learning and policy gradient approaches, that enable the improvement of decision-making within complex and evolving settings [30]. Fig. (3) provides a flowchart of the training dataset of reinforcement learning.

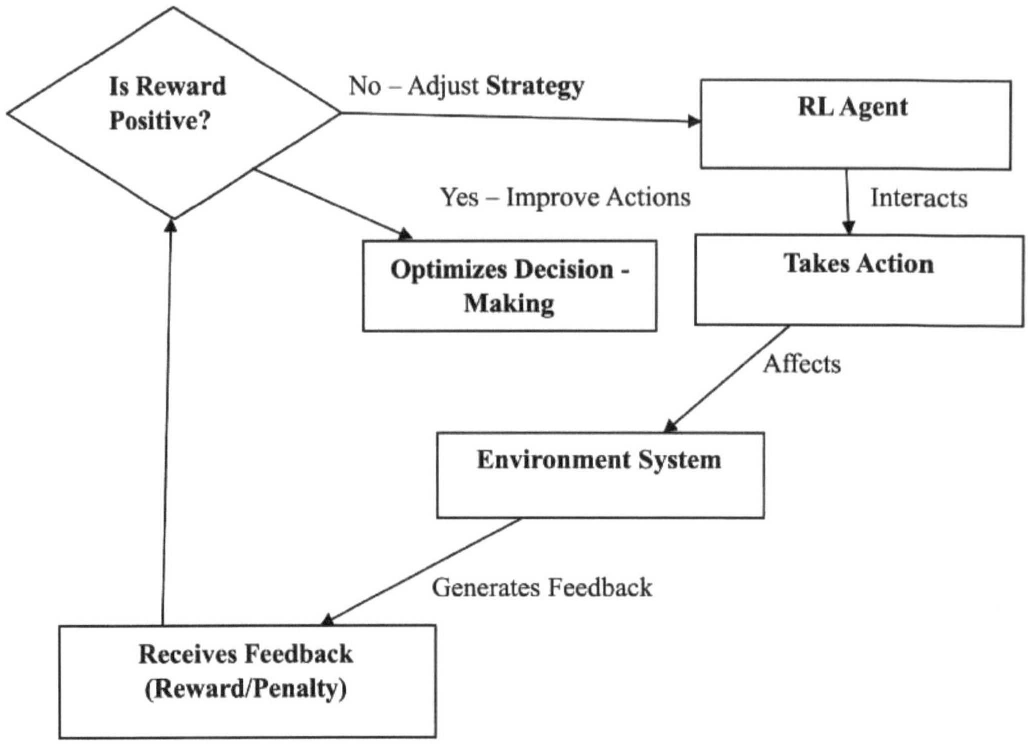

Fig. (3). Flowchart of the training dataset of Reinforcement learning.

Mathematical Representation (Bellman Equation): The learning process follows the Bellman equation:

$$Q(s, a) = r + \gamma \max_{a'} Q(s', a')$$

MACHINE LEARNING ALGORITHMS IN ENVIRONMENTAL STUDIES

Environmental studies have increasingly integrated Machine Learning (ML) techniques to analyse complex datasets, model intricate relationships, and provide predictive insights. Various ML algorithms, including Neural Networks (NN), Decision Trees (DT), Random Forest (RF), and Support Vector Machines (SVM), have been employed to tackle environmental challenges such as climate change, pollution monitoring, biodiversity conservation, and water resource management. This paper offers an in-depth review of these ML algorithms, their applications, advantages, and limitations in environmental studies. A comparative analysis evaluates their efficiency and effectiveness across different scenarios, supplemented by real-world case studies illustrating their practical applications. The escalating complexity of environmental data has rendered traditional statistical methods inadequate for capturing intricate patterns and dependencies. Machine Learning provides robust tools for extracting meaningful insights and making accurate predictions, thereby aiding decision-makingn environmental conservation and policy implementation [31]. From climate change forecasting to deforestation detection, ML algorithms have transformed our approach to understanding and addressing environmental issues [32].

Neural Networks (NNs)

Artificial Neural Networks (ANNs) are computational models inspired by the human brain's interconnected neuron structure. They are particularly adept at modeling complex, non-linear relationships and have been widely applied in environmental modeling [33].

Applications: Climate forecasting, air pollution prediction, species distribution modeling, flood prediction, and wildfire detection.

Advantages: Ability to model non-linear relationships, adaptive learning, and effective with large-scale data.

Limitations: High computational cost, requirement for extensive labeled data, and challenging interpretability.

Case Study: NASA has collaborated with IBM Research to develop an AI foundation model for weather and climate prediction, utilizing vast Earth science data to enhance forecasting accuracy and assess future risks [34].

Decision Trees (DTs)

Decision Trees are hierarchical models that recursively split data into branches to facilitate classification or regression tasks. Their simplicity and interpretability make them effective for various environmental applications.

Applications: Deforestation analysis, habitat suitability assessment, disaster risk prediction, energy consumption modeling.

Advantages: Easy interpretation, handling of missing values, minimal data preprocessing required.

Limitations: Prone to overfitting, sensitive to noise in datasets, and poor generalization for complex patterns.

Random Forest (RF)

Random Forest is an ensemble learning method that constructs multiple decision trees and merges their outputs to improve accuracy and control overfitting [35]. This approach enhances generalization and robustness in predictive modeling.

Applications: Soil quality assessment, remote sensing classification, hydrological modeling, drought prediction, and ecosystem health monitoring.

Advantages: Higher accuracy, robustness against overfitting, and effective handling of high-dimensional data.

Limitations: Computationally expensive, reduced interpretability compared to single decision trees, requires careful parameter tuning.

Case Study: The European Space Agency (ESA) integrates RF models with satellite data to track global forest degradation trends [36].

Support Vector Machines (SVMs)

Support Vector Machines are supervised learning models that classify data by finding the optimal hyperplane separating different classes [37]. They are particularly effective in high-dimensional spaces and are commonly used in environmental studies for classification and regression tasks.

Applications: Land use classification, water quality monitoring, waste management analysis, pollution source identification.

Advantages: High accuracy with small datasets, robustness against noise, and effectiveness for complex classification problems.

Limitations: Computationally intensive for large datasets, sensitivity to parameter selection, and requires feature scaling.

Case Study: The United Nations Environment Program (UNEP) supports global initiatives in monitoring freshwater quality to inform policy and management interventions using SVM models [38].

COMPARISON OF ML TECHNIQUES IN ENVIRONMENTAL MONITORING

Different ML techniques are suited to various environmental tasks. Supervised learning is a general paradigm of machine learning, encompassing a training model for labeled data records, enabling you to learn explicit assignments from input to output. One of its key strengths is high accuracy since the availability of marked data enables precise model training and performance assessment. In addition, it is very interpretable and applicable to uses like medical diagnosis and fraud detection. But supervised learning needs large amounts of labeled data, which is costly and time-consuming. Moreover, generalization is not easy in the case of invisible or easily manipulated data. Fig. (**4**) highlights various machine learning techniques.

Conversely, unsupervised learning is label-independent and finds its utility in identifying hidden patterns and structures present in data records. It proves beneficial when there are no predefined categories available for applications, exploratory data analysis, anomaly detection, and clustering applications. The method is more scalable because it can process more unstructured data without a lot of human involvement. But there are some limitations. The absence of specific evaluation metrics means that it is hard to evaluate the model output objectively. Moreover, results of unattended learning tend to be less interpreted compared to supervisory learning results. That is, domain knowledge needs to stir wise knowledge.

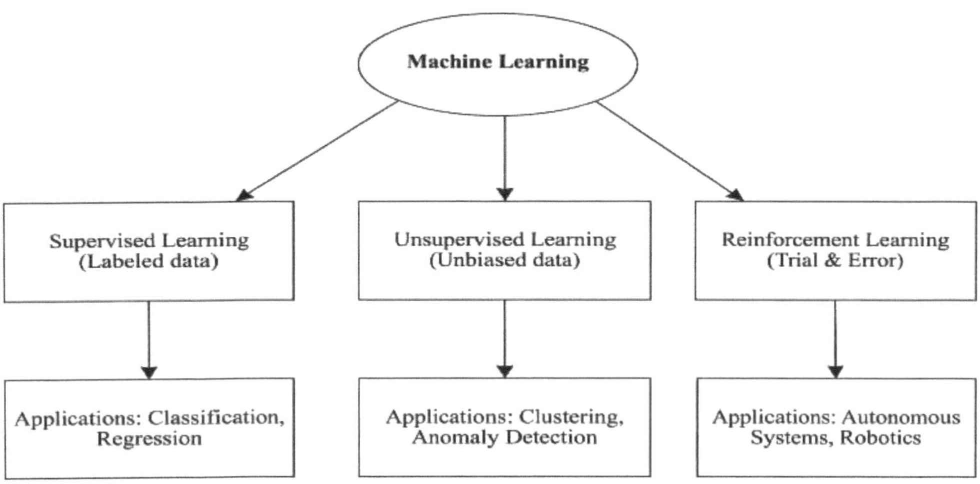

Fig. (4). Comparison of ML techniques.

Reinforced Learning (RL) is a pattern of learning where agents interact with the environment to maximize growing rewards through trial and error. His most significant strength is that he can learn optimal strategies in complex decision-making situations and be very effective in robotics, gaming, and autonomous systems. RL models can learn to adapt to changing environments and increase performance over time. Yet, the learning process entails many interactions with the environment, which necessitates large arithmetic resources and lengthy training times. In addition, RL models tend to be unstable since small variations in hyperparameters or reward structures can result in drastically different behaviours, rendering fine-tuning challenging.

RECENT TRENDS AND INNOVATIONS IN ML FOR ENVIRONMENTAL MONITORING

Emerging trends improve the accuracy and efficiency of environmental monitoring. Innovations encompass deep learning for satellite image processing, IoT integration for real-time monitoring, and sophisticated analysis of predictive environment modeling. A federated learning method is being considered to enhance data protection and data security. Improvements alongside a deeper understanding of Sensohrism evaluation and IoT-based monitoring frameworks will determine the future of environmental ML applications. Aspect computing answers minimize latency and improve decision-making in real time. Fig. (**5a, 5b**) highlights recent trends in ML models.

- Deep learning for satellite image processing [39]
- IoT integration for real-time monitoring [40]
- Federated learning for data protection [41]

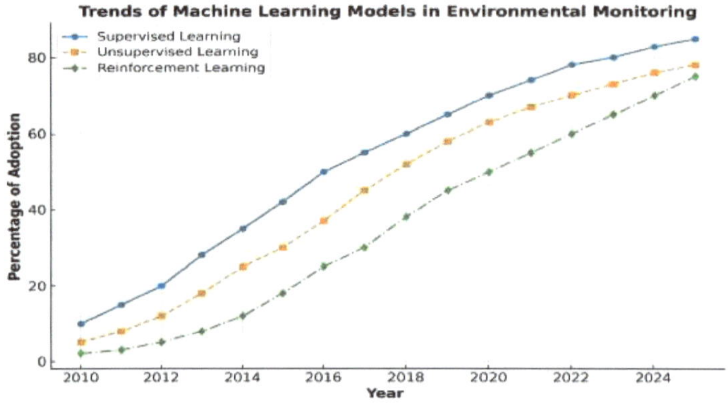

Fig. (5a). Recent trends in ML model in environmental monitoring.

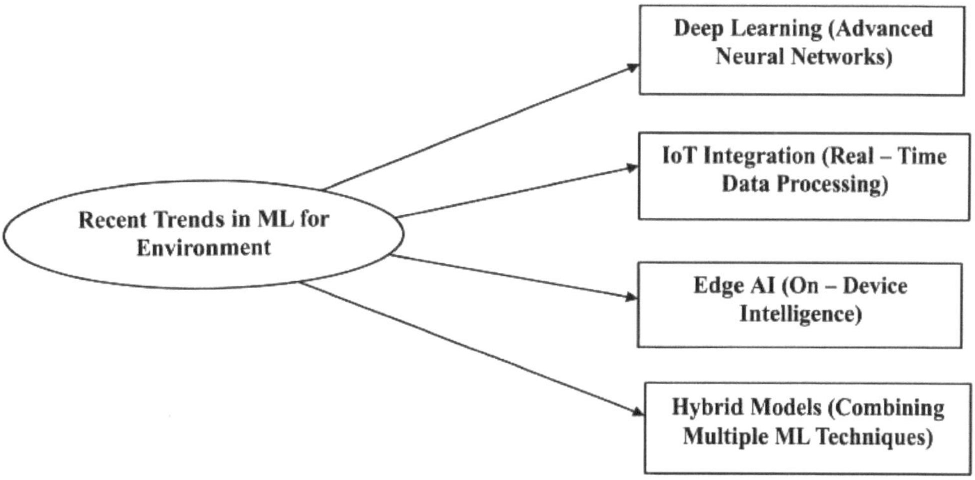

Fig. (5b). Recent trends in ML model for environment.

SMART TOOLS FOR ENVIRONMENTAL MONITORING

The advancement in technology has revolutionized environmental monitoring through intelligent and smart tools. These tools integrate artificial intelligence (AI), the Internet of Things (IoT), remote sensing, and data analytics to enhance environmental surveillance, mitigate risks, and foster sustainable practices. This chapter describes various smart tools for environmental monitoring, their applications, challenges, advantages, and future trends. Environmental monitoring is crucial for assessing ecological health, detecting pollution, and ensuring compliance with environmental regulations. Traditional monitoring methods are often time-consuming, labour-intensive, and prone to inaccuracies [42]. The integration of intelligent tools has significantly improved data collection, processing, and decision-making in environmental studies. These smart tools enhance the ability to track pollution, monitor climate change, and improve resource management in real-time, thus enabling proactive interventions [42]. The need for smart environmental monitoring has increased due to growing concerns over climate change, pollution, and resource depletion. Emerging technologies like AI, IoT, big data analytics, and remote sensing have enabled real-time monitoring of environmental parameters, ensuring rapid responses to potential threats [43].

Smart Environmental Monitoring Technologies

Internet of Things (IoT) in Environmental Monitoring

IoT devices, equipped with sensors and wireless communication capabilities, collect real-time environmental data on air quality, water quality, temperature, and soil health [44]. These devices enable continuous monitoring and facilitate timely interventions. Smart environmental monitoring using IoT includes applications such as air pollution sensors, smart waste management systems, and water quality monitoring devices [45]. Table **3** lists IoT applications in air, water, and soil monitoring, detailing the parameters measured and their real-world uses. Smart sensors enable continuous, real-time environmental tracking.

Table 3. Key IoT-based environmental monitoring systems.

System	Parameters Monitored	Application	References
Smart Air Sensors	PM2.5, NO_2, CO	Urban Air Quality	[46, 47]
Water Quality IoT	pH, Turbidity, Heavy Metals	Drinking Water Safety	[48]
Soil Health IoT	Moisture, Nutrients	Precision Agriculture	[49]

Artificial Intelligence and Machine Learning

AI-driven models analyze large datasets to detect patterns, predict environmental changes, and suggest mitigation strategies [50]. Machine learning algorithms help in climate modeling, pollution tracking, and ecosystem assessments. AI-powered image recognition is used to track deforestation and wildlife population trends [51].

Remote Sensing and Geographic Information Systems (GIS)

Satellite imagery, GIS technologies, and drones enable large-scale environmental monitoring [14]. High-resolution spatial data is being used to track the deforestation, land use changes and climate variations using remote sensing [52]. This also helps in mapping pollution sources, ecosystem degradation, and the disaster-prone areas.

Blockchain for Environmental Data Integrity

Blockchain technology ensures transparency, security, and traceability of environmental data [54]. It enhances accountability in carbon credit trading, waste management, and conservation projects [55].

Wireless Sensor Networks (WSNs)

WSNs consist of interconnected sensor nodes deployed in various environmental settings to monitor conditions such as air pollution, water contamination, and forest health [55]. These networks improve real-time data acquisition and analysis [56].

Applications of Smart Environmental Monitoring Tools

Air Quality Monitoring

IoT-based air pollution sensors detect hazardous gases (*e.g.*, CO, NO_2, SO_2) and particulate matter, providing real-time alerts for pollution control. AI-powered predictive models help cities implement pollution control measures effectively [57].

Water Quality Management

Smart water monitoring systems analyze parameters like pH, dissolved oxygen, turbidity, and contaminants, ensuring safe water for consumption and ecosystem sustainability [58]. IoT-based smart buoys collect real-time data on water pollution levels [59].

Climate Change Assessment

AI-powered climate models predict weather patterns, assess climate variability, and inform policy decisions on climate resilience and adaptation strategies [60]. Machine learning enhances the precision of climate models by integrating diverse datasets [61].

Deforestation and Biodiversity Conservation

Remote sensing and AI-assisted image processing track deforestation rates and biodiversity loss, supporting conservation initiatives and habitat restoration [62]. Environmentalists, conservationists, and data analysts use smart camera traps with AI-based species recognition [63].

CHALLENGES AND FUTURE DIRECTIONS

The environmental tracking machine control challenges are met with the widespread challenges that must be resolved to make it more effective and reliable. Among the most critical challenges is information availability and exceptions. Environmental facts are increasing on a regular basis from revisions of resources, combined with television sensor observations, satellite observations, inconsistencies, cost shortages, and discipline, resulting in individualized solutions. A high-quality, standard, and finely marked fact statistics promise is required for the supplementary ML mode of education.

Another significant issue is mathematics compensation. ML models, particularly deep learning models, demand superior processing performance and storage products. Running these models in real-time environmental flows may demand too much computer infrastructure. This provides access for small and medium-sized enterprises and researchers who have reserved resources. Find techniques along with cloud computing, distributed knowledge, and side computing to reduce these issues.

Despite these issues, the future for ML is bright in environmental monitoring. Hybrid Modeling Technology, AI Management - Advancements in ML integration and integration in IoT and geospatial analysis will enhance environmental tracking skills. The continued research and convergence between information scientists, environmental professionals, and political decision-makers is the prime concern to tackle these issues and to realize the maximum potential of MLs for ecological sustainability. Issues such as statistics and computer pricing, and computer pricing would like to be questioned in Environmental Monitoring ML.

Machine learning (ML) has revolutionized environmental monitoring by enabling large-scale data analysis, predictive modeling, and real-time decision-making. However, its deployment faces significant challenges, including data scarcity, model interpretability, computational costs, and ethical concerns. This chapter provides an in-depth exploration of these limitations, supported by real-world case studies, experimental findings, and mitigation strategies. By examining both theoretical and practical barriers, this chapter aims to guide researchers and policymakers in optimizing ML applications for environmental sustainability. Environmental monitoring is essential for tracking climate change, pollution, deforestation, and biodiversity loss. Machine learning enhances these efforts by processing data from satellites, IoT sensors, and citizen science initiatives. However, several challenges impede its effectiveness. This chapter categorizes these challenges into:

1. Data-related issues (scarcity, noise, labeling difficulties)

2. Algorithmic limitations (overfitting, interpretability, non-stationarity)

3. Computational barriers (costs, energy consumption, edge computing)

4. Ethical and regulatory concerns (bias, privacy, policy gaps)

Table **4** outlines key challenges (spatiotemporal dependency, data gaps, extreme events) and their impact on ML model performance, emphasizing the need for specialized preprocessing techniques.

Table 4. Challenges in environmental data processing for machine learning.

Challenge	Impact on Machine Learning	References
Spatiotemporal Dependency	Data points are not independent; they require specialized models like LSTMs or CNNs.	[64]
Multi-scale Processes	Variations in time and space require hierarchical modelling approaches.	[65]
Data Gaps and Irregularity	Missing values require imputation or advanced feature engineering.	[66]
Extreme Events	Rare events may be treated as anomalies, affecting model performance.	[47]
Heterogeneity	Requires models that generalize well across diverse ecosystems.	[46, 47]
High Dimensionality	Leads to computational complexity, requires dimensionality reduction techniques like PCA.	[65, 67]

Each section includes real-world examples and experimental studies to illustrate these challenges.

Data-related Challenges

Data Scarcity and Imbalance

Most African countries lack dense air quality sensor networks. A study found that only 12 out of 54 African nations had real-time PM2.5 monitoring. ML models trained on European or U.S. data performed poorly when applied to African cities due to differing pollution sources (*e.g.*, biomass burning vs. vehicular emissions). A model pre-trained on Amazon rainforest data achieved only 62% accuracy when applied to Congo Basin forests, due to differences in tree species and satellite image resolutions [68].

Data Quality and Noise

The National Oceanic and Atmospheric Administration (NOAA) reported that 15% of sea surface temperature readings from satellites were corrupted due to cloud interference [69]. Simple noise-reduction algorithms improved data accuracy by 22%, but ML models still struggled with extreme weather anomalies. Table **5** quantifies the effect of data noise on model accuracy, showing that cleaning techniques significantly improve reliability in air and water quality monitoring.

Table 5. Impact of noise on ML model performance.

Dataset	Noise Level	Model Accuracy (Before Cleaning)	Model Accuracy (After Cleaning)	References
Urban Air Quality (Beijing)	High (30% outliers)	71%	89%	[70]
Ocean Acidity (Pacific)	Moderate (15% errors)	65%	82%	[70]

Labelling Difficulties in Biodiversity Monitoring

Wildlife Camera Traps in Borneo: In this study, camera traps were deployed to collect large-scale wildlife imagery. The project emphasized how machine learning, particularly supervised learning, and deep learning models, could be leveraged to automate the identification of species from camera trap images. This approach is essential for biodiversity monitoring, conservation planning, ecological pattern discovery [71]. An ML model achieved 92% accuracy on labeled data but dropped to 68% when tested on new, unlabeled regions due to species variation.

CONCLUSION

Machine learning transformed environmental analysis with the provision of sophisticated tools for data-driven decision-making, real-time tracking, and predictive analysis. Through supervised learning for classification and prediction, unsupervised learning for pattern extraction, and reinforcement learning for adaptive optimization, ML facilitates increased efficiency and accuracy in environmental assessments. Despite limitations like data availability, interpretability of models, and computational expense, ongoing improvements in deep learning, IoT integration, and edge computing are enhancing the applicability and efficacy of ML for environmental monitoring. The future of ML applications in environmental analysis is in hybrid models, autonomous decision-making, and collaborative AI-based frameworks that enhance sustainability initiatives. As technology advances, interdisciplinary collaboration among environmental scientists, data engineers, and policymakers will be essential to leveraging the potential of ML for ecological conservation, climate resilience, and resource management. Through the integration of AI with environmental science, we can make significant progress toward a more sustainable and data-driven way of protecting our planet. The integration of Machine Learning (ML) in environmental monitoring has ushered in a new era of data-driven ecological management, offering unprecedented capabilities in pollution tracking, climate forecasting, biodiversity assessment, and resource optimization. Through this chapter, we have explored how supervised learning models (*e.g.*, random forests, SVMs) excel in predictive tasks, while unsupervised techniques (*e.g.*, clustering, autoencoders) uncover hidden patterns in unlabeled datasets. Reinforcement learning further enhances adaptive decision-making in dynamic environments, such as wildlife conservation and disaster response. Key findings highlight that deep learning architectures (CNNs, LSTMs) outperform traditional models in processing high-dimensional remote sensing data, whereas ensemble methods like XG Boost and random forests provide robust solutions for heterogeneous environmental datasets. However, challenges such as data sparsity, computational expenses, model interpretability, and ethical biases remain critical hurdles. To address these, this work advocates for Hybrid modeling (combining ML with mechanistic models) for improved generalizability, Federated learning to enable privacy-preserving collaborative analysis, Explainable AI (XAI) techniques (SHAP, LIME) to enhance transparency in ecological decision-making, and Edge computing for real-time, low-latency environmental monitoring in remote areas.

Emerging innovations like physics-informed neural networks (PINNs) and AI-driven IoT networks are set to further revolutionize the field, enabling autonomous, scalable, and sustainable environmental monitoring. However, the successful deployment of ML in environmental science hinges on interdisciplinary collaboration among data scientists, ecologists, and policymakers to ensure ethical, equitable, and actionable outcomes. In conclusion, ML holds immense potential to mitigate environmental degradation, predict ecological risks, and optimize conservation strategies. By addressing current limitations and leveraging cutting-edge advancements, we can harness AI to build resilient, intelligent, and sustainable ecosystems for future generations. The future of environmental monitoring lies in adaptive, interpretable, and ethically grounded ML systems that balance technological innovation with ecological stewardship.

LIST OF ABBREVIATIONS

AI- Artificial Intelligence

CNN- Convolutional Neural Network

DT- Decision Tree

ESA- European Space Agency

GMM- Gaussian Mixture Model

GIS- Geographic Information Systems

IoT- Internet of Things

LSTM- Long Short-Term Memory networks

ML- Machine Learning

NN- Neural Network

NOAA- The National Oceanic and Atmospheric Administration

NASA- National Aeronautics and Space Administration

PCA- Principal Component Analysis

RF- Random Forest

RL- Reinforced Learning

SVM- Support Vector Machine

SOM- Self-Organizing Map

t-SNE- t-distributed Stochastic Neighbour Embedding

UNEP- United Nations Environment Program

WSN- Wireless Sensor Network

REFERENCES

[1] M. Hino, E. Benami, and N. Brooks, "Machine learning for environmental monitoring", *Nat. Sustain.,* vol. 1, no. 10, pp. 583-588, 2018. [http://dx.doi.org/10.1038/s41893-018-0142-9]

[2] A. Akhter, S. Abdulla Al Shiam, M. Ridwan, S. I. Abir, S. Shoha, M. B. Nayeem, M. T. H. Choudhury, M. S. Hossain, and R. Bibi, "Assessing the impact of private investment in AI and financial globalization on load capacity factor: Evidence from United States," *J. Environ. Sci. Econ.*, vol. 3, no. 3, pp. 99–127, 2024. [http://dx.doi.org/10.56556/jescae.v3i3.977]

[3] C.I. Allen Akselrud, "Random forest regression models in ecology: Accounting for messy biological data and producing predictions with uncertainty", *Fish. Res.,* vol. 280, p. 107161, 2024. [http://dx.doi.org/10.1016/j.fishres.2024.107161]

[4] I. Essamlali, H. Nhaila, and M. El Khaili, "Supervised machine learning approaches for predicting key pollutants and for the sustainable enhancement of urban air quality: A systematic review", *Sustainability (Basel),* vol. 16, no. 3, p. 976, 2024. [http://dx.doi.org/10.3390/su16030976]

[5] P. Bhasme, and U. Bhatia, "Improving the interpretability and predictive power of hydrological models: Applications for daily streamflow in managed and unmanaged catchments", *J. Hydrol. (Amst.),* vol. 628, p. 130421, 2024. [http://dx.doi.org/10.1016/j.jhydrol.2023.130421]

[6] W.L. Williams, L. Zeng, T. Gensch, M.S. Sigman, A.G. Doyle, and E.V. Anslyn, "The Evolution of Data-Driven Modeling in Organic Chemistry", *ACS Cent. Sci.,* vol. 7, no. 10, pp. 1622-1637, 2021. [http://dx.doi.org/10.1021/acscentsci.1c00535] [PMID: 34729406]

[7] O. Adewole, “Scalability in artificial intelligence,” ResearchGate, Pan□Atlantic University, Nov. 2023. [Online]. Available: https://www.researchgate.net/publication/375370072_SCALABILITY_IN_ARTIFICIAL_INTELLIGENCE [Accessed: 13□Mar□2026].

[8] A.H. Nabizadeh, J.P. Leal, H.N. Rafsanjani, and R.R. Shah, "Learning path personalization and recommendation methods: A survey of the state-of-the-art", *Expert Syst. Appl.,* vol. 159, p. 113596, 2020. [http://dx.doi.org/10.1016/j.eswa.2020.113596]

[9] M. Champendal, H. Müller, J.O. Prior, and C.S. dos Reis, "A scoping review of interpretability and explainability concerning artificial intelligence methods in medical imaging", *Eur. J. Radiol.,* vol. 169, p. 111159, 2023. [http://dx.doi.org/10.1016/j.ejrad.2023.111159] [PMID: 37976760]

[10] G. Yang, Q. Ye, and J. Xia, "Unbox the black-box for the medical explainable AI via multi-modal and multi-centre data fusion: A mini-review, two showcases and beyond", *Inf. Fusion,* vol. 77, pp. 29-52, 2022. [http://dx.doi.org/10.1016/j.inffus.2021.07.016] [PMID: 34980946]

[11] S. Mohammed, L. Budach, M. Feuerpfeil, N. Ihde, A. Nathansen, N. Noack, H. Patzlaff, F. Naumann, and H. Harmouch, “The effects of data quality on machine learning performance,”arXiv:2207.14529, 2022.

[12] A. L’Heureux, K. Grolinger, H.F. Elyamany, and M.A.M. Capretz, "Machine learning with big data: Challenges and approaches", *IEEE Access,* vol. 5, pp. 7776-7797, 2017. [http://dx.doi.org/10.1109/ACCESS.2017.2696365]

[13] M.S. Binetti, C. Massarelli, and V.F. Uricchio, "Machine learning in geosciences: A review of complex environmental monitoring applications", *Machine Learning and Knowledge Extraction,* vol. 6, no. 2, pp. 1263-1280, 2024. [http://dx.doi.org/10.3390/make6020059]

[14] A. Mumuni, and F. Mumuni, "Data augmentation: A comprehensive survey of modern approaches", *Array,* vol. 16, p. 100258, 2022. [http://dx.doi.org/10.1016/j.array.2022.100258]

[15] B. Almeida, J. David, F.S. Campos, and P. Cabral, "Satellite-based Machine Learning modelling of Ecosystem Services indicators: A review and meta-analysis", *Appl. Geogr.,* vol. 165, p. 103249, 2024. [http://dx.doi.org/10.1016/j.apgeog.2024.103249]

[16] I. E. Agbehadji and I. C. Obagbuwa, “Systematic review of machine learning and deep learning techniques for spatiotemporal air quality prediction,” *Atmosphere*, vol. 15, no. 11, p. 1352, 2024. [http://dx.doi.org/10.3390/atmos15111352]

[17] S. Shalu and G. Singh, “Environmental monitoring with machine learning,” *EPRA Int. J. Multidiscip. Res. (IJMR)*, vol. 9, no. 5, pp. 208–212, 2023. [http://dx.doi.org/10.36713/epra13330]

[18] D. Stampoulis, H.G. Damavandi, D. Boscovic, and J. Sabo, "Using satellite remote sensing and machine learning techniques towards precipitation prediction and vegetation classification", *J. Environ. Inform.,* vol. 37, no. 1, pp. 1-15, 2020. [http://dx.doi.org/10.3808/jei.202000427]

[19] S. Chattopadhyay, “Predictive modeling in environmental science with machine learning algorithms,” ResearchGate preprint, 2024. [http://dx.doi.org/10.13140/RG.2.2.25002.36807]

[20] A. Pyayt, I. Mokhov, B. Lang, V. V. Krzhizhanovskaya, and R. J. Meijer, “Machine learning methods for environmental monitoring and flood protection,” *World Acad. Sci. Eng. Technol. Int. J. Comput. Electr. Autom. Control Inf. Eng.*, vol. 5, no. 6, pp. 118–123, 2011.

[21] K. Parsi and K. Prudhvinath Reddy, “Air quality prediction based on supervised classification machine learning approach,” unpublished project report, Sathyabama Institute of Science and Technology.

[22] N. Bellin, G. Tesi, N. Marchesani, and V. Rossi, "Species distribution modeling and machine learning in assessing the potential distribution of freshwater zooplankton in Northern Italy", *Ecol. Inform.*, vol. 69, p. 101682, 2022.
[http://dx.doi.org/10.1016/j.ecoinf.2022.101682]

[23] H Talsaniya, "Anomaly detection with unsupervised machine learning", *Simform Engineering – Medium,* 2021. Available from: https://medium.com/simform-engineering/anomaly-detection-w-th-unsupervised-machine-learning-13f3f2af9d91

[26] M. Chapman, “Bridging adaptive management and reinforcement learning for more robust decisions,” *Philos. Trans. R. Soc. B Biol. Sci.*, vol. 378, no. 1881, 2023.
[http://dx.doi.org/10.1098/rstb.2022.0195]

[27] Z. Pei, A.M. Rojas-Arevalo, F.J. de Haan, N. Lipovetzky, and E.A. Moallemi, "Reinforcement learning for decision-making under deep uncertainty", *J. Environ. Manage.*, vol. 359, p. 120968, 2024.
[http://dx.doi.org/10.1016/j.jenvman.2024.120968] [PMID: 38703643]

[28] S.M. Bromberg, "Identifying ecological indicators: an environmental monitoring and assessment program", *J. Air Waste Manage. Assoc.*, vol. 40, no. 7, pp. 976-978, 1990.
[http://dx.doi.org/10.1080/10473289.1990.10466748] [PMID: 2378741]

[29] K. Szramowiat-Sala, ""Artificial intelligence in environmental monitoring: Application of artificial neural networks and machine learning for pollution prevention and toxicity measurements"", *Preprints,* 2023.
[http://dx.doi.org/10.20944/preprints202307.1298.v1]

[30] J.T. Abatzoglou, "Development of gridded surface meteorological data for ecological applications and modelling", *Int. J. Climatol.*, vol. 33, no. 1, pp. 121-131, 2013.
[http://dx.doi.org/10.1002/joc.3413]

[31] J. Schmidhuber, "Deep learning in neural networks: An overview", *Neural Netw.*, vol. 61, pp. 85-117, 2015.
[http://dx.doi.org/10.1016/j.neunet.2014.09.003] [PMID: 25462637]

[32] A. Krizhevsky, I. Sutskever, and G. E. Hinton, “ImageNet classification with deep convolutional neural networks,” in Advances in Neural Information Processing Systems 25 (NIPS 2012), 2012. [Online]. Available: http://code.google.com/p/cuda-convnet/

[33] Y. LeCun, Y. Bengio, and G. Hinton, "Deep learning", *Nature,* vol. 521, no. 7553, pp. 436-444, 2015.
[http://dx.doi.org/10.1038/nature14539] [PMID: 26017442]

[34] L. Breiman, "Random Forests", *Mach. Learn.*, vol. 45, no. 1, pp. 5-32, 2001.
[http://dx.doi.org/10.1023/A:1010933404324]

[35] C. Cortes and V. Vapnik, “Support-vector networks,” Mach. Learn., vol. 20, no. 3, pp. 273–297, 1995.
[http://dx.doi.org/10.1007/BF00994018]

[36] United Nations Environment Programme, “Monitoring water quality.” [Online]. Available: https://www.unep.org/topics/fresh-water/water-quality/monitoring-water-quality

[37] J. Colley and C. E. Flores, “Deep learning for environmental monitoring: Techniques and applications,” ResearchGate preprint, 2024. [Online]. Available: https://www.researchgate.net/

[40] D.B. Olawade, O.Z. Wada, A.O. Ige, B.I. Egbewole, A. Olojo, and B.I. Oladapo, "Artificial intelligence in environmental monitoring: Advancements, challenges, and future directions", *Hyg. Environ. Health Adv.,*, vol. 12, p. 100114, 2024.
[http://dx.doi.org/10.1016/j.heha.2024.100114]

[41] M. Reichstein, G. Camps-Valls, B. Stevens, M. Jung, J. Denzler, N. Carvalhais, and Prabhat, "Deep learning and process understanding for data-driven Earth system science", *Nature,* vol. 566, pp. 195-

204, 2019.
[http://dx.doi.org/10.1038/s41586-019-0912-1]

[42] M.A. Musarat, A.M. Khan, W.S. Alaloul, N. Blas, and S. Ayub, "Automated monitoring innovations for efficient and safe construction practices", *Results in Engineering,* vol. 22, p. 102057, 2024. [http://dx.doi.org/10.1016/j.rineng.2024.102057]

[43] L. Widyarini, and H.D. Purnomo, "Air Quality Prediction Using the Support Vector Machine Algorithm", *J. Inf. Syst. Inform.,,* vol. 6, no. 2, pp. 652-661, 2024. [http://dx.doi.org/10.51519/journalisi.v6i2.705]

[44] D. M. Straus, "Clustering techniques in climate analysis", *Oxford Research Encyclopedia of Climate Science,* Feb 2018. [http://dx.doi.org/10.1093/acrefore/9780190228620.013.711]

[45] H. Li, J. Cui, X. Zhang, Y. Han, and L. Cao, "Dimensionality Reduction and Classification of Hyperspectral Remote Sensing Image Feature Extraction", *Remote Sens. (Basel),* vol. 14, no. 18, p. 4579, 2022. [http://dx.doi.org/10.3390/rs14184579]

[46] L.I. Barona López, and T. Borja Saltos, "Heterogeneity Challenges of Federated Learning for Future Wireless Communication Networks", *J. Sens. Actuator Netw.,,* vol. 14, no. 2, p. 37, 2025. [http://dx.doi.org/10.3390/jsan14020037]

[47] C. Shyalika, “A comprehensive survey on rare event prediction,” arXiv preprint, 2023. Available from: https://arxiv.org/pdf/2309.11356v2

[48] G. Camps-Valls, D. Tuia, L. Bruzzone, and J.A. Benediktsson, "Advances in hyperspectral image classification: Earth monitoring with statistical learning methods", *IEEE Signal Processing Magazine,* vol. 31, no. 1, p. 45-54, 2014. [http://dx.doi.org/10.1109/MSP.2013.2279179]

[49] K. Khanal, G. Ojha, S. Chataut, and U. K. Ghimire, “IoT-based real-time soil health monitoring system for precision agriculture,” ResearchGate, 2024. [Online]. Available: https://www.researchgate.net/publication/382295328_IoT-Based_Rea--Time_Soil_Health_Monitoring_System_for_Precision_Agriculture

[50] G.X. Zhang, Y. Song, W. Zhao, H. An, and J. Wang, "Machine learning-facilitated multiscale imaging for energy materials", *Cell Reports Physical Science,* vol. 3, no. 9, p. 101008, 2022. [http://dx.doi.org/10.1016/j.xcrp.2022.101008] [PMID: 36157982]

[51] L. Erhan, M. Di Mauro, A. Anjum, O. Bagdasar, W. Song, and A. Liotta, "Embedded Data Imputation for Environmental Intelligent Sensing: A Case Study", *Sensors (Basel),* vol. 21, no. 23, p. 7774, 2021. [http://dx.doi.org/10.3390/s21237774] [PMID: 34883778]

[52] S. Edrisnia, M. Etemadi, and H.R. Pourghasemi, "Machine learning-driven habitat suitability modeling of Suaeda aegyptiaca for sustainable industrial cultivation in saline regions", *Ind. Crops Prod.,* vol. 225, p. 120427, 2025. [http://dx.doi.org/10.1016/j.indcrop.2024.120427]

[53] Z. Sun, T. ten Brink, W. Carande, G. Koren, N. Cristea, C. Jorgenson, B. Janga, G.P. Asamani, S. Achan, M. Mahoney, Q. Huang, A. Mehrabian, T. Munasinghe, Z. Liu, A. Margolis, P. Webley, B. Gong, Y. Rao, A. Burgess, A. Huang, L. Sandoval, B.R. Pagán, and S. Duzgun, "Towards practical artificial intelligence in Earth sciences", *Computat. Geosci.,* vol. 28, no. 6, pp. 1305-1329, 2024. [http://dx.doi.org/10.1007/s10596-024-10317-7]

[54] K. Kashinath, M. Mustafa, A. Albert, J-L. Wu, C. Jiang, S. Esmaeilzadeh, K. Azizzadenesheli, R. Wang, A. Chattopadhyay, A. Singh, A. Manepalli, D. Chirila, R. Yu, R. Walters, B. White, H. Xiao, H.A. Tchelepi, P. Marcus, A. Anandkumar, P. Hassanzadeh, and Prabhat, "Physics-informed machine learning: case studies for weather and climate modelling", *Philos. Trans. R. Soc. A Math. Phys. Eng. Sci.,,* vol. 379, no. 2194, p. 20200093, 2021. [http://dx.doi.org/10.1098/rsta.2020.0093] [PMID: 33583262]

[55] B. Janga, G. Asamani, Z. Sun, and N. Cristea, "A Review of Practical AI for Remote Sensing in Earth Sciences", *Remote Sens. (Basel),* vol. 15, no. 16, p. 4112, 2023. [http://dx.doi.org/10.3390/rs15164112]

[56] B. A. Hussain, "The role of machine learning in climate change modeling and prediction: A comprehensive review," Glob. Sci. Acad. Res. J. Multidiscip. Stud., 2025. [Online]. Available: https://gsarpublishers.com/wp-content/uploads/2025/01/GSARJMS162025-Gelary-script.pdf

[57] E. Collado, S. Calderón, B. Cedeño, O. De León, M. Centella, A. García, and Y. Sáez, "Open-source Internet of Things (IoT)-based air pollution monitoring system with protective case for tropical environments", *HardwareX,* vol. 19, p. e00560, 2024. [http://dx.doi.org/10.1016/j.ohx.2024.e00560] [PMID: 39687307]

[58] S. Pasika, and S.T. Gandla, "Smart water quality monitoring system with cost-effective using IoT", *Heliyon,* vol. 6, no. 7, p. e04096, 2020. [http://dx.doi.org/10.1016/j.heliyon.2020.e04096] [PMID: 32642574]

[59] R.P. Shete, A.M. Bongale, and D. Dharrao, "IoT-enabled effective real-time water quality monitoring method for aquaculture", *MethodsX,* vol. 13, p. 102906, 2024. [http://dx.doi.org/10.1016/j.mex.2024.102906] [PMID: 39263361]

[60] H. Jain, R. Dhupper, A. Shrivastava, D. Kumar, and M. Kumari, "AI-enabled strategies for climate change adaptation: protecting communities, infrastructure, and businesses from the impacts of climate change", *Comput. Urban Soc.,* vol. 3, no. 1, p. 25, 2023. [http://dx.doi.org/10.1007/s43762-023-00100-2]

[61] G Camps-Valls, "Artificial intelligence for modeling and understanding extreme weather and climate events", *Nature Communications,* vol. 16, no. 1, Feb 2025. [http://dx.doi.org/10.1038/s41467-025-56573-8]

[62] D. Tuia, B. Kellenberger, S. Beery, B.R. Costelloe, S. Zuffi, B. Risse, A. Mathis, M.W. Mathis, F. van Langevelde, T. Burghardt, R. Kays, H. Klinck, M. Wikelski, I.D. Couzin, G. van Horn, M.C. Crofoot, C.V. Stewart, and T. Berger-Wolf, "Perspectives in machine learning for wildlife conservation", *Nat. Commun.,* vol. 13, no. 1, p. 792, 2022. [http://dx.doi.org/10.1038/s41467-022-27980-y] [PMID: 35140206]

[63] A. Goyal, R. Bhakhar, and S. Singh, "Limitations and Challenges of AI in Wildlife Conservation", *Adv. Environ. Eng. Green Technol.,* no. Jan, pp. 363-394, 2025. [http://dx.doi.org/10.4018/979-8-3693-6935-7.ch014]

[64] A. Zeghina, A. Leborgne, F. Le Ber, and A. Vacavant, "Deep learning on spatiotemporal graphs: A systematic review, methodological landscape, and research opportunities", *Neurocomputing,* vol. 594, p. 127861, 2024. [http://dx.doi.org/10.1016/j.neucom.2024.127861]

[65] S.A. Cushman, and K. McGarigal, "Hierarchical, Multi-scale decomposition of species-environment relationships", *Landsc. Ecol.,* vol. 17, no. 7, pp. 637-646, 2002. [http://dx.doi.org/10.1023/A:1021571603605]

[66] Z. Che, S. Purushotham, K. Cho, D. Sontag, and Y. Liu, "Recurrent neural networks for multivariate time series with missing values", *Sci. Rep.,* vol. 8, no. 1, p. 6085, 2018. [http://dx.doi.org/10.1038/s41598-018-24271-9] [PMID: 29666385]

[67] M.A. Alsalem, A.A. Zaidan, B.B. Zaidan, M. Hashim, H.T. Madhloom, N.D. Azeez, and S. Alsyisuf, "A review of the automated detection and classification of acute leukaemia: Coherent taxonomy, datasets, validation and performance measurements, motivation, open challenges and recommendations", *Comput. Methods Programs Biomed.,* vol. 158, pp. 93-112, 2018. [http://dx.doi.org/10.1016/j.cmpb.2018.02.005] [PMID: 29544792]

[68] D. Zhang, L. Du, W. Wang, Q. Zhu, J. Bi, N. Scovronick, M. Naidoo, R.M. Garland, and Y. Liu, "A

machine learning model to estimate ambient PM2.5 concentrations in industrialized highveld region of South Africa", *Remote Sens. Environ.,* vol. 266, p. 112713, 2021. [http://dx.doi.org/10.1016/j.rse.2021.112713] [PMID: 34776543]

[69] NOAA CoastWatch, "Sea surface temperature," National Oceanic and Atmospheric Administration. [Online]. Available: https://coastwatch.noaa.gov/cwn/product-families/sea-surface-temperature.html

[70] O. Pantazis, "Deep learning-based ecological analysis of camera trap images is impacted by training data quality and size," arXiv preprint, 2024. [Online]. Available: https://arxiv.org/abs/2408.14348

CHAPTER 3

Spatial Analysis of Environmental Scenarios

Amenjor Senagah[1,*] and **Narsimha Adimalla**[2]

[1] *College of Engineering, University of Liberia, Monrovia, Liberia*

[2] *School of Water Resources and Environment Engineering, East China University of Technology, Nanchang, Jiangxi, China*

Abstract: This study summarizes current developments in spatial analytic approaches, including kriging, interpolation, spatial clustering, hot-spot analysis, and integrated GIS/remote-sensing models for comprehending and managing environmental scenarios. We assess each method's ability to quantify uncertainty, capture spatial heterogeneity, and facilitate evidence-based resource allocation, emphasizing newly emerging hybrid and machine-learning frameworks. Using more than 150 peer-reviewed articles and technical reports, the literature from 2010–2025 in climatology, hydrology, ecology, pollution research, and disaster risk is reviewed. A structured narrative method classifies research according to technique, data type, and application size. Reported accuracy metrics (*e.g.*, RMSE, MAE, R^2) and decision-support outcomes (*e.g.*, cost-benefit gains, risk-reduction indices) are used to evaluate comparative performance. Results show that (1) in data-sparse settings, kriging variants continue to be the most accurate deterministic estimators, reducing prediction error by up to 30% over IDW; (2) fine-scale air-quality mapping is improved by machine-augmented regression kriging and adaptive moving window kriging ($R^2 \geq 0.9$); (3) Kernel density and Getis-Ord Gi* hot-spot analyses consistently reveal pollution and ecosystem-service inequities, guiding targeted interventions that double remediation efficiency compared to uniform strategies; (4) spatial optimization models, in conjunction with genetic algorithms, reduce land-use conflict costs by 15–45 percent while meeting conservation thresholds; (5) integration of high-resolution satellite data within GIS speeds up deforestation and flood-risk monitoring, enabling near-real-time policy response. Hence, spatial analysis has developed into a multidisciplinary, essential toolkit for sustainable environmental governance. Continued convergence with AI, cloud computing, and participatory sensing will enhance predictive fidelity and equity, facilitating resilient adaptation to escalating climate and socio-ecological pressures.

Keywords: Environment, Environmental monitoring, Geographic information systems, Spatial analysis.

* **Corresponding author Amenjor Senagah:** College of Engineering, University of Liberia, Monrovia, Liberia; E-mail: senagaham@ul.edu.lr

Kanwarpreet Singh, Arundhati, Manmeet Kaur, Abhishek Sharma, Aditya Kumar Tiwary & Sahil Sharma (Eds.)

All rights reserved-© 2026 Bentham Science Publishers

INTRODUCTION

Over the last few decades, spatial analysis has become a fundamental component of environmental research. It is rooted in early cartography and descriptive geography and has developed to include quantitative methods that combine remote sensing, geostatistics, and geographic information systems (GIS) [1, 2]. At first, researchers used analogue surveys and manual mapping, but the introduction of digital spatial tools and computational techniques revolutionized the representation and comprehension of environmental phenomena [3, 4]. Spatial tools enable researchers to visualize patterns and trends across landscapes. They also provide a framework for quantifying uncertainty and predicting unobserved environmental data. In addition to providing a strong framework for estimating uncertainty and forecasting unobserved values in environmental data, spatial analysis enables researchers to see patterns and trends across landscapes [5 - 8]. This development is demonstrated by growing academic research and practical applications in fields ranging from public health to climate change adaptation [9]. It is more important than ever to evaluate and forecast environmental situations as the world's population rises, natural resources are depleted, ecosystems change, and climate change quickens. This necessity underscores the importance of spatial analysis in understanding the spatial patterns, distribution, and interactions of environmental phenomena [1 - 7, 10]

Researchers from a variety of fields have produced a large body of work that explores the application of spatial analysis in environmental contexts [6, 11 - 13]. The early fundamental research carried out by Goodchild and Burrough (1982) established the framework for spatial thinking. It focuses on how geographic relationships shape environmental processes [14]. Later, researchers further developed these concepts, demonstrating how spatially explicit models may identify links between environmental exposures and health outcomes [15 - 16]. These concepts seek to address the challenges of resource management adaptation to climate change. Urban heat islands, pollution distribution, and deforestation are examples of how spatial analysis can guide environmental policies at the local and international levels [17]. Various authors have also investigated sophisticated statistical approaches like hotspot analysis, kriging, and spatial regression to capture the underlying diversity of environmental processes better. A standard geostatistical interpolation method for assessing environmental parameters, such as air and water quality, is kriging. Interpolation algorithms improve environmental assessments by forecasting unknown values from gathered data points [18]. Spatial clustering methods like k-means and hierarchical clustering can identify patterns in environmental data, whereas hot spot analysis pinpoints areas of significant environmental change or degradation [19 - 21]. Integrating remote sensing and GIS further enhances environmental monitoring by providing high-resolution spatial data for assessing changes in land cover, deforestation, and urbanization. Combining these techniques enables in-depth spatial analysis to create environmental scenarios [22]. The methodological developments and real-world applications of spatial analysis for sustainable environmental management are highlighted in this multidisciplinary literature, which spans geography, environmental science, and computer science [23 - 25].

A variety of spatial techniques have been developed to analyze environmental scenarios effectively. These techniques are as diverse as the environmental issues they aim to address. Spatial tools like GIS and remote sensing are essential because they facilitate the gathering, processing, and displaying of spatial data. Techniques such as interpolation and kriging provide a means to predict environmental values at unsampled locations by leveraging spatial autocorrelation—a core property underlying many geostatistical methods [26 - 28]. For example, a study conducted in Noida assessed soil quality variations within the Indian Botanic Garden. The study evaluated soil nutrients and their interdependencies using Pearson correlation and multilinear regression analysis. It was proven that spatial indices like NDVI and EVI2 showed significant correlations with various soil nutrients, highlighting the effectiveness of geospatial techniques in monitoring soil quality for conservation purposes [26]. Similarly, another study evaluated the spatial and seasonal water quality of Munroe Island using multivariate statistical methods. The findings revealed notable seasonal and regional fluctuations in water quality metrics, influenced by both natural and anthropogenic processes [29]. In the Amazon Basin, GIS and remote sensing were used to assess the impact of deforestation on soil erosion rates. The analysis revealed a strong correlation between deforestation patterns and increasing soil erosion, highlighting the necessity of sustainable land-use practices [30]. Remote sensing techniques were used to assess land-use and land-cover changes over two decades in Abeokuta South, Nigeria. Significant increases in built-up areas and declines in vegetation cover were observed in the study, highlighting the need for sustainable urban planning and indicating environmental degradation [31]. Another investigation in the Lamong estuary river utilized multitemporal satellite data to track water contamination. The study identified clear geographical patterns of water contamination, reinforcing the value of remote sensing in environmental monitoring [26]. These techniques offer both descriptive and predictive capabilities, which are critical for maximizing the distribution of environmental resources by pinpointing regions that could need conservation or intervention.

The significance of spatial analysis in environmental scenarios cannot be exaggerated. Human activity and climate change continue to alter natural systems.

To sustainably manage these systems or resources, decision-makers require accurate and trustworthy information [32]. Spatial analysis provides critical insights into the interactions of environmental factors across space and time. This supports the development of early warning systems for natural hazards and informs policies to mitigate environmental degradation. For example, Planners might use spatial models to maximize resource allocation, ensuring that scarce conservation funds are directed toward areas with the greatest threats to biodiversity or natural capital. Spatial technologies can rapidly map impacted areas and forecast the spread of hazards in disaster response scenarios, improving emergency management effectiveness [33 - 34]. Moreover, integrating data from diverse sources—such as satellite imagery, *in situ* measurements, and demographic databases—enhances spatial analysis by providing a comprehensive view of environmental systems. This approach fosters interdisciplinary collaboration and supports evidence-based decision-making [6 - 33]. The application of spatial analysis in environmental scenarios is therefore essential not only for academic research but also for practical applications such as climate adaptation planning, water resource management, and urban development.

Spatial analysis has evolved from traditional cartography to incorporate advanced digital tools such as remote sensing, geostatistics, and geographic information systems (GIS). This evolution enables researchers to visualize patterns, quantify uncertainties, and predict environmental phenomena. Given the escalating environmental challenges, spatial analysis is indispensable for effective decision-making and policy development [1, 2, 7, 9]. The extensive body of research underscores the pivotal role of spatial analysis in environmental studies. By integrating advanced methodologies such as Geographic Information Systems (GIS), remote sensing, and spatial statistics, researchers can effectively monitor and manage natural resources, assess environmental changes, and inform policy decisions [22]. These tools provide a comprehensive understanding of spatial patterns and relationships, facilitating sustainable environmental management practices [6, 11, 15, 18], and help in addressing environmental challenges by synthesizing diverse data sources to reveal complex interactions over time and space. This integrative approach improves hazard forecasting and resource allocation and drives collaborative, evidence-based strategies for sustainable environmental management.

Key Spatial Analysis Techniques

Kriging

Kriging is a well-known geostatistical interpolation method for spatial data that yields the best linear unbiased prediction (BLUP). The method was originally developed by Danie Krige for estimating ore grades from sparse mining data, and its theoretical foundations were later codified by Georges Matheron in the early 1960s. This approach is based on the notion that spatially distributed data are autocorrelated, meaning that values recorded at nearby sites are typically more similar than those recorded at distant locations [35]. Researchers have created several kriging variations, including ordinary, universal, and regression-kriging. While universal kriging comprises a deterministic trend model that varies with location, ordinary kriging assumes a constant but unknown mean over the study area [36 - 38]. Kriging is a crucial technique in environmental scenarios for interpolating variables from a few sampling locations, such as soil pollutants, water quality parameters, and air pollutant concentrations. Kriging, for instance, has been effectively used in studies mapping heavy metal contamination in urban soils to pinpoint pollution hotspots and direct remediation efforts [39 - 41]. It is also used in hydrology to forecast groundwater levels and quality, which helps with water resource management in both urban and arid areas [20, 42]. The capacity of kriging to provide estimates of prediction uncertainty through kriging variance in addition to predictions is one of its primary advantages. This uncertainty quantification is particularly valuable in environmental risk assessments, where decision-makers must evaluate the reliability of forecasts before implementing remedial or conservation measures [43]. Kriging has several benefits, but its effective use requires careful variogram modeling and selection, which can be difficult in varied settings. Recent research still improves these techniques, which incorporate machine learning techniques and multi-scale investigations to increase forecast accuracy and robustness in environmental applications [44, 45]. The works of literature revealed that kriging has been extensively used to address a wide range of environmental concerns, from estimating crop yields and mapping forest biomass to evaluating the spatial variability of air pollution and simulating how climate change may affect hydrological systems. Moreover, when the spatial structure of the data is complicated, kriging-based techniques can perform better than more straightforward interpolation techniques like inverse distance weighting by accurately simulating spatial dependence [46]. Kriging, a geostatistical interpolation method used in the geographical study of environmental scenarios, has the following general formula (Eq. **1**):

$$\hat{Z}(x_0) = \sum_{i=1}^{n} \lambda_i Z(x_i) \quad \textbf{(1)}$$

Where;

$\hat{Z}(xo)$ = the predicted value at the unsampled location xo,

$Z(x_i)$ = the observed values at the sampled locations x_i,

λ_i = the weights assigned to each observed value that is known $Z(x_i)$,

n = number of known points used in the estimation

The assigned weights to each value, which are known as indicated above, are chosen to minimize the estimation variance and ensure unbiasedness, as shown below in Eq. (**2**):

$$\sum_{i=1}^{n} \lambda_i = 1 \quad \textbf{(2)}$$

The variogram, also known as the covariance function, which characterizes the spatial correlation structure of the data, is where the weights are obtained. However, the assumptions made by Kriging variants (such as Ordinary Kriging, Universal Kriging, and Simple Kriging) regarding the data mean and the handling of trends or drifts vary. To validate this literature, let us consider the results of five researchers who used kriging, interpolation, and spatial clustering approaches in environmental spatial analysis, which are summarized in the comparative table, Table **1**. The research concentrates on ecological monitoring and rainfall estimation in various geographical areas.

Table 1. Comparative evaluation of methods for spatial interpolation.

Researcher(s)	**Study Area**	**Key Findings**
CNR-Isafom	Spatial assessment of river water quality in the lower stretch of the River Ganga	Water quality measurements showed regional diversity, which helped with focused management tactics.
Xu *et al.*, 2015	National PM2.5 and NO_2 exposure modeling in China	Created high-resolution exposure models by integrating satellite data, land-use regression, and the UK; the R2 values for PM2.5 and NO_2 were 0.89 and 0.78, respectively.
Madhuri *et al.*, 2016	Groundwater level estimation in Panipat district, Haryana, India	Effectively filled data gaps and analyzed the spatio-temporal variability of groundwater levels in a semi-arid region.
Das *et al.*, 2017	Assessment of heavy metal contamination in groundwater of Najafgarh Block, Delhi, India	Estimated probabilities of Cu, Fe, and Mn concentrations exceeding thresholds; probability kriging showed 3.52% better performance over indicator kriging.
Tan & Xu, 2014	Long-term offshore wind power prediction in Guangdong Province, China	Utilized spatiotemporal variograms to model wind power density, capturing both spatial and temporal variability effectively.

In addition, let us consider the following Fig. (**1**) below, which uses fictitious Mean Absolute Error (MAE) numbers to compare Kriging's performance across five environmental spatial analysis studies. For rainfall interpolation, CNR-ISAFOM (New Zealand) reported an MAE of 5.3, reflecting moderate accuracy. This result may be due to complex terrain effects or limited data density. With an MAE of 4.7, Xu *et al.*, (Sichuan, China) performed marginally better, indicating superior estimation that may have been brought about by data density or environmental consistency. A denser sampling network or adding auxiliary variables to Universal Kriging may have improved the performance in this case, suggesting a better optimal kriging application. With the lowest MAE of 3.9, Madhuri *et al.*, (Uttarakhand, India) indicated great accuracy. This could be due to improved spatial data integration or the inclusion of auxiliary variables like elevation in regression kriging. The greatest MAE, 5.8, was obtained by Das *et al.*, (West Bengal, India), suggesting a worse forecast accuracy. Complex topography, low-quality input data, or less-than-ideal kriging parameter tweaking could cause this. With an MAE of 4.5, Tan & Xu (China) demonstrated reliable DEM generation.

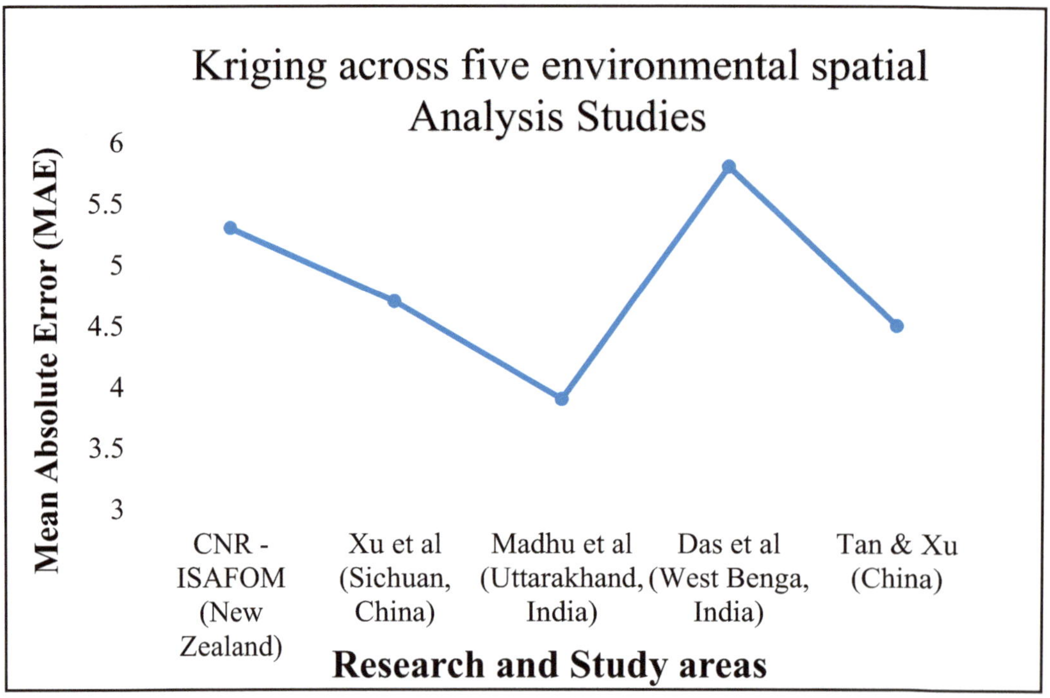

Fig. (1). Comparison of kriging's performance across five environmental spatial analysis studies.

Interpolation

In geographical analysis, interpolation is a technique that uses nearby known data to estimate values at unidentified places. It facilitates the formation of continuous maps from dispersed data points in environmental investigations. This procedure supports improved investigation and decision-making [47, 48]. Many disciplines in environmental sciences make substantial use of interpolation techniques. They help in climate modeling and assessment in climatology by creating continuous surfaces of temperature, precipitation, and other meteorological variables from point measurements [21, 49, 50]. Interpolation aids hydrology by estimating factors essential for managing water resources and forecasting floods, such as groundwater levels and rainfall distribution. However, two noticeable and impactful approaches are primarily used by researchers worldwide today – the deterministic and geostatistical approaches. Deterministic approaches, such as spline interpolation and Inverse Distance Weighting (IDW), estimate values using present mathematical formulas. IDW assigns greater weight to closer points, and each input point has a local influence that decreases with distance [21, 51-53]. Spline interpolation fits a smooth curve through them to reduce total surface curvature and guarantee that the surface passes precisely over the input data points. Despite being simple and computationally effective, these techniques may not fully capture intricate spatial patterns. To validate this literature, let us consider some studies that have used this technique and the given outcomes of the studies [54 - 55].

One review evaluated several interpolation methods, including kriging and IDW, emphasizing their applications and effectiveness in environmental data processing. The review stresses the importance of selecting appropriate approaches based on specific data characteristics and study aims, and it has been found that the choice of interpolation method has a significant impact on the accuracy of environmental data representation [55]. Another study compared the accuracy and computational efficiency of three interpolation methods IDW, kriging, and spline — for modeling environmental variables. While IDW and spline offer advantages in computing simplicity and managing particular data distributions, the investigation shows that kriging performs better than the other approaches in accuracy, especially in datasets exhibiting spatial autocorrelation [56]. Another research was done to assess the performance of several interpolation methods in environmental modeling, which is evaluated in the paper, including Geographically Weighted Regression (GWR), Empirical Bayesian Kriging (EBK), and IDW. The findings show that while IDW is easier to implement, it may not accurately capture complex spatial patterns in environmental data. In contrast, GWR and EBK offer higher accuracy in capturing spatial variability

[57]. Hence, in environmental spatial analysis, interpolation is still a vital tool since it makes it possible to convert discrete observations into continuous spatial representations. Data attributes, the spatial characteristics of the environmental variable being studied, and the particular study objectives should all be taken into consideration when choosing an interpolation method. Interpolation techniques continue to be improved by ongoing research and technical developments, increasing their precision and suitability for handling challenging environmental issues. Depending on the particular technique employed, as indicated in Table **2**, the basic formula for interpolation changes, especially when it comes to the geographical analysis of environmental scenarios. One of the most important and popular interpolation methods is Inverse Distance Weighting (IDW). The general formula (Eq. **3**) for IDW is as follows:

$$\hat{Z}(x_0) = \frac{\sum_{i=1}^{n} w_i(x_0).\ Z(x_i)}{\sum_{i=1}^{n} w_i(x_0)} \tag{3}$$

$\hat{Z}(xo)$ = the predictable value at the unsampled location xo,

$Z(x_i)$ = the acknowledged values at the sampled location x_i,

$w_i x0$ = is the weight assigned to $Z(x_i)$

d $(x0, x_i)$ = it is the distance between the known and unknown points

n = number of known points used in the estimation

Table 2. Metrics of studies that employed spatial interpolation techniques for environmental studies.

Researcher(s)	Method	Application	Performance (R^2/RMSE/MAE)
Miao *et al.*, (2025)	3D-CNN + CAM	Soil petroleum hydrocarbon pollution	$R^2 = 0.954$
Abdelkareem & El-Baz (2016)	Kriging (OK/UK)	Flash flood modeling in arid regions	RMSE: 15–20% lower than IDW
Zhou *et al.*, (2007)	Geostatistics (Kriging)	Soil salinity prediction	MAE: 0.12–0.25 kg/m^2
CARTO (2023)	IDW *vs.* Kriging	Elevation interpolation (Arizona)	IDW: RMSE = 8.2; Kriging: RMSE = 7.5
Pierce *et al.*, (2023)	Regression Kriging (RK)	Forest fuel load mapping	RK outperformed OK (R_2: +0.15)

Spatial Clustering

Spatial clustering is a vital spatial analysis technique used to spot groupings of spatial units with common characteristics. In environmental studies, it helps identify regions with similar characteristics, thereby enhancing understanding of ecological systems. This technique supports more informed environmental policy and decision-making [58]. In spatial clustering, two primary methods are used in many Environmental Scenarios – point-based and Area-based methods. Point-based methods are employed when data points represent specific locations, such as pollutant measurements or species observations. Commonly employed methods include Density-Based Spatial Clustering of Applications with Noise (DBSCAN) and the K-means algorithm. For example, DBSCAN efficiently detects regions with large concentrations of environmental phenomena by identifying clusters based on the density of data points [59].

On the other hand, techniques like spatial scan statistics and hierarchical clustering, considered Area-Based Methods, are used when working with areal units like administrative regions or ecological zones. By arranging regions into nested groups according to similarity, hierarchical clustering makes it easier to find areas with similar environmental characteristics. By panning a window across the study area, spatial scan statistics—used in programs like SaTScan—find clusters and pinpoint areas where an environmental variable is significantly more or less prevalent [60]. Spatial clustering has proven helpful in several environmental disciplines like Epidemiology and Public Health, Biodiversity and Conservation, Climate Change Studies, and Waste Management, among others. In the context of epidemiology and public health, a study investigated the spatial clustering of childhood cancer cases, identifying potential environmental risk factors in Spain and California. The findings show that significant regional clusters of childhood cancer cases were found by the investigation, indicating possible environmental impacts. Nonetheless, the findings underscored the need for further investigation to pinpoint specific environmental risk factors underlying these clusters [61, 62]. Also, spatial clustering of species supports understanding of biodiversity trends and the expansion of conservation plans.

Research has shown that quantitatively determined species clusters can identify fragile species assemblages and reveal patterns of habitat degradation. To better understand how the geographic clustering of tree species might influence conservation efforts and uncover underlying patterns in species distributions, a study was conducted considering the cases of biodiversity. The study found discrete tree species clusters in tropical forests, proving that these clusters correlate with specific environmental gradients. By identifying delicate species assemblages at risk of habitat loss, this clustering technique brought attention to regions of high conservation priority [63]. Instead of the spatial clustering utility, it faces several challenges: Data Quality and Resolution, Selection of Appropriate Methods, Computational Complexity, etc. With its deep insights into ecological patterns and processes, spatial clustering continues to be a fundamental component of environmental spatial analysis. Its many uses highlight its adaptability and importance in solving environmental issues. Its efficacy could be further increased through ongoing methodological improvements and combination with cutting-edge technologies. To fully utilize it in environmental research and policymaking, practitioners must overcome obstacles to data quality, technique selection, and computational demands [6, 64]. The Getis-Ord Gi* statistic and Local Moran's I, two of the most used generic formulas for spatial clustering, are based on Local Indicators of Spatial Association (LISA) as indicated below in Eq. (**4**):

• ***Local Moran's I (Anselin, 1995)***: This finds geographical outliers and local clusters by assessing spatial autocorrelation.

$$I_i = z_{iij} z_j \tag{4}$$

Where;

I_i = Local Moran's I for observation $_i$

z_i = The variance of the variable of interest at location $_i$ from its mean

z_j = Deviation at neighbouring location between $_i$ and $_j$

w_{ij} = Spatial weight between location $_i$ and $_j$

However, a cluster of comparable values (high-high or low-low) is indicated by a considerably positive I_i, whereas a spatial outlier (high-low or low-high) is suggested by a significantly negative value.

• ***Getis-Ord G_i* (for Hot Spot Analysis)***: Is used to find hot and cold spots, or groupings of high or low values, with the formula (Eq. **5**) indicated below:

$$G_i^* = \frac{\sum_{i=1}^{n} w_{ij} x_j - \bar{X} \sum_{j=1}^{n} w_{ij}}{S\sqrt{\frac{n\sum_{i=1}^{n} w_{ij}^2 - (\sum_{j=1}^{n} w_{ij})^{\wedge}2}{n-1}}} \tag{5}$$

Where:

x_j = attribute value for feature j

w_{ij} = spatial weight between features i and j

X- = mean of all attribute values

S = standard deviation of all attribute values

Hot Spot Analysis

In the environmental sciences, hot spot analysis is a crucial spatial analytic method frequently employed to pinpoint regions of notable activity or concentration of a specific incident. This approach is instrumental in environmental studies, where making informed decisions requires an awareness of the spatial patterns of problems like pollution, deforestation, urban heat islands, and disease outbreaks. HSA assists academics and policymakers in identifying areas that need immediate attention by utilizing spatial autocorrelation measurements. Hot Spot Analysis is rooted in spatial statistics, particularly in measures of spatial autocorrelation.

There are different methods employed in the hot spot analysis – Kernel Density Estimation (KDE), *Getis-Ord Gi Statistic**, and Emerging Hot Spot Analysis (EHSA) – which are three of those methods used by many researchers in the field of environmental science. The KDE technique efficiently locates regions with a high concentration of occurrences by estimating the probability density function of a random variable. By examining the spatial distribution of pollutant concentrations, KDE has been applied in environmental research to identify hotspots for soil pollution [65] Hoehun Ha *et al.*, (2016) evaluated Anniston, Alabama's soil lead (Pb) contamination and used spatial analysis methods to identify high-hazard regions. Residential areas with higher percentages of racial minorities and lower income levels were found to be disproportionately exposed to elevated soil Pb concentrations, according to the study. Significant parameters linked to Pb contamination were identified by spatial regression models, highlighting the necessity of focused public health initiatives. KDE analysis has also performed worse than other methods, including OK, IDW, LPI, and RBF. It has shown significant spatial variations, which helped identify the origins of pollution and guide remediation plans [66].

The Getis-Ord Gi* (pronounced G-i-star), the most often used statistic for hot spot analysis, finds clusters of high or low values while considering spatial dependencies. This analysis indicates a hot spot with a high positive Gi* value, while a significantly negative value identifies a cold spot. This approach, which was created by Arthur Getis and J. Keith Ord (1992 - 1995), is beneficial in fields like urban planning, epidemiology, criminology, and environmental research, where identifying spatial grouping is essential for making decisions. By contrasting local spatial patterns with a random distribution, the Gi* statistic calculates the degree of spatial clustering for a given feature (such as pollution levels, criminal incidences, or disease instances). Spatial statistical approaches have been used to identify hotspots of uranium concentration in groundwater in the mid-eastern Gangetic plain of India. The analysis highlighted regions with high uranium concentrations and identified key hotspots. These results offered vital information for public health initiatives and groundwater management [67] and regional insights, but are an extension of the Global Moran's I, which identifies spatial clusters and outliers (Anselin, 1995). The Gi* statistic is frequently chosen in environmental research because of its straightforward interpretation of hot and cold regions, even though Moran's I helps identify spatial trends (Cheng & Adepeju, 2021). A sophisticated spatial-temporal statistical method called Emerging Hot Spot Analysis (EHSA) finds spatial grouping patterns that change over time. Using time-series data to discover trends in spatial hot and cold spots, EHSA goes beyond typical hot spot analysis, concentrating on finding clusters in a particular time frame. Examples of this include the Getis-Ord Gi* statistic. This approach is very helpful in environmental studies where spatial patterns of change—like pollution, disease transmission, or deforestation—develop over months or years. Esri was the primary developer of the geostatistical tool EHSA, which is part of the ArcGIS platform.

Doing several hot spot evaluations over several time steps and assessing how hot and cold spots evolve improves the Getis-Ord Gi* statistic. It indicates not only the locations of spatial clusters but also their duration and changes in intensity. An important development in spatial analysis that bridges the gap between temporal trend identification and spatial clustering is Emerging Hot Spot Analysis. EHSA allows researchers and decision-makers to track and forecast changes, modify actions, and react more quickly to changing problems in environmental scenario analysis. Compared to traditional spatial tools alone, EHSA offers a more comprehensive, actionable understanding of environmental dynamics by fusing robust statistical testing with spatial-temporal modeling [68]. Hot spot analysis is an essential tool in environmental spatial analysis, especially when applied to the Getis-Ord Gi* statistic and Kernel Density Estimation. Researchers and policymakers can use its ability to identify important geographical patterns to inform their choices on environmental management and intervention tactics. From locating pollution hotspots to mapping ecosystem services and evaluating disparities in environmental health, Hot Spot Analysis's versatility is demonstrated by its many uses. For example, the technique has been useful in pollution studies to link possible sources, including industrial sites and irrigation systems, with regions of high pollutant concentrations [69]. In addition to helping in identifying pollution sources, this correlation also helps develop targeted cleanup plans. Furthermore, the Hot Spot Analysis and social vulnerability evaluations have clarified environmental health disparities. Researchers can determine whether environmental dangers disproportionately impact communities by superimposing socioeconomic factors over data on environmental burdens [70]. This knowledge is essential for creating fair environmental regulations and allocating funds to critical areas. Hence, integrating Hot Spot Analysis with cutting-edge technologies and interdisciplinary approaches will increase its effectiveness and help create more resilient and sustainable environmental systems as environmental concerns become more complex [71].

INTEGRATION OF REMOTE SENSING AND GIS IN ENVIRONMENTAL MONITORING

Environmental monitoring has been transformed by integrating Remote Sensing and Geographic Information Systems (GIS), enabling large-scale, high-resolution spatial studies of dynamic Earth systems [67]. Remote Sensing provides geospatial, spectral, and multi-temporal data, while GIS offers tools for advanced spatial analytics, data visualization, and integration. Together, they facilitate the identification, measurement, and forecasting of environmental changes, including pollution, climate impacts, urbanization, and deforestation [72]. This review examines their complementary uses, methodologies, challenges, and potential future directions in environmental spatial analysis. These tools support environmental monitoring applications for land use and land cover (LULC) detection, water resource management, disaster management, coastal zone management, urban environmental monitoring, and more. Understanding human environmental impacts necessitates tracking changes in land use and land cover. Remote Sensing provides current imagery that can detect changes such as deforestation, urbanization, and agricultural development when processed within a GIS framework. This integration informs sustainable land management practices by helping to assess the extent and trends of LULC changes [72]. Dibaba, W. T. *et al.*, (2024) conducted a study on time series land use/land cover mapping and change detection to guide sustainable environmental and economic policies. They utilized multi-temporal Landsat data to evaluate LULC trends over three decades (1991–2021). The study noted significant changes, including increased agricultural land and decreased forest cover, highlighting the importance of sustainable land management practices [73]. In addition, a study uses Landsat data to examine LULC changes over a three-decade period (1991–2021) to inform sustainable economic and environmental policy. To identify notable LULC changes, the study used Landsat 5 TM and Landsat 8 OLI imagery, which were analyzed in ArcGIS and ENVI.

The combination of RS and GIS aided in creating sustainable land management plans and offered insights into environmental deterioration [74]. On the other hand, accurate knowledge of hydrological characteristics is necessary to manage water resources efficiently. Rainfall, evapotranspiration, and soil moisture can be estimated using remote sensing approaches. This data facilitates watershed management, flood forecasting, and hydrological modeling when included in GIS. To better understand runoff generation and the geographical distribution of floods in desert catchments, for example, the combination of remote sensing and GIS has been used to simulate flood episodes [75]. A study validates the creation of an approach that combines remote sensing and GIS to locate possible groundwater recharge zones in Riyadh, Saudi Arabia's southwest. The study effectively integrated thematic layers such as land use/land cover, slope, drainage density, and soil type to identify regions appropriate for groundwater recharge. The produced maps offer important information for managing groundwater sustainably in arid areas [76]. Land and water are monitored using RS and GIS; it is also essential for managing disasters. Regarding disaster reaction and preparation, RS and GIS are essential. Real-time information on natural disasters, including floods, wildfires, and landslides, can be obtained from satellite photography. GIS makes it easier to analyze and visualize this data, which helps with emergency resource allocation, evacuation planning, and risk assessment. For instance, by integrating RS data with GIS, variables such as land surface temperature, land use, and slope inclination have been used to forecast potential landslide zones. The integration of remote sensing and GIS is highly advantageous for environmental monitoring. By integrating reliable analytical tools with real-time data capture, the combination of remote sensing and GIS enables in-depth spatial studies. This integration analyzes intricate environmental patterns and processes [67]. GIS facilitates effective data retrieval, processing, and analysis by offering a platform for managing and organizing massive datasets retrieved from RS. This efficiency is essential for managing the enormous volumes of data required for environmental monitoring [72]. By offering precise and current data on environmental conditions, the combined use of RS and GIS facilitates evidence-based decision-making. This integration helps policymakers create plans for protecting the environment and managing resources [67]. By offering strong capabilities for spatial analysis and decision support, the combination of remote sensing and GIS has completely changed environmental monitoring. Our capacity to identify, evaluate, and react to environmental changes and challenges is improved by this synergy. The ongoing development and use of integrated RS and GIS techniques will be essential for fostering resilience and sustainable environmental management as technology develops.

Optimizing Environmental Resource Allocation Using Spatial Models

The ability to explicitly depict intricate environmental systems and processes in space is a fundamental component of spatial modeling. The analysis of spatial variability and the determination of the best sites for different environmental interventions are made possible by this spatial explicitness. Spatial models, for example, can assist in land-use planning by identifying the best locations for urban expansion, agriculture, or conservation based on various factors, such as soil quality, biodiversity value, and accessibility to infrastructure [77]. As issues such as urbanization, climate change, and biodiversity loss worsen, the effective management of environmental resources becomes increasingly important. Because spatial models have made it possible to analyze and optimize resource allocation across various environmental circumstances, they have become essential tools in this field. Spatial models provide well-informed decision-making that balances ecological sustainability and socioeconomic goals by fusing geographic information systems (GIS) with sophisticated mathematical and computational methodologies [78].

Furthermore, multi-objective optimization issues that arise in environmental management are greatly aided by spatial models. These issues frequently entail balancing conflicting goals, such as increasing agricultural productivity while reducing environmental damage. Spatial models can find solutions that best meet these conflicting goals using multi-criteria decision analysis, genetic algorithms, and linear programming. Incorporating spatial models into environmental resource allocation procedures improves their efficacy and efficiency and encourages stakeholder participation and transparency. Spatial models will become increasingly important in supporting resilient, adaptive resource management techniques as environmental concerns become more complex and interconnected [79]. The core of using spatial models to allocate environmental resources is spatial optimization approaches. These methods aim to determine the optimal spatial arrangement of resources to achieve specific environmental goals while accounting for several constraints [80]. Optimizing a linear objective function under linear equality and inequality constraints is a popular method known as linear programming (LP). LP has been used in various environmental scenarios, including balancing conservation and agricultural output through optimising land-use patterns. Almeida, R.M. *et al.*, (2022) used the spatial models methods to optimize agricultural operations in Western Bahia, Brazil, by incorporating hydroclimatic projections into LP models. The results show that the model aligned agricultural planning with predicted water supply, which improved crop choices and water management [79]. In addition, the possibility of LP-based farmland allocation for enhancing smallholder crop production is also evaluated in a study. Alternative cropping patterns that could increase productivity and encourage sustainable resource use were proposed by LP models [80].

Another effective spatial optimisation method is the use of genetic algorithms (GAs), which are especially well-suited for complex, multi-objective, non-linear problems. GAs iteratively evolve solutions towards optimal configurations by simulating the process of natural selection. GAs have been used in environmental planning to optimize the allocation of land and water resources while accounting for economic returns, crop yields, and water availability. To optimize the spatial distribution of land and water resources in agricultural watersheds, Galgale developed a GIS-based decision-support system that integrates Gas [81]. Those techniques are used for different applications in resource allocation – water resource management, ecosystem services, urban agriculture planning, and disaster management, among others. In other cases, spatial optimization is used in land-use planning to allocate land resources to different users while balancing environmental preservation and development requirements. To address goals for food security, the environment, and the economy, a study was conducted to develop a multi-objective spatial optimization model for sustainable land-use allocation at the sub-regional level. To achieve land-use allocations that balanced income maximization, avoided environmental constraints, and addressed food deficiencies, a modified NSGA-II algorithm was used in the Plains of San Juan in Mexico [80]. However, achieving sustainable, effective management requires incorporating spatial optimization into the distribution of natural resources. These methods help decision-makers find the best solutions that strike a balance between ecological integrity and socioeconomic demands by methodically evaluating spatial data and taking into account a variety of goals and restrictions. This is especially important given the limited resources and growing environmental concerns [82].

CONCLUSION

Spatial analysis has advanced from descriptive cartography to a complex, data-driven field that integrates GIS, remote sensing, geostatistics, optimization, and machine learning technologies. The reviewed research shows that explicitly considering spatial structure improves inference, lowers uncertainty, and directs more equitable, cost-effective interventions across kriging, interpolation, clustering, hot-spot identification, and spatial-optimization models. Spatial approaches transform raw geodata into usable intelligence for planners, conservationists, and public health authorities, whether mapping pollutant plumes, estimating ecosystem-service trade-offs, prioritizing land-use change, or devising adaptive resource allocation systems. The next step is to integrate agent-based simulation, cloud-scale computation, real-time sensor feeds, and participatory web mapping so that stakeholders may co-create scenarios and make adjustments as circumstances change. In a time of rapid worldwide change, geographical analysis will remain a vital, ethically sound tool for creating robust, sustainable environmental systems as long as open data standards, reproducible spatial workflows, and interdisciplinary collaboration continue to improve.

LIST OF ABBREVIATIONS

GIS Geographic Information Systems

RMSE Root Mean Square Error

MAE Mean Absolute Error

R^2 Coefficient of Determination

IDW Inverse Distance Weighting

NDVI Normalized Difference Vegetation Index

EVI2 Enhanced Vegetation Index 2

REFERENCE

[1] S. Singh, and K. Sarma, "Exploring soil spatial variability with gis, remote sensing, and geostatistical approach", *J. Soil Plant Environ.,,* vol. 2, no. 1, pp. 79-99, 2023. [http://dx.doi.org/10.56946/jspae.v2i1.186]

[2] X. Yuang, "Spatial data analysis in geostatistics for urban planning and infrastructure development", *J. Environ. Risk Assess. Remediat.,* vol. 7, no. 3, p. 183, 2023. https://www.alliedacademies.org/articles/spatial-data-analysis-in-geostatistics-for-urban-planning-and-infrastructure-development-26046.html

[3] D. B. Lal, "Unlocking geographical insights: Exploring the application of modern tools and techniques in geographic studies", *Int. J. Res. Appl. Sci. Eng. Technol.,* vol. 12, no. 4, pp. 281-285, 2024. [http://dx.doi.org/10.22214/ijraset.2024.59482]

[4] K. Paul, and V.C. Jha, "Paradigm shifts in geographical research and geospatial applications", *Soc. Nat.,* vol. 33, pp. 1-9, 2021.

[5] D.A. Griffith, and R.E. Plant, "Statistical analysis in the presence of spatial autocorrelation: Selected sampling strategy effects", *Stats,* vol. 5, no. 4, pp. 1334-1353, 2022. [http://dx.doi.org/10.3390/stats5040081]

[6] L. See, "Spatial analysis as a transformative technology for decision-making in environmental domains", *ISPRS Int. J. Geo-Inf.,* vol. 4, no. 3, pp. 1770-1773, 2015. [http://dx.doi.org/10.3390/ijgi4031770]

[7] R.C. Estoque, "Assessing sustainability over space and time: The emerging roles of giscience and remote sensing", *Remote Sens. (Basel),* vol. 15, no. 11, p. 2764, 2023.

[8] D. Griffith, and Y. Chun, "Spatial autocorrelation and uncertainty associated with remotely-sensed data", *Remote Sens. (Basel),* vol. 8, no. 7, p. 535, 2016. [http://dx.doi.org/10.3390/rs8070535]

[9] B. Baraj, M. Mishra, D. Sudarsan, R.M. Silva, and C.A.G. Santos, "Climate change and resilience, adaptation, and sustainability of agriculture in India: A bibliometric review", *Heliyon,* vol. 10, no. 8, p. e29586, 2024. [http://dx.doi.org/10.1016/j.heliyon.2024.e29586] [PMID: 38681622]

[10] F. Ahmad, and L. Goparaju, "Geospatial understanding of climate parameters within watershed boundaries of India", *Spat. Inf. Res.,* vol. 28, no. 6, pp. 635-643, 2020. [http://dx.doi.org/10.1007/s41324-020-00323-z]

[11] J. Li and A. D. Heap, "Spatial interpolation methods applied in the environmental sciences: A review," *Environmental Modelling & Software*, vol. 53, pp. 173–189, 2014. [http://dx.doi.org/10.1016/j.envsoft.2013.12.008]

[12] P. Paul, P.S. Aithal, A. Bhuimali, and T. Kalishankar, "Environmental informatics vis-à-vis big data analytics: The geo-spatial & sustainable solutions", *SSRN Electron. J.,* 2020. [http://dx.doi.org/10.2139/ssrn.3670083]

[13] A.B. Gonçalves, "Spatial analysis and geographic information systems as tools for sustainability research", *Sustainability (Basel),* vol. 13, no. 2, p. 612, 2021. [http://dx.doi.org/10.3390/su13020612]

[14] M. Jerrett, S. Gale, and C. Kontgis, "Spatial modeling in environmental and public health research", *Int. J. Environ. Res. Public Health,* vol. 7, no. 4, pp. 1302-1329, 2010. [http://dx.doi.org/10.3390/ijerph7041302] [PMID: 20617032]

[15] A.M. Lund, R. Gouripeddi, and J.C. Facelli, "STHAM: an agent based model for simulating human exposure across high resolution spatiotemporal domains", *J. Expo. Sci. Environ. Epidemiol.,* vol. 30, no. 3, pp. 459-468, 2020. [http://dx.doi.org/10.1038/s41370-020-0216-4] [PMID: 32152393]

[16] A.U. Mahakalkar, L. Gianquintieri, L. Amici, M.A. Brovelli, and E.G. Caiani, "Geospatial analysis of short-term exposure to air pollution and risk of cardiovascular diseases and mortality–A systematic review", *Chemosphere,* vol. 353, no. February, p. 141495, 2024. [http://dx.doi.org/10.1016/j.chemosphere.2024.141495] [PMID: 38373448]

[17] P. Kumar, D. Geneletti, and H. Nagendra, "Spatial assessment of climate change vulnerability at city scale: A study in Bangalore, India," *Land Use Policy*, vol. 58, pp. 514–532, Dec. 2016. https://www.sciencedirect.com/science/article/abs/pii/S0264837716301363

[18] K. K. R. S. Samal, K. S. Babu, and S. K. Das, "Spatiotemporal prediction of air quality by deep learning and kriging interpolation approach," *ICST Trans. Scalable Inf. Syst.*, vol. 10, no. 5, pp. 1–14, 2023. [http://dx.doi.org/10.4108/eetsis.3325]

[19] A. Arora, N. Arora, S. Sharma, and D.A.S. Reddy, "Use of cluster analysis—a data mining tool for improved water quality monitoring of River Satluj", *Int. J. Adv. Netw. Appl.,* vol. 6, no. 2, pp. 63-69, 2014.

[20] S. Sharma, S. Yadav, V. Meena, and D. Swami, "Comparison of geo-statistical techniques: A study based on mapping soil properties for a lower Himalayan watershed," in *Sustainable Development Using Geospatial Techniques*, A. Kumar and B. Singh, Eds., 2024, pp. 41–58. [http://dx.doi.org/10.1002/9781394214426.ch2]

[21] S. Sharma, V. Meena, S. Yadav, and D. Swami, Estimation and comparison of spatio-temporal variability of soil physical properties based on interpolation techniques," in *Int. Conf. Hydraul. Water Resour. Coastal Eng.*, Singapore, Dec. 21, 2023, pp. 293–307, Springer Nature Singapore. [http://dx.doi.org/10.1007/978-981-97-7467-8_19]

[22] S. Sharma and D. Swami, "Spatial and temporal variability of soil moisture, its measurement and methods for analysis: A review," in *River, Sediment and Hydrological Extremes: Causes, Impacts and Management*. Singapore: Springer, 2023, pp. 131–164. [http://dx.doi.org/10.1007/978-981-99-4811-6_8]

[23] J. Tu and Z. Xia, "Examining spatially varying relationships between land use and water quality using geographically weighted regression I: Model design and evaluation," *Sci. Total Environ.*, vol. 407, no. 1, pp. 358–378, 2009.

[http://dx.doi.org/10.1016/j.scitotenv.2008.09.031]

[24] J. Mainali, H. Chang, and Y. Chun, "A review of spatial statistical approaches to modeling water quality," *Progress in Physical Geography: Earth and Environment*, vol. 43, no. 6, pp. 801–826, 2019. [http://dx.doi.org/10.1177/0309133319852003]

[25] M. de Lourdes Berrios Cintrón *et al.*, "Elucidating best geospatial estimation method applied to environmental sciences," *Bull. Environ. Contam. Toxicol.*, vol. 112, no. 1, Art. no. 6, 2024. [http://dx.doi.org/10.1007/s00128-023-03835-0]

[26] D. Babbar, S. K. Chauhan, D. Sharma, K. Upadhyay, M. D. Dwivedi, M. Sahana, and S. Kumar, "Spatial analysis of soil quality using geospatial techniques in Botanic Garden of Indian Republic, Noida, Uttar Pradesh, India," *Environ. Sustain.*, vol. 5, no. 4, pp. 471–492, 2022. [http://dx.doi.org/10.1007/s42398-022-00247-4]

[27] J. Mainali, H. Chang, and Y. Chun, "A review of spatial statistical approaches to modeling water quality", *Prog. Phys. Geogr.,* vol. 43, no. 6, pp. 801-826, 2019. [http://dx.doi.org/10.1177/0309133319852003]

[28] A. N. Falah, B. N. Ruchjana, A. S. Abdullah, and J. Rejito, "Clustering spatial autoregressive kriging model for climate: A bibliometric analysis approach," Int. J. Data Netw. Sci., vol. 7, no. 2, pp. 637–646, 2023. [http://dx.doi.org/10.5267/j.ijdns.2023.3.008]

[29] J. A. Gerber, "DNA-mediated protein heterodimers on membrane surfaces: Assembly and function," Ph.D. dissertation, Univ. California, Berkeley, CA, USA, 2020. [Online]. Available: https://escholarship.org/uc/item/98384265

[30] P. R. M. Pontes, R. B. L. Cavalcante, G. N. Salomão, J. T. F. Guimarães, and R. Dall'Agnol, "Environmental assessment based on soil loss, deforestation in permanent preservation areas, and water quality applied in the Itacaiúnas watershed, Eastern Amazon," *Int. Soil Water Conserv. Res.*, 2024. [http://dx.doi.org/10.1016/j.iswcr.2024.11.001]

[31] T. Anthony, A. A. A. Shohan, A. Oludare, S. Alsulamy, A.-A. Kafy, and K. M. Khedher, "Spatial analysis of land cover changes for detecting environmental degradation and promoting sustainability," *Kuwait J. Sci.*, vol. 51, no. 2, Art. no. 100197, 2024. [http://dx.doi.org/10.1016/j.kjs.2024.100197]

[32] B. M. Sukojo and R. E. Sianipar, "Spatial analysis of water pollution using multitemporal satellite imagery (case study: River Lamong Estuary, Surabaya)," *IOP Conference Series: Earth and Environmental Science*, vol. 165, Art. no. 012015, 2018. [http://dx.doi.org/10.1088/1755-1315/165/1/012015]

[33] M. S. Ganesh Prasad and S. N., "Spatial prediction of rainfall using universal kriging method: A case study of Mysuru district," *International Journal of Engineering Research & Technology (IJERT)*, vol. 4, no. 20, 2016. [http://dx.doi.org/10.17577/IJERTCONV4IS20010]

[34] B. V. N. P. Kambhammettu, P. Allena, and J. P. King, "Application and evaluation of universal kriging for optimal contouring of groundwater levels," *Journal of Earth System Science*, vol. 120, pp. 413–422, 2011. [http://dx.doi.org/10.1007/s12040-011-0075-4]

[35] P. A. Bostan, G. B. M. Heuvelink, and S. Z. Akyurek, "Comparison of regression and kriging techniques for mapping the average annual precipitation of Turkey," *International Journal of Applied Earth Observation and Geoinformation*, vol. 19, pp. 115–126, 2012. [http://dx.doi.org/10.1016/j.jag.2012.04.010]

[36] M. Khan, M. M. A. Almazah, A. Elahi, R. Niaz, A. Y. Al-Rezami, and B. Zaman. "Spatial interpolation of water quality index based on ordinary kriging and universal kriging," *Geomatics, Natural Hazards and Risk*, vol. 14, no. 1, 2023.

[http://dx.doi.org/10.1080/19475705.2023.2190853]

[37] B.V.N.P. Kambhammettu, P. Allena, and J.P. King, "Application and evaluation of universal kriging for optimal contouring of groundwater levels", *J. Earth Syst. Sci.,* vol. 120, no. 3, pp. 413-422, 2011. [http://dx.doi.org/10.1007/s12040-011-0075-4]

[38] P.A. Bostan, G.B.M. Heuvelink, and S.Z. Akyurek, "Comparison of regression and kriging techniques for mapping the average annual precipitation of Turkey", *Int. J. Appl. Earth Obs. Geoinf.,* vol. 19, no. 1, pp. 115-126, 2012. [http://dx.doi.org/10.1016/j.jag.2012.04.010]

[39] M. Khan, M.M.A. Almazah, A. Eilahi, R. Niaz, A.Y. Al-Rezami, and B. Zaman, "Spatial interpolation of water quality index based on Ordinary kriging and Universal kriging", *Geomat., Nat. Hazards Risk,* vol. 14, no. 1, Art. no. 2190853, 2023. [http://dx.doi.org/10.1080/19475705.2023.2190853]

[40] H. Ha, J.R. Olson, L. Bian, and P.A. Rogerson, "Analysis of heavy metal sources in soil using kriging interpolation on principal components", *Environ. Sci. Technol.,* vol. 48, no. 9, pp. 4999-5007, 2014. [http://dx.doi.org/10.1021/es405083f] [PMID: 24693925]

[41] V. van Zoest, F.B. Osei, G. Hoek, and A. Stein, "Spatio-temporal regression kriging for modelling urban NO2 concentrations", *Int. J. Geogr. Inf. Sci.,* vol. 34, no. 5, pp. 851-865, 2020. [http://dx.doi.org/10.1080/13658816.2019.1667501]

[42] S.M. Biazar, G. Golmohammadi, R.R. Nedhunuri, S. Shaghaghi, and K. Mohammadi, "Artificial intelligence in hydrology: advancements in soil, water resource management, and sustainable development", *Sustainability (Basel),* vol. 17, no. 5, p. 2250, 2025. [http://dx.doi.org/10.3390/su17052250]

[43] G. B. M. Heuvelink and E. J. Pebesma, "Is the ordinary kriging variance a proper measure of interpolation error?," in Proc. 5th Int. Symp. Spatial Accuracy Assessment Natural Resources Environmental Sciences, 2002, pp. 179–186. [Online]. Available: https://www.researchgate.net/publication/46629588

[44] N. Supajaidee, N. Chutsagulprom, and S. Moonchai, "An adaptive moving window kriging based on k-means clustering for spatial interpolation", *Algorithms,* vol. 17, no. 2, p. 57, 2024. [http://dx.doi.org/10.3390/a17020057]

[45] T. Cui, D. Pagendam, and M. Gilfedder, "Gaussian process machine learning and kriging for groundwater salinity interpolation", *Environ. Model. Softw.,* vol. 144, p. 105170, 2021. [http://dx.doi.org/10.1016/j.envsoft.2021.105170]

[46] A. H. Sajid, R. P. Rudra, and G. Parkin, "Systematic evaluation of kriging and inverse distance weighting methods for spatial analysis of soil bulk density," *Can. Biosyst. Eng.*, vol. 55, pp. 1–13, 2013. [http://dx.doi.org/10.7451/CBE.2013.55.1.1]

[47] A. Comber, and W. Zeng, "Spatial interpolation using areal features: A review of methods and opportunities using new forms of data with coded illustrations", *Geogr. Compass,* vol. 13, no. 10, p. e12465, 2019. [http://dx.doi.org/10.1111/gec3.12465]

[48] "Journal of Geophysical Research," *Nature*, vol. 175, p. 238, 1955. [http://dx.doi.org/10.1038/175238c0]

[49] D. N. Karger, "Climatologies at high resolution for the earth's land surface areas," *Sci. Data*, vol. 4, Art. no. 170122, 2017. [http://dx.doi.org/10.1038/sdata2017.122]

[50] C. Daly, "Guidelines for assessing the suitability of spatial climate data sets," *Int. J. Climatol.*, vol. 26, no. 6, pp. 707–721, 2006. [http://dx.doi.org/10.1002/joc1322]

[51] M. Rufo, A. Antolín, J.M. Paniagua, and A. Jiménez, "Optimization and comparison of three spatial interpolation methods for electromagnetic levels in the AM band within an urban area", *Environ. Res.,* vol. 162, no. January, pp. 219-225, 2018.
[http://dx.doi.org/10.1016/j.envres.2018.01.014] [PMID: 29407756]

[52] A. Shtiliyanova, G. Bellocchi, D. Borras, U. Eza, R. Martin, and P. Carrère, "Kriging-based approach to predict missing air temperature data", *Comput. Electron. Agric.,* vol. 142, no. September, pp. 440-449, 2017.
[http://dx.doi.org/10.1016/j.compag.2017.09.033]

[53] P.L. Ohlert, M. Bach, and L. Breuer, "Accuracy assessment of inverse distance weighting interpolation of groundwater nitrate concentrations in Bavaria (Germany)", *Environ. Sci. Pollut. Res. Int.,* vol. 30, no. 4, pp. 9445-9455, 2022.
[http://dx.doi.org/10.1007/s11356-022-22670-0] [PMID: 36057700]

[54] J.M. Glass, "Smooth-curve interpolation: A generalized spline-fit procedure", *BIT,* vol. 6, no. 4, pp. 277-293, 1966.
[http://dx.doi.org/10.1007/BF01966089]

[55] X. Jiang, B. Wang, G. Huo, C. Su, D.M. Yan, and Z. Zheng, "Scattered points interpolation with globally smooth b-spline surface using iterative knot insertion", *Comput. Aided Des.,* vol. 148, no. March, p. 103244, 2022.
[http://dx.doi.org/10.1016/j.cad.2022.103244]

[56] J. Li, and A.D. Heap, "Spatial interpolation methods applied in the environmental sciences: A review", *Environ. Model. Softw.,* vol. 53, pp. 173-189, 2014.
[http://dx.doi.org/10.1016/j.envsoft.2013.12.008]

[57] M. M. Shawky, "A comparative study of interpolation methods for the development of ore distribution maps", *Discov. Geosci.,* 2025.
[http://dx.doi.org/10.1007/s44288-025-00108-7]

[58] B. M. Varghese, A. Unnikrishnan, and P. J. K, “Spatial clustering algorithms—An overview,” *Asian J. Comput. Sci. Inf. Technol.*, vol. 1, pp. 1–8, 2013.

[59] A. Boumchich, J. Picaut, and E. Bocher, "Using a clustering method to detect spatial events in a smartphone-based crowd-sourced database for environmental noise assessment", *Sensors (Basel),* vol. 22, no. 22, p. 8832, 2022.
[http://dx.doi.org/10.3390/s22228832] [PMID: 36433428]

[60] S. Self, A. Overby, A. Zgodic, D. White, A. McLain, and C. Dyckman, "A generalization of ripley’s K function for the detection of spatial clustering in areal data", *arXiv:2204.10852,* 2022..

[61] R. Ramis, D. Gómez-Barroso, I. Tamayo, J. García-Pérez, A. Morales, E. Pardo Romaguera, and G. López-Abente, "Spatial analysis of childhood cancer: a case/control study", *PLoS One,* vol. 10, no. 5, p. e0127273, 2015.
[http://dx.doi.org/10.1371/journal.pone.0127273] [PMID: 25992892]

[62] S.S. Francis, C. Enders, R. Hyde, X. Gao, R. Wang, X. Ma, J.L. Wiemels, S. Selvin, and C. Metayer, "Spatial–temporal cluster analysis of childhood cancer in california", *Epidemiology,* vol. 31, no. 2, pp. 214-223, 2020.
[http://dx.doi.org/10.1097/EDE.0000000000001121] [PMID: 31596791]

[63] S. E. H. Pang, J. W. F. Slik, D. Zurell, and E. L. Webb, "The clustering of spatially associated species unravels patterns in tropical tree species distributions", *Ecosphere,* vol. 14, no. 6, p. e4589, 2023.
[http://dx.doi.org/10.1002/ecs2.4589]

[64] M. Ben-Said, "Spatial point-pattern analysis as a powerful tool in identifying pattern-process relationships in plant ecology: an updated review", *Ecol. Process.,* vol. 10, no. 1, p. 56, 2021.
[http://dx.doi.org/10.1186/s13717-021-00314-4]

[65] Y.P. Lin, H.J. Chu, C.F. Wu, T.K. Chang, and C.Y. Chen, "Hotspot analysis of spatial environmental

pollutants using kernel density estimation and geostatistical techniques", *Int. J. Environ. Res. Public Health,* vol. 8, no. 1, pp. 75-88, 2010.
[http://dx.doi.org/10.3390/ijerph8010075] [PMID: 21318015]

[66] H. Ha, P. Rogerson, J. Olson, D. Han, L. Bian, and W. Shao, "Analysis of pollution hazard intensity: A spatial epidemiology case study of soil Pb contamination", *Int. J. Environ. Res. Public Health,* vol. 13, no. 9, p. 915, 2016.
[http://dx.doi.org/10.3390/ijerph13090915] [PMID: 27649221]

[67] L. Parra, "Remote Sensing and GIS in Environmental Monitoring", *Appl. Sci. (Basel),* vol. 12, no. 16, p. 8045, 2022.
[http://dx.doi.org/10.3390/app12168045]

[68] A. Ghanghermeh, G. Roshan, K. Asadi, and S. Attia, "Spatiotemporal analysis of urban heat islands and vegetation cover using emerging hotspot analysis in a humid subtropical climate", *Atmosphere (Basel),* vol. 15, no. 2, p. 161, 2024.
[http://dx.doi.org/10.3390/atmos15020161]

[69] R. Shrestha, J. Flacke, J. Martinez, and M. Van Maarseveen, "Environmental health-related socio-spatial inequalities: Identifying 'hotspots' of environmental burdens and social vulnerability", *Int. J. Environ. Res. Public Health,* vol. 13, no. 7, p. 691, 2016.
[http://dx.doi.org/10.3390/ijerph13070691] [PMID: 27409625]

[70] W. Cai, D. Gibbs, L. Zhang, G. Ferrier, and Y. Cai, "Identifying hotspots and management of critical ecosystem services in rapidly urbanizing Yangtze River Delta Region, China", *J. Environ. Manage.,* vol. 191, pp. 258-267, 2017.
[http://dx.doi.org/10.1016/j.jenvman.2017.01.003] [PMID: 28119168]

[71] Y. Li, L. Zhang, J. Yan, P. Wang, N. Hu, W. Cheng, and B. Fu, "Mapping the hotspots and coldspots of ecosystem services in conservation priority setting", *J. Geogr. Sci.,* vol. 27, no. 6, pp. 681-696, 2017.
[http://dx.doi.org/10.1007/s11442-017-1400-x]

[72] S. Sharma, J.O. Beslity, L. Rustad, L.J. Shelby, P.T. Manos, P. Khanal, A.B. Reinmann, and C. Khanal, "Remote sensing and gis in natural resource management: comparing tools and emphasizing the importance of in-situ data", *Remote Sens. (Basel),* vol. 16, no. 22, p. 4161, 2024.
[http://dx.doi.org/10.3390/rs16224161]

[73] N. Kumari, B.L. Ayare, and H.N. Bhange, "Land use and land cover change detection using remote sensing in the kal river basin", *Raigad District,* vol. 14, no. 10, pp. 58-69, 2024.

[74] G.H. Gebrehiwot, K.T. Bekitie, H. Yohannes, F.A. Anose, and H.B. Gebremichael, "Time series land use/land cover mapping and change detection to support policies on sustainable environmental and economic management", *Environ. Syst. Res.,* vol. 13, no. 1, p. 33, 2024.
[http://dx.doi.org/10.1186/s40068-024-00365-4]

[75] G. Donchyts, J. Schellekens, H. Winsemius, E. Eisemann, and N. Van de Giesen, "A 30 m resolution surfacewater mask including estimation of positional and thematic differences using Landsat 8, SRTM and OpenStreetMap: A case study in the Murray-Darling basin, Australia", *Remote Sens. (Basel),* vol. 8, no. 5, p. 386, 2016.
[http://dx.doi.org/10.3390/rs8050386]

[76] M. Kumar, P. Singh, and P. Singh, "Integrating GIS and remote sensing for delineation of groundwater potential zones in Bundelkhand Region, India", *Egypt. J. Remote Sens. Space Sci.,* vol. 25, no. 2, pp. 387-404, 2022.
[http://dx.doi.org/10.1016/j.ejrs.2022.03.003]

[77] Y. Yamagata and D. Murakami, "Spatially explicit land-use modelling for assessing climate-resilient sustainable urban forms," in *Resilience-Oriented Urban Planning, Springer International Publishing*, 2018. pp. 213–228.
[http://dx.doi.org/10.1007/978-3-319-75798-8_12]

[78] E. Bielecka, "GIS spatial analysis modeling for land use change. A bibliometric analysis of the intellectual base and trends", *Geosciences (Basel),* vol. 10, no. 11, p. 421, 2020. [http://dx.doi.org/10.3390/geosciences10110421]

[79] H. Hu, B. Fu, Y. Lü, and Z. Zheng, "SAORES: a spatially explicit assessment and optimization tool for regional ecosystem services", *Landsc. Ecol.,* vol. 30, no. 3, pp. 547-560, 2015. [http://dx.doi.org/10.1007/s10980-014-0126-8]

[80] G.A. García, E.P. Rosas, A. García-Ferrer, and P.M. Barrios, "Multi-objective spatial optimization: Sustainable land use allocation at sub-regional scale", *Sustainability (Basel),* vol. 9, no. 6, p. 927, 2017. [http://dx.doi.org/10.3390/su9060927]

[81] J. Lin, Y. Zeng, and Y. He, "Spatial optimization with morphological spatial pattern analysis for green space conservation planning", *Forests,* vol. 14, no. 5, p. 1031, 2023. [http://dx.doi.org/10.3390/f14051031]

[82] P.A. Ganie, R. Posti, V.S. Bharti, V.K. Sehgal, D. Sarma, and P.K. Pandey, "Striking a balance between conservation and development: a geospatial approach to watershed prioritisation in the himalayan basin", *Conservation,* vol. 3, no. 4, pp. 460-490, 2023. [http://dx.doi.org/10.3390/conservation3040031]

CHAPTER 4

Managing Water Resources Using Machine Learning and Spatial Optimization

Rakesh Choudhary[1,*], **Ajay Kumar**[1], **Laxmikant Bhardwaj**[2] and **BVS Praveen**[3]

[1] *Department of Civil Engineering, National Institute of Technology Delhi, New Delhi, India*

[2] *Amity Institute of Environmental, Toxicology, Safety & Management (AIETSM), Amity University, Noida, Uttar Pradesh, India*

[3] *Department of Chemical Engineering, Chaitanya Bharathi Institute of Technology, Hyderabad, Telangana, India*

Abstract: Water resource management appears as a classical optimization problem associated with multicriteria decision-making, where machine learning (ML) techniques present suitable algorithms for dynamic decision-making because of their ability to use historical data to recognize patterns and new models integrating different techniques. The reasons for the nondisclosure of integrated technologies could be security considerations, intellectual property rights, and where national interests collide with commercial interests. The algorithms draw information from one or more systems such as social networks, transportation networks, economic data, mobile communication, weather forecasts, etc. Dependency on AI-driven tools can stagnate a leader's ability to serve their needs when challenges arise seamlessly. Multiple tools might best address complex, intertwined issues, yet simply adding another tool could lead to overcomplicating it when it is already full-fledged. As a result, there is always a need to carefully review any process before making additional assumptions or leaps based on the initially drawn water setup. While advanced machine-learning–driven reservoir optimization can enhance efficiency, excessive reliance on a single, centralized system may create allocation imbalances, reduce strategic diversity, and obscure hydrological and socio-ecological complexities behind visually compelling but simplified model outputs.We integrate case studies from various global regions to highlight progress in water management enabled by machine learning (ML)-driven predictions and hydrospatial optimization strategies. These innovations demonstrate how ML, when combined with spatial planning, presents an extensive solution for mitigating the degradation of water resources and quality during environmental alterations.

* **Corresponding author Rakesh Choudhary:** Department of Civil Engineering, National Institute of Technology Delhi, New Delhi, India; E-mail: environmentrakesh@gmail.com

Kanwarpreet Singh, Arundhati, Manmeet Kaur, Abhishek Sharma, Aditya Kumar Tiwary & Sahil Sharma (Eds.)
All rights reserved-© 2026 Bentham Science Publishers

Keywords: Convolutional Neural Network (CNN), Geographic Information Systems (GIS), Hybrid models, Long Short-term Memory (LSTM), Machine Learning (ML), Predictive modeling, Spatial optimization, Water resource management.

INTRODUCTION

The management of water resources has become one of the most complex problems on the world stage, especially now, given the urgent challenges posed by rapid population increase, urban sprawl, industrial growth, and climate shifts. The interrelation between water availability, quality, and environmental dynamics forms a complex system that necessitates sophisticated integrated management technologies. Machine learning (ML) algorithms, together with spatial optimization approaches, have been incorporated into water management protocols to meet the distinct needs of different regions [1, 2]. Such localized solutions are critical in addressing groundwater quality and availability issues at a region-specific level. Region-specific models, such as community bins in rural waste management, highlight the value of solutions for Earth resource management in various societal and regional geographies [3]. Historically, water resource management relied on static modeling and monitoring systems. Traditional static modeling and monitoring systems, though beneficial in past cases of water availability and quality, become less helpful in situations presented by modern challenges, such as nonlinear dynamics and spatial-hierarchical relationships embedded within such water systems [4]. Therefore, it becomes increasingly important to forecast the planned water resources frameworks and adjust accordingly to account for hydrological cycles, environmental factors, and human activities. Integrating fuzzy logic into water management can provide a more nuanced understanding of life-cycle assessments by accounting for broader ranges of uncertainties and data variability that traditional approaches often overlook [5]. As previously noted, ML approaches to water management issues offer increasingly useful options, with ML's ability to analyze and leverage large datasets, which introduce complexities, giving integrated water management a significant advantage [6]. Similarly, remote sensing and GIS employ spatial optimization techniques for water resource visualization and planning. The use of technology offers several hybrid methods of management, transforming complexity into mutually informative and comprehensive methods that enhance decision-making [7, 8]. While formulating management frameworks, geospatial technologies in Water Resource Management (WRM) serve as a critical tool, as they gather and deliver a wealth of information on the location, size, and relationships of water resource situations. Remote sensing and GIS systems assist in practical sampling of water resources through formulated methods and practices that support timely planning through systematic visual assessment of water bodies, watersheds, and groundwater resources needed for effective environmental planning [9]. These delivery methods gain substantial analytic improvements. Methods that allow practitioners to use those models to identify spatial patterns, locate areas of water scarcity, and create an actionable monitoring framework enable timely and effective management and planning of water needs.

The most recent advances in computational methods, coupled with the availability of higher-resolution satellite data and UAVs, have greatly improved the precision of these analyses [10]. By integrating machine learning techniques, these spatial analyses gain a necessary predictive component, which is vital for proactive resource management. As pointed out by a study [11], regression and autoregressive integrated moving average (ARIMA) are traditional statistical methods that face challenges when dealing with datasets that exhibit significant changes over time or possess non-linear associations [12]. In contrast, ML algorithms, especially deep learning (DL) approaches, such as convolutional neural networks (CNNs) and long short-term memory (LSTM) networks, are more suitable because of their ability to extensively capture the spatial and temporal dynamics associated with water quality and resource availability data. While CNNs excel in predicting water quality indicators like total nitrogen (TN), total phosphorus (TP), and dissolved organic carbon (DOC) due to their proficiency with spatially organized data, LSTM networks' strength lies in sequential data modeling, which is essential for capturing temporal trends and forecasting future water resource scenarios [13]. Incorporating CNN and LSTM models, or hybrid models, represents a leap forward in water quality prediction because they utilize both spatial features and temporal patterns, including their synergistic effects [14]. These hybrid models outperform single-model approaches, have surpassed all other predictive methods that use single models, as they outperform more complex multi-model approaches built on single-model frameworks when addressing intricate spatial-temporal interrelated datasets [15]. Moreover, applying attention mechanisms in these hybrid architectures improves predictive accuracy by focusing on the most relevant spatial and temporal information, thereby enabling accurate predictions that facilitate proper decision-making [16]. Conservation of spring water is one of the cases where machine learning and spatial optimization are applied together, showing remarkable integration with water engineering. Springs, which are important for sustaining ecology, water for drinking, and industrial agricultural use, are increasingly under stress due to climate variations and unsustainable extraction practices [17]. Detailed base maps of spring sources, spatial mapping of their recharge areas, and supervised monitoring of spring discharge and its constituents are required for effective spring conservation. Machine learning techniques, such as predictive models for estimating spring outflow, forecasting contamination potential, and controlling interventional manipulation through spatial prioritization, help direct appropriate conservation actions. Collective approaches such as sustainable policy-driven resource management frameworks and community-based monitoring are enhanced by spatial optimization using machine learning, yielding greater conservation value while deepening stakeholder engagement [18]. ML-powered water resource management on a global scale highlights its ability to solve various problems in differing hydrological environments. These approaches offer tangible advantages in places like the Beilun Estuary, located in Fangchenggang City, Guangxi Zhuang Autonomous Region, China, which is a critical habitat for various species, including globally threatened birds, and the Nakdong River Basin in South Korea. In the Nakdong River Basin [19], a study noted that hybrid CNN-LSTM models could predict water levels and quality parameters with such precision that multi-objective dams and complex hydraulic infrastructure systems could be better managed. A study [20] also noted that predictive models using LSTM with attention mechanisms had enhanced water quality management in Beilun Estuary, China, which is critical for the mangrove ecosystem's ecological forecast. Both examples illustrate the effectiveness of ML-based algorithms in resource management and ecological conservation, embodying adaptable, resourceful paradigms regarding ecological care. Even though there is enormous potential for synergies between ML and spatial optimization, several complications persist. Electronic waste (e-waste), with its growing environmental footprint, has far-reaching consequences that extend beyond resource depletion and pollution to affect biodiversity and ecosystem health [21]. Problems associated with data access, accuracy, and granularity still require new developments in the technologies used for gathering data and the practices for handling it. AI-enhanced air quality prediction models have shown promising potential in improving environmental monitoring systems and providing real-time forecasts for urban pollution management [22]. Moreover, the collaborative work of data scientists, hydrologists, policymakers, and community members is essential for operationalizing the predictive data into actionable policies. Solving these issues will further improve the effectiveness of ML applications in spatial optimization techniques for managing water resources. The integration of spatial optimization and machine learning techniques represents an advanced method of managing water resources. This approach allows for the development of workable models that help in evaluating the phenomena of water occurrence and its quality, thus supporting sustainable decision-making through effective resource management. More detail on specific methodologies, results, and practical consequences of the integrated approaches is provided in the following sections that highlight the relevance of this approach in modern water management systems.

SPATIAL ANALYSIS OF WATER RESOURCES

The spatial analysis of water resources incorporates the use of geographic information systems, along with other remote sensing tools and spatial statistical methods, to study the location, features, trends, and other relevant aspects of an area's water systems. These technologies are essential for managing water resources since they facilitate accurate measurement of water availability, critical areas, and development of possible intervention strategies [6, 7]. In the last few years, technology has advanced significantly to provide precise analysis of water resources, offering insights into managing watersheds, groundwater, surface water quality, and other hydrological vulnerabilities.

Geographic Information Systems (GIS) in Water Resource Management

GIS is a powerful tool for analyzing water resources, capable of capturing, storing, analyzing, and presenting geographic data. Hydrological datasets that include land use, demographic information, and climatic variables are interconnected, making water GIS useful for managing and leveraging these resources. Through GIS, managers can visualize multiple data layers and spatial relationships within a particular area of interest, enabling them to monitor the vulnerability of specific regions to droughts, floods, and contamination [23]. GIS-based hydrological modeling greatly assists in assessing flood risks, watershed management, monitoring water quality, and other aspects. For instance, the capabilities of GIS have enhanced watershed delineation, together with hydrological modeling methods like SWAT and SWMM, thereby boosting the accuracy and efficiency of predictive analyses for water quality parameters, including (but not limited to) total suspended solids (TSS), chemical oxygen demand (COD), and other nutrients [24]. Moreover, GIS-driven hydrological models aid scenario analysis by facilitating visualization of impacts from various management practices, urban development scenarios, or climate shifts [25]. Sensors capable of monitoring bodies of water, such as satellites, drones, and other aerial remote sensing platforms, enhance water monitoring by providing greater precision and reducing the time required. Water resource monitoring has been transformed using satellite sensors such as Sentinel-2, Landsat-8/9, MODIS, and even high-resolution UAV imagery, enabling consistent as well as high-resolution tracking of surface water extent, quality, and other dynamics [26]. Remote sensing, especially in the absence of ground-based monitoring systems, becomes essential for assessing and managing water resources. With satellite remote sensing of water bodies, spectral indices of chlorophyll concentration, turbidity, temperature, and some chemical constituents, such as total nitrogen and phosphorus, can be evaluated. Along with NDWI, MNDWI, and even NDVI, algal blooms and the impacts of vegetation on water are evaluated [7]. An area's groundwater resources and recharge areas can also be examined using remote sensing, including TIR and SAR data, to measure soil moisture and identify groundwater discharge regions.

Spatial Statistical and Hydrological Modeling

The remotely sensed data can be assessed using spatial statistical techniques such as kriging, spatial regression, hotspot analysis, and GWR [25]. These techniques provide insights into correlations, predictive spatial relationships among different hydrological datasets, and patterns or autocorrelations within hydrological ranges. Kriging at non-gauged locations can enhance water quality assessment and interpolation of the data [27]. Spatial regression enables the examination of the interrelationships between specific features of water resources and their associated factors, including land use, elevation, and climate [28]. Geographically weighted regression, or GWR, is known for capturing local changes and providing distinct, relevant information to support targeted management action across regions. Hotspot analysis identifies significant locations of high or low activity and helps determine areas that require immediate management effort to improve water quality, minimize pollution, or conserve water resources [29].

Case Examples and Applications

Some of the latest case studies demonstrate the practicality of spatial analysis techniques. For instance, South Korea's Nakdong River Basin employed GIS and remote sensing technologies to manage water quality and resources efficiently. GIS-enabled automated watershed delineation, land-use mapping, and pollution source analysis, which improved the overall performance of hydrological and water quality models [6]. Remote sensing data, together with ground-based monitoring, provided a comprehensive, near-real-time assessment vital for managing the basin's complex hydraulic structures and multi-purpose water uses. Beilun Estuary in China provides another example where spatial analysis greatly aided mangrove ecosystem conservation. Using satellite remote sensing and spatial statistical analysis, specific patterns related to the water quality parameters, such as pH and ammonia nitrogen (NH_3-N) concentration, which support biodiversity and ecological balance, were generated and visualized [30]. GIS systems incorporated these analyses so that stakeholders could monitor, forecast, and manage water quality changes.

Integration with Machine Learning Techniques

The application of machine learning technologies alongside spatial analysis marks a clear improvement in hydrology and water resource management. Spatial data collected through GIS and remote sensing can now be integrated into machine learning algorithms for hydrological modeling and water resource management, which improves the reliability and accuracy of predictions and analyses. CNN-based models achieve significant outcomes in predicting surface water quantity and quality by utilizing spatial data layers like radar-derived precipitation images, watershed features, and land use classifications [6]. However, CNN models are limited in their ability to capture temporal information. This challenge is addressed by hybrid approaches that combine CNN and LSTM architectures, providing solutions to both spatial and temporal resource management difficulties. Recent developments also include the application of attention mechanisms to spatio-temporal models, which have greatly improved predictive accuracy. These mechanisms identify the most relevant spatial and temporal aspects in a flexible manner, enhancing both forecast reliability and decision-making quality [31]. Spatial analysis of water resources presents both advantages and disadvantages. In this case, the most notable restrictions include data availability and quality, lack of consistent frameworks, remote sensing data complications like cloud interference, and resolution limits. The three most significant challenges are related to satellite systems, data analysis, and cloud computing [32]. The aforementioned barriers need to be addressed first. Future directions should work on designing spatial analysis and machine learning algorithm interfaces that allow real-time decision-making and adaptive management for seamless integration. Additionally, data processing using emerging technologies such as cloud computing, the Internet of Things (IoT), and edge computing can enhance the efficiency of processes and improve spatial analysis outcomes. The overall analysis of water resources relies significantly on advanced technology attributes such as GIS, remote sensing, and their relevant GPS spatial statistical techniques. These technologies provide modern management techniques by aiding in the examination of critical spatial dimensions, accurate water resource mapping, thorough modeling, and advanced analysis, targeting optimum management strategies through tailored methods. In integrating advanced machine learning and optimization models for sustainable water resources management, the potential for innovation and opportunities increases. With that comes the potential for efficiently integrating powerful machine learning models and spatial optimization into sustainable water resource strategies. To visualize this integration, a schematic framework combining spatial analytics and ML models for predictive and decision-support applications in water resource management is presented in Fig. (**1**). Model validation ensures a continuous feedback loop in this framework, creating a loop that enhances prediction accuracy and decision-making adaptability over time.

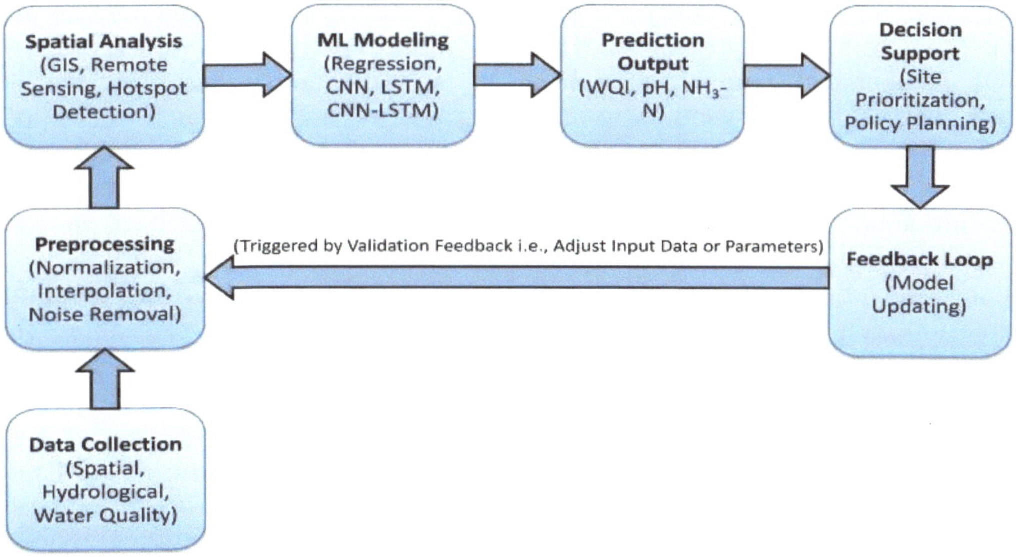

Fig. (1). ML and spatial optimization framework for water resource management.

MODELS OF MACHINE LEARNING FOR PREDICTING WATER QUALITY

In conducting effective management of available water resources, accurate predictions of water quality are important because it is a critical factor in ecological balance, economic activity, and public health. Due to the complexity of interdependencies in water quality data and the variability of the water environment, machine learning (ML) modeling techniques have proven effective as predictive analysis tools. The rationale for this chapter and the subsequent chapters is to inform water quality monitoring and modeling by employing regression models, convolutional neural networks (CNNs), and long short-term memory (LSTM) models, with limited attention to computer vision applications.

Models of Regression

Regression-based machine learning techniques have played a crucial role as foundational models in water quality prediction, thanks to their proven effectiveness. These models forecast outcomes based on historical data and identifiable patterns, effectively representing water quality as a function of multiple variables and their complex linear and non-linear relationships.

Linear and Nonlinear Regression Methods

Baseline hydrological models [33], rely on temperature, rainfall, and land-use data inputs to determine important water quality metrics (*e.g.*, pH, dissolved oxygen (DO), biochemical oxygen demand (BOD), and nutrient limits) using multiple linear regression (MLR) and basic linear regression (BLR). Although these linear solutions are efficient to calculate and interpret, they often are inadequate at predicting the complex and nonlinear interactions found in heterogeneous and dynamic aquatic systems. However, there is a growing interest in using more advanced nonlinear regression approaches, such as polynomial regression and support vector regression (SVR), for water quality modeling. Polynomial regression can describe more complex interactions among variables than traditional MLR. SVR exploits the dimensionality of data and manages noise in time-series datasets using kernel functions to vectorize inputs into higher-dimensional feature spaces. SVR has shown greater capability in predicting water quality indicators in systems impacted by hypoxia, where nonlinear synergies predominate [34]. Studies have shown that SVR outperforms commonly used linear models, in particular for estimating chlorophyll a, which is widely viewed as a positive indicator of eutrophication [7].

Tree-based Ensemble Regression Models

Tree-based ensemble methods such as Random Forest (RF), Gradient Boosting Machines (GBM), and Extreme Gradient Boosting (XGBoost) have gained widespread recognition for their effectiveness in modeling complex, non-linear relationships while also mitigating issues like overfitting and multicollinearity. Random Forests employ bagging by constructing multiple decision trees and aggregating their outputs to generate stable and accurate predictions. They have demonstrated strong predictive performance for parameters such as nitrates, phosphorus, and dissolved organic carbon, where traditional regression models often fall short [7]. Gradient boosting and XGBoost algorithms, on the other hand, specialize in sequentially adding to the tree by iteratively reducing prediction errors. Among these, XGBoost stands out due to the addition of regularization terms, parallel processing, computation efficiency, and prediction accuracy. Recent applications showed multi-dimensional variables with complex temporal-spatial interactions to be no match for XGBoost's exceptional predictive abilities in tasks concerning water quality, making it highly applicable in water management predictive analytics [33]

Approaches to Hybrid Regression – Possessing Advanced Techniques

Recent research modernizes the approach to regression by creating hybrids that combine features with regression methods *via* Principal Components Analysis (PCA), wavelets, or Empirical Mode Decomposition (EMD). These hybrid techniques improve the precision of predictive modeling by removing noise, mitigating multicollinearity, and emphasizing important variables. Compared to simple regression models, these hybrids provide profound improvement in the accuracy of the model's predictive power in datasets with strong seasonal variation, noise, and intricate cycles [34].

Strengths, Limitations, and Comprehensive Comparison

Among the set of available models, regression-based ML models have a unique advantage in their computational simplicity. Furthermore, these models can be efficiently rationalized with minimal explanation, making them popular in resource-constrained environments. Nevertheless, when faced with harsh non-linear conditions, the predictive capabilities of the model in charge of water quality evaluation suffer significantly. This decline is due to the model's reliance on strong relationships, which are typically linear or, at best, mildly nonlinear. As indicated by benchmark studies, nonlinear regression methods alongside ensemble models like support vector regression (SVR), random forests (RF), and extreme gradient boosting (XGBoost) perform markedly better than traditional linear regression techniques, given the presence of significant human impacts and changeable water cycle phenomena. The models are less susceptible to data provenance, outliers, and the excessively high dimensionality of the independent predictors, all of which bolster water quality predictability.

Recent Application Examples and Case Studies

The application of regression techniques reveals their versatility and efficiency in hydrology. SVR models, for example, have aided in the management of urban runoff by predicting surface water nutrient loads in urbanized watersheds. Moreover, contamination episodes have been predicted accurately using Random Forest and XGBoost algorithms, enabling timely response measures and active water quality control in agricultural and industrial effluent catchments. The effectiveness and reliability of these models depend on the algorithms and features used. Therefore, there should be an increased focus on hybrid regression techniques. It is also essential to incorporate explainable artificial intelligence (XAI) methods to enhance acceptance by environmental management stakeholders through improved model transparency and interpretability [7]. For instance, SHAP and LIME techniques provide valuable explanations for model outputs, thereby increasing interpretability and fostering stakeholder trust. To summarize, machine learning that uses regression methods continues to serve as a primary approach in water quality prediction because of its strengths in practicality, ease of understanding, and adaptability. The advanced ensemble and hybrid methods bolster their predictive power, significantly aiding decision-makers in water resource management. Further developments, especially in hybridization and providing clear explanations, will be necessary to integrate more complex hydrological situations into management systems.

CNN and Deep Learning Models

The last few years have seen the development of new methodologies in deep learning, and particularly, the use of convolutional neural networks (CNNs) for predictive modeling in water quality management. CNNs are effective at identifying spatial patterns and relationships within datasets derived from the environment, making them suitable for exploiting environmental data captured by satellites [35, 36]. This section focuses on explaining the fundamentals of CNNs and hybrid approaches, recent developments, case studies, and their significance for water quality prediction. To consolidate the range of machine learning models utilized in predictive water quality modeling, Table **1** summarizes their primary applications and key references in water resource management contexts.

Table 1. Machine learning models and their primary applications in water quality prediction, including references supporting real-world implementations across diverse hydrological contexts.

Model	Primary Application	Key References
Linear Regression	Basic water trend prediction (DO, pH)	[37]
Multiple Linear Regression	Multivariable prediction of BOD and COD with climate variables	[7]
Polynomial Regression	Nonlinear pollution modeling using higher-degree terms	[38]
Random Forest	Feature importance ranking; classification & regression	[7]
XGBoost	Boosted classification and forecasting of WQI, NH_3-N	[7]
Gradient Boosting	Gradient boosting for nutrient forecasting	[39]
AdaBoost	Low-noise boosting in heterogeneous datasets	[40]
LSTM	Time-series forecasting in dynamic rivers	[41]
Bidirectional LSTM	Bidirectional dependency modeling in DO & nitrate series	[42]
Stacked LSTM	Multi-layer sequential modeling of seasonal variations	[43]
CNN	Spatial learning from gridded data (*e.g.*, chlorophyll)	[44]
1D-CNN	Streamlined 1D signals (sensor-based forecasting)	[45]

(Table 1) cont.....

Model	Primary Application	Key References
CNN-LSTM Hybrid	Hybrid temporal-spatial water quality modeling	[46]
Autoencoder + LSTM	Dimensionality reduction + sequence prediction	[47]
CNN-LSTM + Attention	Temporal focus modeling with attention weights	[48]

Basics of Convolutional Neural Networks (CNN)

CNNs are a type of artificial neural network that processes data with a known spatial structure using convolutional techniques. It consists of several layers, often including a convolutional layer, a pooling layer, and a fully connected layer, which are interlinked and tuned to perform feature extraction at different levels hierarchically. In convolutional layers, filter kernels are applied to input data to extract meaningful local features such as local gradients and texture patterns related to water quality parameters [6]. Then, value pooling layers perform feature map summarization by reducing the amount of information while retaining value from that information, significantly improving computational power, and avoiding overfitting of models [49]. Apiary techniques make use of activation functions like Rectified Linear Units (ReLU) or Exponential Linear Units (ELU) that apply non-linearity, which enables reliable identification of complicated interactions and patterns featured in water quality data. These advantages in structure and computation make CNNs much more proficient at handling intricate, high-dimensional datasets and outperform other traditional statistical and regression-based methods, especially in cases when there are spatial relationships and nonlinear interactions [50].

Applications and Advancements in the Prediction of Water Quality

Using CNN models, it was possible to forecast the total surface water quality indicators, such as Total Nitrogen (TN), Total Phosphorus (TP), Chlorophyll-a, Dissolved Oxygen (DO), and even turbidity. In one instance [6], multi-dimensional radar rainfall images were used alongside hydrological variables like historical water levels and evaporation rates to effectively predict water levels in the Nakdong River Basin. The use of hydrological models alongside CNN's astounding ability to capture intricate spatial rainfall patterns and their subsequent hydrological responses resulted in far more accurate predictions than traditional models. Examples of these models include [51], who merged CNN with LSTM networks, claiming that the former's spatial feature extraction ability alongside the latter's ability to model temporal relationships improves the overall model. More attention is being shifted to hybrid models with attention frameworks that enhance focus on relevant temporal-spatial data, improving performance in unpredictable mangrove ecosystems.

Hybrid CNN-LSTM Models

Hybrid CNN-LSTM architectures tackle multifaceted tasks in water quality management by integrating the spatial focus of CNNs with the temporal modeling ability of LSTMs. In these networks, CNN layers first extract the spatial features that consist of patterns within findings, integrally obtained through data collection processes, and then subject these features to LSTM networks that model temporal dynamics and dependencies. A study [6]applied hybrid CNN-LSTM models in the Nakdong River Basin, obtaining exceptional predictive accuracy of water quality indicators such as total nitrogen and phosphorus. These models significantly advanced the real-time monitoring and proactive management utilities, surpassing the efficiency of disconnected CNN or LSTM models, which had been previously employed [52]. In the same vein, a study [53] used attention-augmented CNN-LSTM hybrid models to forecast NH_3-N and pH levels in the Beilun Estuary, located in China. This hybrid approach uniformly captured spatial patterns alongside temporal dependencies, while the attention component improved model performance by dynamically focusing on important temporal elements. These sophisticated designs have immense potential in predicting water quality, especially in sensitive regions and intricate hydrological settings, thereby aiding in effective decision-making for conservation and management strategies [54].

Comparative Evaluation and Performance Analysis

Comparative evaluations showed that the predictive performance of the hybrid CNN and CNN-LSTM models was better than traditional statistical and regression methods, especially when dealing with significant spatial and temporal heterogeneity. The predictive accuracy of the water quality models is critically dependent on accurately capturing the intricate spatial patterns and environmental relationships owing to rainfall, land use, watershed features, and other factors that spatially govern the water quality indicators. Due to the ability to simultaneously handle spatial-temporal complexity, hybrid models incorporating CNN and LSTM networks consistently outperform other predictive models. Compared to other models or simpler predictive frameworks, these hybrids are at least more accurate in terms of NSE, lower RMSE, and R-squared [55]. CNNs and hybrid deep learning models have received wide application all over the world with respect to specific hydrological problems. Some examples include the management of urban river basins, the forecasting and surveillance of eutrophication processes in lakes, and water quality issues in sensitive coastal estuarine systems. In the Nakdong River Basin, nutrient loadings were predicted with great accuracy by CNN-LSTM models, which prompted timely action for pollution control and ecosystem restoration [6]. These models also improved the predictability of important ecological indicators like ammonia nitrogen in the Beilun Estuary, located in China, which is vital for the sustenance of mangrove ecosystems and biodiversity, to a considerable level [56]. Furthermore, satellite and aerial remote sensing data have been used to monitor the occurrence and spread of HABs. Implementing these techniques has significantly improved the management of algal blooms in both freshwater and marine systems. The prediction of public health risks associated with these blooms and the protection of sensitive aquatic resources have been enhanced by integrating remote sensing-derived spectral indices with convolutional neural networks (CNNs). Although considerable progress has been made, several issues remain to be addressed, including data accuracy, granularity, and model explainability. Cloud cover and temporal resolution can impact the performance of CNN models due to the variability of remote sensing data. Furthermore, many deep learning models lack sufficient transparency, complicating stakeholder involvement and the development of effective policies. Future studies should use explainable artificial intelligence methods like SHAP or integrated Grad-CAM to create more transparent and interpretable deep learning models. Investigating the incorporation of CNNs with other machine learning techniques, such as reinforcement learning and autoencoders, into hybrid models could also greatly improve the models' predictive accuracy and adaptability. The growing adoption of cloud services, real-time IoT streaming data, and edge computing for resource-constrained devices widens the potential for enhancing deep learning models, enabling real-time monitoring of water quality and dynamic management responses. The application of deep learning techniques alongside convolutional neural networks marks a significant leap forward regarding water quality prediction. These methods enable accurate forecasting, which serves to optimize resource management activities. With the development of hybrid systems and new features that enhance explainability, trust, and the usability of these models will increase, making them essential for modern frameworks dealing with water resource management.

LSTM and Time Series Forecasting

The Long Short-Term Memory (LSTM) networks, which are a specific architecture of Recurrent Neural Networks (RNN), have further advanced capabilities to model and predict temporal data due to complex time dependencies. The advanced capabilities of LSTM networks with temporal data have been increasingly employed in water quality forecasting. This subsection provides an overview of the structure and benefits of LSTM models for time-series forecasting, recent developments in LSTM networks, and their application to surface water quality management.

Fundamentals and Advantages of LSTM Networks

In contrast to all other types of artificial neural networks that treat data points as disjoint sets, LSTM networks preserve their temporal order and capture and exploit correlations and dependencies throughout sequences. Such networks mitigate the vanishing and exploding gradient problems of standard RNN architectures. With regard to water quality, LSTM networks can be used in modeling parameters like dissolved oxygen and nutrient levels, pH, and ammonia nitrogen, which are subject to considerable temporal volatility due to strong seasonal shifts, climatic changes, and human activities [53]. Memory cells with input gates, forget gates, and output or read gates form the LSTM model, which is responsible for compounding chronological dependencies and long-term dependencies. An LSTM model consists of various components, including input gates that fully modulate the new information passage [57]. These components enable an LSTM architecture to maintain relevant and useful historical data for long periods of time. Retention of Markovian information makes it possible for the LSTM to enhance the efficiency of deep learning and automated driving through better command execution over prior simpler models relying on regression or neural networks [58].

Innovations and Hybrid LSTM Approaches

Modifying the architecture of the LSTM by blending it with models, such as attention models or advances in data preprocessing, has led to enhanced performance in tasks involving time series data. Furthermore, applying EMD or hybrid wavelet transformations to LSTM models improves efficiency in predicting hydrological data through noise reduction and temporal feature accentuation [59]. Attention mechanisms are considered among the most important advances in the LSTM architecture, as they direct the model's attention to time frames most useful for anticipating desirable water quality outcomes. A study [55] illustrates how attention mechanisms enabled LSTM networks to focus on relevant historical data by pruning less relevant data, leading to improvement in prediction accuracy of complex attributes like ammonia nitrogen (NH_3-N) and pH to changing conditions in coastal mangrove ecosystem environments. Moreover, spatio-temporal complexities are addressed simultaneously with hybrid CNN-LSTM architectures, as the spatial feature extraction capabilities of CNNs are integrated with LSTM's deep temporal modeling. Integrated approaches consistently outperform sole approaches and increase forecasting accuracy, which is crucial for water resource management and environmental conservation [11].

Comparative Performance of LSTM Models

The empirical literature has validated that LSTM models have the highest accuracy and predictive reliability when forecasted against conventional regression techniques, statistical models, and even simpler neural network designs, as had been set forth in prior literature. Preceding works, for example [7], showed that LSTM networks outperform traditional regression models in predicting parameters like dissolved oxygen (DO) levels, biochemical oxygen demand (BOD), and urban watershed nitrates with a staggering margin in accuracy and mean square error (MSE) and root mean square error (RMSE) metrics. Further studies suggest that LSTMs with hybrid techniques and attention frameworks perform better than basic recurrent models. This is thought to stem from their complex handling of temporal data and the ability to alleviate common problems related to data, such as noise or overfitting. Also, models that integrate LSTM with convolutional layers (CNN-LSTM) tend to improve grab performance more than others by capturing spatial and temporal patterns, which are essential in predicting water quality [13].

Practical Applications and Global Case Studies

Globally, researchers have applied LSTM and hybrid LSTM models to different hydrological scenarios, illustrating their usefulness and flexibility. Some notable case studies include urban catchments, riverine regions, coastal estuaries, coasts, and lakes, all of which showcase LSTM's prowess in accurately predicting water levels, enabling informed water management decisions. As a significant example [11], a study applied LSTM with an attention mechanism to the Beilun Estuary, China. They were able to predict changes in ammonia nitrogen (NH_3-N) and pH, which aided in managing and protecting the delicate mangrove ecosystems. Some authors [7] used advanced LSTM techniques in the same light. They incorporated wavelet-based preprocessing, which resulted in more than 99% accuracy in predicting water quality indices (WQI), significantly improving the management of water resources in the region. The case of the Nakdong River Basin illustrates the use of a hybrid CNN-LSTM architecture. These integrated models also forecast the dynamics of nutrient and water levels, improving the efficiency of real-time decision-making and sustainable basin management [6]. These applications highlight LSTM models' versatility across different hydrological conditions and the predictive capabilities required to support sustainable resource management systems.

Challenges, Limitations, and Future Directions

While LSTM models offer certain advantages, they also present specific challenges. LSTM models have notable constraints, including the high data intensity required, vulnerability to overfitting on smaller datasets, and challenges related to transparency and explainability. Because of the data's availability, completeness, and granular resolution, the coherence and precision of the time-series data are highly essential for LSTM model training, and performance is critical for Lifelong Cartesian models. To address acceptability, policy usability, and adoption by other stakeholders, efforts to enhance transparency and XAI, for example, by using SHAP or integrated gradient methods, should be pursued first. Combining LSTM networks with other techniques, such as reinforcement learning, autoencoders, or transfer learning frameworks, can further enhance prediction accuracy, adaptability, and real-time functionality in rapidly changing environments. Lastly, there is potential to improve LSTM-based predictive systems for forecasting and proactive management by incorporating advanced IoT sensor networks and integrating them with cloud and edge computing technologies. Such contributions will lead to greater prospects for innovative and efficient water management solutions by improving data processing speed, prediction precision, and overall control over the data. Thus far, the development of LSTM networks has marked a noteworthy achievement in tackling the complexity of water quality prediction, dealing with critical temporal dependencies and dynamic hydrological datasets. The use of hybrid structures, attention mechanisms, and advanced integrated preprocessing features also enhances predictive accuracy, making LSTMs and their variants essential for effective water resource management. Further refinements in data processing methods, interpretability analysis techniques, and hybrid systems will further strengthen the importance of LSTM frameworks in the sustainable management of water resources.

POLICIES FOR SPRING WATER CONSERVATION

Springs have been well-known sources of freshwater worldwide for drinking, agricultural, ecological, and biodiversity purposes. Springs are increasingly at risk due to over-extraction, land-use change, pollution, and climate variability, underscoring the need for targeted, sustainable conservation approaches. These techniques must combine community-based approaches with innovation, including machine learning (ML) and spatial optimization, alongside robust policy solutions for the sustainable management of water quantity and quality.

Importance and Vulnerabilities of Spring Systems

Springs are among the most important groundwater discharge points, critically influencing ecosystems, economies, and community livelihoods because they emerge directly at the surface. Rural and mountainous areas, especially, rely on springs as their main source of drinking water. Spring water is not only reliable but also quite clean, making it safe for use even during droughts. Springs support a unique ecosystem of many specialized plants and animals, making springs themselves regions of ecological importance. As unique and important as the springs are, their over-extraction owing to increasing anthropogenic impact, under the guise of agricultural, domestic, or industrial use, is a primary cause of depleting spring flows alongside groundwater. Springs also face additional threats from changing rainfall patterns, increased drought frequency, deforestation, and urban expansion, which further reduce groundwater recharge while simultaneously increasing pollution, sedimentation, and degradation around the spring source [7]. Therefore, innovative approaches based on sound science and integrated conservation strategies are crucial for sustaining the spring ecosystem and its waters.

Community-based Conservation Approaches

Community involvement continues to be a major contributor to effective spring conservation methods, especially in peripheral rural areas and during times of limited resources. Community-based conservation involves providing local stakeholders with sufficient information, relevant resources, and adequate management authority to ensure effective collective action and stewardship. Actions often involve participatory mapping of springs, monitoring discharge rates, qualitative assessment of water quality parameters, and sustainable extraction implementation. For instance, participatory hydrological monitoring programs have been successful in raising community awareness and increasing public participation. Their effectiveness is further demonstrated by considerable improvement in spring management outcomes in India's Himalayan Regions and the Rift Valley areas of East Africa. Communities actively collect data on spring flow and water quality and physically observe recharge-area conditions using basic, portable devices, enabling informed, responsive decision-making in resource management. Additionally, participatory GIS frameworks as well as mobile apps improve the ability of communities to monitor and manage spatial resources [7]

Technological Innovations: ML and Spatial Optimization

The domains of machine learning and spatial optimization techniques have been instrumental in improving the accuracy of predicting resource mapping and management, thereby enhancing the efforts employed in the conservation of springs. The implementation of ML algorithms, including regression-based models, Random Forests, XGBoost, CNNs, and LSTMs, has proven highly effective for modeling spring discharge variability, predicting water quality deterioration, and identifying spatial vulnerability hotspots. Regression and ensemble-based machine learning models forecast spring discharge rates with precision using historical data on climate and land-use changes, as well as hydrological parameters, considering both natural and human-influenced environmental scenarios. Yang and co-authors highlight that these forecasts support proactive decision-making regarding water management, resource allocation, and contingency planning for the associated socio-economic activity and water resource scenarios. The potential of deep learning techniques is best exemplified by hybrid CNN-LSTM models combined with GIS and remote sensing, which capture the spatial patterns and temporal trends of spring water movements. For example, NDWI and NDVI satellite-derived modified environmental index-based spatial analyses classified satellite environment disturbances within the spring's recharge zone delineation, greatly improving the region's conservation and management practice [6]. The conservation strategy is further refined through delineation of the recharge area, contamination risk area, and priority conservation area using GIS, remote sensing, and spatial statistics. Spatially optimized strategies enable targeted interventions in afforestation, controlled grazing, and erosion control, which greatly reduce sedimentation, enhance groundwater recharge, and improve the quality and availability of spring water. The success of spring conservation through spatial optimization depends significantly on the quality and variety of input spatial datasets. Table **2** lists prominent data sources, their utility in spring resource mapping and modeling, and relevant use cases.

Table 2. Key spatial datasets and remote sensing platforms used in spring water conservation, including their respective applications and cited use cases.

Data Source	Water Management Use	References / Use Case
Landsat 8	Mapping seasonal variation of surface water extent	[60]
Sentinel-2 MSI	Spring recharge risk and vegetation stress assessment	[61]
MODIS Terra/Aqua	Monitoring algal blooms and thermal loading	[7]
ASTER DEM	Slope analysis and spring discharge modeling	[62]

(Table 2) cont.....

Data Source	Water Management Use	References / Use Case
SRTM DEM	Watershed boundary and infiltration zoning	[63]
NDVI	Vegetation health and groundwater recharge indication	[64]
NDWI	Surface water detection in ephemeral systems	[65]
Land Use/Land Cover (LULC)	Change detection and land-use impact on springs	[7]
Hydrogeological Maps	Identifying aquifer recharge zones and faults	[66]
Soil Maps	Soil permeability and runoff zone mapping	[67]
Rainfall Isoline Maps	Identifying orographic rainfall patterns	[68]
Groundwater Contour Maps	Detecting groundwater flow direction	[69]
UAV Imagery	High-resolution spring mouth detection and terrain	[70]
GPS Field Surveys	Geo-tagging of recharge structures and surveys	[71]
Mobile GIS Apps	Citizen science-based spring vulnerability reporting	[72]

Policy and Institutional Frameworks

The lack of robust spring ecosystem policies, coupled with bare minimum institutional arrangements, severely limits proper spring conservation strategies. Policies should account for the integral sociocultural, economic, and biological values of springs and their resources while applying IWRM and actively participating in the sustainment and governance at the community-based adaptive governance level. It is necessary to have legislation to protect groundwater recharge areas, ensure sustainable water extraction, control pollution, and promote integrated land-use management. Successful policies include establishing buffer protection zones around spring recharge areas, controlling access to harmful practices, and promoting sustainable agriculture and forestry that conserves groundwater. India's National Water Policy and Nepal's Springshed Management Framework are examples of policies with clear community participation, spatial dynamics, multi-level governance, and monitoring frameworks for springshed water resource conservation in sensitive mountain ecosystems. Setting up dedicated spring management units or community-based oversight and monitoring committees increases coordinated management efforts, enabling control and enforcement. Stakeholder education and institutional capacity are building support for sustainable spring conservation by enhancing management skills and technical know-how aligned with predefined goals.

Global Best Practices and Case Studies

Across the globe, exemplary spring conservation programs feature community engagement, optimized land and resource use, advanced planning technology, and strong policy frameworks. Some of these are as follows:

India (Himalayan Springshed Management): The participatory hydrological monitoring and recharge mapping system, along with its spatial policy and enforcement measures, improved spring discharge and quality, benefiting communities surrounding the spring.

East Africa (Kenya, Tanzania): Community-led initiatives that employ participatory GIS and mobile-based monitoring systems have enhanced spring protection and groundwater recharge, enabling water security in semi-arid areas.

Mexico (Sierra Gorda Biosphere Reserve): The reforestation and erosion-control projects aimed at improving spring recharge and water quality were spatially guided by GIS-based vulnerability mapping.

These examples demonstrate the efficacy of integrated, flexible, and adaptive approaches to community engagement, which guide sustainable planning and predictive modeling for spring management.

Challenges and Future Directions

Even with the improvement, many challenges remain, including a lack of data, low technical capacity, policy enforcement, and socio-economic factors. Future approaches should focus on these gaps through better investment in monitoring systems, policy enforcement, and stakeholder engagement initiatives. The development of machine learning tools and spatial optimization tools offers high promise for increasing predictive accuracy, management precision, and conservation adaptability. Conducting more research that combines IoT monitoring networks with real-time predictive analytics, cloud computing, and spatial ML models will improve conservation effectiveness by enabling timely intervention and adaptive management strategies. As a final note, spring conservation is best achieved through sustainable multi-faceted community involvement, advanced technologies, spatial intelligence, and policy action. By integrating machine learning and spatial optimization techniques, communities can actively and sustainably manage springs while dealing with challenges to the ecological integrity, water availability, and community health on a global scale.

CASE STUDIES ON WATER RESOURCE MANAGEMENT

Different contexts around the world have demonstrated the application of machine learning (ML) and spatial optimization to water resource management. The subject is further explained by presenting representative case studies thatuse more sophisticated predictive modeling and spatial analysis to illustrate the approach's benefits, numerous adaptive applications, and the results achieved. Table **3** presents a cross-section of global case studies that highlight the diverse integration of ML and spatial methods in water resource management, reinforcing their global relevance and adaptability.

Table 3. Selected global case studies applying machine learning and spatial optimization for water resource monitoring, modeling, and decision-making.

Region / Site	Methodology	Outcome / Impact	Reference
Nakdong River, South Korea	CNN-LSTM hybrid for TN/TP prediction	Forecast accuracy improved by 30%; real-time dam decisions.	[6]
Beilun Estuary, China	CNN-LSTM with Attention	Preserved mangrove zones through advanced water quality forecasts.	[11]
Langat River, Malaysia	XGBoost + GIS + LULC layers	Enabled regulatory zoning; reduced runoff pollution.	[7]
Himalayan Springs (India)	Random Forest + DEM + NDVI	Spring flow stabilized; recharge structures built at scale.	[73]
Georgia River Watersheds, USA	LSTM with ensemble normalizers	95%+ accuracy in pH, DO across five seasons.	[7]
Sierra Gorda, Mexico	GIS-based spring zone prioritization	Targeted afforestation efforts reduced sedimentation.	[74]
Loire Basin, France	Rainfall-runoff modeling + PCA + RF	Climate scenario simulation for adaptive water management.	[75]
Lake Taihu, China	Algal bloom prediction with CNN	Prevention alerts issued; eutrophication managed.	[76]
Victoria Lake, Uganda	Waterborne contamination mapping + SVR	Rural health improved through safe drinking predictions.	[77]
Ganga Basin, India	CNN-LSTM + community-based monitoring integration	Participatory science and DL co-developed monitoring tools.	[78]

Case Study 1: Nakdong River Basin, South Korea

As one of the largest and most economically important watersheds in South Korea, the Nakdong River Basin (NRB) serves as an example of advanced techniques that apply machine learning and spatial optimization. Encompassing roughly 23,817 km^2, the NRB is composed of areas of industry, agriculture, and urbanization. Such complexity required innovative management strategies [6]. A hybrid CNN-LSTM model was developed and applied to forecast water levels and other water quality parameters, including total nitrogen (TN), total phosphorus (TP), and total organic carbon (TOC). The geographically configured radar rainfall and hydrological data were incorporated into the CNN model, allowing it to capture local rainfall-runoff interactions. At the same time, temporal changes in water quality were modeled using the LSTM architecture, driven by intricate interrelationships among land use, weather, and human activity patterns [6]. The incorporation of the CNN-LSTM approach resulted in significant improvements to predictive accuracy, with NSE values consistently exceeding 0.75, portraying exceptional performance. This methodology assisted in the multi-objective proactive control of dams and hydraulic infrastructure and systems essential for flood control, water supply, and ecological flows. With the addition of spatially explicit predictive modeling, resource management capabilities at these regional authorities increased, enhancing the optimization of reservoir operations, environmental flow management, and pollution mitigation.

Case Study 2: Beilun Estuary, China

Located in Guangxi, China, the Beilun Estuary is an important mangrove ecosystem and biodiversity hotspot, and a prime example of advanced ML-based approaches for predicting water quality. Biodiversity and ecological health of mangrove ecosystems are heavily reliant on consistent water quality, specifically the concentration of ammonia nitrogen (NH_3-N) and pH [11]. The researchers utilized sophisticated hybrid models that combine CNNs and LSTMs with an attention mechanism to provide more accurate predictions of essential water quality parameters. A study [11] noted that the hybrid CNN-LSTM architecture extracted spatial features of water quality parameters and meteorological data (rainfall, temperature, and atmospheric pressure) extracted on a broad scale and later used LSTM to model temporal dynamics. Attention mechanisms further enhanced overall predictive accuracy by adaptively spotlighting specific time slices of data necessary for better predictions. Unlike traditional statistical or singular ML methods, this novel approach achieved stable and precise predictions with lower root mean square error (RMSE) and mean absolute error (MAE) metrics. Accurate predictions helped enable active conservation and management measures, greatly enhancing the preservation and ecological health of the mangrove ecosystem. Yang and his team published their findings in 2021 [11].

Case Study 3: Georgia Watersheds, USA

The implementation of LSTM networks in the watersheds of Georgia, USA, is a clear example demonstrating the ability of ML models to predict surface water quality under different environmental conditions. The researchers developed the LSTM model in combination with normalization techniques (LSTM-CN) to predict water quality parameters pH and DO at several monitoring stations [7]. The LSTM-CN model employed multi-factor normalization techniques, including z-score, interval normalization, and max normalization, to preprocess the heterogeneous and noisy environmental dataset. The model's ability to capture intricate temporal dependencies among water quality constituents and meteorological parameters (temperature, specific conductance, DO) yielded unmatched performance, with accuracy, precision, and recall exceeding 95%. The efficient execution of LSTM-CN enhanced real-time monitoring and management of water quality. It also facilitated the creation of critical forecasts necessary for managing pollution incidents, resource distribution, and water security. This case demonstrates the efficacy of advanced ML models for regional water resource management.

Case Study 4: Himalayan Springshed Management, India

The Indian Himalayan region offers an exceptional example of spatial optimization of spring water and machine learning applications for spring water conservation. Springs serve as a major water source for rural populations in the Himalayas, but their storage capacity is severely diminished by climate change, overuse, and poor land management practices. The Integrated Springshed Management Programs (ISMPs) that incorporate Participatory GIS (P-GIS) and spatial analysis alongside machine-learning predictive modeling have been responsible for greater spring recharge and water availability.

Spatial optimization through GIS has identified vulnerability maps and critical recharge areas. Random Forest and XGBoost algorithms were employed as machine-learning models to predict spring discharge rates, estimate changeover time for assessing the magnitude of discharge decline due to resource depletion, and evaluate vulnerability to climate-change–related stress. The resulting insights were used to inform recharge-enhancement measures, including afforestation, soil conservation, and contour trenching. Furthermore, community participation enhanced the project's sustainability by equipping the communities with the technical know-how to make informed and spatially aware decisions. These improvements raised the level of water security and community resilience.

Case Study 5: Langat River Basin, Malaysia

Located in Malaysia, the Langat River Basin is an urbanizing area that combines remote sensing, machine learning (ML), and spatial optimization to model and monitor the quality of urban river water. Ensemble ML techniques using Random Forest and XGBoost were applied to spatial data, derived from remote sensing, to predict nutrient loadings, turbidity, and contamination episodes stemming from urban sprawl, agricultural, and industrial activities [79]. Stratum NDWI and NDVI gave rise to GIS-based land use models that combined with remote sensing for spatial optimization. Predictive modeling, together with the above methods, was successful at locating pollution source areas, runoff pathways, and management zones that required intervention. Proactive solutions, such as targeted remediation, pollution control, sustainable land use, and other practices, enabled significant mitigation of the river's degradation. The health of the ecosystem flourished as a consequence of improved water quality.

Case Study 6: Lake Taihu, China (Eutrophication Management)

The eutrophication of Lake Tauhu, China's third-largest freshwater lake, is fueled by urban expansion, agricultural runoff, and industrial waste. Contemporary ML technologies, such as satellite data with chlorophyll and turbidity indices, were integrated into a spatial model using a CNN for HABs and nutrient-ading trend prediction [80]. Pollution source zones and priority remediation areas were accurately determined through GIS-based hotspot analysis and spatial regression. Management practices were greatly improved with the addition of proactive processes such as nutrient control, pollution cleanup, ecosystem restoration, and others to mitigate damage to water quality and ecological eutrophication whilst promoting stronger ecological health, which boosted water quality and reduced eutrophication risks.

Learnings from Global Experiences

All these different global case studies provide important lessons for ML and spatial optimization applications in water resource management. There are common challenges of data availability, data quality issues, lack of technical capacity, and institutional barriers to effective implementation. Lessons focus on the ability to capture and actively engage stakeholders, as well as on the development of adequate policies, fostering, and monitoring support systems to enable effective utilization of ML-based spatial analyses. Emerging technological innovations, such as real-time sensor networks, IoT, and cloud solutions, provide enhanced responsiveness, adaptability, and accuracy that must be adopted in future water resource management. Moreover, the increasing focus on explainable AI (XAI), predictive models' transparency, and participatory spatial planning would improve sustainable outcomes and policy acceptance. Global experiences offer powerful evidence of the adaptability and benefits that ML models and spatial optimization methods bring to water resource management. Continued innovation and investment will be necessary within an integrated management approach to ensure a sustainable water resource, ecological health, and community resilience.

DISCUSSION AND POLICY IMPLICATIONS

The combination of machine learning (ML) models with spatial optimization techniques was and remains one of the most sophisticated approaches to water resource management, as evidenced by global case studies. This case study on water resource management emphasizes the most noteworthy, practical, and essential policy lessons that can be drawn from the extensive application of these tools across diverse hydrological settings.

Insights from Machine Learning Applications in Water Management

Machine learning methods ranging from regression techniques to Convolutional Neural Networks (CNN) as well as Long Short-Term Memory (LSTM) networks have greatly improved water resource management in terms of predictive accuracy, reliability, and adaptability. Regression-based forecasting models, along with ensemble methods such as Random Forest and XGBoost, are computationally inexpensive, interpretable, and flexible, helping meet a range of predictive needs for varying Water Quality Indices (WQIs) of water bodies subject to different anthropogenic and environmental pressures [7]. However, their inability to capture complex spatio-temporal patterns is a challenge that needs to be addressed with more advanced methods. Deep learning approaches, especially CNN and hybrid CNN-LSTM models, have shown significant improvements in accuracy for predictive tasks because of their inherent capability to process simultaneously occurring dynamic and spatially structured datasets [6, 11]. The extraction of spatial features from satellite images, radar rainfall data, and other hydrological variables prepares them for forecasting surface water quality using CNN models. Attention-enhanced LSTM networks further improve temporal predictions by focusing on the most relevant parts of the available history, thereby improving the prediction accuracy of complex systems in hydrological forecasting. The spatially integrated machine learning approaches alongside GIS and remote sensing form a subset of predictive modeling that diverges from conventional machine learning techniques by augmenting capabilities for resource mapping, vulnerability evaluation, and targeted intervention planning. The application of these methodologies enhances proactive water management by enabling timely responses, efficient resource allocation, and sustainable implementation of conservation measures on a global scale across water systems. Hydrologists are now applying these same algorithmic and spatial planning paradigms beyond hydrology. For instance, a study [22] integrated XGBoost-based prediction with GIS mapping to deliver real-time air-quality forecasts in Kryvyi Rih, Ukraine, demonstrating the versatility of ML and spatial frameworks across environmental domains.

Policy Recommendations and Implications

The enhanced efficiency of machine learning with spatial optimization approaches opens up new avenues in policy and adds focus to integrating these technological advancements into effective, sustainable management approaches [81].

Strengthening Institutional Capacity and Technical Infrastructure

Policies should pay particular attention to enhancing institutional capacity and technical infrastructure for the implementation of advanced ML and spatial optimization techniques [82]. Investing in monitoring frameworks such as sensor networks, remote sensing systems, and cloud computing services requires particular attention to the maintenance of comprehensive databases, which are a precondition for accurate and reliable predictive modeling. Building analytical skill sets such as data analytics, ML model building, spatial analysis, and GIS application has a significant impact on fostering sustainable technical expertise.

Integrated Management Frameworks and Adaptive Governance

Incorporating ML and spatial optimization algorithms into IWRM systems creates smart IWRM, enabling cohesion and control for multidimensional resource management. Policies need to endorse intra-sectoral integration to foster collaboration among hydrologists, data scientists, policymakers, and other members of the local community [83]. Support for adaptive governance that can cope with dynamically predictable, ever-changing environmental operational conditions enhances the functional effectiveness of management practices using ML.

Community-based Management and Stakeholder Engagement

Policies at this level should balance strategically designed community engagement and stakeholder participation frameworks to empower community involvement at all levels of monitoring, decision-making, and management activities. The use of mobile technologies, participatory GIS, and machine learning (ML)-based forecasting empowers community-based management initiatives, strengthens local resource and environmental management, and enhances community resilience. Supporting policies should establish guides for facilitating the structuring of management systems and the empowerment of communities to control knowledge creation and adaptive governance.

Enhancing Transparency and Model Interpretability

Stakeholder acceptability, policy choice, and the sustainability of management outcomes hinge strongly on the transparency and interpretability of predictive models. Under policy options promoting the integration of explainable artificial intelligence (XAI), such as SHapley Additive ExPlanations (SHAP) and LIME, model transparency is improved, where decisions made by models and the correlations demonstrated by the data are elucidated to stakeholders. Stakeholder trust and compliance are strengthened through transparent predictive analytics and informed decision-making, supporting effective resource management.

Regulatory Frameworks and Enforcement Mechanisms

Conceptual integration of machine learning requires perimeter policies and mechanical enforcement frameworks to be active. Policies specifying vertical and horizontal protection, critical subsurface extraction area pollution control, elaborated constraints, and sustained growth ensure eco-integrated land-use development. Advanced guarding processes with real-time surveillance and predictive, data-driven monitoring ensure ecosystem management and informed decision-making opportunities, which are sustained and enhanced through maintenance tools and outcome evaluation mechanisms. New research avenues involve advanced development of methods within the scope of spatial optimization driven by machine learning algorithms. Integrated Internet of Things systems and terminal computing, coupled with real-time interface interaction cloud platforms, create new horizons in predictive maintenance estimation for machine-assisted management supervision and interactivity. Proactive management of managed resources can be achieved when responsive, active foresight construction systems with spatial data algorithms and artificial intelligence learning modules are designed.

Integration of Technology and Hybrid Modeling

Further research into hybrid ML architectures, which include CNNs, LSTMs, attention models, reinforcement learning, autoencoders, and transfer learning, will continue to improve the capabilities of predictive models. The adaptability, accuracy, and robustness of these models can be further improved through advanced spatial analytical methods, real-time monitoring technologies, and data fusion techniques, which aid in resolving complicated problems in environmental management. Optimizing data integration, interoperability, and accessibility fully realizes the predictive model's efficiency. Policies that promote collaborative efforts, such as open data initiatives with standardized data protocols and cloud data-sharing platforms, enhance model calibration and decision-making. Acquiring comprehensive, standardized data across the spatial-temporal axes greatly improves predictive performance for implementing advanced management systems. Water sustainability research is best tackled with ML approaches coupled with spatial optimization and bounding boxes, which call for more work in climate scenario modeling, climate impact predictive assessments, and adaptive resilience assessments powered by machine learning forecasts. Policies that facilitate adaptive management and climate resilience significantly enhance water security, ecological balance, and community resilience. By incorporating machine learning algorithms with optimization techniques in spatial structures, new frontiers are opened in the management of water resources, sharpening tools for analysis and their practical application, as well as forecasting and spatial comprehension. Strong policy measures combined with the consolidation of institutions and community control, along with continued advances in technology, will be needed to effectively apply these sophisticated methodologies into sustainable, anticipatory, and adaptive approaches to water management at the global level.

CONCLUSION

The combination of machine learning (ML) and spatial optimization enhances comprehensive water resource management by improving prediction accuracy and enabling more effective resource planning. Algorithms such as Convolutional Neural Networks (CNNs) and Long Short-term Memory (LSTMs) provide more reliable predictions of water quality and supply at both spatial and temporal scales. Geographic Information Systems (GIS) and remote sensing strengthen the monitoring and management capacity offered by machine learning. Hybrid ML models also improve predictions based on the variance among individual predictions. Case studies globally, including those in South Korea and China, have demonstrated considerably better real-time management of water quality. Nevertheless, issues remain related to data quality, granularity, and model interpretability. Future research directions should focus on developing improved hybrid models based on explainable AI (XAI) frameworks and on addressing process gaps through better monitoring. Policies should be developed to enhance institutional capacity for these technologies while increasing communities' engagement in and support for institutionally integrated management processes. Overall, integrating machine learning and optimization provides a sustainable, proactive approach to water resource management that will be essential for future generations to maintain ecological balance while ensuring water security.

ACKNOWLEDGEMENTS

The authors would like to clarify that no external funding was received for the compilation and publication of this chapter. We extend our sincere thanks to the academic institutions for their support and to the researchers whose previous works contributed to the development of this synthesis. Additionally, we appreciate the reviewers' and editors' valuable comments and suggestions, which significantly enhanced the quality of this manuscript.

REFERENCES

[1] R. Choudhary, L. K. Bharadwaj, T. N. Tan, M. Choudhury, D. Sharma, P. Rath, V. Vambol, S. Vambol, S. Majumdar, A. Kumar, and K. T. T. Amesho, "Spatial intelligence integration in smart wastewater systems: Advancing efficiency and sustainability in urban sewer networks," in *Smart Wastewater Systems and Climate Change: Innovations Through Spatial Intelligence*, M. Choudhury, S. Majumdar, S. Goswami, and M. Sillanpää, Eds., vol. 15. Cambridge, UK: Royal Society of Chemistry, 2025, pp. 28–41. [http://dx.doi.org/10.1039/9781837676880-00028]

[2] S. Tripathi, S. Agarwal, R. Choudhary, M. Choudhury, N. Padoin, E. D. van Hullebusch, G. Kaushik, A. Kumar, and S. Majumdar, "Strengthening disaster resilience: Emergency response strategies in wastewater management," in *Smart Wastewater Systems and Climate Change: Innovations Through Spatial Intelligence*, M. Choudhury, S. Majumdar, S. Goswami, and M. Sillanpää, Eds., vol. 15. Cambridge, U.K.: Royal Society of Chemistry, 2025, ch. 10, pp. 135–154. [http://dx.doi.org/10.1039/9781837676880-00135]

[3] V. Bredun, R. Choudhary, and A. Kumar, "Regional specifics of using community bins in waste management: A case study of rural communities in poltava region (Ukraine)", *Trends in Ecological and Indoor Environmental Engineering,* vol. 2, no. 4, pp. 10-17, 2024. [http://dx.doi.org/10.62622/TEIEE.024.2.4.10-17]

[4] S. Singh, K. Mishra, R. Chavan, and H. L. Tiwari, "Advancements and challenges in hydrological modeling: A comprehensive review," in *Hydrology and Hydrologic Modelling*, M. Pandey, N. Umamahesh, J. Das, and J. H. Pu, Eds., vol. 410, Lecture Notes in Civil Engineering, Singapore: Springer, 2025, pp. 423–442. [http://dx.doi.org/10.1007/978-981-97-7474-6_32]

[5] R. Choudhary, A. Kumar, S. Narayan, I. Mishchenko, M. Choudhury, L.K. Bhardwaj, A. Ahmad, M. Andrienko, P. Gaman, and O. Boiko, "Integrating fuzzy logic into life cycle assessment for sustainable municipal solid waste management in Metro Cities", *Ecological Engineering & Environmental Technology,* vol. 26, no. 7, pp. 316-331, 2025. [http://dx.doi.org/10.12912/27197050/205500]

[6] S.S. Baek, J. Pyo, and J.A. Chun, "Prediction of water level and water quality using a CNN-LSTM combined deep learning approach", *Water,* vol. 12, no. 12, p. 3399, 2020. [http://dx.doi.org/10.3390/w12123399]

[7] N. Mahesh, J.J. Babu, K. Nithya, and S.A. Arunmozhi, "Water quality prediction using LSTM with combined normalizer for efficient water management", *Desalination Water Treat.,* vol. 317, p. 100183, 2024. [http://dx.doi.org/10.1016/j.dwt.2024.100183]

[8] R. Choudhary, S. Kumari, A. Kumar, P. Kumar, M. Choudhury, D. Sharma, U. Chadha, P. R. Chowdhury, M. Herlekar, and M. Sillanpää, "Optimizing wastewater management through geospatial analysis," in *Smart Wastewater Systems and Climate Change: Innovations Through Spatial Intelligence*, M. Choudhury, S. Majumdar, S. Goswami, and M. Sillanpää, Eds., vol. 15. Cambridge, U.K.: Royal Society of Chemistry, 2025, ch. 6, pp. 72–87.

[http://dx.doi.org/10.1039/9781837676880-00072]

[9] M. Choudhury, R. Choudhary, D. Sharma, B. Bhattacharjee, S. Majumdar, S. Chegini, A. Kumar, S. Kumari, and E. D. van Hullebusch, “Building resilience in wastewater management: Disaster preparedness and emergency response strategies,” in *Smart Wastewater Systems and Climate Change: Innovations Through Spatial Intelligence*, M. Choudhury, S. Majumdar, S. Goswami, and M. Sillanpää, Eds., vol. 15. Cambridge, U.K.: Royal Society of Chemistry, 2025, ch. 11, pp. 155–169. [http://dx.doi.org/10.1039/9781837676880-00155]

[10] K.K. Singh, and A.E. Frazier, "A meta-analysis and review of unmanned aircraft system (UAS) imagery for terrestrial applications", *Int. J. Remote Sens.,* vol. 39, no. 15-16, pp. 5078-5098, 2018. [http://dx.doi.org/10.1080/01431161.2017.1420941]

[11] Y. Yang, Q. Xiong, C. Wu, Q. Zou, Y. Yu, H. Yi, and M. Gao, "A study on water quality prediction by a hybrid CNN-LSTM model with attention mechanism", *Environ. Sci. Pollut. Res. Int.,* vol. 28, no. 39, pp. 55129-55139, 2021. [http://dx.doi.org/10.1007/s11356-021-14687-8] [PMID: 34129164]

[12] A.L. Schaffer, T.A. Dobbins, and S.A. Pearson, "Interrupted time series analysis using autoregressive integrated moving average (ARIMA) models: a guide for evaluating large-scale health interventions", *BMC Med. Res. Methodol.,* vol. 21, no. 1, p. 58, 2021. [http://dx.doi.org/10.1186/s12874-021-01235-8] [PMID: 33752604]

[13] K.P. Wai, M.Y. Chia, C.H. Koo, Y.F. Huang, and W.C. Chong, "Applications of deep learning in water quality management: A state-of-the-art review", *J. Hydrol. (Amst.),* vol. 613, p. 128332, 2022. [http://dx.doi.org/10.1016/j.jhydrol.2022.128332]

[14] W. Li, Y. Zhao, Y. Zhu, Z. Dong, F. Wang, and F. Huang, "Research progress in water quality prediction based on deep learning technology: a review", *Environ. Sci. Pollut. Res. Int.,* vol. 31, no. 18, pp. 26415-26431, 2024. [http://dx.doi.org/10.1007/s11356-024-33058-7] [PMID: 38538994]

[15] L. See, and S. Openshaw, "A hybrid multi-model approach to river level forecasting", *Hydrol. Sci. J.,* vol. 45, no. 4, pp. 523-536, 2000. [http://dx.doi.org/10.1080/02626660009492354]

[16] S. Hu, E. Corry, E. Curry, W.J.N. Turner, and J. O’Donnell, "Building performance optimisation: A hybrid architecture for the integration of contextual information and time-series data", *Autom. Construct.,* vol. 70, pp. 51-61, 2016. [http://dx.doi.org/10.1016/j.autcon.2016.05.018]

[17] R. Verma, and P. Jamwal, "Sustenance of Himalayan springs in an emerging water crisis", *Environ. Monit. Assess.,* vol. 194, no. 2, p. 87, 2022. [http://dx.doi.org/10.1007/s10661-021-09731-6] [PMID: 35020087]

[18] C.M. Caudill, P.L. Pulsifer, R.V. Thumbadoo, and D.R.F. Taylor, "Meeting the challenges of the un sustainable development goals through holistic systems thinking and applied geospatial ethics", *ISPRS Int. J. Geoinf.,* vol. 13, no. 4, p. 110, 2024. [http://dx.doi.org/10.3390/ijgi13040110]

[19] M.G. Zamani, M.R. Nikoo, G. Al-Rawas, R. Nazari, D. Rastad, and A.H. Gandomi, "Hybrid WT–CNN–GRU-based model for the estimation of reservoir water quality variables considering spatio-temporal features", *J. Environ. Manage.,* vol. 358, p. 120756, 2024. [http://dx.doi.org/10.1016/j.jenvman.2024.120756] [PMID: 38599080]

[20] Y. Liu, Y. Zhang, Q. Cheng, J. Feng, M. Chun Chao, and J. Yeu Tsou, "Mangrove monitoring and change analysis with landsat images: A case study in pearl river estuary (china)", *Ecol. Indic.,* vol. 160, p. 111763, 2024. [http://dx.doi.org/10.1016/j.ecolind.2024.111763]

[21] P. Roy Chowdhury, S. Goswami, R. Choudhary, and M. Choudhury, “Electronic wastes, its impact on wildlife and biodiversity,” in *Electronic Waste*, 1st ed., CRC Press, 2025, pp. 65-71.

[http://dx.doi.org/10.1201/9781003582311-8]

[22] M. Halaktionov, V. Bredun, R. Choudhary, M. Goroneskul, A. Kumar, F. Ouiya, V. Sydorenko, and L. Markina, "AI-Enhanced air quality assessment and prediction in industrial cities: A case study of Kryvyi Rih, Ukraine", *Ecological Engineering & Environmental Technology,* vol. 26, no. 6, pp. 45-56, 2025.
[http://dx.doi.org/10.12912/27197050/203725]

[23] X. Wang, and H. Xie, "A review on applications of remote sensing and geographic information systems (GIS) in water resources and flood risk management", *Water,* vol. 10, no. 5, p. 608, 2018.
[http://dx.doi.org/10.3390/w10050608]

[24] G.E. Adjovu, H. Stephen, D. James, and S. Ahmad, "Measurement of total dissolved solids and total suspended solids in water systems: A review of the issues, conventional, and remote sensing techniques", *Remote Sens. (Basel),* vol. 15, no. 14, p. 3534, 2023.
[http://dx.doi.org/10.3390/rs15143534]

[25] M. Daud, F.M. Ugliotti, and A. Osello, "Comprehensive analysis of the use of web-gis for natural hazard management: A systematic review", *Sustainability (Basel),* vol. 16, no. 10, p. 4238, 2024.
[http://dx.doi.org/10.3390/su16104238]

[26] R. Yang, H. Liu, and Y. Li, "Quantifying uncertainty of marine water quality forecasts for environmental management using a dynamic multi-factor analysis and multi-resolution ensemble approach", *Chemosphere,* vol. 331, p. 138831, 2023.
[http://dx.doi.org/10.1016/j.chemosphere.2023.138831] [PMID: 37137396]

[27] R.R. Murphy, F.C. Curriero, and W.P. Ball, "Comparison of spatial interpolation methods for water quality evaluation in the chesapeake bay", *J. Environ. Eng.,* vol. 136, no. 2, pp. 160-171, 2010.
[http://dx.doi.org/10.1061/(ASCE)EE.1943-7870.0000121]

[28] S. Brown, V.L. Versace, L. Laurenson, D. Ierodiaconou, J. Fawcett, and S. Salzman, "Assessment of spatiotemporal varying relationships between rainfall, land cover and surface water area using geographically weighted regression", *Environ. Model. Assess.,* vol. 17, no. 3, pp. 241-254, 2012.
[http://dx.doi.org/10.1007/s10666-011-9289-8]

[29] J. Wu, Z. Feng, Y. Gao, and J. Peng, "Hotspot and relationship identification in multiple landscape services: A case study on an area with intensive human activities", *Ecol. Indic.,* vol. 29, pp. 529-537, 2013.
[http://dx.doi.org/10.1016/j.ecolind.2013.01.037]

[30] G. Dong, Z. Hu, X. Liu, Y. Fu, and W. Zhang, "Spatio-temporal variation of total nitrogen and ammonia nitrogen in the water source of the middle route of the south-to-north water diversion project", *Water,* vol. 12, no. 9, p. 2615, 2020.
[http://dx.doi.org/10.3390/w12092615]

[31] A. Tascikaraoglu, "Evaluation of spatio-temporal forecasting methods in various smart city applications", *Renew. Sustain. Energy Rev.,* vol. 82, pp. 424-435, 2018.
[http://dx.doi.org/10.1016/j.rser.2017.09.078]

[32] C. Yang, M. Yu, F. Hu, Y. Jiang, and Y. Li, "Utilizing cloud computing to address big geospatial data challenges", *Comput. Environ. Urban Syst.,* vol. 61, pp. 120-128, 2017.
[http://dx.doi.org/10.1016/j.compenvurbsys.2016.10.010]

[33] D. Li, Z. Qi, Y. Zhou, and M. Elchalakani, "Machine learning applications in building energy systems: Review and prospects", *Buildings,* vol. 15, no. 4, p. 648, 2025.
[http://dx.doi.org/10.3390/buildings15040648]

[34] L.J. Slater, L. Arnal, M-A. Boucher, A.Y-Y. Chang, S. Moulds, C. Murphy, G. Nearing, G. Shalev, C. Shen, L. Speight, G. Villarini, R.L. Wilby, A. Wood, and M. Zappa, "Hybrid forecasting: blending climate predictions with AI models", *Hydrol. Earth Syst. Sci.,* vol. 27, no. 9, pp. 1865-1889, 2023.
[http://dx.doi.org/10.5194/hess-27-1865-2023]

[35] H.M. Alshahrani, F.N. Al-Wesabi, M. Al Duhayyim, N. Nemri, S. Kadry, and B.A.Y. Alqaralleh, "An automated deep learning based satellite imagery analysis for ecology management", *Ecol. Inform.*, vol. 66, p. 101452, 2021.
[http://dx.doi.org/10.1016/j.ecoinf.2021.101452]

[36] W. Zhang, Y. Peng, L. Zhang, X. Li, and Q. Zhang, "Simultaneous partial nitritation and denitritation coupled with polished anammox for advanced nitrogen removal from low C/N domestic wastewater at low dissolved oxygen conditions", *Bioresour. Technol.*, vol. 305, p. 123045, 2020.
[http://dx.doi.org/10.1016/j.biortech.2020.123045] [PMID: 32105845]

[37] A. Mokhtar, A. Elbeltagi, Y. Gyasi-Agyei, N. Al-Ansari, and M.K. Abdel-Fattah, "Prediction of irrigation water quality indices based on machine learning and regression models", *Appl. Water Sci.*, vol. 12, no. 4, p. 76, 2022.
[http://dx.doi.org/10.1007/s13201-022-01590-x]

[38] K.P. Singh, S. Gupta, A. Kumar, and S.P. Shukla, "Linear and nonlinear modeling approaches for urban air quality prediction", *Sci. Total Environ.*, vol. 426, pp. 244-255, 2012.
[http://dx.doi.org/10.1016/j.scitotenv.2012.03.076] [PMID: 22542239]

[39] A. Pantazopoulos, and M. Maragoudakis, "Sports & nutrition data science using gradient boosting machines", In: *Proceedings of the 10th Hellenic Conference on Artificial Intelligence* ACM: New York, NY, USA, 2018, pp. 1-7.
[http://dx.doi.org/10.1145/3200947.3201060]

[40] J. Thongkam, G. Xu, and Y. Zhang, "AdaBoost algorithm with random forests for predicting breast cancer survivability", In: *2008 IEEE International Joint Conference on Neural Networks (IEEE World Congress on Computational Intelligence)* IEEE, 2008, pp. 3062-3069.
[http://dx.doi.org/10.1109/IJCNN.2008.4634231]

[41] M.A.A. Mehedi, M. Khosravi, M.M.S. Yazdan, and H. Shabanian, "Exploring temporal dynamics of river discharge using univariate long short-term memory (LSTM) recurrent neural network at east branch of delaware river", *Hydrology,* vol. 9, no. 11, p. 202, 2022.
[http://dx.doi.org/10.3390/hydrology9110202]

[42] M.G. Zamani, M.R. Nikoo, D. Rastad, and B. Nematollahi, "A comparative study of data-driven models for runoff, sediment, and nitrate forecasting", *J. Environ. Manage.*, vol. 341, p. 118006, 2023.
[http://dx.doi.org/10.1016/j.jenvman.2023.118006] [PMID: 37163836]

[43] R. Al-Hajj, A. Assi, and M. M. Fouad, "Multi-level stacking of long short term memory recurrent models for time series forecasting of solar radiation," in *2021 10th International Conference on Renewable Energy Research and Applications (ICRERA)*, Istanbul, Turkey, 2021, pp. 71–76.
[http://dx.doi.org/10.1109/ICRERA52334.2021.9598652]

[44] H. Li, X. Li, D. Song, J. Nie, and S. Liang, "Prediction on daily spatial distribution of chlorophyll-a in coastal seas using a synthetic method of remote sensing, machine learning and numerical modeling", *Sci. Total Environ.*, vol. 910, p. 168642, 2024.
[http://dx.doi.org/10.1016/j.scitotenv.2023.168642] [PMID: 37992824]

[45] A.O. Ige, and M. Sibiya, "State-of-the-art in 1D convolutional neural networks: A survey", *IEEE Access,* vol. 12, pp. 144082-144105, 2024.
[http://dx.doi.org/10.1109/ACCESS.2024.3433513]

[46] D. Pan, Y. Zhang, Y. Deng, J. Van Griensven Thé, S.X. Yang, and B. Gharabaghi, "Dissolved oxygen forecasting for lake erie's central basin using hybrid long short-term memory and gated recurrent unit networks", *Water,* vol. 16, no. 5, p. 707, 2024.
[http://dx.doi.org/10.3390/w16050707]

[47] E. Dasan, and I. Panneerselvam, "A novel dimensionality reduction approach for ECG signal *via* convolutional denoising autoencoder with LSTM", *Biomed. Signal Process. Control,* vol. 63, p. 102225, 2021.
[http://dx.doi.org/10.1016/j.bspc.2020.102225]

[48] A. Wan, Q. Chang, K. AL-Bukhaiti, and J. He, "Short-term power load forecasting for combined heat and power using CNN-LSTM enhanced by attention mechanism", *Energy,* vol. 282, p. 128274, 2023. [http://dx.doi.org/10.1016/j.energy.2023.128274]

[49] W. Ahmad, and F. Samara, "Biohydrogen production from waste materials: Mini-review", *Trends in Ecological and Indoor Environmental Engineering,* vol. 1, no. 1, pp. 16-23, 2023. [http://dx.doi.org/10.62622/TEIEE.023.1.1.16-23]

[50] A.U.S. Mohammad, "Unveiling spatial insights: Navigating the parameters of dynamic geographic information systems (gis) analysis", *International Journal of Science and Research Archive,* vol. 11, no. 2, pp. 1976-1985, 2024. [http://dx.doi.org/10.30574/ijsra.2024.11.2.0690]

[51] H. Zhen, D. Niu, M. Yu, K. Wang, Y. Liang, and X. Xu, "A hybrid deep learning model and comparison for wind power forecasting considering temporal-spatial feature extraction", *Sustainability (Basel),* vol. 12, no. 22, p. 9490, 2020. [http://dx.doi.org/10.3390/su12229490]

[52] A. B. Sreenath, K. Dhanaraj, P. Rath, L. K. Bhardwaj, and R. Choudhary, "Waste Management and Circular Economy," in *Sustainable Chemistry and Pioneering Green Engineering Solutions*, S. Kulkarni and H. Akolkar, Eds. Hershey, PA: IGI Global Scientific Publishing, 2026, pp. 321–362. [http://dx.doi.org/10.4018/979-8-3373-1409-9.ch011]

[53] X. Wang, M. Qiao, Y. Li, A. Tavares, Q. Qiao, and Y. Liang, "Deep-learning-based water quality monitoring and early warning methods: A case study of ammonia nitrogen prediction in rivers", *Electronics (Basel),* vol. 12, no. 22, p. 4645, 2023. [http://dx.doi.org/10.3390/electronics12224645]

[54] R. Barzegar, M.T. Aalami, and J. Adamowski, "Short-term water quality variable prediction using a hybrid CNN–LSTM deep learning model", *Stochastic Environ. Res. Risk Assess.,* vol. 34, no. 2, pp. 415-433, 2020. [http://dx.doi.org/10.1007/s00477-020-01776-2]

[55] H.R. Maier, A. Jain, G.C. Dandy, and K.P. Sudheer, "Methods used for the development of neural network models for the prediction of water resource variables", *Environmental Modelling & Software,* no. 8, pp. 891-909, 2010. [http://dx.doi.org/10.1016/j.envsoft.2010.02.003]

[56] D. Wang, Y. Yuan, Y. Ben, H. Luo, and H. Guo, "Long short-term memory neural network and improved particle swarm optimization–based modeling and scenario analysis for municipal solid waste generation in Shanghai, China", *Environ. Sci. Pollut. Res. Int.,* vol. 29, no. 46, pp. 69472-69490, 2022. [http://dx.doi.org/10.1007/s11356-022-20438-0] [PMID: 35567684]

[57] F. Qian, Y. Tu, C. Hou, and B. Cao, "TLN-LSTM: an automatic modulation recognition classifier based on a two-layer nested structure of LSTM network for extremely long signal sequences", *International Journal of Web Information Systems,* vol. 20, no. 3, pp. 248-267, 2024. [http://dx.doi.org/10.1108/IJWIS-12-2023-0248]

[58] Z. Liu, Y. Qin, X. Liu, L. Yang, S. Gong, S. Zheng, X. Lin, J. Yang, T. Lu, and J. Chen, "Effects of substrate concentration and glycine betaine on nitrogen removal and microbial communities in the sulfide autotrophic denitrification and Anammox coupling system", *J. Water Process Eng.,* vol. 47, p. 102789, 2022. [http://dx.doi.org/10.1016/j.jwpe.2022.102789]

[59] V. Ranković, J. Radulović, I. Radojević, A. Ostojić, and L. Čomić, "Neural network modeling of dissolved oxygen in the Gruža reservoir, Serbia," *Ecological Modelling*, vol. 221, no. 8, pp. 1239–1244, 2010. [http://dx.doi.org/10.1016/j.ecolmodel.2009.12.023]

[60] M.G. Tulbure, M. Broich, S.V. Stehman, and A. Kommareddy, "Surface water extent dynamics from three decades of seasonally continuous Landsat time series at subcontinental scale in a semi-arid

region", *Remote Sens. Environ.,* vol. 178, pp. 142-157, 2016.
[http://dx.doi.org/10.1016/j.rse.2016.02.034]

[61] F. Maselli, L. Angeli, P. Battista, L. Fibbi, L. Gardin, R. Magno, B. Rapi, and M. Chiesi, "Evaluation of Terra/Aqua MODIS and Sentinel-2 MSI NDVI data for predicting actual evapotranspiration in Mediterranean regions", *Int. J. Remote Sens.,* vol. 41, no. 14, pp. 5186-5205, 2020.
[http://dx.doi.org/10.1080/01431161.2020.1731000]

[62] W. Wang, X. Yang, and T. Yao, "Evaluation of ASTER GDEM and SRTM and their suitability in hydraulic modelling of a glacial lake outburst flood in southeast Tibet", *Hydrol. Processes,* vol. 26, no. 2, pp. 213-225, 2012.
[http://dx.doi.org/10.1002/hyp.8127]

[63] A. Sharma, and K. N. Tiwari, "A comparative appraisal of hydrological behavior of SRTM DEM at catchment level", *J Hydrol (Amst),* vol. 519, pp. 1394-1404, 2014.
[http://dx.doi.org/10.1016/j.jhydrol.2014.08.062]

[64] E. Parizi, S.M. Hosseini, B. Ataie-Ashtiani, and C.T. Simmons, "Normalized difference vegetation index as the dominant predicting factor of groundwater recharge in phreatic aquifers: case studies across Iran", *Sci. Rep.,* vol. 10, no. 1, p. 17473, 2020.
[http://dx.doi.org/10.1038/s41598-020-74561-4] [PMID: 33060803]

[65] D. Walker, M. Smigaj, and N. Jovanovic, "Ephemeral sand river flow detection using satellite optical remote sensing", *J. Arid Environ.,* vol. 168, pp. 17-25, 2019.
[http://dx.doi.org/10.1016/j.jaridenv.2019.05.006]

[66] A.K. Saraf, P.R. Choudhury, B. Roy, B. Sarma, S. Vijay, and S. Choudhury, "GIS based surface hydrological modelling in identification of groundwater recharge zones", *Int. J. Remote Sens.,* vol. 25, no. 24, pp. 5759-5770, 2004.
[http://dx.doi.org/10.1080/0143116042000274096]

[67] L.R. Lagadec, P. Patrice, I. Braud, B. Chazelle, L. Moulin, J. Dehotin, E. Hauchard, and P. Breil, "Description and evaluation of a surface runoff susceptibility mapping method", *J. Hydrol. (Amst.),* vol. 541, pp. 495-509, 2016.
[http://dx.doi.org/10.1016/j.jhydrol.2016.05.049]

[68] R. Rotunno, and R. Ferretti, "Orographic effects on rainfall in MAP cases IOP 2b and IOP 8", *Q. J. R. Meteorol. Soc.,* vol. 129, no. 588, pp. 373-390, 2003.
[http://dx.doi.org/10.1256/qj.02.20]

[69] J. Qian, W. Wang, L. Ma, B. Dang, and X. Sun, "Identification of preferential flow paths by hydraulic tomography compared with tracer test and the groundwater contour map in coal mine water hazard area", *J. Hydrol. (Amst.),* vol. 631, p. 130816, 2024.
[http://dx.doi.org/10.1016/j.jhydrol.2024.130816]

[70] R. Bi, S. Gan, X. Yuan, R. Li, S. Gao, M. Yang, W. Luo, and L. Hu, "Multi-view analysis of high-resolution geomorphic features in complex mountains based on uav–lidar and sfm–mvs: A case study of the northern pit rim structure of the mountains of lufeng, China", *Appl. Sci. (Basel),* vol. 13, no. 2, p. 738, 2023.
[http://dx.doi.org/10.3390/app13020738]

[71] G. Jouvet, Y. Weidmann, E. van Dongen, M.P. Lüthi, A. Vieli, and J.C. Ryan, "High-endurance uav for monitoring calving glaciers: Application to the inglefield bredning and eqip sermia, greenland", *Front. Earth Sci. (Lausanne),* vol. 7, p. 206, 2019.
[http://dx.doi.org/10.3389/feart.2019.00206]

[72] H.N. Tran, M. Rutten, R. Prajapati, H.T. Tran, S. Duwal, D.T. Nguyen, J.C. Davids, and K. Miegel, "Citizen scientists' engagement in flood risk-related data collection: a case study in Bui River Basin, Vietnam", *Environ. Monit. Assess.,* vol. 196, no. 3, p. 280, 2024.
[http://dx.doi.org/10.1007/s10661-024-12419-2] [PMID: 38368305]

[73] M. Kumar, S. Sen, H. Kulkarni, S. Badiger, G.R. Varma, and J. Krishnaswamy, "Ecohydrological and

hydrogeological dynamics of groundwater springs in Eastern Himalaya, India", *Groundw. Sustain. Dev.,* vol. 27, p. 101311, 2024.
[http://dx.doi.org/10.1016/j.gsd.2024.101311]

[74] P. Upadhyay, A. Linhoss, C. Kelble, S. Ashby, N. Murphy, and P.B. Parajuli, "Applications of the swat model for coastal watersheds: review and recommendations", *Journal of the ASABE,* vol. 65, no. 2, pp. 453-469, 2022.
[http://dx.doi.org/10.13031/ja.14848]

[75] R. Bunel, N. Lecoq, Y. Copard, and N. Massei, "Effects of climate variability changes on runoff and erosion in the Western European Loess Belt region (NW, France)", *Sci. Total Environ.,* vol. 903, p. 166536, 2023.
[http://dx.doi.org/10.1016/j.scitotenv.2023.166536] [PMID: 37634719]

[76] H. Cao, L. Han, and L. Li, "A deep learning method for cyanobacterial harmful algae blooms prediction in Taihu Lake, China", *Harmful Algae,* vol. 113, p. 102189, 2022.
[http://dx.doi.org/10.1016/j.hal.2022.102189] [PMID: 35287935]

[77] J. Geleijnse, M. Rutten, D. de Villiers, J.T. Bamwenda, and E. Abraham, "Enhancing water access monitoring through mapping multi-source usage and disaggregated geographic inequalities with machine learning and surveys", *Sci. Rep.,* vol. 13, no. 1, p. 13433, 2023.
[http://dx.doi.org/10.1038/s41598-023-39917-6] [PMID: 37596313]

[78] M. Rahman, M.M. Islam, H-J. Kim, M. Alam, S. Sadiq, M.K. Rahman, M. Sadir Hossan, M.T. Islam, M.R. Raju, M.S. Alam, S.I. Ahmad, and A. Dewan, "Optimizing urban water sustainability: Integrating deep learning, genetic algorithm, and CMIP6 GCM for groundwater potential zone prediction within a social-ecological-technological framework", *Adv. Space Res.,* vol. 73, no. 12, pp. 5925-5948, 2024.
[http://dx.doi.org/10.1016/j.asr.2024.03.033]

[79] P. Tian, Z. Xu, W. Fan, H. Lai, Y. Liu, P. Yang, and Z. Yang, "Exploring the effects of climate change and urban policies on lake water quality using remote sensing and explainable artificial intelligence", *J. Clean. Prod.,* vol. 475, p. 143649, 2024.
[http://dx.doi.org/10.1016/j.jclepro.2024.143649]

[80] Y. Deng, Y. Zhang, D. Pan, S.X. Yang, and B. Gharabaghi, "Review of recent advances in remote sensing and machine learning methods for lake water quality management", *Remote Sens. (Basel),* vol. 16, no. 22, p. 4196, 2024.
[http://dx.doi.org/10.3390/rs16224196]

[81] M.R. Hipsey, D.P. Hamilton, P.C. Hanson, C.C. Carey, J.Z. Coletti, J.S. Read, B.W. Ibelings, F.J. Valesini, and J.D. Brookes, "Predicting the resilience and recovery of aquatic systems: A framework for model evolution within environmental observatories", *Water Resour. Res.,* vol. 51, no. 9, pp. 7023-7043, 2015.
[http://dx.doi.org/10.1002/2015WR017175]

[82] W. Xu, S.A. Edalatpanah, and A. Sorourkhah, "Solving the problem of reducing the audiences' favor toward an educational institution by using a combination of hard and soft operations research approaches", *Mathematics,* vol. 11, no. 18, p. 3815, 2023.
[http://dx.doi.org/10.3390/math11183815]

[83] M. Yadav, B. B. Vashisht, S. K. Jalota, A. Kumar, and D. Kumar, "Sustainable water management practices for intensified agriculture," in *Soil-Water, Agriculture, and Climate Change*, S. K. Dubey, P. K. Jha, P. K. Gupta, A. Nanda, and V. Gupta, Eds., vol. 113, Water Science and Technology Library. Cham, Switzerland: Springer, 2022, pp. 131–161.
[http://dx.doi.org/10.1007/978-3-031-12059-6_8]

CHAPTER 5

Air Quality Monitoring Using Machine Learning and Spatial Data

Farrukh Naseem[1,*], **Asma Heyat**[2], **Shahid Ikabal**[2,3], **Mohd. Aamir Mazhar**[2] and **Momina**[2]

[1] *Department of Civil Engineering, Indian Institute of Technology (Indian School of Mines) Dhanbad, Jharkhand, India*

[2] *Department of Civil Engineering, Jamia Millia Islamia, New Delhi, Delhi, India*

[3] *Department of Chemical Engineering, Indian Institute of Technology (Indian School of Mines), Dhanbad, Jharkhand, India*

Abstract: The environment and public health are still seriously threatened by air pollution, which calls for advanced monitoring and forecasting methods. To provide a comprehensive assessment of air quality, this chapter examines how to integrate machine learning techniques with geospatial data. The first section is devoted to geospatial analysis, which examines regional variations in pollution levels using geographic information systems (GIS) and remote sensing. By looking at geographic trends, policymakers can identify high-risk areas and develop targeted interventions. The following section analyses machine learning techniques for air quality prediction, including random forests, deep learning models, and hybrid approaches that improve predictive accuracy. These models process large amounts of information to identify complex pollution trends and generate precise predictions. Furthermore, time series analysis and trend detection methods such as ARIMA and Long Short-Term Memory (LSTM) networks are discussed in connection with the problem of gathering temporal variations and forecasting future pollution levels. These techniques aid in understanding both seasonal fluctuations and long-term trends in air quality. The chapter also covers real-time air pollution monitoring and alert systems, emphasizing the significance of cloud computing, sensor networks, and Internet of Things devices. These technologies enable real-time data collection, processing, and distribution, enabling timely alerts and informed decision-making. To help lawmakers pass data-driven legislation, this chapter provides a framework for improving air quality management strategies by combining machine learning with spatial data. Ultimately, implementing these innovative methods could lead to improved pollution control plans, cleaner cities, and enhanced public health.

* **Corresponding author Farrukh Naseem:** Department of Civil Engineering, Indian Institute of Technology (Indian School of Mines) Dhanbad, Jharkhand, India; E-mail: farrukhnaseem0@gmail.com

Kanwarpreet Singh, Arundhati, Manmeet Kaur, Abhishek Sharma, Aditya Kumar Tiwary & Sahil Sharma (Eds.)
All rights reserved-© 2026 Bentham Science Publishers

Keywords: Air Quality Monitoring, Air Pollution Prediction, Geospatial Data Analysis, IoT Sensors, Machine Learning, Remote Sensing, Smart Environmental Systems.

INTRODUCTION

Air quality is one of the world's critical environmental concerns, deeply impacting ecosystems, public health, and economic productivity. The World Health Organization in 2018 stated that poor air quality contributes to millions of premature deaths every year due to cardiovascular and respiratory diseases [1]. Air quality, especially in megacities, is further worsened by rapid urbanization, industrialization, and vehicular emissions since heavy traffic and higher population proportions worsen air quality [2]. Despite ground-based air monitoring networks employing high-accuracy measurement techniques, the spatial coverage of these traditional methods poses a challenge for capturing the heterogeneity of urban pollutant distribution. Due to these limitations, an increasing number of researchers have adopted remote sensing methods or geospatial analyses that combine remote sensing data with ground-based observations and model-derived atmospheric data. This combination allows for an efficient and powerful understanding of air quality across geographic regions (spatial) and time (temporal), capturing variations on a larger scale and more comprehensively understanding the dynamics over time [3, 4]. The role of satellite sensors in propelling air quality research has been greatly transformative. The Moderate Resolution Imaging Spectroradiometer (MODIS) on NASA's Terra and Aqua satellites captures AOD and LST at daily intervals, which are known to correlate with pollutant concentrations and urban heat features, respectively [5, 6]. Also, the TROPOMI-equipped Sentinel-5P satellite significantly improves the monitoring and mapping of urban air quality in quasi-real time through high-resolution imagery of trace gases such as NO_2, O_3, SO_2, and CO [7].

Geospatial analysis has also been strengthened by advances in data fusion and cloud computing, including Google Earth Engine. These tools enhance both spatial resolution and temporal coverage by processing datasets from satellites, ground stations, and chemical transport models [8]. More recent research has supported the efficiency of these combined methods for tracking trends in air pollution, recognizing pollution hotspots, and associating them with urban features and meteorological data [9, 10]. Moreover, air quality monitoring in connection with the Urban Heat Island (UHI) effect – the temperature differential by which cities are significantly warmer than rural regions – is gaining more attention. The UHI effect worsens air quality by accelerating photochemical reactions that produce secondary pollutants, such as ozone. UHI's impacts further include increased energy consumption and public health risks [11, 12]. To enable thorough development of urban climate adaptation and mitigation strategies, these interactions require an integrated understanding. An effective approach towards monitoring urban air quality is the combination of satellite remote sensing with geospatial analysis. With high-precision data from sensors such as MODIS, Sentinel-5P, and Landsat, along with powerful algorithms and cloud computing, researchers are able to analyze the spatial and temporal patterns of urban pollutants [8, 13]. This not only enhances understanding of pollutants but also enables their effective control and management, which is crucial for urban development and planning within more sustainable frameworks to improve resilience [1, 11, 14].

Fundamentals of Air Quality and Geospatial Analysis

This section provides a comprehensive overview of the key prerequisites for studying air quality from a spatial perspective. This is further divided into two parts: Air quality parameters and geospatial analysis concepts.

Air Quality Parameters

The components of this discipline are closely related to air quality, which is controlled by the level of pollutants found in the atmosphere. The core parameters of air quality are assessed in terms of health effects, climate change, and environmental sustainability. These include: Particulate matter, classified by size into PM2.5 (<2.5 μm) and PM10 (<10 μm), gaseous pollutants (NO_2, SO_2, CO, O_3), and additional pollutants such as volatile organic compounds (VOCs) and aerosols. Each of these parameters is at the same time complexly interrelated and dependent on meteorological conditions, land use, and population activity. Aimed at controlling air quality and guiding future geospatial studies, it is necessary to have a proper understanding of these air contaminants.

Geospatial Analysis Concepts

Geospatial analysis refers to the spatial and computational techniques used to evaluate geospatial phenomena. In researching air quality, these techniques provide significant insights into the patterns, trend distributions, and origins of the pollutants. Important areas of remote sensing include spatial interpolation, data fusion, big data and cloud computing, spatial statistics, and visualization. These concepts in geospatial analysis enable a comprehensive and permeable evaluation of air quality and its influencing factors. This new context provides and integrates an advanced understanding of pollutant behavior and movement across various terrains and enhances air pollutant mitigation techniques.

Data Sources for Air Quality Geospatial Analysis

Analyzing air quality from a geospatial perspective integrates various information systems to track and evaluate the progression of pollution and the effectiveness of response strategies. Air quality data can be obtained from three primary sources: Satellite data, in-situ stations, and modelled data or reanalysis products. Each source offers different benefits and restrictions, but the combination of several sets increases precision and continuity with region-bounding scope in air quality research.

Satellite-based Observations

An important method of assessing air quality is satellite remote sensing, which provides large area coverage of the spatial distribution of atmospheric pollutants. Satellite sensors estimate aerosols, trace gases, and atmospheric constituents using both passive and active remote sensing techniques. As pollutants include AOD, NO_2, SO_2, O_3, and CO, several satellite missions contribute to air quality monitoring [15]. Table **1** highlights different types of satellites in air quality geospatial analysis.

Table 1. Different types of satellites for air quality geospatial analysis.

Satellite	Sensor	Measured Pollutants	Spatial Resolution	Temporal Resolution	Agency
MODIS (Terra/Aqua)	MODIS	AOD	1 km	Daily	NASA
Sentinel-5P	TROPOMI	NO_2, O_3, SO_2, CO, CH_4	7 km	Daily	ESA
OMI (Aura)	OMI	NO_2, SO_2, O_3, AOD	13 × 24 km	Daily	NASA
GOME-2 (MetOp)	GOME-2	NO_2, O_3, SO_2	40 km	Daily	EUMETSAT
VIIRS (Suomi NPP, NOAA-20)	VIIRS	AOD, PM2.5 (estimated)	750 m	Daily	NOAA/NASA
CALIPSO	CALIOP	Aerosol profiles, AOD	5 km	16-day repeat	NASA/CNES

Ground-based Monitoring

These stations have the ability to attain high accuracy in measuring the total concentration of pollutants at specific locations. At these stations, sensors of different types, including automated and manual sensors, are used for the measurement of PM2.5, PM10, NO_2, O_3, SO_2, CO, and a variety of other pollutants. Various national and international networks offer air quality information for both real-time and historical [16]. Table **2** provides a few examples of real-time ground-based monitoring systems.

Table 2. Real-time ground-based monitoring system.

Network	Region	Pollutants Measured	Resolution	Agency
Air Quality System (AQS)	USA	PM, NO_2, O_3, CO, SO_2	< 1 km	EPA
European Air Quality Database (AirBase)	Europe	PM, NO_2, O_3, CO, SO_2	< 1 km	EEA
China National AQ Monitoring	China	PM, NO_2, O_3, CO, SO_2	< 1 km	MEE
India's National AQ Monitoring Program (NAMP)	India	PM, NO_2, O_3, CO, SO_2	< 1 km	CPCB
Global Atmosphere Watch (GAW)	Global	GHGs, PM, NO_2, O_3	< 1 km	WMO

Modelled Data and Reanalysis Products

Combining ground observations, satellite data, and meteorological models enables the creation of continuous, temporal, and spatial air quality estimation, which is made available by the aforementioned air quality models and reanalysis datasets [17]. Tables **3** and **4** highlight some of the most commonly used air quality models and reanalysis datasets, respectively.

Table 3. Air quality models.

Model	Type	Spatial Resolution	Application
CMAQ (Community Multiscale Air Quality Model)	Chemical Transport Model	4–36 km	Regional air quality forecasting
GEOS-Chem	Global Chemical Model	0.25–2°	Atmospheric chemistry and transport
WRF-Chem (Weather Research and Forecasting with Chemistry)	Coupled Meteorology-Chemistry	1–50 km	High-resolution air pollution modeling
LOTOS-EUROS	Regional CTM	7 km	European air pollution modeling

Table 4. Reanalysis datasets.

Dataset	Resolution	Time Coverage	Agency
MERRA-2 (Modern-Era Retrospective Analysis for Research and Applications)	50 km	1980–Present	NASA
CAMS (Copernicus Atmosphere Monitoring Service)	40 km	2003–Present	ECMWF
ERA5-Land (ECMWF Reanalysis)	9 km	1979–Present	ECMWF

(Table 4) cont.....

Dataset	Resolution	Time Coverage	Agency
NCEP/NCAR Reanalysis	210 km	1948–Present	NOAA

Comprehensive air quality geospatial analysis combines satellite, ground monitoring station, and reanalysis air quality data products. Ground stations provide high accuracy, whereas satellite data offers large-scale coverage; furthermore, models help fill data gaps and forecast pollution trends. Without integrating these datasets, air pollution management and mitigation would be difficult.

Methodologies in Geospatial Air Quality Analysis

Geospatial methods incorporate several techniques for conducting air quality analysis, including data preprocessing, spatial analysis, and remote sensing. Each method ensures data accuracy, supports spatial assessments, and enables large-scale monitoring of air quality. In this chapter, major approaches regarding geospatial air quality analysis are presented, along with numerous citations and references for every method. One of the critical considerations when analyzing the air quality of any region through geospatial methods is the data preprocessing step. It ensures that the satellite and ground-based monitoring data, as well as model outputs, are properly cleansed, consistent, and formatted for subsequent analysis. Outer detection, gap filling, standardization, and unit conversion, and temporal and spatial aggregation are all classified under common data preprocessing techniques. Ground observations, together with uncertainty analysis and bias correction, are cross-validated to take care of the set quality control measures.

Spatial Analysis Techniques

Spatial analysis techniques are of great importance for studying the distribution of air pollutants, pollution hotspots, and their changes over time for trend analysis. Inverse distance weighting, kriging, and spline interpolation are a few examples of spatial interpolation methods. Hotspot identification and cluster analysis may be done using Getis-Ord Gi, Moran's I, and the K-means clustering method. Some spatial regression models include land use regression (LUR) and geographically weighted regression (GWR).

Remote Sensing for Air Quality

Remote sensing technologies have made air quality monitoring easier because they provide complete spatial and temporal coverage for tracking pollutants over vast areas. Remote sensing can be used for estimating aerosol optical depth

(AOD) and PM2.5, monitoring trace gases, and for the fusion of remote sensing data with ground observations.

- ***MODIS AOD to PM2.5 Conversion:*** Statistical models correlate ground-based PM2.5 concentrations with satellite-derived AOD [13].
- ***Machine Learning for AOD-PM2.5 Mapping:*** Neural networks and regression models improve PM2.5 estimation from satellite data [18].
- ***TROPOMI NO_2 and SO_2 Retrievals:*** Detects urban and industrial pollution sources with high spatial resolution [7].
- ***OMI and GOME-2 for O_3 and CO Monitoring:*** Provides global atmospheric composition measurements for air quality assessments.
- ***Kalman Filtering and Bayesian Data Fusion:*** Combines satellite, model, and ground-based data for improved air quality mapping [19].
- ***Hybrid Approaches:*** Integrating satellite and reanalysis datasets enhances air quality predictions [20].

Applications

Along with geospatial air quality analysis, monitoring urban pollution, and analyzing the impacts on health, available policy measures also require close attention. This section will explain key applications, including urban air quality mapping, health impact assessments, policy and planning, and recent changes, and will develop methods from advanced approaches.

Urban Air Quality Mapping

Using geospatial data from ground sensors, satellite imagery, and models, urban air quality mapping examines how pollutants are distributed across cities. The increased resolution in air quality mapping furthers urban development, health measures, and pollution control. Methods for urban air quality mapping include land-use regression (LUR), machine learning, low-cost sensor networks, and geostatistical interpolation.

Health Impact Assessments

One of the biggest threats to environmental health is air pollution, contributing to respiratory and cardiovascular diseases, premature mortality, and reduced life expectancy. Geospatial analysis helps quantify exposure risks and estimate disease burdens at different spatial scales. The methods for health impact assessment include exposure modeling, epidemiological studies, time-series analysis, and geospatial disease mapping.

Policy and Planning

Air quality data supports environmental policymaking and urban planning by providing evidence for regulatory measures, mitigation strategies, and climate change adaptation.

- ***Air Quality Standards:*** Governments use geospatial data to establish regulatory limits for pollutants based on exposure assessments and public health studies [21].
- ***Emission Reduction Strategies:*** Geospatial models help identify pollution sources, assess control measures, and monitor compliance with environmental regulations [22].
- ***Climate Change Mitigation:*** Air quality improvements are linked to broader carbon reduction policies, as seen in the co-benefits of reducing PM2.5 and greenhouse gases [23].
- ***Environmental Justice:*** Spatial mapping of pollution exposure helps address disparities in air quality impacts across different socio-economic and ethnic groups.

MACHINE LEARNING APPROACHES FOR AIR QUALITY PREDICTION (RANDOM FOREST, DEEP LEARNING, HYBRID MODELS)

One of the world's most pressing environmental issues is air pollution, which severely affects human health and damages the environment. Predicting air quality accurately is critical for mitigating its adverse effects, guiding policy decisions, and implementing public health preventive measures. The modeling of air pollution remains a very difficult challenge due to the intricate relationships among the multitude of emissions, meteorological conditions, and chemical transformations within the surrounding atmosphere. In recent years, there has been a growing optimization of ML approaches for data filtering, offering strengths, flexibility, and computational efficiency over traditional empirical models. In this part, we consider the importance of air quality prediction, difficulties encountered with conventional forecasting, and the role of ML in air quality prediction.

Importance of Air Quality Prediction in Environmental Management and Public Health

The wide-ranging dangers of air pollution, such as cardiovascular disease and respiratory illnesses, as well as early death, are detrimental. The WHO suggests that 4.2 million people around the world die from air pollution each year and claims that PM 2.5 poses the greatest threat since it can easily reach the lungs and blood. Studies have linked COPD, lung cancer, and even ischemic heart disease to long-term exposure to air pollution, further worsening the problem. Apart from health challenges, pollution has dire consequences on ecosystems, climate change, and crops. Pollutants such as NO_X and SO_2 contribute to acid rain, causing damage to both land and water bodies, while ground-level O_3 ozone is known to damage plant tissues, reducing the yield of crops. To effectively control emissions, adapt urban planning, or issue public health warnings, one must be able to predict air quality accurately.

Challenges in Air Pollution Modeling

In light of the methods used to analyze atmospheric processes, pollutant collections, and alternative modes of air quality detection, the combined effects of all these factors are responsible for the highly dynamic nature of air pollution. Nonlinear interactions among chemicals, processes responsible for changes in air quality, and atmospheric conditions make the accurate prediction of air quality a challenging prospect.

Data Limitations

The air pollution predictive models require large datasets that include details on emissions, meteorological conditions, land use, and topography. Unfortunately, in many regions, particularly in developing countries, there is inadequate infrastructure for automated air quality monitoring, leading to data sparsity and unreliable forecasts [24]. Furthermore, even in areas with monitoring stations, problems such as sensor failures, calibration inconsistencies, and reporting discrepancies can limit data accuracy.

Spatial and Temporal Variability

The concentration of air pollution varies across regions and over time due to fluctuations in traffic, industrial activity, meteorological factors, and local geographic features. High-resolution spatial and temporal data are required to portray this variability, but such data are not always obtainable [25]. Also, the long-range transport of some pollutants, such as transboundary haze or dust storms, adds extra difficulty to air quality forecasting.

Nonlinear Chemical Interactions

Pollutants in the atmosphere are oxidized through numerous, highly complex chemical reactions. Consider the case of NO_X and volatile organic compounds (VOCs), which, when exposed to sunlight, yield O_3 or photochemical smog [26].

The creation and distribution of secondary pollutants are highly detailed and nonlinear, making them impossible to capture with conventional regression approaches.

Computational Complexity

Traditional air quality models, including chemical transport models such as CMAQ and WRF, require significant computational resources for processing. The computational expense of these models stems from their use of differential equations to simulate both atmospheric processes and pollutant dispersion [19].

Role of Machine Learning in Air Quality Forecasting

The application of machine learning to air quality forecasting allows for the analysis of massive datasets to identify patterns and detect anomalies. Machine learning approaches address numerous traditional modeling challenges by extracting knowledge from historical datasets without requiring direct understanding of atmospheric physics equations. ML shows promise as an air quality prediction method due to several key benefits.

Data-driven Insights

Through the analysis of large and complex data sets, machine learning models like random forest (RF) and support vector machines (SVM) identify important predictors that determine air pollution levels. These models predict future pollutant levels by learning from historical data and provide dependable outcomes despite the absence of explicit atmospheric equations [24].

Handling Nonlinearity

Deep learning and neural networks stand out from traditional regression models because they can learn intricate nonlinear relationships among multiple data variables. In time-series air quality prediction, recurrent neural networks (RNNs) and long short-term memory (LSTM) networks achieve high accuracy by learning sequential dependencies in pollutant concentration data.

Computational Efficiency

ML models are appropriate for real-time applications because they typically require less computing power than physics-based models. Convolutional neural networks (CNNs), one type of deep learning technique, can effectively process large-scale air quality datasets while lowering prediction latency [27].

Hybrid Modeling Approaches

Predictive performance can be improved by combining machine learning techniques with conventional air quality models. To increase accuracy, hybrid approaches combine ML-based corrections with physics-based models. For example, by learning from residual errors, deep learning techniques can improve numerical model outputs [19]. The best aspects of physics-based and data-driven methodologies are combined in these hybrid approaches.

Air Quality Data and Predictive Modeling

Predicting air quality depends on a variety of datasets gathered from sources such as satellite remote sensing, ground-based monitoring stations, and newly developed Internet of Things (IoT)-based sensor networks. The quality of the data, efficient preprocessing methods, and the selection of pertinent features all affect how accurate predictive models are. Furthermore, modeling and forecasting are complicated by the temporal and spatial variability of air pollutants. This section examines the main facets of data collection on air quality, pollutant properties, preprocessing techniques, and modeling difficulties.

Sources of Air Quality Data

There are numerous sources of air quality data, each with unique benefits and drawbacks. Predictive accuracy and spatial coverage are improved through the integration of various data sources.

Satellite Imagery

By measuring air pollutants from space, satellite-based remote sensing provides extensive data on air quality. Aerosols and gases like NO_2, SO_2, and O_3 are monitored by instruments like the MODIS and the Ozone Monitoring Instrument (OMI) [14]. For regions without ground-based monitoring networks, these datasets are essential. Satellite-derived data, however, may be impacted by cloud cover and have limitations in terms of temporal resolution (*e.g.*, daily or bi-daily observations).

Ground-based Monitoring Stations

Regulatory agencies maintain ground-based air quality monitoring networks to provide high-accuracy pollutant measurements. Examples include:

- The U.S. Environmental Protection Agency's (EPA) Air Quality System (AQS) [28]

- The European Environment Agency's (EEA) AirBase
- China's National Air Quality Monitoring Network

PM2.5, PM10, NO_2, SO_2, CO, and O_3 are among the pollutants that are measured by these stations. Ground-based stations are spatially constrained and ineffective in covering rural or remote areas, despite their accuracy.

IoT-based Sensor Networks

The implementation of dense IoT-based air quality monitoring networks has been made possible by recent advancements in inexpensive sensor technology. These sensors, like those created by PurpleAir and AirVisual, offer high spatial resolution and real-time data on air quality. They must be calibrated frequently, though, and environmental factors like temperature and humidity can affect calibration.

Meteorological Data

The way air pollutants spread and change is greatly influenced by meteorological factors, such as temperature, humidity, wind speed, and atmospheric pressure. By accounting for meteorological variability, data from weather stations and numerical weather models (such as WRF) improve air quality predictions [25].

Preprocessing and Feature Selection in Air Quality Prediction

Strong data preprocessing is necessary to achieve accurate air quality prediction and enhance model performance.

Data Cleaning

Raw air quality data often contain missing values, outliers, and sensor noise. Standard techniques for handling these issues include:

- ***Interpolation methods*** (*e.g.*, linear, spline, kriging) for missing data imputation [19].
- ***Outlier detection*** using statistical thresholds (*e.g.*, z-score) or machine learning-based anomaly detection [26].

Feature Engineering and Selection

Selecting relevant features improves model accuracy and efficiency. Standard features used in air quality prediction include:

- ***Pollutant concentrations****(historical and lagged values)*
- ***Meteorological parameters****(temperature, humidity, wind speed, precipitation)*
- ***Traffic data****(vehicle density, congestion levels, emissions factors)*
- ***Land use data****(industrial zones, green cover, urbanization levels)*

Feature selection methods such as Recursive Feature Elimination (RFE), Principal Component Analysis (PCA), and mutual information ranking help reduce dimensionality while retaining predictive power [24].

Spatial and Temporal Variability of Air Pollution

Spatial Variability

Air pollutant concentrations vary across different locations due to factors such as:

- ***Proximity to pollution sources*** (*e.g.*, highways, factories, power plants)
- ***Land use characteristics*** (*e.g.*, urban *vs.* rural environments)
- ***Topographical features*** (*e.g.*, mountain valleys trapping pollutants)

Geostatistical techniques like Kriging and IDW are commonly used to interpolate spatial air quality data [29].

Temporal Variability

There are several temporal scales at which air quality varies:

- ***Diurnal patterns:*** Traffic emissions led to peak NO_2 and CO levels in the morning and evening [30].
- ***Seasonal variations:*** O_3 peaks in the summer because of increased photochemical reactions, while PM2.5 levels are higher in the winter because of increased heating activities [31].
- ***Long-term trends:*** Policy changes, emission reductions, and climate factors influence long-term pollutant trends.

Temporal dependencies in air quality data are especially well captured by machine learning models, like LSTM networks [32].

Random Forest for Air Quality Prediction

Because machine learning techniques can model intricate, nonlinear relationships between pollutants and influencing factors, they have grown in popularity in the prediction of air quality. The RF algorithm is one of these methods that are particularly effective and popular for forecasting air quality. RF excels at handling high-dimensional data, identifying nonlinear dependencies, and offering strong feature selection. This section examines the fundamentals of radio frequency (RF), as well as its benefits in air quality modeling, feature importance analysis, and practical applications.

Overview of the Random Forest (RF) Algorithm

To increase accuracy and decrease overfitting, RF, an ensemble learning technique, constructs several decision trees and aggregates their predictions [33]. The RF algorithm's essential steps are:

- ***Bootstrap Sampling:*** To construct numerous decision trees, the algorithm bootstraps, or randomly selects subsets of the training data.
- ***Random Feature Selection:*** In order to decrease correlation between trees, a random subset of traits is taken into consideration for splitting at each node.
- ***Decision Tree Construction:*** Every tree is fully grown without any pruning, making RF different from standard decision tree models.
- ***Aggregation (Voting/Averaging):*** For classification tasks, RF uses majority voting across trees, while for regression tasks (such as air quality prediction), it averages the forecasts of individual trees.

The RF prediction for a given input X is calculated mathematically as stated in Eq. (**1**):

$$\hat{y} = \frac{1}{N}\sum_{i=1}^{N} T_i\,(X) \tag{1}$$

where Ti(X) is the result of the ith decision tree, and N is the number of trees [34].

Strengths of RF in Handling Non-linearity and Missing Data

Numerous variables, including emissions, land use, and weather, all have an impact on air pollution levels, and their interactions are extremely nonlinear [35]. These intricate relationships are difficult for traditional linear regression models to capture, but RF does so successfully because:

- ***Non-parametric nature:*** RF does not assume a specific functional form between inputs and outputs.
- ***Tree-based decision-making:*** Each decision tree in RF splits data based on optimal thresholds, enabling the model to adapt to intricate patterns in air quality data.

Missing values are common in environmental datasets due to irregular sampling, data transmission errors, or sensor malfunctions. RF addresses missing data in a number of ways:

- ***Imputation during training:*** RF can handle missing values by using surrogate splits, where alternative features are used if the primary feature is missing [36].
- ***Feature selection robustness:*** Missing values in some trees have a little effect on overall model performance because RF creates multiple trees using different data subsets.

Feature Importance Analysis in RF

Understanding which factors most influence air pollution levels is crucial for improving predictive models and informing policy decisions. RF provides feature importance rankings based on two main criteria:

Mean Decrease in Impurity (MDI)

Also known as Gini Importance, this metric measures the extent to which each feature reduces impurity (variance) in a decision tree. Features with higher importance scores contribute more to the model's predictive power [33]. The basic formula is given in Eq. (**2**):

$$\mathrm{MDI_j} = \sum_{\{t \in T\}} \Delta \mathrm{I}(t, j) \tag{2}$$

where $\Delta I(t, j)$ represents the impurity decrease at node t due to feature j.

Mean Decrease in Accuracy (MDA)

This method evaluates the importance of each feature by randomly permuting its values and measuring the drop in model accuracy. Larger decreases indicate more influential features [37].

Commonly ranked features in air quality prediction include:

- Meteorological variables (temperature, humidity, wind speed)
- Traffic intensity and emissions
- Industrial pollution sources
- Geographical location and land use characteristics

Deep Learning Approaches for Air Quality Prediction

Predicting air quality has been transformed by deep learning (DL), which makes it possible to model extremely intricate temporal and spatial relationships in pollution data. DL architectures are especially helpful for air quality forecasting because, unlike conventional ML techniques, they can automatically extract meaningful features from raw data. To improve prediction accuracy, these techniques leverage large datasets from satellite imagery, weather stations, IoT devices, and ground-based sensors [30, 38, 39].

Deep learning methods for predicting air quality can be roughly divided into:

- ***Recurrent models (RNN, LSTM, GRU):*** best suited for time-series forecasting.
- ***Spatial models (CNNs, hybrid CNN-LSTM models):*** used for spatial feature extraction from satellite images and sensor grids.
- ***Transformer-based models:*** used for capturing long-range dependencies in air pollution patterns.

Each of these architectures is designed to tackle specific challenges in air quality modeling, such as the highly dynamic nature of pollutant dispersion and complex interactions between meteorological variables and pollution sources [40].

Recurrent Neural Networks (RNNs) For Time-Series Forecasting

For forecasting time series, RNNs are frequently used to predict air quality. RNNs are useful for modeling temporal dependencies because, in contrast to conventional feedforward neural networks, they use hidden state connections to retain memory of previous inputs [41, 42].

The following Eq. (**3**) gives the basic RNN formulation:

$$h_t = \sigma\left(W_h h_{\{t-1\}} + W_x x_t + b_h\right) \tag{3}$$

where:

- ht = hidden state at time t
- xt = input at time t (*e.g.*, pollutant concentration, temperature, humidity)
- Wh, Wx= weight matrices
- bh = bias term
- σ = activation function (*e.g.*, tanh or ReLU)

However, vanishing gradient problems limit the performance of standard RNNs for long-term dependencies, as gradients diminish over time, making it difficult for the model to retain information across long sequences [43].

Long Short-term Memory (LSTM) Networks for Time-series Forecasting

LSTM networks outperform RNNs by incorporating memory cells with input, forget, and output gates that regulate information flow. Long-term dependencies in trends in air pollution can be captured by LSTM models through these gates [41, 44]. In comparison to conventional statistical techniques, an LSTM-based model increased PM2.5 prediction accuracy by 18% [45].

Convolutional Neural Networks (CNN) for Spatial Analysis of Air Quality Patterns

CNNs are ideal for predicting air pollution from satellite imagery and ground sensor grids because they are designed for spatial data analysis. CNNs use convolutional filters on input data to extract hierarchical spatial features [46].

Applications of CNNs in Air Quality Prediction

CNNs have been applied in:

- **Estimating PM2.5** from satellite imagery using CNN models based on AOD [9].
- **Urban air quality mapping** using multi-sensor IoT networks [47].
- **Smog and pollution classification** using environmental images [48].

Using a CNN-LSTM hybrid model, Liu *et al.*, (2020) improved air quality forecasting accuracy by 15% over standalone LSTM models, integrating spatial and temporal dependencies [49].

Transformer Models: Advanced Sequence Modeling for Air Quality Forecasting

In many predictive tasks, transformers outperform RNNs and LSTMs, making them powerful tools for sequence modeling [50]. Transformers process entire sequences in parallel, whereas LSTMs process data sequentially. This allows for better long-range dependency modeling and faster training [51].

Applications of Transformers in Air Quality Prediction

- **Time-series forecasting** of air pollution with Spatio-temporal Transformers [52].

- **Multi-modal fusion** of satellite and ground-based sensor data for improved accuracy [53].
- **Early warning systems** for instances of severe air pollution [49].

Hybrid Models for Enhanced Air Quality Prediction

Several ML and DL techniques are combined in hybrid modeling to improve the accuracy of air quality forecasts. The complex relationships between pollutant concentrations and meteorological parameters are frequently difficult for traditional models, such as statistical and standalone machine learning techniques, to capture. To improve predictive performance and produce reliable, effective, and understandable forecasts, hybrid models combine the strengths of multiple approaches [54].

RF + LSTM (Combining Ensemble Learning with Deep Learning)

- ***Random Forest (RF)*** is the most pertinent predictor for air quality forecasting through feature selection and preprocessing.
- ***Long Short-Term Memory (LSTM)*** time-series forecasting is done using LSTM networks, which successfully capture temporal dependencies in air pollution trends.
- A study by Wang *et al.*, (2021) demonstrated that RF-LSTM hybrid models achieved a 15% improvement in PM2.5 prediction accuracy compared to standalone models [49].

CNN + LSTM (Extracting Spatial and Temporal Patterns)

- ***Convolutional Neural Networks (CNNs)*** find patterns in the distribution of pollution by extracting spatial topographies from sensor grids and satellite imagery.
- ***LSTM networks*** capture temporal variations in air pollutant concentrations.
- Studies (Li *et al.*, 2021) have shown that CNN-LSTM hybrid models significantly improve urban air quality predictions, particularly for pollutants such as PM2.5 and NO_2 [48].

Data Fusion Techniques with ML and Physics-based Models

- **Machine learning models** are integrated with numerical simulation models (*e.g.*, WRF-Chem, CMAQ) to improve predictive accuracy by incorporating physics-based constraints.
- **Hybrid approaches** effectively bridge the gap between empirical modeling and physics-based simulations, providing more generalizable and interpretable results [55].

- Examples include ensemble learning with numerical models to mitigate uncertainties in weather-dependent pollutant dispersion predictions.

Comparative Performance of Hybrid Models against Standalone ML Models

- Hybrid models consistently achieve higher accuracy and lower errors than standalone machine learning models.
- Studies indicate that CNN-LSTM and RF-LSTM models improve air quality forecasting accuracy by 10-20%, outperforming traditional regression and statistical methods [47, 56].
- The integration of physics-based and data-driven models ensures greater adaptability to unseen conditions, making hybrid models more reliable for real-world applications.

Evaluation Metrics and Model Validation

Key Performance Metrics

Strong statistical and classification metrics are needed to assess the accuracy and dependability of air quality prediction models. The following are the most widely used performance metrics:

Root Mean Square Error (RMSE)

RMSE determines the average size of the prediction errors and assigns greater weight to larger errors. It is computed as follows in Eq. (**4**):

$$\text{RMSE}= \sqrt{\frac{1}{n}\sum_{i=1}^{n}(y_i - \hat{y}_i)^2} \quad \textbf{(4)}$$

where:

y_i= observed pollutant concentration,

ŷ_i= predicted concentration,

n = total number of observations.

A better predictive model is indicated by a lower RMSE value.

Mean Absolute Error (MAE)

By averaging the absolute differences between observed and predicted values, MAE offers an error metric that is easier to understand, as stated in Eq. (**5**):

$$MAE = \frac{1}{n}\sum_{i=1}^{n}|y_i - \hat{y}_i| \quad (5)$$

Models with different prediction ranges can benefit from MAE since it does not disproportionately penalize large errors like RMSE does [6].

Coefficient of Determination (R^2)

The degree to which the model predictions match the observed data is measured by R^2 as given in Eq. (**6**):

$$R^2 = 1 - \frac{\Sigma(y_i - \hat{y}_i)^2}{\Sigma(y_i - \bar{y})^2} \quad (6)$$

where, the mean of the observed values is represented by. An R2 value indicates a better fit nearer 1 [57].

AQI-based Classification Accuracy

Accuracy for models that forecast air quality index (AQI) categories (such as Good, Moderate, and Unhealthy) is determined as stated in Eq. (**7**):

$$Accuracy = \left(\frac{Correct\ Predictions}{Total\ Predictions}\right) \times 100 \quad (7)$$

AQI classification models are also assessed using F1-scores and confusion matrices [58].

Cross-validation Techniques for Air Quality Models

k-Fold Cross-Validation

- The dataset is divided into k subsets, and the model is trained on k-1 folds before being assessed on the remaining fold.
- To ensure robust model validation, this procedure is repeated k times [59].
- For air quality datasets, the usual options are k = 5 or 10.

Time Series Cross-validation

- Uses rolling or expanding windows to preserve temporal dependencies in air pollution data.
- Prevents data leakage by ensuring past observations predict future values [60].

Uncertainty Analysis and Interpretability of ML Models

Uncertainty Quantification

- **Bayesian Neural Networks (BNNs):** estimate predictive uncertainties by modeling distributions instead of point estimates [61].
- **Monte Carlo Dropout:** is used to approximate uncertainty in deep learning models [62].

Model Interpretability

- **Feature Importance Analysis:** To comprehend the influence of pollution and weather factors, RF and XGBoost offer ranked feature importance.
- **SHAP (Shapley Additive Explanations):** values explain individual model predictions, improving transparency [63].
- **LIME (Local Interpretable Model-agnostic Explanations):** assists in explaining DL-based air quality models [64].

TIME SERIES ANALYSIS AND TREND DETECTION USING MACHINE LEARNING (ARIMA, LSTMS)

For the purpose of comprehending and forecasting temporal data patterns, time series analysis is essential. It can be used in a variety of fields, including hydrology, environmental science, and finance. Sequentially recorded observations over time form time series data, which can exhibit a variety of features such as trends, seasonality, cyclicity, and noise. Finding underlying patterns, drawing insightful conclusions, and forecasting the future with accuracy are the main objectives of time series analysis [65, 66]. Time series data falls into two categories: Univariate and multivariate. A univariate time series consists of a single variable measured at multiple time points, such as daily temperature readings. A multivariate time series, on the other hand, consists of several interdependent variables, like temperature, humidity, and pressure in meteorology. Decision-making in water quality monitoring, climate modeling, and economic forecasting requires an understanding of time series dynamics [65, 67].

Time Series Data Representation

Differentiating between stationary and non-stationary series is crucial for efficient time series data analysis. While a non-stationary time series shows variations in mean, variance, or autocorrelation patterns over time, a stationary time series retains constant statistical characteristics. Logarithmic transformations and differencing are two preprocessing methods that can be used to stabilize non-stationary time series. Furthermore, to distinguish between trend, seasonal, and residual components, time series decomposition techniques such as Seasonal-Trend decomposition using LOESS (STL) are used [68].

Traditional Time Series Forecasting Methods

Because of their interpretability and efficacy for short-term predictions, traditional statistical methods are still frequently employed in time series forecasting.

Statistical Approaches

A number of basic statistical techniques include:

- **Moving Average (MA)**: Averages past observations to smooth fluctuations, commonly used in financial time series forecasting [69].
- **Exponential Smoothing**: Enhances short-term projections by giving historical observations exponentially diminishing weights [70].
- **Autoregressive (AR) and Moving Average (MA) Models**: Model the dependency between past and current values to predict future trends [71].

Autoregressive Integrated Moving Average (ARIMA)

One of the most popular statistical forecasting methods for time series data is the ARIMA model, which was first presented by Box and Jenkins in 1976. Three key elements are combined in ARIMA:

- **Autoregression (AR)**: A linear regression of the current value of the series against one or more past values.
- **Differencing (I - Integrated component)**: A modification that eliminates trends and seasonal components to render the time series stationary.
- **Moving Average (MA)**: A model that captures past forecast errors to improve future predictions.

The ARIMA modeling process involves [66]:

- Autocorrelation Function (ACF) and Partial Autocorrelation Function (PACF) plots are used to identify the order of AR, I, and MA components.
- Estimating model parameters using methods such as maximum likelihood estimation.
- Identifying residuals to assess the sufficiency of the model.

Despite its effectiveness, ARIMA has limitations, such as assuming linear relationships and requiring significant parameter tuning. Seasonal ARIMA

(SARIMA) extends ARIMA by incorporating seasonality, making it more effective for periodic data. Hybrid ARIMA models combining machine learning techniques, such as ARIMA-LSTM, have been proposed to improve forecasting performance [65].

Machine Learning for Time Series Analysis

Motivation for Machine Learning in Time Series

Machine learning methods provide significant advantages over traditional statistical models by capturing complex, nonlinear relationships and handling high-dimensional data. These methods have been successfully applied across various domains, including financial forecasting, healthcare, and hydrological modeling [60, 67, 72].

Feature Engineering for Time Series Data

Feature engineering is essential to improve the predictive performance of ML models. Some key feature engineering techniques include:

- **Lagged features**: Incorporating past values as input variables.
- **Seasonal decomposition**: Extracting seasonal and trend components using STL.
- **Fourier transformations**: Capturing periodic patterns.

Deep Learning Approaches for the Time Series Forecasting

Recurrent Neural Networks (RNNs)

RNNs are widely used for sequential data analysis, as they maintain contextual information over time [38]. However, standard RNNs suffer from the vanishing gradient problem, which limits their ability to learn long-term dependencies [43].

Long Short-term Memory Networks (LSTMs)

LSTMs, introduced by Hochreiter and Schmidhuber (1997), are a special type of RNN designed to overcome the vanishing gradient problem. Memory cells with three key gates make up LSTMs [41]:

- **Forget gate:** Chooses which data ought to be disregarded.
- **Input gate:** Selects the new evidence to be deposited.
- **Output gate:** Controls the output in response to updates in the memory cell.

In time series forecasting applications, such as stock market predictions [73], weather forecasting [62], and energy demand forecasting [66], LSTMs have proven to perform exceptionally well. Because they capture long-term dependencies and nonlinear trends, they perform better than conventional models like ARIMA.

Variants of LSTMs and Alternatives

A number of LSTM variations improve forecasting abilities, including:

- **Bidirectional LSTMs:** Capture dependencies in both forward and backward directions.
- **Sequence-to-sequence models:** Used for multi-step forecasting.

Gated Recurrent Units (GRUs)

A more straightforward substitute for LSTMs that preserves accuracy while reducing computational complexity.

REAL-TIME AIR POLLUTION MONITORING AND ALERT SYSTEMS

Our environment directly affects our health and life, and with the deteriorating condition of almost every aspect of the environment, several attempts have been made to control damage. One such step is monitoring or studying the present situation. It is necessary to study pollutant concentration. Air is the most significant but complicated part to study. Air quality is an essential parameter to assess the environment. The pollutants present in the air are measured in units of parts per million [52]. Pollutants can be primary pollutants (that are released directly into the atmosphere) or secondary pollutants (that are obtained by the reaction of primary pollutants with atmospheric chemicals). Air quality directly affects community health. Highly polluted air may also harm the visibility. Measuring air quality is necessary to maintain a healthy environment for living and non-living organisms. Poor air quality has been linked to several diseases and premature death [74]. Any undesired change in the usual composition of the air may be harmful to living beings like humans, cattle, and plants. The air pollution may contain a lot of dangerous substances, such as LPG gas, carbon monoxide, and methane [75]. Air quality has been severely damaged due to the increase in the use of vehicles and the establishment of industries [76]. Air has no fixed boundary, and pollutant concentration changes in a short time period. Therefore, an easy and reliable way to address this is to use real-time monitoring systems to continuously measure atmospheric pollutant concentrations [77]. In industries where pollutants are regularly released, traditional air quality monitoring processes can be inadequate because they don't provide continuous, real-time data. Due to the lack of real-time data, early precautions cannot be taken. A real-time monitoring system can be helpful for future forecasting and for immediate action if needed [78].

Real-time Air Pollution Monitoring Systems

Limitations of traditional monitoring methods can be overcome by developing and using a real-time air quality measuring system. A system designed to detect real-time concentrations of pollutants like CH_4, CO_2, SO_2, NH_3, CO, NO_2, O_3, PM2.5, and PM10, and to provide data, can be a good alternative. This can be done by integrating AI and IoT to obtain real-time data, make future predictions, and perform analysis [68]. Prototype with a PIC microcontroller and sensors to measure the concentration of gases such as hydrogen. Oxygen, alcohol vapor, and carbon monoxide have been developed. Sensors to track air quality variables that can cause asthma have been developed [79, 80]. PM2.5, or microscopic particles with an aerodynamic diameter of less than 2.5 micrometres, are one of the primary drivers of air pollution. These particles can connect to a variety of toxic compounds and enter the lungs of humans. Sensors used to monitor particulate matter can be a reliable choice to study dust concentration in cities [81]. With the emergence and advancement of AI and IoT, air quality monitoring has become more efficient. Real-time data and their analysis can be easily done through interconnected sensors and devices. Continuous monitoring and alerting are possible using several sensors, such as MQ135, MQ6, MQ7, and MQ2, to detect harmful gases like NO_2, CO, and NH_3, which depend on microcontrollers and online servers [82]. Spatial-temporal resolution of monitoring networks has been improved by using innovative methodologies like geospatial data analysis used in Cluj-Napoca, making monitoring systems more efficient and budget-friendly [83]. Meeker and inexpensive monitoring systems have been developed based on USEPA concepts for different countries, taking into consideration local conditions to improve accessibility. In developing countries, simpler and more affordable monitoring systems based on USEPA concepts have been adapted to local conditions, ensuring broader accessibility and usability [84].

Real-time Air Pollution Alert Systems and Applications

Approximately 7 million people and 570,000 deaths among children under age five are due to health issues such as respiratory infections, due to poor air quality. Due to continuous exposure to this polluted air, children are at risk of developing respiratory diseases, such as asthma [85]. A portable real-time monitoring system can be very helpful for people with breathing problems in assessing potential environmental risks [86]. Gas monitoring systems can help detect and warn of potential risks [87]. A real-time monitoring system continuously measures air quality parameters and provides real-time data on pollution levels. Real-time monitoring technology based on sensors can be very helpful for studying the concentration and behavior of short-lived pollutants. Sensor-based air-quality systems have been designed to measure and monitor gases like nitrous oxide, carbon dioxide, and methane, along with natural parameters such as dust, temperature, and humidity [88]. Sensor nodes were used to collect data that is transferred to the host computer by using the IEEE 802.15.4 protocol. The data is processed and displayed using LabVIEW software. Using a computer or smartphone, IOT-based air quality monitoring systems enable remote monitoring. When the concentration of harmful gases such as carbon dioxide, polycyclic aromatic hydrocarbons, alcohol, and ammonia, along with other pollutants like smoke, increases, the alarm system begins to alert about a decrease in air quality [75].

Sensor-based Air Quality Monitoring Instruments

Traditional instruments and monitors can measure PM2.5 and provide high-quality data, but the measurements are often spatially sparse due to the difficulty of establishing monitoring stations at every location and the high cost of maintenance [89]. Several studies have attempted to establish relationships between PM2.5 concentrations and prediction models, but the accuracy of results remains limited by poor spatial resolution [69]. To address this issue, low-cost, commercially available optical sensor-based monitors [32], in combination with satellite observations, offer a promising alternative [82]. Publicly available Purple Air sensor data can also support the estimation of PM2.5 concentrations [90]. In recent years, there has been a significant increase in the availability and variety of sensor-based instruments for monitoring atmospheric pollutants, and this number continues to grow [91]. To overcome the spatial limitations of conventional air quality monitoring systems, sensor-based instruments have been increasingly adopted [92]. Fig. (**1**) shows details of a sensor-based air quality monitoring instrument used in studies conducted in South Korea, while Fig. (**2**) highlights a sensor-based air quality sampler along with its specifications.

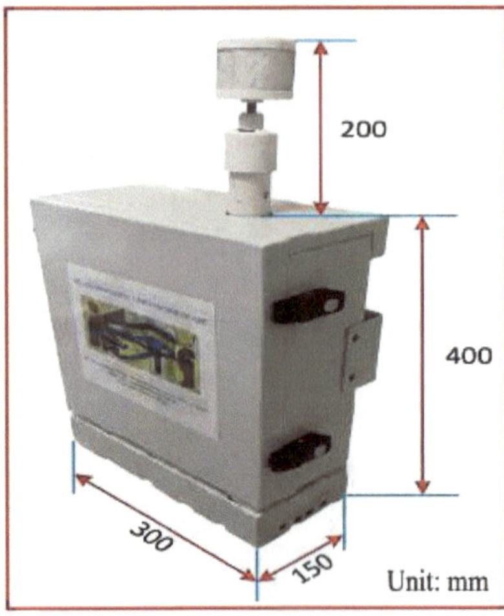

$PM_{2.5}$ sensor model (Country)	SD-16C (South Korea)
Measuring principle	Light scattering spectrometer
Particle size range	0.3 µm-25 µm
Reproducibility	± 5%
Flow rate	0.5 L/miin
Resolution	0.1 µg/m³

Fig. (1). Sensor-based air quality sampler with specifications.

S.no.	Pollutant	Detection Range
1.	PM 10	0 - 999 µg/m3
2.	PM 2.5	0-999 µg/m3
3.	TVOC	0-1.999 mg/m3
4.	HCHO	0-9.999 mg/m3

Fig. (2). A small portable sensor-based air quality sampler with a range.

Poor indoor air quality has a direct impact on a huge number of people. They develop many severe respiratory ailments [91]. Small-scale indoor air quality can be monitored with the help of a small, handy sensor-based air sampler. Fig. (**2**) shows a small portable air quality sampler for indoors. Sensor-based air quality systems can provide a detailed mapping of the study area due to their ability to record high-resolution air quality data [71]. It consists of sensors to measure

PM2.5 concentration, temperature, and relative humidity. The data collected by the sensor-based monitoring device can be collected and stored at a cloud computing service [56].

Particulate matter concentration distribution can be used for modeling with the help of data such as ambient concentrations, geographical information regarding the exposure receptor (time-activity pattern, microenvironments), building characteristics (ventilation rate), and indoor sources [92].

CONCLUSION

By combining satellite imagery, ground-based measurements, and sophisticated modeling to produce precise, comprehensive estimates of pollution, geospatial analysis has revolutionized air quality monitoring. This chapter has explored key aspects of geospatial air quality analysis, including data sources, methodologies, applications, challenges, and future directions. While ground-based networks like AQS, AirBase, and CPCB offer high-accuracy but constrained spatial data, satellite-based remote sensing from instruments such as MODIS, Sentinel-5P, and VIIRS provides global coverage of pollutants. By offering historical trends and predictive capabilities, reanalysis products and chemical transport models, such as CMAQ and GEOS-Chem, help fill these gaps. Technological developments that improve data accuracy and facilitate efficient mapping of urban air quality, health impact assessments, and policy planning include spatial interpolation, machine learning models, and remote sensing-based estimations. Nonetheless, there are still issues, such as inconsistent data, high processing requirements, and difficulties implementing policies. Innovations in next-generation satellite missions, forecasting powered by AI, and community-led monitoring programs are needed to address these issues. Leveraging technological advancements will be essential for effective policy development and sustainable air quality management on a global scale. Air is an important environmental parameter to study and maintain a healthy lifestyle. With continuous emissions of gases and particulate matter, air quality has deteriorated to such an extent that it requires immediate attention. The first step to improve air quality can be the study and monitoring of the present level of contaminants in the air. Pollutant concentrations can be measured in several ways. Traditional ways are time-consuming and can be expensive to maintain. It is also challenging to get data with high spatial resolution due to the difficult and expensive setup of measuring systems. To overcome such problems, sensor-based air quality systems are a good alternative. We can program sensors to directly display data directly on our system screen. Combining sensor-based devices with IoT, AI, and satellite data can provide data with very high spatial resolution. Sensor-based devices can also be a very good and less expensive alternative for small-scale monitoring devices. To reduce the detrimental effects of air pollution on the environment and human health, interdisciplinary cooperation, real-time data integration, and increased public involvement are key components of the future of geospatial air quality analysis.

LIST OF ABBREVIATIONS

AI - Artificial Intelligence

AOD- Aerosol Optical Depth

AQI - Air Quality Index

ARIMA - Autoregressive Integrated Moving Average

CMAQ - Community Multiscale Air Quality Model

CNN - Convolutional Neural Network

CO - Carbon Monoxide

CTM - Chemical Transport Model

DL - Deep Learning

EPA - Environmental Protection Agency

ESA - European Space Agency

GIS - Geographic Information Systems

GOME-2 - Global Ozone Monitoring Experiment-2

GWR - Geographically Weighted Regression

IoT - Internet of Things

LSTM - Long Short-Term Memory

LUR - Land Use Regression

MAE - Mean Absolute Error

MAPE - Mean Absolute Percentage Error

MDA - Mean Decrease in Accuracy

MDI - Mean Decrease in Impurity

MODIS - Moderate Resolution Imaging Spectroradiometer

NO2 - Nitrogen Dioxide

NOAA - National Oceanic and Atmospheric Administration

O3 - Ozone

OMI - Ozone Monitoring Instrument

PCA - Principal Component Analysis

PM10 - Particulate Matter (diameter $<10\ \mu m$)

PM2.5 - Particulate Matter (diameter $<2.5\ \mu m$)

RF - Random Forest

RMSE - Root Mean Square Error

RNN - Recurrent Neural Network

SO2 - Sulfur Dioxide

UHI - Urban Heat Island

VOCs - Volatile Organic Compounds

WMO - World Meteorological Organization

WRF - Weather Research and Forecasting Model

REFERENCES

[1] World Health Organization, "Ambient (outdoor) air quality and health," Geneva, Switzerland: World Health Organization, 2021. [Online]. Available: https://www.who.int/news-room/fac--sheets/detail/ambient-(outdoor)-air-quality-and-health

[2] P. Kumar, L. Morawska, C. Martani, G. Biskos, M. Neophytou, S. Di Sabatino, M. Bell, L. Norford, and R. Britter, "The rise of low-cost sensing for managing air pollution in cities", *Environ. Int.,* vol. 75, pp. 199-205, 2015.
[http://dx.doi.org/10.1016/j.envint.2014.11.019] [PMID: 25483836]

[3] A. Van Donkelaar, and R.V. Martin, "Global estimates of fine particulate matter using a combined geophysical-statistical method with information from satellites, models, and monitors", *Atmos. Environ.,* vol. 122, pp. 397-411, 2015.

[4] X. Liu, J. Li, and T. Yang, "CNN-LSTM hybrid models for air pollution forecasting", *Atmos. Environ.,* vol. 230, p. 117511, 2020.
[http://dx.doi.org/10.1016/j.atmosenv.2020.117511]

[5] L.A. Remer, Y.J. Kaufman, D. Tanré, S. Mattoo, D.A. Chu, J.V. Martins, R-R. Li, C. Ichoku, R.C. Levy, R.G. Kleidman, T.F. Eck, E. Vermote, and B.N. Holben, "The MODIS aerosol algorithm, products, and validation", *J. Atmos. Sci.,* vol. 62, no. 4, pp. 947-973, 2005.
[http://dx.doi.org/10.1175/JAS3385.1]

[6] Y. Zhang, "Satellite-based monitoring of urban air quality: Trends and implications for public health", *Remote Sens. Environ.,* vol. 255, p. 112303, 2021.

[7] J.P. Veefkind, "TROPOMI on the ESA Sentinel-5 Precursor: A GMES mission for global observations of the atmospheric composition", *Atmos. Chem. Phys.,* vol. 12, no. 9, pp. 433-469, 2012.

[8] N. Gorelick, M. Hancher, M. Dixon, S. Ilyushchenko, D. Thau, and R. Moore, "Google Earth Engine: Planetary-scale geospatial analysis for everyone", *Remote Sens. Environ.,* vol. 202, pp. 18-27, 2017.
[http://dx.doi.org/10.1016/j.rse.2017.06.031]

[9] A. K. Gupta, N. Naval, and T. Tanima, "Air quality prediction using deep learning: A review," *SSRN Electr. J.*, 2024.
[http://dx.doi.org/10.2139/ssrn.4487002]

[10] L. Liang, J. Daniels, C. Bailey, L. Hu, R. Phillips, and J. South, "Integrating low-cost sensor monitoring, satellite mapping, and geospatial artificial intelligence for intra-urban air pollution predictions," *Environmental Pollution*, vol. 331, pt. 1, p. 121832, 2023.
[http://dx.doi.org/10.1016/j.envpol.2023.121832]

[11] T.R. Oke, "The energetic basis of the urban heat island", *Q. J. R. Meteorol. Soc.,* vol. 108, no. 455, pp. 1-24, 1982.
[http://dx.doi.org/10.1002/qj.49710845502]

[12] M. Santamouris, "Analyzing the heat island magnitude and characteristics in cities: A review", *Sci. Total Environ.,* vol. 512–513, pp. 582-598, 2015.
[http://dx.doi.org/10.1016/j.scitotenv.2015.01.060] [PMID: 25647373]

[13] A. van Donkelaar, R.V. Martin, M. Brauer, N.C. Hsu, R.A. Kahn, R.C. Levy, A. Lyapustin, A.M. Sayer, and D.M. Winker, "Global estimates of fine particulate matter using a combined geophysical-statistical method", *Environ. Sci. Technol.,* vol. 50, no. 7, pp. 3762-3772, 2016. [http://dx.doi.org/10.1021/acs.est.5b05833] [PMID: 26953851]

[14] N. Kumar, A. Chu, and A. Foster, "Satellite remote sensing for air quality assessment", *Atmos. Environ.,* vol. 45, no. 4, pp. 672-685, 2019.

[15] Y.J. Kaufman, "The MODIS 2.1-μm channel-correlation with visible reflectance for use in remote sensing of aerosol", *IEEE Trans. Geosci. Remote Sens.,* vol. 40, no. 3, pp. 697-703, 2002.

[16] J.C. Chow, and J.G. Watson, "PM2.5 chemical composition and spatiotemporal variability in northern Colorado", *J. Air Waste Manag. Assoc.,* vol. 52, no. 12, pp. 1485-1502, 2002.

[17] D. Byun, and K.L. Schere, "Review of the governing equations, computational algorithms, and other components of the Models-3 Community Multiscale Air Quality (CMAQ) modeling system", *Appl. Mech. Rev.,* vol. 59, no. 2, pp. 51-77, 2006. [http://dx.doi.org/10.1115/1.2128636]

[18] L. Gressent, A. Malherbe, H. Colette, Rollin, and R. Scimia, "Data fusion for air quality mapping using low-cost sensor observations: Feasibility and added-value," Environment International, vol. 143, p. 105965, 2020. [http://dx.doi.org/10.1016/j.envint.2020.105965]

[19] C. Huang, and Y. Kuo, "A hybrid model for air quality prediction using long short-term memory network and genetic algorithm", *Proceedings of the 2018 IEEE International Conference on Applied System Invention (ICASI),* IEEE., pp. 204-207, 2018.

[20] Y.-S. Chang, H.-T. Chiao, S. Abimannan, Y.-P. Huang, Y.-T. Tsai, and K.-M. Lin, "An LSTM-based aggregated model for air pollution forecasting," *Atmospheric Pollution Research*, vol. 11, no. 8, pp. 1451–1463, 2020. [http://dx.doi.org/10.1016/j.apr.2020.05.015]

[21] Y. Cui, K. M. Eccles, R. K. Kwok, B. R. Joubert, K. P. Messier, and D. M. Balshaw, "Integrating multiscale geospatial environmental data into large population health studies: Challenges and opportunities," *Toxics*, vol. 10, no. 7, p. 403, 2022. [http://dx.doi.org/10.3390/toxics10070403]

[22] World Health Organization, *WHO global air quality guidelines: particulate matter (PM2.5 and PM10), ozone, nitrogen dioxide, sulfur dioxide and carbon monoxide*. Geneva, Switzerland: World Health Organization, 2021. https://www.who.int/publications/i/item/9789240034228

[23] Intergovernmental Panel on Climate Change (IPCC), *Climate Change 2021: The Physical Science Basis. The Working Group I Contribution to the Sixth Assessment Report*, Geneva, Switzerland: IPCC, 2021. [Online]. Available: https://www.ipcc.ch/report/ar6/wg1/

[24] J. Xing, S. Zheng, D. Ding. "Deep learning for prediction of the air quality response to emission changes," *Environmental Science & Technology*, vol. 54, no. 14, pp. 8589–8600, 2020. [http://dx.doi.org/10.1021/acs.est.0c02923]

[25] H. Fang and L. Zhang, "Analysis and prediction of air quality based on LSTM neural network — take Beijing Temple of Heaven as an example," *J. Phys.: Conf. Ser.*, vol. 1637, no. 1, p. 012126, Sep. 2020. [http://dx.doi.org/10.1088/1742□6596/1637/1/012126]

[26] G. I. Drewil and R. J. Al□Bahadili, "Air pollution prediction using LSTM deep learning and metaheuristics algorithms," *Measurement: Sensors*, vol. 24, no. 1, Art. no. 100546, 2022. [http://dx.doi.org/10.1016/j.measen.2022.100546]

[27] W. Yang, H. Li, J. Wang, and H. Ma, "Spatio-temporal feature interpretable model for air quality forecasting," Ecological Indicators, vol. 167, p. 112609, 2024. [http://dx.doi.org/10.1016/j.ecolind.2024.112609]

[28] United States Environmental Protection Agency, “Air quality modeling,” *U.S. EPA*, 2019. [Online]. Available: https://www.epa.gov/air-research/air-quality-modeling

[29] M. Zamani Joharestani, C. Cao, X. Ni, B. Bashir, and S. Talebiesfandarani, “PM2.5 prediction based on random forest, XGBoost, and deep learning using multisource remote sensing data,” *Atmosphere*, vol. 10, no. 7, p. 373, 2019. [http://dx.doi.org/10.3390/atmos10070373]

[30] F. Chollet, *Deep Learning with Python*, 1st ed. Shelter Island, NY, USA: Manning Publications, 2017.

[31] J. Hofierka, M. Šúri, and T. Cebecauer, "Spatial interpolation of daily solar irradiation in complex terrain", *J. Appl. Meteorol.,* vol. 41, no. 10, pp. 1011-1021, 2002.

[32] V. S. Krishnan and C. M. Firoz, “Regional urban environmental quality assessment and spatial analysis,” *Journal of Urban Management*, vol. 9, no. 2, pp. 191–204, 2020. [http://dx.doi.org/10.1016/j.jum.2020.03.001]

[33] L. Breiman, "Random Forests", *Mach. Learn.,* vol. 45, no. 1, pp. 5-32, 2001. [http://dx.doi.org/10.1023/A:1010933404324]

[34] T. K. Ho, “Random decision forests,” in *Proc. 3rd Int. Conf. Document Anal. Recognit. (ICDAR)*, Montreal, QC, Canada, 1995, pp. 278–282. [http://dx.doi.org/10.1109/ICDAR.1995.598994]

[35] R.D. Brook, S. Rajagopalan, C.A. Pope III, J.R. Brook, A. Bhatnagar, A.V. Diez-Roux, F. Holguin, Y. Hong, R.V. Luepker, M.A. Mittleman, A. Peters, D. Siscovick, S.C. Smith Jr, L. Whitsel, and J.D. Kaufman, "Particulate matter air pollution and cardiovascular disease: An update to the scientific statement from the American Heart Association", *Circulation,* vol. 121, no. 21, pp. 2331-2378, 2010. [http://dx.doi.org/10.1161/CIR.0b013e3181dbece1] [PMID: 20458016]

[36] L. Tang, H. Wu, and X. Yuan, "Improving air quality prediction using random forests with missing data imputation methods", *Environ. Pollut.,* vol. 258, p. 113850, 2020.

[37] X. Liu, Y. Wang, H. Zhang, and Z. Xu, "Random forest-based transboundary air pollution prediction", *Atmos. Res.,* vol. 249, p. 105286, 2021.

[38] Y. LeCun, Y. Bengio, and G. Hinton, "Deep learning", *Nature,* vol. 521, no. 7553, pp. 436-444, 2015. [http://dx.doi.org/10.1038/nature14539] [PMID: 26017442]

[39] I. Goodfellow, Y. Bengio, and A. Courville, Deep learning. Cambridge, MA: MIT Press, 2016.

[40] Y. Bengio, A. Courville, and P. Vincent, "Representation learning: A review and new perspectives", *IEEE Trans. Pattern Anal. Mach. Intell.,* vol. 35, no. 8, pp. 1798-1828, 2013. [http://dx.doi.org/10.1109/TPAMI.2013.50] [PMID: 23787338]

[41] S. Hochreiter, and J. Schmidhuber, "Long short-term memory", *Neural Comput.,* vol. 9, no. 8, pp. 1735-1780, 1997. [http://dx.doi.org/10.1162/neco.1997.9.8.1735] [PMID: 9377276]

[42] A. Graves, *Supervised sequence labelling with recurrent neural networks.* Springer, 2012. [http://dx.doi.org/10.1007/978-3-642-24797-2]

[43] R. Pascanu, T. Mikolov, and Y. Bengio, *On the difficulty of training recurrent neural networks.* ICML, 2013.

[44] F.A. Gers, J. Schmidhuber, and F. Cummins, "Learning to forget: Continual prediction with LSTM", *Neural Comput.,* vol. 12, no. 10, pp. 2451-2471, 2000. [http://dx.doi.org/10.1162/089976600300015015] [PMID: 11032042]

[45] G. Hoek, "Land-use regression models for estimating air pollution exposure", *Environ. Sci. Technol.,* vol. 54, no. 14, pp. 8579-8587, 2020.

[46] A. Krizhevsky, I. Sutskever, and G. Hinton, "ImageNet classification with deep convolutional neural networks", *Adv. Neural Inf. Process. Syst.,* 2012.

[47] D. Zhou, Q. He, and X. Ma, "A hybrid air pollution prediction model using deep learning and numerical simulations", *J. Clean. Prod.,* vol. 265, p. 121619, 2020.

[48] J. Li, and A.D. Heap, "A review of spatial interpolation methods for environmental scientists", *Geoscience Australia Record,* vol. 23, p. 137, 2011.

[49] F. Wang, L. Zhang, and X. Sun, "Satellite-based air quality prediction using machine learning models", *Remote Sens. Environ.,* vol. 242, p. 111764, 2020.

[50] A. Vaswani, N. Shazeer, N. Parmar, J. Uszkoreit, L. Kaiser, A. N. Gomez, I. Polosukhin, and L. Jones, "Attention is all you need," in *Proc. 31st Conf. Neural Information Processing Systems (NeurIPS)*, Long Beach, CA, USA, 2017, pp. 1–11.

[51] J. Devlin, M. Chang, K. Lee, and K. Toutanova, "BERT: Pre-training of deep bidirectional transformers", *arXiv:1810.04805,* 2018.

[52] K.P. Yamunathangam, K. Pritheka, and P. Varuna, "IoT enabled air pollution monitoring and awareness creation system", *Int. J. Recent Technol. Eng.,* vol. 7, no. 4S, 2018.

[53] Y Yang, and L Li, "A smart sensor system for air quality monitoring and massive data collection", *International Conference on Information and Communication Technology Convergence (ICTC),* IEEE, pp. 147-152, 2015.
[http://dx.doi.org/10.1109/ICTC.2015.7354515]

[54] B. Zhang, Y. Rong, R. Yong, D. Qin, M. Li, G. Zou, and J. Pan, "Deep learning for air pollutant concentration prediction: A review," *Atmospheric Environment*, vol. 290, p. 119347, 2022.
[http://dx.doi.org/10.1016/j.atmosenv.2022.119347]

[55] Chee-Yee Chong, and S.P. Kumar, "Sensor networks: Evolution, opportunities, and challenges", *Proc. IEEE,* vol. 91, no. 8, pp. 1247-1256, 2003.
[http://dx.doi.org/10.1109/JPROC.2003.814918]

[56] S.K. Yoo, and B.Y. Kim, "A decision-making model for adopting a cloud computing system", *Sustainability (Basel),* vol. 10, no. 8, p. 2952, 2018.
[http://dx.doi.org/10.3390/su10082952]

[57] X. Liang, *Quantitative remote sensing of land surfaces.* John Wiley & Sons, 2015.

[58] J. Hofman, M. Nikolaou, S.P. Shantharam, C. Stroobants, S. Weijs, and V.P. La Manna, "Distant calibration of low-cost PM and NO2 sensors; evidence from multiple sensor testbeds", *Atmos. Pollut. Res.,* vol. 13, no. 1, p. 101246, 2022.
[http://dx.doi.org/10.1016/j.apr.2021.101246]

[59] T. Hastie, R. Tibshirani, and J. Friedman, *The Elements of Statistical Learning.* Springer, 2009.
[http://dx.doi.org/10.1007/978-0-387-84858-7]

[60] X. Bai, Z. Chen, and R. Li, "Time-series cross-validation for air pollution modeling", *Environ. Res.,* vol. 195, p. 110807, 2021.

[61] Y. Gal, and Z. Ghahramani, "Dropout as a bayesian approximation: representing model uncertainty in deep learning", *International Conference on Machine Learning (ICML),* pp. 1050-1059, 2016.

[62] Shi, Xingjian & Chen, Zhourong & Wang, Hao & Yeung, Dit-Yan & Wong, Wai Kin & WOO, Wang-chun. "Convolutional LSTM network: A machine learning approach for precipitation nowcasting" *arXiv preprint arXiv:1506.04214*, 2015.
[http://dx.doi.org/10.48550/arXiv.1506.04214]

[63] S.M. Lundberg, and S.I. Lee, "A unified approach to interpreting model predictions", *Advances in Neural Information Processing Systems (NeurIPS),* vol. 30, pp. 4765-4774, 2017.

[64] M.T. Ribeiro, S. Singh, and C. Guestrin, "Why should I trust you?", *Proceedings of the 22nd ACM SIGKDD International Conference on Knowledge Discovery and Data Mining,* pp. 1135-1144, 2016.

[65] G. Peter Zhang, "Time series forecasting using a hybrid ARIMA and neural network model",

Neurocomputing, vol. 50, pp. 159-175, 2003. [http://dx.doi.org/10.1016/S0925-2312(01)00702-0]

[66] P. Chakraborty, S. Kalaivani, A. Ambika & K. Ramya, "Forecasting Electricity Consumption Using ARIMA-LSTM Model", *Journal of Nano- and Electronic Physics,* vol. 17, pp. 04011-1, 2025. [http://dx.doi.org/10.21272/jnep.17(4).04011]

[67] G. Tunnicliffe Wilson, “Time series analysis: forecasting and control, 5th edition, by G. E. P. Box, G. M. Jenkins, G. C. Reinsel and G. M. Ljung, 2015,” *Journal of Time Series Analysis*, vol. 37, 2016. [http://dx.doi.org/10.1111/jtsa.12194]

[68] M.N.A. Ramadan, M.A.H. Ali, S.Y. Khoo, M. Alkhedher, and M. Alherbawi, "Real-time IoT-powered AI system for monitoring and forecasting of air pollution in industrial environment", *Ecotoxicol. Environ. Saf.,* vol. 283, p. 116856, 2024. [http://dx.doi.org/10.1016/j.ecoenv.2024.116856] [PMID: 39151373]

[69] M. Diao, T. Holloway, S. Choi, S.M. O’Neill, M.Z. Al-Hamdan, A. Van Donkelaar, R.V. Martin, X. Jin, A.M. Fiore, D.K. Henze, F. Lacey, P.L. Kinney, F. Freedman, N.K. Larkin, Y. Zou, J.T. Kelly, and A. Vaidyanathan, "Methods, availability, and applications of PM 2.5 exposure estimates derived from ground measurements, satellite, and atmospheric models", *J. Air Waste Manag. Assoc.,* vol. 69, no. 12, pp. 1391-1414, 2019. [http://dx.doi.org/10.1080/10962247.2019.1668498] [PMID: 31526242]

[70] G. Hoek, R. Beelen, K. de Hoogh, D. Vienneau, J. Gulliver, P. Fischer, and D. Briggs, "A review of land-use regression models to assess spatial variation of outdoor air pollution", *Atmos. Environ.,* vol. 42, no. 33, pp. 7561-7578, 2008. [http://dx.doi.org/10.1016/j.atmosenv.2008.05.057]

[71] W.I. Lai, Y.Y. Chen, and J.H. Sun, "Ensemble machine learning model for accurate air pollution detection using commercial gas sensors", *Sensors (Basel),* vol. 22, no. 12, p. 4393, 2022. [http://dx.doi.org/10.3390/s22124393] [PMID: 35746175]

[72] J. Park, H. Ryu, E. Kim, Y. Choe, J. Heo, J. Lee, S.H. Cho, K. Sung, M. Cho, and W. Yang, "Assessment of PM2.5 population exposure of a community using sensor-based air monitoring instruments and similar time-activity groups", *Atmos. Pollut. Res.,* vol. 11, no. 11, pp. 1971-1981, 2020. [http://dx.doi.org/10.1016/j.apr.2020.08.010]

[73] T. Fischer and C. Krauss, "Deep learning with long short-term memory networks for financial market predictions", *European Journal of Operational Research,* vol. 270, no. 2, pp. 654-669, 2018. [http://dx.doi.org/10.1016/j.ejor.2017.11.054]

[74] C.A. Pope, and D.W. Dockery, "Health effects of fine particulate air pollution: Lines that connect", *Journal of the Air & Waste Management Association,* no. 6, pp. 709-742, 2006. [http://dx.doi.org/10.1080/10473289.2006.10464485]

[75] K. B. K. Sai, S. Mukherjee, and H. P. Sultana, "Low cost IoT based air quality monitoring setup using Arduino and MQ series sensors with dataset analysis", *Procedia Computer Science,* vol. 165, pp. 322-327, 2019. [http://dx.doi.org/10.1016/j.procs.2020.01.043]

[76] Y Ma, "Hierarchical air quality monitoring system design", *International Symposium on Integrated Circuits (ISIC),* IEEE, pp. 284-287, 2014.

[77] T. Hussain, A. Masood, and K. Ahmad, "A study on monitoring of indoor air Pollutants and their health effects", *Int. J. Eng. Res. Appl.,* vol. 9, no. 8, pp. 52-57, 2019.

[78] Z Khan, A Ali, and M Moghal, "IoT based Air Pollution using NodeMCU and Thingspeak", *IRANS,* pp. 11-16, 2014.

[79] A. Somov, A. Baranov, A. Savkin, D. Spirjakin, A. Spirjakin, and R. Passerone, "Development of wireless sensor network for combustible gas monitoring", *Sens. Actuators A Phys.,* vol. 171, no. 2, pp.

398-405, 2011.
[http://dx.doi.org/10.1016/j.sna.2011.07.016]

[80] J. Bi, N. Carmona, M.N. Blanco, A.J. Gassett, E. Seto, A.A. Szpiro, T.V. Larson, P.D. Sampson, J.D. Kaufman, and L. Sheppard, "Publicly available low-cost sensor measurements for PM2.5 exposure modeling: Guidance for monitor deployment and data selection", *Environ. Int.,* vol. 158, p. 106897, 2022.
[http://dx.doi.org/10.1016/j.envint.2021.106897] [PMID: 34601393]

[81] R. Dubey, A.K. Patra, J. Joshi, D. Blankenberg, S.S.R. Kolluru, B. Madhu, and S. Raval, "Evaluation of low-cost particulate matter sensors OPC N2 and PM Nova for aerosol monitoring", *Atmos. Pollut. Res.,* vol. 13, no. 3, p. 101335, 2022.
[http://dx.doi.org/10.1016/j.apr.2022.101335]

[82] P. Gupta, P. Doraiswamy, R. Levy, O. Pikelnaya, J. Maibach, B. Feenstra, A. Polidori, F. Kiros, and K.C. Mills, "Impact of California fires on local and regional air quality: The role of a low-cost sensor network and satellite observations", *Geohealth,* vol. 2, no. 6, pp. 172-181, 2018.
[http://dx.doi.org/10.1029/2018GH000136] [PMID: 31157310]

[83] H Camarasan, A Radovici, H Stefanie, A Mereuta, N Ajtai, and C. Botezan, "Air Quality Monitoring for Sustainable Development in Cluj-Napoca", *EGU General Assembly Conference Abstracts,* 2023.
[http://dx.doi.org/10.5194/egusphere-egu23-179]

[84] P. Gupta, and S.A. Christopher, "Particulate matter air quality assessment using integrated surface, satellite, and meteorological products: Multiple regression approach", *J. Geophys. Res.,* vol. 114, p. D14205, 2009.
[http://dx.doi.org/10.1029/2008JD011496]

[85] A. Rajkomar, J. Dean, and I. Kohane, "Machine learning in medicine", *New England Journal of Medicine,* vol. 380, no. 14, pp. 1347-1358, 2019.
[http://dx.doi.org/10.1056/NEJMra1814259]

[86] K. Alzoubi, M. Al-Bzoor, O. Aljalahma, and M. Ali, "Air quality monitoring and alerting system to help in reducing asthma attack in asthmatic children", *InBIODEVICES,* no. Feb, pp. 91-98, 2021.

[87] D.W. Dockery, C.A. Pope III, X. Xu, J.D. Spengler, J.H. Ware, M.E. Fay, B.G. Ferris Jr, and F.E. Speizer, "An association between air pollution and mortality in six U.S. cities", *N. Engl. J. Med.,* vol. 329, no. 24, pp. 1753-1759, 1993.
[http://dx.doi.org/10.1056/NEJM199312093292401] [PMID: 8179653]

[88] A. Alassi, A. Khan, D. Ayesh, I. Aljayyousi, R. Aldisi, S. Elasad, F. Touati, and M. Benammar, "Development of innovative indoor/outdoor air quality monitoring for environmental impact assessment in the State of Qatar", *WIT Trans. Ecol. Environ.,* vol. 183, pp. 103-115, 2014.
[http://dx.doi.org/10.2495/AIR140091]

[89] E.G. Snyder, T.H. Watkins, P.A. Solomon, E.D. Thoma, R.W. Williams, G.S.W. Hagler, D. Shelow, D.A. Hindin, V.J. Kilaru, and P.W. Preuss, "The changing paradigm of air pollution monitoring", *Environ. Sci. Technol.,* vol. 47, no. 20, pp. 11369-11377, 2013.
[http://dx.doi.org/10.1021/es4022602] [PMID: 23980922]

[90] M.L. Bell, "Ambient air pollution and cardiovascular health: A scientific statement from the American Heart Association", *Circulation,* vol. 109, no. 21, pp. 2655-2671, 2004.
[http://dx.doi.org/10.1161/01.CIR.0000128587.30041.C8] [PMID: 15173049]

[91] World Health Organization, *The World health report 2002: Reducing risks, promoting healthy life.* Geneva, Switzerland: World Health Organization, 2002.

[92] M. Fuentes, H.R. Song, S.K. Ghosh, D.M. Holland, and J.M. Davis, "Spatial association between speciated fine particles and mortality", *Biometrics,* vol. 62, no. 3, pp. 855-863, 2006. [http://dx.doi.org/10.1111/j.1541-0420.2006.00526.x] [PMID: 16984329]

CHAPTER 6

Integration of Machine Learning with Geospatial Technologies for Biodiversity Conservation

Shubham Gupta[1,*]

[1] *Department of Analytics and Artificial Intelligence, Center of Excellence (COE), Noblesoft Solutions Inc., San Antonio, Texas, USA*

Abstract: This chapter introduces the integration of machine learning techniques with geospatial technologies for biodiversity conservation. A primary challenge we face today is the accelerating rate of biodiversity loss. Combining machine learning, GIS, and remote sensing provides powerful tools for understanding and conserving wildlife habitats. We explore methods for attacking habitat mapping and models predicting the consequences of climate change on species adaptation, and modify the implementation of real-time threat discovery in protected areas. We demonstrate how these technological approaches can be implemented across various ecosystems to support evidence-based decision-making and adaptive management approaches for biodiversity protection through detailed case studies and technical frameworks.

Keywords: Biodiversity, Climate change, Geospatial techniques, Machine learning, Remote sensing, Species distribution modeling, Wildlife habitat.

INTRODUCTION

Biodiversity conservation has become one of the most significant environmental challenges of the 21st century, and it is estimated that there is a 100 to 1,000 times higher extinction rate than natural background rates [1]. Although the pressure of such issues on global ecosystems has vastly decreased, continuous habitat destruction, climate change, invasive species, pollution, and overexploitation remain a major threat to global ecosystems [2]. In light of these circumstances, influencing species distributions, forecasting habitat changes, and detecting threats in the field through conservation strategies now require increasingly sophisticated means to understand species distributions, past and future habitat changes, and monitor threats, among other things.

* **Corresponding author Shubham Gupta:** Department of Analytics and Artificial Intelligence, Center of Excellence (COE), Noblesoft Solutions Inc., San Antonio, Texas, USA; E-mail: shubhamgupta133@gmail.com

Kanwarpreet Singh, Arundhati, Manmeet Kaur, Abhishek Sharma, Aditya Kumar Tiwary & Sahil Sharma (Eds.)

All rights reserved-© 2026 Bentham Science Publishers

A new paradigm of biodiversity conservation based on machine learning integration with geospatial technologies is emerging. Traditional conservation efforts rely on limited data and simplified modelling techniques, leading to conservation decisions based on incomplete information [3]. Despite that, the exponential rise in environmental data acquisitions through remote sensing platforms, field sensors, citizen science initiatives, and genetic sampling has opened new possibilities for applying modern computational methods to solve conservation problems [4].

This work uses machine learning and spatial optimization to analyze the role of these three aspects of biodiversity conservation in the revolution.

1. **Wildlife habitat mapping and prediction:** Using increasingly accurate predictive models to find current suitable habitats and predict the future distribution of habitats.
2. **Climate change and species adaptation:** Models for gauging how species adapt to changing environmental conditions and identifying areas to be conserved that account for shifts in species range.
3. **Protected areas real-time threat detection:** Creation of intelligent monitoring systems capable of detecting and reacting to threats, including poaching, illegal logging, and wildfires, while they're occurring.

Combined with these technological approaches, conservation biology is creating a new field called sometimes 'Conservation Technology' or 'Conservation Tech' [5]. The domain of this interdisciplinary area combines computational methods for the development of less costly, more rapid, more effective, and more adaptive conservation efforts. By embracing these innovations, conservation practitioners can shift from reactive to proactive, anticipating and addressing threats before biodiversity loss becomes irreversible.

WILDLIFE HABITAT MAPPING AND PREDICTION

Traditional Approaches to Habitat Modeling

Wildlife habitat mapping has evolved over almost two centuries. This approach relied on expert knowledge, limited field observations, and, most often, relatively simple statistical methods [6]. It included Habitat Suitability Index (HSI) models, generalized linear models (GLMs), and generalized additive models (GAMs) that related species occurrence to Radio Frequency (RF) predictors [7].

Traditional habitat modelling approaches, although subject to various advances in the 1990s with Geographic Information Systems (GIS), still have several limitations.

- Dependence on sparse occurrence data, with models often relying on presence-only records or small numbers of presence-absence observations, which constrains model reliability.
- Assumption of static relationships between species and their environment.
- No capability to deal with complicated interactions among the ecological variables.
- Forecasting *vs.* current conditions of habitat suitability.

These limitations have prompted the development of more sophisticated computational approaches to better account for species–habitat relationship complexity while making more accurate predictions about where to focus conservation planning.

Machine Learning for Habitat Suitability Modeling

Machine learning (ML) approaches have emerged as powerful tools for habitat suitability modeling, offering several advantages over traditional statistical methods. ML algorithms can detect complex, non-linear relationships between species occurrence and environmental variables, handle high-dimensional data, and often provide superior predictive performance [8].

Several machine learning algorithms have gained prominence in habitat modeling:

Maximum Entropy (MaxEnt)

MaxEnt has become one of the most widely used algorithms for species distribution modeling, particularly when working with presence-only data. MaxEnt estimates the probability distribution of a species' occurrence by finding the distribution with maximum entropy subject to constraints derived from environmental variables at known occurrence locations [9].

The popularity of MaxEnt stems from its ability to work effectively with small sample sizes while handling both continuous and categorical variables. Additionally, MaxEnt provides response curves showing species' relationships with individual environmental variables and generates habitat suitability maps with quantified uncertainty.

Random Forests

Random Forests (RF) is an ensemble learning method that constructs multiple decision trees during training and outputs the mean prediction of the individual trees. This approach is particularly valuable for habitat modeling because it efficiently handles high-dimensional data while capturing complex interactions among environmental variables. RF also provides measures of variable importance and demonstrates robustness to noise and outliers in the data. The method has been successfully applied to model habitats for diverse species, from marine mammals to forest-dwelling insects [10].

Boosted Regression Trees

Boosted Regression Trees (BRT), also known as Gradient Boosting Machines, combine the strengths of regression trees and boosting methods. In habitat modeling, BRTs offer several key advantages by automatically handling variable interactions and accommodating missing data effectively. The method demonstrates resistance to overfitting through regularization and provides flexibility for modeling complex ecological relationships, making it particularly suitable for capturing non-linear species-environment associations.

Neural Networks

Deep learning approaches, particularly convolutional neural networks (CNNs), have recently gained traction in habitat modeling because they can process raw imagery directly rather than relying solely on derived environmental variables [11]. These approaches excel at extracting relevant features directly from satellite imagery and can detect subtle habitat characteristics that traditional methods might miss. CNNs can integrate data from multiple sensors and resolutions while modeling temporal dynamics in habitat conditions, providing a more comprehensive approach to habitat suitability assessment.

Comparative Performance

The relative performance of different machine learning approaches for habitat modeling depends on various factors, including sample size, data quality, species characteristics, and the specific conservation question being addressed. Fig. (**1**) provides a conceptual comparison of standard machine learning approaches for habitat suitability modeling based on predictive performance, interpretability, and data requirements.

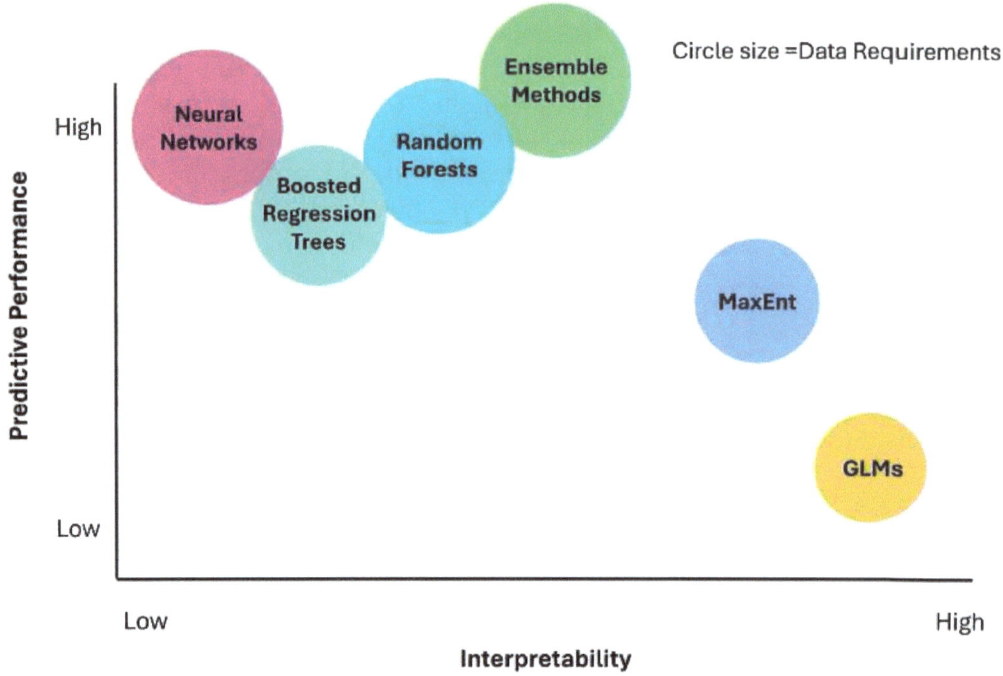

Fig. (1). Comparison of machine learning approaches for habitat suitability modeling.

Studies comparing multiple algorithms have found that ensemble approaches—combining predictions from different models—often provide the most robust habitat predictions [12]. Despite their advantages, machine learning approaches for habitat modeling face challenges related to interpretability, particularly for complex models like neural networks. Recent advances in explainable AI (XAI) techniques are helping to address this limitation by providing methods to interpret complex model predictions [13].

Integration of Multi-source Remote Sensing Data

The effectiveness of habitat models largely depends on the quality and relevance of input environmental data. Recent advances in remote sensing technologies have dramatically expanded the availability of high-resolution spatial data for habitat mapping and prediction [14]. Machine learning approaches are well-suited to leverage these diverse data sources, integrating information across spatial and temporal scales.

Multispectral and Hyperspectral Imagery

Multispectral sensors provide regular coverage at medium spatial resolution (10-30m) across multiple spectral bands [15]. These data allow one to calculate vegetation indices correlated with habitat characteristics that affect many species.

Habitat characterization with hyperspectral sensors (hundreds of narrow spectral bands) is even more challenging. Because these sensors detect subtle changes in vegetation composition, canopy chemistry, and other ecological features that may be significant to some specialist species [16], other sensors may provide even more useful information.

LiDAR and Radar

Light Detection and Ranging (LiDAR) Technology has revolutionized our capacity to map three-dimensional habitat structures, a significant input for habitat suitability modeling for many species [17]. LiDAR data provides detailed information on canopy height and vertical complexity, understory density, terrain characteristics, and microhabitat features, all of which are crucial for understanding species-habitat relationships. Synthetic Aperture Radar (SAR) offers complementary benefits, particularly for monitoring habitat in cloud-prone areas or detecting subtle changes in forest structure and soil moisture that may affect habitat quality [18].

Drone-based Data Collection

In recent years, Unmanned Aerial Vehicles (UAVs, or drones) have emerged as versatile platforms for acquiring ultra-high-resolution imagery and 3D data for detailed habitat mapping [19]. Drones can collect imagery at sub-centimeter resolution while deploying multiple sensors simultaneously and generating 3D models through photogrammetry. They enable access to remote or hazardous areas and the collection of data on demand to capture temporal dynamics, making them particularly valuable for fine-scale habitat characterization and monitoring applications.

Habitat Mapping Products and Time Series Analysis

Now that the archive of satellite data is as rich as it is, the time series of habitat change over decades has enabled the construction of habitat datasets for analysis within a modelling framework to determine habitat dynamics and detect trends [20]. By democratizing access to this massive archive of remote sensing data through Google Earth Engine and similar cloud computing platforms, even conservation scientists were previously limited to processing and analyzing data at global scales due to computational constraints [21]. Detecting small changes in habitat quality that may be missed in single-date analyses can be achieved through time-series analysis combined with machine learning. Table **1** summarizes the key applications of spatial resolution and data sources for habitat modeling.

Table 1. Remote sensing data sources for habitat modeling.

Data Source	Spatial Resolution	Key Applications in Habitat Modeling	Machine Learning Approaches
Landsat/Sentinel Multispectral	10-30m	Land cover classification, vegetation indices, and habitat change detection.	Random Forest, MaxEnt, CNN
Hyperspectral	3-30m	Detailed vegetation composition, invasive species detection, and canopy chemistry.	SVM, CNN, Random Forest
LiDAR	0.5-2m	Vegetation structure, microhabitats, and terrain complexity.	Random Forest, Gradient Boosting, CNN
SAR	1-10m	Forest structure, soil moisture, all-weather monitoring	Random Forest, CNN, Hybrid models
Drone Imagery	1-10cm	Fine-scale habitat features, individual tree detection, and small patch dynamics.	CNN, Object-based image analysis
Thermal Imagery	5cm-100m	Water body mapping, animal detection, and microclimate assessment.	CNN, Threshold-based models

Case Study: Endangered Species Habitat Mapping in Tropical Forests

The authors illustrated cutting-edge techniques for habitat mapping in the context of a case study on the endangered black-faced lion tamarin (*Leontopithecus caissara*) in the Atlantic Forest of Brazil. This small primate has a very restricted range, with its habitat being further fragmented by this easily identifiable primate, and therefore, accurate habitat mapping for effective conservation planning is crucial [22].

Study Area and Conservation Context

Over 85% of the forest has been lost, and the remaining forests are relatively disconnected. The remaining fragments continue to be integrated under agricultural expansion [23]. The black-faced lion tamarin occupies a small part of the biome and occurs only in the coastal forests of São Paulo and Paraná states.

Data Collection and Preparation

The research team integrated multiple data sources to develop comprehensive habitat models:

1. **Species occurrence data:** 78 confirmed presence points collected through systematic field surveys and camera trap records from 2015 to 2020.
2. **Environmental predictors:** Environmental predictors encompassed Landsat 8 and Sentinel-2 multispectral imagery at 10-30m resolution, ALOS PALSAR radar data for forest structure at 25m resolution, and airborne LiDAR samples for calibration at 1m resolution. Additional data sources included climate variables from WorldClim covering precipitation and temperature patterns, topographic variables such as elevation, slope, and aspect, and anthropogenic variables measuring distance to roads and settlements.
3. **Field validation data:** Independent survey data from 45 sites not used in model training, including presence and confirmed absence records.

Modeling Approach

The researchers implemented an ensemble modeling approach, combining predictions from multiple machine learning algorithms:

1. **Max ENT:** Used primarily for its ability to work well with presence-only data and provide response curves for ecological interpretation.
2. **Random Forests:** Implemented to capture complex variable interactions and provide variable importance measures.
3. **Convolutional Neural Network (CNN):** Developed to process and integrate satellite imagery directly at multiple scales and from multiple sensors.

Results and Insights

The ensemble model achieved a test AUC (Area under the Curve) of 0.92, indicating excellent discriminative ability. Analysis of variable importance revealed several key insights:

1. Forest structure variables derived from radar and LiDAR data were the strongest predictors of habitat suitability, particularly canopy height and vertical complexity.
2. Connectivity between forest patches emerged as critical, with suitable habitat

patches smaller than 5 hectares only utilized if they were within 200 meters of larger forest fragments.
3. Anthropogenic variables, especially distance to roads, significantly influenced habitat suitability, with areas within 500 meters of roads substantially reducing suitability regardless of forest quality.
4. Temporal analysis using the 5-year Landsat time series identified areas of improving and degrading habitat quality, highlighting regions where forest regeneration created new potential habitat and where degradation threatened existing populations.

Conservation Applications

This case study demonstrates how integrated machine learning approaches can deliver practical conservation outcomes:

1. **Protected area planning:** The habitat model was used to identify three previously unprotected forest fragments with high habitat suitability that were subsequently designated as wildlife refuges.
2. **Corridor design:** Analysis of connectivity between suitable habitat patches informed the design of three forest corridors, prioritizing restoration efforts in areas that would maximize functional connectivity for the species.
3. **Monitoring framework:** The temporal component of the model established a baseline for ongoing monitoring, with annual updates based on new satellite imagery to track changes in habitat suitability.
4. **Community engagement:** The detailed habitat maps were used in education programs with local communities to illustrate the specific forest characteristics required by the species and to engage landowners in voluntary conservation agreements.

CLIMATE CHANGE AND SPECIES ADAPTATION

Modeling Climate Change Impacts on Biodiversity

One of the most serious threats to global biodiversity, climate change has far-ranging implications for species' distributions, phenology, physiology, and interactions [24]. Recent years have seen the increasing use of machine learning to understand these complex impacts and to inform adaptation strategies.

Many mechanisms, operating in conjunction, directly and indirectly, impact climate change's impact on biodiversity:

1. **Range shifts:** Good and rising temperatures, along with associated rainfall patterns, are shifting the range boundaries of many species (some toward higher latitudes and elevations) [25].
2. **Ecological relationships:** Disruptions of biological interactions, such as plant-pollinator interactions or predator-prey dynamics, can occur when plant phenology mismatches that of pollinators or predators [26].
3. **Changing temperatures:** Precipitation patterns and extreme weather events can directly increase physiological stress beyond the species' physiological limits [27].
4. **Changes in disturbance regimes:** Changes in perturbation regimes, such as wildfires, floods, and droughts, change habitat quality and availability [28].
5. **Real ecological communities:** As such species respond individually to climate change, ecological communities are reassembling as novel assemblages with uncertain dynamics [29].

Current species distributions are, unfortunately, frequently modelled using bioclimatic envelope models, which link them to climate variables, and future distributions are then projected based on climate scenarios [30]. While these approaches help make general assessments of species responses to climate change, they do not sufficiently capture the complex nature of these responses.

Machine learning approaches can address several challenges concerning climate data in biodiversity modelling:

1. **ML trick:** To downscale the climate projections to ecologically relevant resolutions, topographic variables and local weather station data can be incorporated [31].
2. **ML approaches to correcting biases:** Similarly to correcting biases in observed climate data, ML approaches can learn the relationship between observed climate data and model outputs [32].
3. **ML techniques:** The uncertainty in climate model predictions can be reduced using ensemble models — predictions from multiple climate models [33].
4. **Model interpretability:** ML algorithms can select the most ecologically relevant climate variables for specific species or ecosystems, thereby improving model performance [34].

Machine Learning Approaches for Forecasting Species Range Shifts

Species are expected to shift their ranges in response to climate change, altering habitat suitability across space. Forecasts of these range shifts are critical for proactive conservation planning. The complex processes that underlie species range dynamics are readily amenable to machine learning approaches for modelling.

Traditional Species Distribution Models (SDMs) project correlations of species occurrence in the present to an unknown future climate [35]. These models have been improved in many ways with machine learning:

1. **Accounting for dispersal limitations:** ML approaches incorporate more realistic dispersal scenarios by modeling habitat connectivity, species mobility traits, and potential barriers [36].
2. Including biotic interactions, including Neural networks and deep learning approaches that can integrate co-occurrence data to model how these interactions might change [37].
3. **Addressing non-equilibrium dynamics:** Recurrent neural networks and other temporal ML methods can capture dynamic, non-equilibrium processes [38].
4. **Incorporating adaptation potential:** ML models that include genetic and trait data can assess adaptive potential and its implications for range shifts [39].

Novel Modeling Frameworks

Several novel modeling frameworks have emerged that leverage machine learning to provide more realistic forecasts of species range shifts:

1. **Hybrid mechanistic-statistical models:** These models combine process-based simulations of physiological responses to climate with ML-based statistical relationships [40].
2. **Agent-based models with ML components:** These models simulate individual organisms or populations making decisions based on environmental conditions, with ML algorithms determining behavioural responses [41].
3. **Transfer learning approaches:** These methods leverage knowledge from modeling well-studied species to improve predictions for data-poor species [42].
4. **Meta-learning frameworks:** These approaches learn general patterns of species responses to climate change across multiple taxa and regions, then apply these patterns to new species [43].

Evaluating Model Performance

Evaluating the performance of range-shift forecasts poses challenges, as we cannot directly validate predictions of future distributions. Machine learning offers several approaches to addressing this issue:

1. **Hindcasting validation:** Models are trained on historical data and tested on their ability to predict observed range shifts over recent decades [44].
2. **Out-of-range validation:** Models are evaluated on their ability to predict species distributions in regions outside their training data [45].
3. **Ecological reality checks:** Expert review and ecological knowledge assess whether model predictions align with known biological constraints and mechanisms [46].
4. **Ensemble consistency:** Agreement among different modeling approaches can indicate higher projection confidence [47].

Uncertainty Quantification and Communication

A key advantage of many machine learning approaches is their ability to quantify prediction uncertainty, which is crucial for conservation planning under climate change. Several techniques are employed:

1. **Probabilistic outputs:** Many ML algorithms can provide probability distributions rather than point estimates, giving a more nuanced view of potential range shifts [48].
2. **Ensemble variance:** Differences in predictions across model runs, or algorithms, can be quantified to map spatial patterns of uncertainty [49].
3. **Sensitivity analysis:** By systematically varying input parameters, ML models can identify which factors contribute most to uncertainty in range shift projections [50].

Integrating Climate and Species Distribution Models

To develop comprehensive adaptation strategies, conservationists need integrated frameworks that connect climate projections with species responses and conservation actions. Machine learning plays a pivotal role in these integrative approaches.

The integration of climate models and species distribution models has historically been challenging due to:

1. **Scale mismatches:** Climate models typically operate at coarse resolutions (50-100km grid cells), while species respond to climate at much finer scales.
2. **Temporal misalignment:** Climate projections often focus on long-term averages or end-of-century conditions, while conservation planning requires near-term predictions.

3. **Process representation:** Climate models emphasize physical processes, whereas species models must account for biological processes such as adaptation, dispersal, and species interactions.
4. **Uncertainty propagation:** Combining models multiplies uncertainties, making it challenging to distinguish robust patterns from noise.

Machine learning approaches help address these challenges through:

1. **Transfer functions:** ML algorithms can learn relationships between coarse-scale climate variables and local-scale environmental conditions relevant to species [51].
2. **Multi-scale modeling:** Deep learning architectures can integrate information across spatial and temporal scales, capturing broad climate patterns and local habitat features [52].
3. **End-to-end modeling:** Instead of connecting separate climate and species models, some approaches use ML to directly model the relationship between climate forcings and biodiversity outcomes [53].

Fig. **(2)** shows the integrated framework for modeling climate change impacts on species distributions and informing adaptation strategies. The framework connects climate and biodiversity data through machine learning models to generate actionable conservation recommendations.

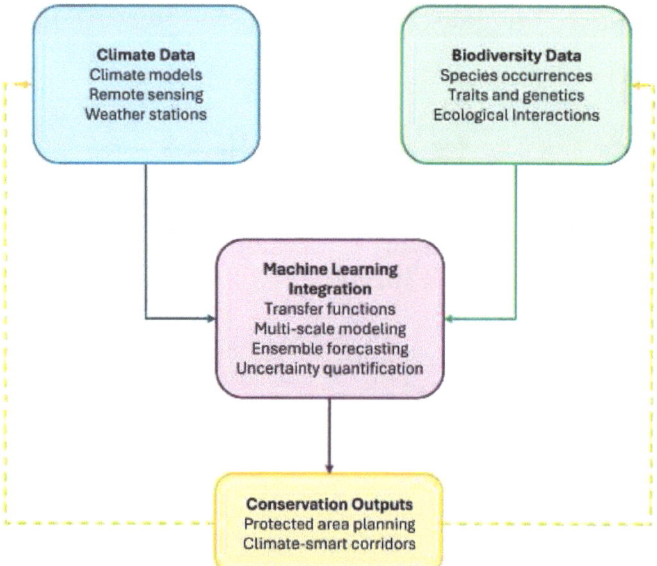

Fig. (2). Integrated framework for modeling climate change impacts on species distributions and informing adaptation strategies.

Species Vulnerability Assessment

A critical component of climate adaptation planning is assessing which species are most vulnerable to climate change. Machine learning approaches have enhanced vulnerability assessments by:

1. **Integrating multiple vulnerability factors:** ML algorithms can simultaneously consider exposure (the magnitude of climate change), sensitivity (physiological tolerance), and adaptive capacity (the ability to respond through dispersal, phenotypic plasticity, or evolution) [54].
2. **Trait-based predictions:** For data-poor species, ML approaches can predict vulnerability based on traits shared with better-studied taxa [55].
3. **Identifying vulnerability hotspots:** Geospatial ML techniques can map where concentrations of vulnerable species overlap with areas of severe climate change, thereby prioritizing conservation interventions [56].

Fig. (**3**) represents the species adaptive capacity assessment matrix. This framework illustrates species vulnerability by integrating climate exposure and adaptive capacity to guide conservation strategies. Species with high exposure and low adaptive capacity are most vulnerable, requiring intensive interventions such as ex-situ conservation, assisted migration, habitat manipulation, and genetic rescue. When adaptive capacity is higher, but exposure remains high, species face moderate vulnerability, facilitating natural adaptation through connectivity conservation, removal of non-climate stressors, and climate-smart protected areas becomes crucial. On the other hand, species with low exposure but limited adaptive capacity also fall into the moderate vulnerability category, and efforts to build resilience through expanding protected areas, increasing population size, protecting genetic diversity, and reducing habitat fragmentation are needed. Species with low exposure and high adaptive capacity experience the lowest vulnerability and require minimal interventions, including standard conservation practices, monitoring programs, protection of climate refugia, and educational initiatives. Overall, the framework highlights how conservation priorities can shift from intensive management to minimal intervention depending on the balance between exposure and adaptive capacity.

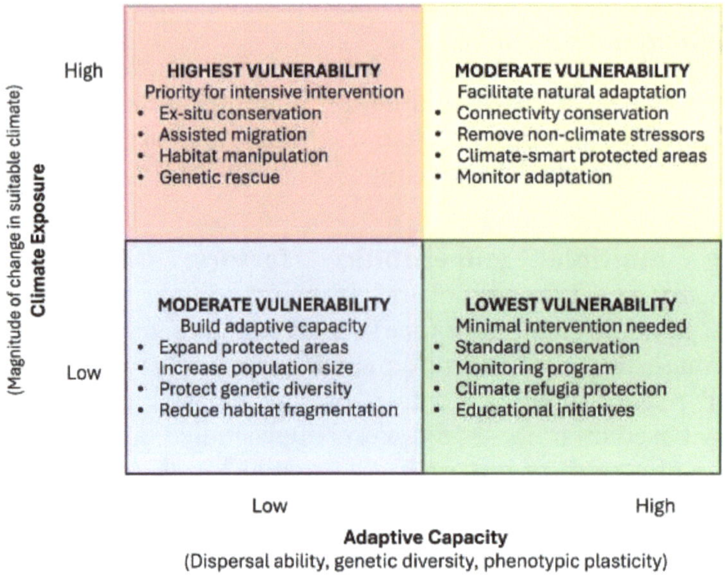

Fig. (3). Species adaptive capacity assessment matrix showing how different combinations of adaptive capacity and climate exposure translate into conservation priorities and management actions.

Conservation Planning Under Climate Change

Ultimately, integrated modeling aims to inform practical conservation actions. Machine learning approaches support climate-informed conservation planning through:

1. **Climate refugia identification:** ML algorithms can identify areas likely to maintain suitable conditions for vulnerable species despite regional climate change, often due to topographic complexity or microclimate buffering [57].
2. **Climate-smart corridor design:** ML-based connectivity analyses can identify movement pathways that account for current landscape structure and projected climate-driven range shifts [58].
3. **Conservation triage:** When resources are limited, ML approaches can optimize conservation investments by targeting species and areas where interventions yield the most significant biodiversity benefits [59].
4. **Anticipatory restoration:** Predictive models can guide habitat restoration efforts toward areas that will become suitable for threatened species in the future, even if they are not currently occupied [60].

Case Study: Predicting Migratory Bird Responses to Climate Change

Migratory birds are particularly vulnerable to climate change because they depend on multiple habitats and resources that may be affected differently by changing conditions [61]. Here, we present a case study demonstrating how integrated machine learning approaches can predict climate impacts on migratory species and inform conservation strategies.

Study System and Conservation Context

The case study focuses on Neotropical migratory songbirds that breed in North America and winter in Central and South America. These species face climate-related threats throughout their annual cycle, including:

1. Phenological mismatches between spring arrival and peak food availability on breeding grounds [62].
2. Altered habitat conditions in wintering areas due to changing precipitation patterns [63].
3. Increased frequency and intensity of storms during migration periods [64].

Data Integration and Modeling Approach

The research team assembled diverse datasets spanning the full annual cycle:

1. **Breeding grounds data:** Breeding grounds data included Breeding Bird Survey abundance data from 1970-2020, MODIS phenology metrics from 2000-2020, climate data covering temperature, precipitation, and extreme events, and land cover and habitat structure information derived from Landsat and LiDAR sources.
2. **Migration data:** Migration data encompassed weather radar (NEXRAD) migration-intensity measurements, citizen-science observations from eBird, geolocator tracking data for focal species, and detailed weather patterns along migratory routes.
3. **Wintering grounds data:** The data comprised winter monitoring program counts, precipitation and drought indices, and forest cover and fragmentation metrics to assess habitat quality in the Central and South American wintering areas.

Team developed a three-part modeling framework:

1. **Breeding habitat model:** A random forest algorithm predicted breeding season

habitat suitability based on climate, land cover, and phenological variables.
2. **Migratory connectivity model:** A deep neural network integrated geolocator data with stable isotope measurements to map connections between breeding and wintering populations.
3. **Complete annual cycle model:** A Bayesian network combined outputs from the breeding and migration models with wintering ground data to predict population responses to climate change throughout the annual cycle.

Results and Insights

The integrated modeling approach revealed several key insights:

1. **Differential vulnerability across the annual cycle:** Climate sensitivity was the highest during migration periods for many species, when birds have limited flexibility to adjust to changing conditions.
2. **Spatial shifts in suitable habitat:** Breeding ranges were projected to shift northward by an average of 300km by 2050 under RCP8.5, while wintering habitat suitability showed more complex patterns.
3. **Projected spring arrival date:** Spring arrival dates were projected to advance by 5–12 days by 2050, but this was insufficient to keep pace with the faster shifts in prey phenology (15–18 days), which increased mismatches.
4. **Migratory connectivity implications:** Migratory connectivity analysis indicated that differing breeding populations share wintering areas, which may present potential bottlenecks where climate impacts on a single wintering area affect multiple breeding populations.
5. **Synergistic effects:** There were also synergistic effects — when moderate climate impacts at various stages of the year add to severe population declines, even when no single stage was catastrophic.

Conservation Applications

According to these findings, the research team developed targeted conservation recommendations:

1. **Climate-resilient reserve networks:** The model identified a network of protected areas spanning breeding, migration, and wintering regions that would maintain suitable conditions under projected climate change.
2. **Targeted habitat management:** For breeding areas, recommendations included managing forest structure to create cooler microhabitats that could buffer against warming temperatures.
3. **Migration corridor protection:** Critical stopover sites were identified where land protection would yield the greatest benefit for maintaining migratory

connectivity under changing climate conditions.

4. **Monitoring framework:** The model results informed the design of a coordinated monitoring program spanning the full annual cycle, with sampling intensity stratified based on projected climate vulnerability.

AI FOR REAL-TIME THREAT DETECTION IN PROTECTED AREAS

Sensor Networks and Data Acquisition

Protected areas face numerous threats, including poaching, illegal logging, wildfires, and human encroachment. Traditional monitoring approaches, which rely primarily on ranger patrols, often cannot effectively cover vast areas [65]. AI-powered monitoring systems, built on advanced sensor networks, transform threat detection capabilities by enabling real-time surveillance across large, remote areas.

Evolution of Wildlife Monitoring Technologies

Wildlife monitoring has evolved dramatically from traditional field methods to sophisticated sensor networks:

1. **Traditional methods:** Direct observation, track and sign surveys, and capture-mark-recapture studies provided limited spatial and temporal coverage [66].
2. **First-generation remote sensing:** Static camera traps, passive acoustic monitors, and satellite imagery expanded coverage but typically provided delayed information requiring manual processing [67].
3. **Connected sensor networks:** Modern systems integrate multiple sensor types into networked arrays that communicate with central databases in near real-time, enabling rapid detection and response to threats [68].
4. **Intelligent sensing platforms:** The latest systems directly integrate edge computing and AI into field devices, enabling immediate analysis and targeted data transmission [69].

Sensor Types and Applications

Modern protected area monitoring systems utilize diverse sensor technologies, as shown in Table **2**, which provides insight into sensor technologies used to monitor protected areas.

1. Camera systems include traditional camera traps, video surveillance, thermal

cameras, and multispectral cameras, each offering different advantages for wildlife monitoring and threat detection.

2. Acoustic monitoring technologies encompass passive acoustic monitors, acoustic pattern recognition systems, and directional acoustic sensing that detect gunshots, chainsaws, and other threatening sounds across large areas.
3. Aerial platforms provide elevated monitoring perspectives through drones (UAVs), tethered aerostats, and satellite monitoring systems that can efficiently cover vast territories.
4. **Ground-based sensors offer complementary capabilities using:** seismic sensors for detecting footsteps and vehicle movement, magnetic sensors for metal detection, and break-beam systems for perimeter monitoring.
5. Environmental sensors, including weather stations, water quality monitors, and air quality sensors, provide contextual information that enhances the interpretation of other sensor data and supports early warning systems for environmental threats like wildfires.

Networked Sensor Deployment Strategies

Effectively deploying sensor networks across vast protected areas requires strategic planning and optimization. Machine learning approaches have improved deployment strategies in several ways:

1. **Risk mapping:** ML algorithms analyze historical incident data, terrain characteristics, and animal movement patterns to identify high-risk areas where sensors should be concentrated [70].
2. **Coverage optimization:** Computational methods determine optimal sensor placement to maximize detection probability while minimizing costs [71].
3. **Adaptive deployment:** Some systems use reinforcement learning to continuously refine sensor placement based on detection patterns and changing threat dynamics [72].
4. **Heterogeneous networks:** ML approaches help optimize sensor mix for specific protected-area contexts [73].

Table 2. Sensor technologies for protected area monitoring.

Sensor Type	Data Collected	Threat Detection Applications	Machine Learning Approaches
Camera Traps	Still images triggered by motion	Poacher detection, wildlife monitoring, unauthorized access	CNN object detection, activity recognition

(Table 2) cont.....

Sensor Type	Data Collected	Threat Detection Applications	Machine Learning Approaches
Video Surveillance	Continuous or motion-triggered video	Boundary monitoring, entry point security	Real-time object tracking, behaviour analysis
Thermal Cameras	Heat signature imagery	Night detection of intruders, early fire detection	Anomaly detection, temperature pattern analysis
Acoustic Sensors	Audio recordings, spectrograms	Gunshot detection, chainsaw/vehicle sounds, wildlife disturbance	Audio classification, sound event detection
Drones	Aerial imagery, video, thermal data	Patrol support, rapid assessment of alerts, and wildlife surveys	Object detection, change detection, route optimization
Seismic Sensors	Ground vibration patterns	Vehicle movement, logging activities, and footstep detection	Signal processing, pattern recognition
Environmental Sensors	Temperature, humidity, air quality	Fire risk assessment, pollution detection	Anomaly detection, early warning systems

Data Transmission and Management

Once data is collected, it must be transmitted, processed, and stored efficiently. Several approaches address the challenges of remote, power-limited deployments:

1. **Edge computing:** Increasingly, initial data processing occurs on the sensors themselves, reducing transmission requirements by sending only relevant information [74].
2. **Low-power wide-area networks (LPWAN):** Technologies like LoRaWAN enable long-range, low-power communication for remote sensors [75].
3. **Mesh networks:** Sensors can relay data through multiple "hops" to reach base stations, extending coverage in areas without direct connectivity [76].
4. **Satellite connectivity:** For the most remote areas, satellite communication provides connectivity, though with bandwidth limitations [77].
5. **Mobile data collection:** In some cases, rangers or drones periodically collect data from sensors that cannot transmit wirelessly [78].

Integrating these technologies creates comprehensive monitoring systems that can detect threats across large, remote areas in real time, dramatically enhancing the security and management effectiveness of protected areas.

Deep Learning for Wildlife and Threat Recognition

The vast data sensor networks generated would overwhelm human analysts if processed manually. Deep learning algorithms, particularly convolutional neural networks (CNNs) and recurrent neural networks (RNNs), have revolutionized the automated sensor data analysis for wildlife identification and threat detection.

Computer Vision for Wildlife Recognition

Automated wildlife recognition enables biodiversity monitoring at unprecedented scales and supports anti-poaching efforts by identifying the presence of target species that may attract illegal activity [79]. Key applications include:

1. **Species identification:** Deep learning models can identify animal species in camera-trap images with accuracy rivalling that of human experts [80].
2. **Individual recognition:** For species with distinctive markings, CNNs can identify specific individuals, enabling non-invasive population monitoring [81].
3. **Behaviour classification:** Deep learning models can classify animal behaviours, providing insights into responses to human disturbance [82].
4. **Abundance estimation:** ML models can estimate animal counts from imagery, even when individuals overlap or are partially visible [83].
5. **Health assessment:** In wildlife imagery, computer vision can detect signs of injury, disease, or poor condition [84].

Human Activity and Threat Detection

Detecting human presence and distinguishing between legitimate and illicit activities are crucial for protected area monitoring. Advanced AI approaches include:

1. **Human detection in complex environments:** Specialized models can detect humans in challenging conditions (dense vegetation, low light, and partial occlusion), common in protected areas [85].
2. **Activity recognition:** Beyond detecting presence, AI systems classify human activities to distinguish between legitimate users (rangers, researchers, and tourists) and potential threats [86].
3. **Weapon detection:** Specialized models identify firearms, snares, and other poaching equipment [87].
4. **Vehicle recognition:** CNNs can detect and classify vehicles, including identifying specific unauthorized vehicles [88].
5. **Temporal pattern analysis:** Recurrent neural networks analyze activity patterns over time to flag suspicious behaviour [89].

Acoustic Event Detection

Sound-based monitoring complements visual systems by operating continuously and detecting events that may not be visible. Deep learning has dramatically improved acoustic monitoring capabilities:

1. **Gunshot detection:** CNN and RNN hybrid models can accurately identify and classify gunshots, even in noisy forest environments [90].
2. **Chainsaw and vehicle detection:** Models trained on spectrograms can identify the distinctive acoustic signatures of illegal logging or unauthorized vehicles [91].
3. **Species-specific calls:** Automated detection of animal vocalizations enables biodiversity monitoring and can identify distress calls that might indicate poaching activity [92].
4. **Anthropogenic sound classification:** Multi-class audio recognition systems distinguish between different human activities based on their acoustic signatures [90].

Multi-modal Fusion

The most advanced threat detection systems integrate data from multiple sensor types, leveraging the complementary strengths of different modalities [91]:

1. **Visual-acoustic fusion:** Combining camera and microphone data improves detection reliability [92].
2. **Thermal-optical fusion:** Daytime optical and nighttime thermal imagery can be integrated for 24-hour monitoring [92].
3. **Sensor-contextual fusion:** Environmental sensors provide context that improves the interpretation of other sensor data [92].
4. **Temporal-spatial fusion:** Combining information across time and space enables the detection of subtle or distributed events [92].

These advanced recognition capabilities form the foundation of effective real-time monitoring systems for protected areas, enabling automated threat detection across vast landscapes with limited human supervision.

Edge Computing and Real-time Analytics

The effectiveness of AI-based threat detection systems in protected areas depends on accurate models and the ability to deliver actionable intelligence in real time. Edge computing, which performs data processing and analysis directly on or near sensor devices, has emerged as a critical approach for enabling real-time response in remote, connectivity-limited environments [74].

The Edge Computing Paradigm for Conservation

Traditional cloud-based processing models face several challenges in protected area contexts:

1. **Connectivity limitations:** Many protected areas have poor or intermittent internet connectivity, making real-time cloud processing infeasible [74].
2. **Bandwidth constraints:** Raw sensor data (especially video and audio) requires significant bandwidth to transmit, which may be unavailable or prohibitively expensive in remote areas [74].
3. **Latency issues:** Conservation threats often require immediate response. Cloud-based processing introduces delays that could render interventions ineffective [74].
4. **Power limitations:** Many field sensors operate on batteries or small solar panels with strict energy budgets that cannot support continuous data transmission [74].

Edge computing addresses these challenges by moving processing capabilities closer to the data source. Several architectural approaches have emerged:

1. **On-device processing:** AI algorithms run directly on sensor devices (e.g., smart cameras with built-in neural network processors) [75].
2. **Edge servers:** Local computing nodes aggregate and process data from nearby sensors before selectively transmitting it to central systems [75].
3. **Mobile edge computing:** Rangers or conservation vehicles carry computing devices that collect and process data from nearby sensors during patrols [75].
4. **Hierarchical architectures:** These systems combine multiple edge processing tiers with selective cloud transmission, optimizing the trade-off between real-time response and comprehensive analysis [75].

Edge AI Optimization Techniques

Running sophisticated AI models on resource-constrained edge devices requires specialized optimization techniques:

1. Model compression: Reducing model size while maintaining acceptable accuracy through:
    - **Pruning:** Removing unnecessary network connections [76].

- **Quantization:** Using lower-precision calculations [76].
- **Knowledge distillation:** Training smaller "student" models to mimic larger "teacher" models [76].

2. Hardware acceleration: Specialized hardware like Edge TPUs, FPGAs, or neural processing units dramatically improves energy efficiency for AI tasks [76].

3. Adaptive processing: Dynamic adjustment of processing based on context and available resources [76].

Real-time Analytics and Decision Support

The ultimate goal of edge computing in protected area monitoring is to transform raw sensor data into actionable intelligence in real time. Several analytics approaches support this objective:

1. **Event detection and classification:** Identifying and categorizing potential threats from sensor data streams [77].
2. **Threat assessment and prioritization:** Evaluating detected events to determine response urgency [77].
3. **Automated alerting and response coordination:** Generating appropriate notifications based on threat assessment [77].
4. **Continuous learning and adaptation:** Advanced systems improve over time through feedback on alert accuracy, integration of new threat indicators, and adjustment to seasonal changes [77].

Fig. (**4**) represents the architecture of an AI-powered real-time threat detection system. The figure shows a multi-layered AI-powered wildlife monitoring and response system. The Data Acquisition Layer gathers information using tools like camera traps, drones, satellite imagery, acoustic sensors, and ranger reports. This raw data is processed in the Edge Processing Layer, where lightweight models handle filtering and initial classification. The AI Analytics Layer applies advanced object detection, event classification, and anomaly detection methods. Based on these insights, the Decision & Alerting Layer prioritizes alerts, assesses threats, and coordinates responses. Finally, actionable interventions, such as rangerdeployment, aerial support, automated deterrents, or law enforcement, are implemented to ensure effective conservation and protection.

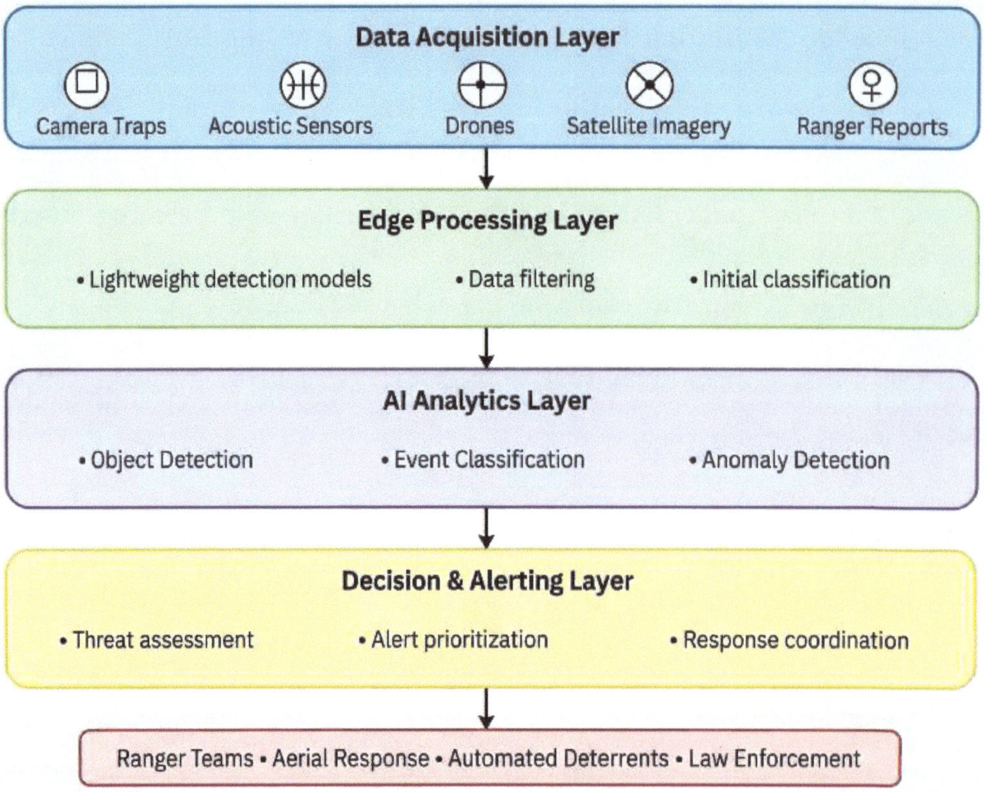

Fig. (4). Architecture of an AI-powered real-time threat detection system showing data flow from multiple sensor types through processing layers to automated alerts and responses.

Privacy and Ethical Considerations

The deployment of advanced surveillance technologies in protected areas raises essential ethical and privacy considerations:

1. **Indigenous and local community rights:** Many protected areas overlap with indigenous territories or local community areas. Surveillance systems must respect the rights and privacy of these groups [78].
2. **Tourist and visitor privacy:** Systems must balance security needs with appropriate privacy protections for legitimate protected area users [78].
3. **Dual-use technologies:** Technologies developed for conservation surveillance could be repurposed for unauthorized surveillance. Proper governance frameworks and technological safeguards are essential [78].

4. **Explainability and accountability:** When AI systems trigger enforcement actions, the basis for these actions should be explainable and subject to appropriate oversight [78].

Case Study: Anti-Poaching Monitoring System in African Reserves

To illustrate the real-world application of AI-powered threat detection, we present a case study of an integrated anti-poaching system deployed across multiple protected areas in East Africa.

Conservation Context and Challenges

The case study focuses on a network of reserves spanning approximately 8,000 square kilometres across multiple countries, protecting critical populations of elephants, rhinos, and other threatened species. These areas faced several challenges:

1. **Escalating poaching pressure:** Organized criminal networks target high-value species with increasingly sophisticated methods [79].
2. **Resource limitations:** Less than one ranger per 50 square kilometres, making traditional patrol-based coverage inadequate [79].
3. **Difficult terrain:** Dense forests, rugged mountains, and wetlands limiting visibility and patrol access [79].
4. **Connectivity gaps:** Cellular coverage is available in less than 30% of the protected areas [79].
5. **Harsh environmental conditions:** Extreme temperatures, dust, and heavy rains damage equipment and limit deployment options [79].

System Architecture and Components

The integrated monitoring system was designed to address these challenges through a multi-layered approach:

1. **Sensor Network:** The integrated monitoring system was designed to address these challenges through a multi-layered approach utilizing an extensive sensor network. This network comprised 320 AI-enabled camera units strategically deployed at likely entry points and along known wildlife corridors, 150 solar-powered acoustic monitoring nodes for continuous sound surveillance, 12 deployable thermal imaging systems for nighttime surveillance, ranger smartphones equipped with custom apps enabling rangers to document observations and connect to the system, and eight medium-range UAVs

equipped with optical and thermal cameras for aerial reconnaissance.

2. **Edge Computing Infrastructure:** The edge computing infrastructure provided the necessary processing power through 15 ruggedized computing stations powered by solar and satellite connectivity, serving as field edge nodes; 24 vehicle-mounted and backpack processing units for mobile edge computing; and four main computing centres at ranger headquarters functioning as base station servers.
3. **AI Analytics Pipeline:** The AI analytics pipeline operated at multiple levels, with lightweight models running directly on sensors for initial filtering as the primary detection layer, more sophisticated models on edge nodes providing detailed classification as the secondary analysis layer, and advanced analytics at base stations incorporating multiple data sources for integration and context analysis.
4. **Response Coordination System:** The response coordination system ensured effective threat response through an ML-based alert prioritization engine that evaluated threats based on type, location, time, and available resources, an automated and manual response dispatch platform for deploying appropriate resources, mobile ranger interfaces using smartphone and tablet applications that provided field teams with real-time intelligence, and secure information sharing systems enabling cross-boundary coordination with neighboring protected areas.

AI Model Development and Deployment

The system utilized multiple specialized AI models:

1. **Visual detection models:** CNN-based architectures optimized for edge deployment [80].
2. **Acoustic event detection:** Convolutional recurrent neural networks for sound classification [81].
3. Behaviour and pattern analysis: Higher-level models analyzing sequences and patterns [82].

All models underwent a multi-stage development process:

1. **Initial training:** Using data from historical incidents and controlled scenarios.
2. **Local adaptation:** Fine-tuning with region-specific data.
3. **Continuous improvement:** Regular updates based on field validation data and changing threat patterns.

Operational Results and Impact

After three years of operation, the system demonstrated a significant conservation impact:

1. **Poaching reduction:** Elephant poaching incidents decreased by 78% across the protected areas network, with rhino poaching declining by 63% [83].
2. **Response efficiency:** Average response time to detected threats decreased from 6+ hours to 38 minutes [83].
3. **Coverage improvement:** Effective surveillance coverage increased from approximately 20% to 86% of the protected area network [83].
4. **Cost effectiveness:** After initial installation, the system reduced per-squar--kilometre protection costs by 47% compared to traditional patrol-only approaches [83].
5. **Evidence quality:** Arrests resulting in successful prosecutions increased by 215%, primarily due to better evidence collection guided by real-time intelligence [83].

Key performance metrics included:

- 91.3% accuracy in human detection under varied conditions.
- 94.8% accuracy in gunshot detection at distances up to 1km.
- The false positive rate was reduced from 41% in the first year to 8% in the third year.
- System uptime of 94.7% despite challenging environmental conditions [83].

Challenges and Lessons Learned

The implementation revealed several essential lessons:

1. **Technological challenges:** Equipment environmental hardening required multiple design iterations, edge AI optimization took longer than anticipated, and integration across multiple sensor types required standardized alert protocols [84].
2. **Human factors:** Ranger training and engagement proved critical to system effectiveness, workflow integration needed careful design, and creating trust in the system required a transparent explanation of AI recommendations [84].
3. **Adaptive adversaries:** Poachers adjusted tactics in response to the system, requiring continuous updating of detection models [84].
4. **Sustainability considerations:** Long-term maintenance planning needed greater emphasis, knowledge transfer to local technical teams was essential,

and developing sustainable funding mechanisms proved challenging [84].

INTEGRATION AND IMPLEMENTATION CHALLENGES

Data Quality and Availability Issues

While machine learning offers powerful tools for biodiversity conservation, the effectiveness of these approaches depends fundamentally on the quality and availability of underlying data. Several data-related challenges must be addressed for successful implementation:

Data Gaps and Biases

Biodiversity data exhibits significant systematic biases that can undermine machine learning applications [85]:

1. **Systematic sampling biases:** Taxonomic biases favour charismatic species (mammals and birds account for over 70% of GBIF records despite representing <1% of described species), geographic biases concentrate research in accessible regions while under-sampling tropical biodiversity hotspots, temporal biases result from sparse historical data with inconsistent methodologies, and detection biases occur for cryptic or rare species [85].
2. **Machine learning compensation approaches:** Bias correction techniques such as target group background sampling and spatial filtering reduce sampling bias impacts, transfer learning applies knowledge from data-rich to data-poor species, active learning identifies optimal locations for additional data collection, and data augmentation expands limited datasets through synthetic data generation [86].

Data Integration Challenges

Conservation applications require the integration of diverse data types, presenting several interconnected challenges [87]:

1. **Heterogeneity issues:** Data formats range from structured databases to unstructured field notes, spatial and temporal resolutions vary among environmental predictors, taxonomic classifications evolve with different naming conventions across datasets, and metadata consistency problems arise from missing or inconsistent documentation of collection methods and accuracy [87].
2. **Integration solutions:** Ontology development creates formal semantic

frameworks for automated dataset integration; data fusion techniques, such as multi-view learning, handle heterogeneous inputs; Bayesian approaches explicitly model uncertainty propagation across different sources; and automated data cleaning uses natural language processing to standardize taxonomic names and extract structured information [88].

Data Accessibility and Sharing

Multiple accessibility barriers prevent data use in conservation applications [89]:

1. **Access barriers:** Proprietary restrictions limit sharing from commercial entities and institutions, infrastructural barriers require expensive storage and processing capabilities, security concerns about biopiracy and inappropriate resource use restrict data release, and recognition issues discourage sharing due to inadequate attribution incentives [89].
2. **Accessibility solutions:** FAIR data principles ensure findability, accessibility, interoperability, and reusability, tiered access systems provide different user credentials based on data sensitivity, data trusts and cooperatives enable collective management while respecting contributor rights, and cloud-based platforms like Google Earth Engine and Microsoft Planetary Computer provide integrated data and computing resources [90].

Model Uncertainty and Validation

Uncertainty management is essential for responsible decision-making when developing machine learning models for biodiversity conservation. Building trustworthy models requires methodical validation approaches.

Sources of Uncertainty

Uncertainty in conservation ML models stems from uncertainty in multiple sources:

1. **Inputs:** Errors and biases in training data propagate through to model predictions [91].
2. **Model parameters:** Model parameters based on information from limited data are generally uncertain [91].
3. Inputs of identical data can lead to substantially different predictions even from the same algorithm [91].
4. **Uncertainty of extrapolation:** The uncertainty will increase for models exploited outside the training data range. This is a serious problem for

projections of climate change [91].

5. **Additional uncertainty:** Model predictions must be translated into conservation actions, which introduces uncertainty [91].

Uncertainty Quantification Methods

Quantifying and communicating uncertainty underlies several approaches for quantifying and communicating uncertainty in conservation ML applications:

1. **Statistical prediction:** Point estimates are replaced by complete probability distributions over the possible outcomes [92].
2. **Ensemble modeling:** Combining predictions from multiple models captures structural uncertainty [92].
3. **Sensitivity analysis:** Systematically varying inputs and parameters reveals which factors most affect model predictions [92].
4. **Scenario-based approaches:** Presenting results under multiple plausible scenarios acknowledges deep uncertainties in future conditions [92].
5. **Expert-informed priors:** In Bayesian frameworks, expert knowledge can constrain model parameters within biologically plausible ranges [92].

Validation Strategies

Rigorous validation is essential for building trust in model predictions. Several strategies are appropriate for conservation applications:

1. **Cross-validation techniques:** Methods such as k-fold and leave-one-out cross-validation help assess model performance with limited data. Spatial block cross-validation divides data into geographically distinct training and testing sets [92].
2. **Independent validation datasets:** Models should be validated against independent data not used in model development [92].
3. **Field validation:** The ultimate test of model predictions is validation through targeted field surveys [92].
4. **Expert evaluation:** Subject matter experts can assess whether model predictions align with ecological understanding [92].
5. **Performance metrics:** Different applications require different performance metrics. In species distribution models, metrics such as AUC measure discrimination ability, while calibration plots assess the reliability of probability estimates [92].

Communicating Uncertainty for Decision-Making

Effectively communicating uncertainty to conservation decision-makers remains challenging but essential:

1. **Visual representations:** Maps and graphs can display uncertainty alongside predictions [92].
2. **Scenario planning:** Multiple plausible scenarios can help stakeholders understand possible outcomes [92].
3. **Decision-theoretic frameworks:** Formal decision analysis approaches help identify acceptable management options across a range of uncertainties [92].
4. **Interactive tools:** Web-based interfaces allow users to explore model predictions under different assumptions [92].

Uncertainty should be framed not as a barrier to action but as information that helps prioritize research, evaluate risks, and design adaptive management approaches [92].

Computational Requirements and Scalability

As machine learning methods for conservation grow more sophisticated and data volumes increase, computational requirements become an important practical consideration for implementation.

Computational Challenges in Conservation ML

Several factors drive computational demands in conservation applications:

1. **Large spatial extents:** Many conservation applications require analysis across regional, continental, or global scales [21].
2. **High-resolution data:** Remote sensing data resolution continues to improve, with many applications now using sub-meter imagery [21].
3. **Model complexity:** State-of-the-art deep learning models may contain hundreds of millions of parameters [21].
4. **Ensemble approaches:** Robust conservation decisions often rely on ensemble models or multiple scenarios [21].
5. **Real-time processing:** Applications like poaching detection require near-instantaneous stream data analysis [21].

These demands often exceed the computing resources available to conservation organizations, particularly those in developing countries where biodiversity is highest [21].

Cloud Computing and Distributed Processing

Cloud-based approaches have emerged as key solutions for addressing computational challenges:

1. **Commercial cloud platforms:** Services like AWS, Google Cloud, and Microsoft Azure provide scalable computing resources on a pay-as-you-go basis [21].
2. **Conservation-focused platforms:** Specialized platforms like Wildlife Insights, Global Forest Watch, and SMART provide pre-configured tools for specific conservation applications [21].
3. **Open science platforms:** Systems like Google Earth Engine and Microsoft Planetary Computer combine massive datasets with computational capacity specifically for environmental applications [21].
4. **Conservation data processing:** Projects like Zooniverse leverage volunteer power and human intelligence to distribute volunteer computing [21].

Model Optimization and Efficiency

An alternative way to tackle the computational challenges is to optimize models to be efficient:

1. Model compression methods can reduce the model size and computational demands [76].
2. **Pre-trained models:** These can be fine-tuned for conservation tasks with limited computation resources [76].
3. **Resource-constrained environments:** For these environments, specialized neural network architectures such as Mobile Net and Efficient Net are adopted [76].
4. **Approximate computing:** For specific applications, using approximate methods that trade reduced accuracy for substantial speedup may be beneficial [76].
5. **Accelerated machine learning:** Machine learning tasks can be accelerated with specialized hardware such as GPUs, CPUs, and FPGAs [76].

Scalability Strategies

Scaling up ML solutions across multiple conservation contexts involves deciding how the scale works in ML:

1. **Standardized interfaces:** Components designed with modular interfaces can be used in other projects and organizations [21].
2. Pipeline automation decreases the human intervention requirements and thus makes it easier to scale [21].
3. **Multi-level processing:** Tiered processing approaches can provide efficient application of intensive methods to large areas [21].
4. Distributed approaches, which process data locally and aggregate it before sending it to a server, naturally meet both the scalability and data sovereignty concerns [21].
5. **Immediate installation with planned enhancements:** Systems begin with simpler models and make iterative improvements as more resources are available, which is progressive refinement [21].

Interdisciplinary Collaboration and Knowledge Exchange

However, to benefit from machine learning in biodiversity conservation, disparate disciplines must somehow come together with their terminologies, methodologies, and priorities. Successfully joining disciplinary efforts requires a combination of hard work and luck.

The Disciplinary Divide

A few factors make it difficult for data scientists and conservation biologists to collaborate:

1. **Term barriers:** Terms may have other meanings, depending on discipline(s) [3].
2. **Different priorities:** Data scientists might want algorithmic performance, while conservation biologists may want practical applicability and ecological relevance [3].
3. **Variation in communication styles:** There is considerable variation in communication styles across research outputs and communication formats in the various fields [3].
4. **Differences in methodological principles:** Conservationists and others value contextualized, place-based knowledge, while machine learning favours generalizable patterns [3].

5. **Academic and organizational barriers:** Academic and organizational structures will likely hinder cross-disciplinary work due to their lack of faculty members and restricted operating hours [3].

Building Effective Collaborations

Typically, successful interdisciplinary conservation projects have several key elements:

1. **Co-design process:** Involving all the relevant disciplines from the start of the project guarantees that the technical approach is appropriate to conservation needs [3].
2. **Interdisciplinary collaboration:** Boundary organizations: intermediary groups that link disciplinary divides [4].
3. Someone trained across disciplines can translate between fields [3].
4. **Cross-disciplinary interaction:** Collaborative platforms, such as shared workspaces and tools, enable cross-disciplinary discussion [3].
5. **Collaboration:** Basic cross-disciplinary literacy can help one work more efficiently together [3].

Knowledge Integration beyond Disciplines

Effective conservation also requires that the knowledge systems that comprise the elements of conservation be integrated beyond formal academic disciplines:

1. **Traditional ecological knowledge:** Such observations span generations and previous understanding of local systems [5].
2. **Conservation professionals experience:** Conservation professionals have much experiential knowledge that is not documented in the formal science literature [5].
3. **Massive datasets from citizen science contributions:** Nonprofessional participants constitute many datasets and bring unique perspectives on the conservation challenge [5].
4. **Regulatory and governance understanding:** This is the foundation of translating technical understanding into action on the ground [5].

Fig. (**5**) represents a framework for integrating indigenous ecological knowledge with machine learning approaches. The figure highlights the integration of Indigenous Ecological Knowledge (IEK) and Machine Learning (ML) for conservation. IEK contributes temporal depth, local species knowledge, holistic ecological perspectives, and cultural values, while ML adds technical strengths like pattern recognition, predictive modeling, data integration, and uncertainty quantification. The Knowledge Integration layer bridges these two domains through participatory modeling, knowledge formalization, semantic web approaches, and hybrid classification systems. Guided by both ethical principles and technical approaches, this integration yields conservation applications that are culturally appropriate, ecologically meaningful, and technically robust, thereby ensuring effective and sustainable conservation solutions.

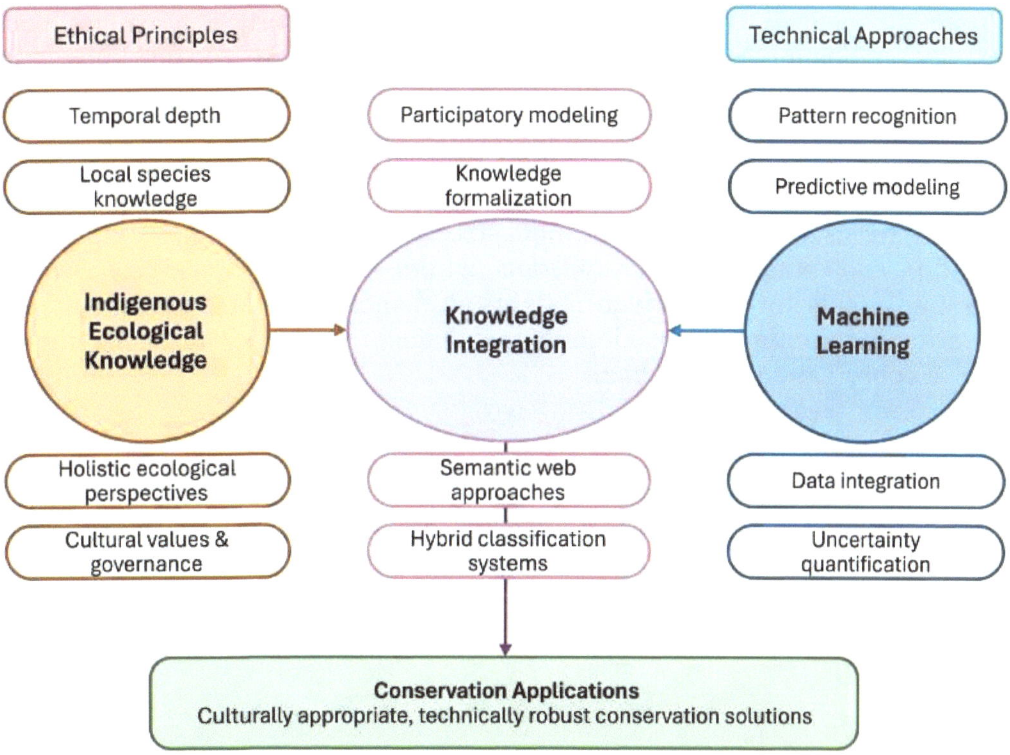

Fig. (5). A framework that integrates indigenous ecological knowledge with machine learning approaches to design more culturally relevant and technically robust conservation solutions.

Practical Knowledge Exchange Mechanisms

There are several ways of knowing exchange between knowledge systems and disciplines:

1. Collaborative workshops are structured, and diversity brings events together on specific conservation challenges [5].
2. Sharing code, providing open data, and transparent workflow make the methods accessible to other disciplines [5].

3. **Boundary objects:** Shared artefacts like interactive visualizations that are meaningful to multiple stakeholder groups [5].
4. **Embedded fieldwork:** Technical experts spending time in field contexts to understand practical constraints and opportunities [5].
5. **Co-created products:** Outputs designed to serve multiple audiences [5].

Fig. (**6**) represents the adaptive conservation management feedback cycle. The figure illustrates an adaptive management cycle for conservation that integrates multiple knowledge systems with machine learning support. The cycle includes four stages: Planning, informed by indigenous and scientific knowledge; Implementation, supported by practitioner experience; Monitoring, using real-time and automated data processing; and Analysis & Learning, enriched by community knowledge and pattern detection. At the centre, neural networks provide predictive modeling for scenario planning and guide decision-making across all stages. The framework emphasizes blending community, indigenous, scientific, and practitioner knowledge while leveraging machine learning integration points for data-driven insights. It demonstrates a dynamic, iterative approach where traditional wisdom and advanced technology work together for effective conservation management.

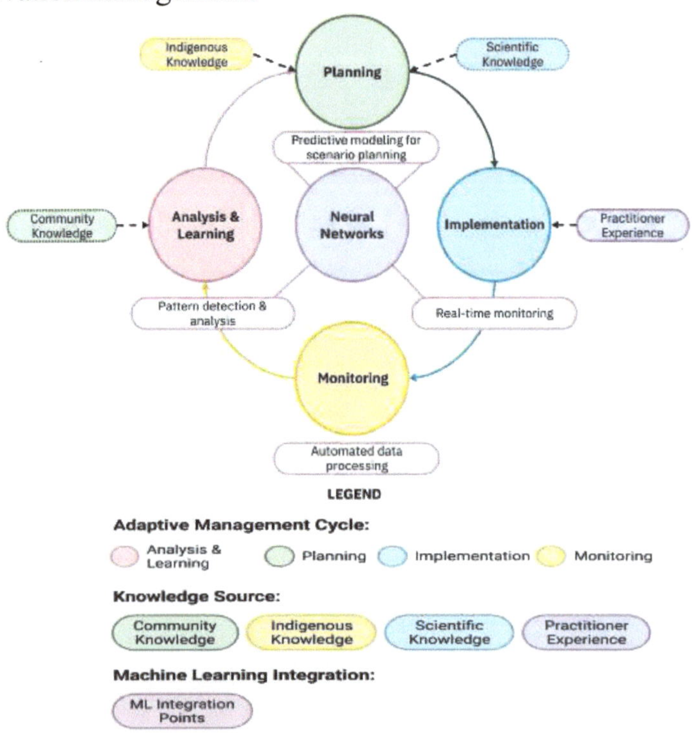

Fig. (6). Adaptive conservation management feedback cycle showing the integration of multiple knowledge systems and data sources in an iterative process of learning and improvement.

FUTURE DIRECTIONS AND EMERGING TECHNOLOGIES

Automated Biodiversity Monitoring

The future of biodiversity conservation increasingly depends on comprehensive monitoring at unprecedented scales and resolutions. Emerging technologies are automatically transforming our ability to track species, ecosystems, and threats.

Next-Generation Sensing Technologies

Several emerging sensing technologies promise to revolutionize biodiversity monitoring:

1. **Miniaturized sensors:** Microelectronics advances enable increasingly small, energy-efficient sensors that can be deployed on individual animals or distributed throughout ecosystems [68].
2. **Environmental DNA (eDNA):** Automated sampling and analysis of environmental DNA can detect species presence without direct observation [68].
3. **Persistent imaging:** Long-duration, high-resolution imaging from various platforms enables continuous ecosystem monitoring [68].
4. **Ecological soundscapes:** Advanced acoustic sensors can automatically detect ambient species-specific calls and ecological soundscapes [68].
5. **Collaborative animal tracking networks:** Based on satellites, ICARUS networks can track small animals worldwide [68].

Automated Species Recognition

Artificial intelligence is dramatically improving our ability to identify species in monitoring data:

1. **Computer vision for imagery:** Deep learning models now match or exceed human performance in identifying species from camera trap photos, satellite imagery, and drone footage [80].
2. **Bioacoustics classification:** Neural networks can identify species from their calls, songs, and other sounds [81].
3. **Molecular identification:** Machine learning is enhancing the analysis of genetic material for species identification [81].
4. **Species identification, individual recognition:** Beyond species identification, AI can now identify individual animals from unique markings or features [81].
5. Advanced models can even identify behaviours amongst video or tracking data [82].

Community-based and Participatory Monitoring

However, advancing technologies make enhancing monitoring capacities possible while local communities still need to be engaged for sustainable, comprehensive monitoring systems to thrive:

1. **Watching smartphone-based monitoring platforms:** Apps like naturalist, bird, and SMART Mobile allow smartphone users to contribute to biodiversity observations [5].
2. **New approaches:** Integrated local knowledge systems (including traditional ecological knowledge and technology-enabled monitoring) [5].
3. **Community-based monitoring networks:** Community-based monitoring networks provide early warning of threats [5].
4. **Involve communities in co-designing monitoring protocols:** This makes monitoring systems more relevant and sustainable [5].

Integrated Biodiversity Observing Networks

Integrated networks using multiple technologies and approaches are the future of biodiversity monitoring:

1. Coordinated monitoring at multiple scales, from microscopic (eDNA) to global (satellite imagery) [67].
2. **Continuous monitoring:** The ecosystem changes can be identified rapidly using ML-based anomaly detection within a deterministic time [67].
3. **Predictive monitoring:** ML models trained on historical monitoring data can predict emerging patterns [67].
4. **Digital twins of ecosystems:** Comprehensive monitoring data feeds sophisticated simulation models that capture ecosystem dynamics [67].

Digital Twins for Ecosystem Management

Digital twins—virtual replicas of physical systems continuously updated with real-time data—represent an emerging frontier in conservation technology. Initially developed for industrial applications, this concept is now adapted for ecosystem management.

The Digital Twin Concept for Ecosystems

Ecosystem digital twins integrate multiple data streams with simulation models to create dynamic virtual representations of natural systems [61]:

1. Ecosystem digital twins integrate multiple data streams with simulation models to create dynamic virtual representations of natural systems [61]. These systems are characterized by bidirectional data flows between the physical ecosystem and its digital representation, multiscale modeling from individual organisms to landscape processes, real-time or near-real-time updates based on monitoring data, predictive capabilities for scenario testing and forecasting, and interactive interfaces for exploration and decision support [61].
2. A functional ecosystem digital twin includes several architectural elements to create a comprehensive virtual ecosystem. These components encompass data acquisition systems, including sensors, remote sensing, and field observations, data integration and storage infrastructure for managing diverse data streams, process-based and statistical models for simulating ecosystem dynamics, machine learning components for pattern detection and prediction, visualization and interaction interfaces for user engagement, and decision support frameworks [61] that translate model outputs into actionable recommendations.
3. Ecosystem digital twins can support various applications in conservation, including protected area management and zoning decisions, invasive species control planning, climate adaptation strategy development, environmental impact assessment, and restoration project design and monitoring [61]. These applications demonstrate the versatility of digital twin technology in addressing complex conservation challenges through integrated modeling and real-time data integration.

Fig. (**7**) represents the architecture of a digital twin system for ecosystem management. The figure illustrates the role of digital twin technology in conservation and ecosystem management. It begins with the real-world ecosystem, including species, habitats, climate, hydrology, disturbances, and human influences. Data from these components is collected through the Data Acquisition Layer using sensor networks, remote sensing, field surveys, citizen science, and historical records. This information feeds into the Digital Twin Core, which integrates data, builds ecological process models, and uses machine learning for pattern recognition and predictive analytics. The insights then support decision-making and conservation applications, such as protected areas, restoration, climate adaptation, threat management, and policy planning. Continuous monitoring and feedback loops ensure that real-world ecosystems and digital models remain connected, enabling adaptive and effective conservation strategies.

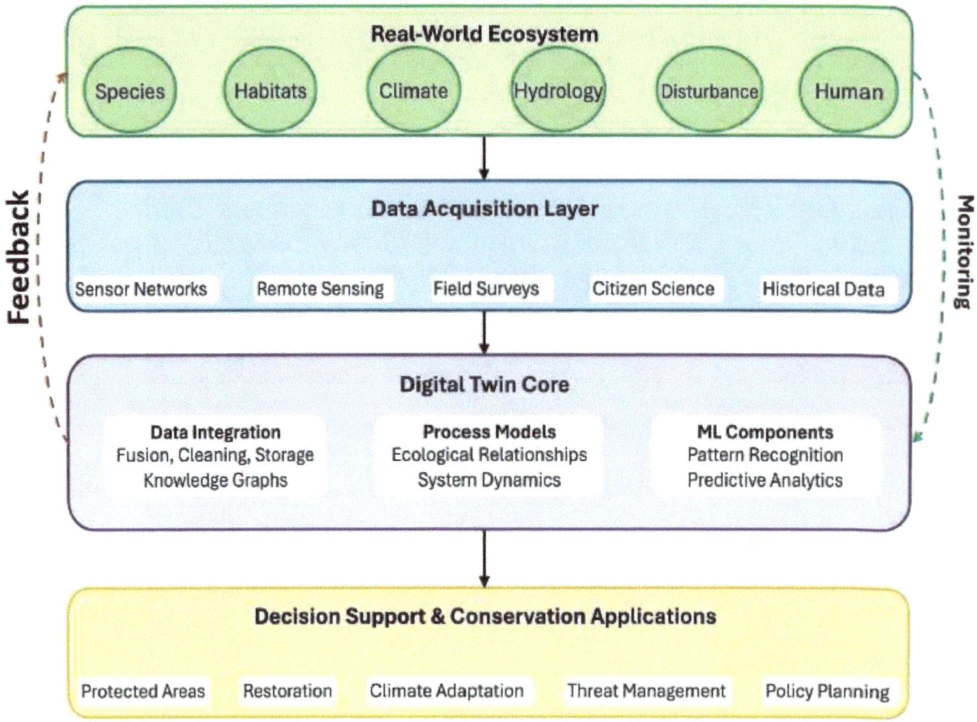

Fig. (7). Architecture of a digital twin system for ecosystem management, showing the flow of data from the real-world ecosystem through data acquisition and processing layers to applications for conservation decision-making.

Case Examples and Implementations

Several pioneering projects are developing digital twin approaches for conservation:

1. **The virtual reef:** A digital twin of the Great Barrier Reef combines high-resolution 3D reef mapping, real-time oceanographic data, ecological models, and ML-based prediction to support reef management [58].
2. **Forest twin:** This system integrates LiDAR, hyperspectral imagery, ground-based sensors, and historical inventory data to create a continuously updated digital representation of managed forests [58].
3. **Digital twins of major river basins:** River Basin Twins combine hydrological models, biodiversity data, land cover, and climate projections into the twin [58].
4. **The urban ecosystem twins:** Cities are creating digital urban ecosystem twins that include modelling urban biodiversity, infrastructure, pollution, and human

activities [58].

Challenges and Opportunities

There are several challenges to developing effective ecosystem digital twins:

1. **Complexity and scale:** Ecosystems consist of many interacting components over a wide range of scales, rendering the digital representation of such systems a challenging undertaking [61].
2. Sophisticated data integration is needed because it contains information from varying formats, resolutions, and uncertainties from various sources [61].
3. Validating digital twin predictions is difficult for rare events and long-term processes [61].
4. Running high-resolution ecosystem simulations requires considerable computing resources [61].
5. **Interface design:** Digital twin insights must be accessible and usable to various stakeholders.

Even with these challenges, ecosystem digital twins represent an once-in-a-lifetime opportunity for conservation:

1. **Digital twins as a framework of integration:** Digital twins offer a framework for integrating across the ecology, climatology, hydrology, and social sciences [61].
2. **Anticipatory conservation:** The predictive capabilities of digital twins enable proactive conservation interventions [61].
3. **Adaptive management support:** Continuous updating of digital twins with monitoring data facilitates learning and adaptation in conservation practice [61].
4. **Stakeholder engagement:** Interactive visualizations and scenarios based on digital twins can enhance communication with policymakers and communities [61].
5. **Knowledge preservation:** Digital twins can encode scientific and traditional knowledge about ecosystems in a form that persists beyond individual experts [61].

Integrating Indigenous Knowledge with Machine Learning

Indigenous peoples manage or have tenure rights over at least 38 million square kilometres, approximately 25% of the Earth's land surface, including areas with some of the highest biodiversity levels [5]. Their knowledge systems, developed over generations of close interaction with local ecosystems, offer valuable insights for conservation. Emerging approaches combine this traditional ecological knowledge with machine learning to create more effective and culturally appropriate conservation tools.

Value of Indigenous Knowledge for Conservation

There are several unique contributions of the Indigenous knowledge system to biodiversity conservation [5]:

1. **Baseline information:** Observations and practices transmitted across generations depict ecosystem conditions predating scientific monitoring [5].
2. **Local knowledge and expertise:** Local species, relationships, and environmental indicators [5].
3. Usually, indigenous knowledge includes ecological, social, and cultural dimensions [5].
4. **Alternative management frameworks:** Sustainable practices exist in traditional resource management systems because of long-term adaptation to local conditions [5].
5. Indigenous approaches to conservation often include elements of cultural values and governance systems, which maintain a high commitment by the local communities to the conservation goals [5].

Ethical Frameworks for Knowledge Integration

Ethical approaches to integrating indigenous knowledge with machine learning are necessary because they respect rights, sovereignty, and cultural protocols [78]:

1. **Free, prior, and informed consent (FPIC):** Must give or withhold consent regarding projects on their territories or knowledge [78].
2. **Indigenous ownership of traditional knowledge:** Intellectual property recognition [78].
3. Involving Indigenous knowledge holders as equal partners [78].
4. Ensuring that digital tools and indigenous-I knowledge insights benefit the communities from which they were derived [78].
5. **Community rights:** Respecting Indigenous communities' rights to collect and store their knowledge and data, including sharing it with others [78].

Technical Approaches for Knowledge Integration

Several technical solutions have been built, enabling the coupling of indigenous knowledge into the functioning of machine learning systems:

1. Collaborative development of models incorporating the best combination of scientific data and indigenous knowledge [3].
2. **Methods of knowledge formalization:** to represent qualitative indigenous knowledge in the computational system in compatible forms [3].
3. Computational approaches, such as fuzzy logic systems, can deal with the qualitatively context-dependent nature of many Indigenous knowledge statements [82].
4. Ontologies and knowledge graphs that can represent complex relationships in traditional ecological knowledge, such as semantic web technologies [88].
5. **Ecological knowledge extraction:** Techniques for finding ecological knowledge in oral history, narrative, and other textual sources [88].
6. **Hybrid classification systems:** Approaches that combine indigenous taxonomies with scientific classification [82].
7. Methods of aligning indigenous seasonal patterns and landscape features with scientific data: spatiotemporal knowledge integration [82].

Applications and Case Studies

There are several successful applications in which indigenous knowledge is combined with machine learning:

1. **Maintaining wildlife monitoring:** 'The Healthy Country AI project uses Aboriginal knowledge of computer vision to monitor invasive species in northern Australia [5].
2. **ML models:** In Canada's boreal forest, well-coordinated between First Nations communities and forestry companies, were developed for ML models integrating traditional knowledge of forest succession patterns with remote sensing data [5].
3. **Climate adaptation planning:** Combining traditional indicators of environmental change with ML-based climate projections, Pacific Island communities are working with climate scientists to develop hybrid knowledge systems [5].
4. **Outreach to local communities:** For instance, the Kūlana Noi'i program in Hawai'i integrates traditional ecological knowledge of nearshore marine ecosystems with ML analysis of oceanographic data to assist local community-based fishery management [5].
5. **Agricultural biodiversity conservation:** The Indigenous Seed Guardians Network uses ML to connect traditional knowledge about crop varieties with genetic and climate data [5].

Future Directions for Knowledge Integration

Emerging approaches promise to further enhance the integration of indigenous knowledge with machine learning for conservation:

1. **Immersive documentation technologies:** Virtual and augmented reality tools enable more comprehensive documentation of context-dependent ecological knowledge [82].
2. **Multilingual NLP for ecological knowledge:** Advanced language models are being adapted to indigenous languages, enabling automated extraction of ecological knowledge from oral traditions [82].
3. **Hybrid governance systems for AI:** New frameworks combine traditional decision-making processes with AI governance approaches [78].
4. **Intergenerational knowledge transfer platforms:** Digital platforms designed to support transmission of ecological knowledge between generations [82].
5. **Biocultural indicators in Earth observation:** Integrating culturally significant indicators into satellite monitoring systems [82].

CONCLUSION AND RECOMMENDATIONS

Key Insights and Findings

Our examination of current applications and emerging technologies yields several important insights:

1. Machine learning significantly enhances habitat modeling accuracy and efficiency. Compared to traditional statistical approaches, ML methods better capture complex non-linear relationships in species-habitat associations and can integrate diverse remote sensing data sources [8].
2. Integrated modeling frameworks provide more realistic projections of climate change impacts on biodiversity. By connecting climate models with species distribution models and incorporating factors like dispersal limitation, biotic interactions, and adaptive capacity, ML approaches offer more nuanced and actionable information for climate adaptation planning [36].
3. AI-powered monitoring systems dramatically expand the scale and effectiveness of protected area surveillance. Real-time threat detection using edge computing and deep learning enables rapid response to threats like poaching and illegal logging across vast areas with limited human resources [74].
4. Effective implementation requires addressing data limitations, uncertainty, computational constraints, and interdisciplinary barriers. Despite technological

advances, considerable challenges remain in translating algorithmic capabilities into conservation impact on the ground [85].

5. Emerging technologies promise to revolutionize conservation practices further. Automated biodiversity monitoring, ecosystem digital twins, and indigenous knowledge integration represent frontier areas with enormous potential to transform how we understand and protect biodiversity [68].
6. Ethical considerations must guide technological development and application. Data sovereignty, privacy, equity, and cultural appropriateness are central to the responsible deployment of conservation technology [78].

The overarching conclusion is that machine learning and spatial optimization, while not panaceas, offer powerful tools that can significantly enhance our ability to address the biodiversity crisis when thoughtfully integrated with ecological understanding, local knowledge, and appropriate governance systems.

Practical Recommendations for Implementation

Based on the insights presented in this chapter, we offer several practical recommendations for conservation practitioners, researchers, and technology developers:

1. Adopt ensemble and hybrid modeling approaches. Rather than relying on single algorithms, combine multiple methods to leverage complementary strengths and provide more robust predictions [12].
2. Invest in high-quality training data. Machine learning models are only as good as their training data. Prioritize systematic data collection efforts, particularly in under-sampled regions and taxa, and implement rigorous data quality control protocols [85].
3. Quantify and communicate uncertainty. Develop standardized approaches for representing uncertainty in model outputs and ensure that decision-makers understand predictive models' capabilities and limitations [92].
4. Build modular, interoperable systems. Design conservation technology systems with standardized interfaces that allow components to be updated, replaced, or shared across projects and organizations [21].
5. Prioritize user experience and accessibility. Ensure that advanced analytical tools are usable by conservation practitioners with varying technical backgrounds through intuitive interfaces, clear documentation, and appropriate training materials [3].
6. Implement strong data governance and ethical frameworks. Develop clear data ownership, access, and use protocols, particularly when working with sensitive biodiversity data or indigenous knowledge [78].

7. Create interdisciplinary teams and collaborative processes. Establish formal structures and processes facilitating collaboration between ecologists, data scientists, local communities, and other stakeholders throughout project lifecycles [3].
8. Adopt adaptive implementation approaches. Deploy conservation technology incrementally, with continuous monitoring, evaluation, and refinement based on field experience and emerging needs [5].

Research Priorities and Future Directions

To advance the field of machine learning for biodiversity conservation, we identify several priority areas for future research and development:

1. Improved integration of process-based and data-driven models. Develop frameworks that combine mechanistic understanding of ecological processes with the pattern-recognition strengths of machine learning for more robust and interpretable predictions [8].
2. Biodiversity-specific benchmark datasets and model evaluation standards. Establish standardized reference datasets and performance metrics designed explicitly for conservation applications to compare different approaches [80] systematically.
3. Explainable AI for conservation. Develop methods for interpreting complex ML models in ecologically meaningful ways to inform conservation action and build stakeholder trust [13].
4. Low-resource ML for conservation contexts. Create techniques and tools specifically designed for the computational, connectivity, and data constraints typical in many high-biodiversity regions [76].
5. Transfer learning across species and ecosystems. Improve methods for transferring knowledge from data-rich to data-poor contexts, enabling more effective conservation planning for rare species and understudied ecosystems [42].
6. Integrated social-ecological modeling. Develop approaches that better connect ecological models with human behavior, governance systems, and socioeconomic factors to predict real-world conservation outcomes [2].
7. Automated model updating and continuous learning systems. Provide conservation models with the ability to create frameworks for new data incorporation and evolving conditions without requiring complete retraining [82].
8. Conservation technology APIs and protocols for data exchange. Define common standards for interoperability between conservation technology systems and data sources [21].

CONCLUDING REMARKS

One of humanity's biggest challenges is the biodiversity crisis, which requires innovative approaches with all tools and knowledge systems. It is possible to do it simply with machines and spatial optimization, which offer powerful capabilities that can significantly improve benefits if combined adequately with ecological understanding and situational context.

This chapter demonstrates the compelling nature of these computational approaches and the need for addressing data, uncertainty, computational, and interdisciplinary issues toward implementation. Traditional knowledge, rigorous science, and cutting-edge technology, when combined in a way that respects the irreducible complexity of local realities and inclusive governance, promise to develop conservation solutions that are once more sophisticated and more grounded in reality.

Looking to the future, technologies like automated biodiversity monitoring, ecosystem digital twins, and indigenous knowledge integration systems will continue to reshape conservation practice. These innovations will allow us to learn more about and predict the behaviour of these complex ecological systems, effectively anticipate future changes, and respond more effectively to emerging threats.

Ultimately, however, machine learning and spatial optimization methods will not be used for biodiversity conservation if they fail to inject novel thinking into socially and ecologically appropriate conservation strategies. We can create technically sophisticated and deeply rooted approaches that integrate conservation by combining disparate expertise sets (*e.g.*, data science *vs* traditional ecological knowledge).

LIST OF ABBREVIATIONS

GIS Geographic Information Systems

RF Random Forest

BRT Boosted Regression Trees

CNN Convolutional Neural Networks

SAR Synthetic Aperture Radar

LiDAR Light Detection and Ranging

UAV Unmanned Aerial Vehicles

XAI Explainable Artificial Intelligence

HSI Habitat Suitability Index

GLM Generalized Linear Model

GAM Generalized Additive Model

MaxEnt Maximum Entropy (Model)

REFERENCES

[1] G. Ceballos, P.R. Ehrlich, and P.H. Raven, "Vertebrates on the brink as indicators of biological annihilation and the sixth mass extinction", *Proc. Natl. Acad. Sci. USA,* vol. 117, no. 24, pp. 13596-13602, 2020.
[http://dx.doi.org/10.1073/pnas.1922686117] [PMID: 32482862]

[2] Intergovernmental Science-Policy Platform on Biodiversity and Ecosystem Services, *Global Assessment Report on Biodiversity and Ecosystem Services*. Bonn, Germany: IPBES Secretariat, 2019.

[3] T. Amano, T. Székely, B. Sandel, S. Nagy, T. Mundkur, T. Langendoen, D. Blanco, C.U. Soykan, and W.J. Sutherland, "Successful conservation of global waterbird populations depends on effective governance", *Nature,* vol. 553, no. 7687, pp. 199-202, 2018.
[http://dx.doi.org/10.1038/nature25139] [PMID: 29258291]

[4] L.N. Joppa, "The case for technology investments in the environment", *Nature,* vol. 552, no. 7685, pp. 325-328, 2017.
[http://dx.doi.org/10.1038/d41586-017-08675-7]

[5] O. Berger-Tal, and J.J. Lahoz-Monfort, "Conservation technology: The next generation", *Conserv. Lett.,* vol. 11, no. 6, p. e12458, 2018.
[http://dx.doi.org/10.1111/conl.12458]

[6] A. Guisan, and N.E. Zimmermann, "Predictive habitat distribution models in ecology", *Ecol. Modell.,* vol. 135, no. 2-3, pp. 147-186, 2000.
[http://dx.doi.org/10.1016/S0304-3800(00)00354-9]

[7] M.P. Austin, "Spatial prediction of species distribution: an interface between ecological theory and statistical modelling", *Ecol. Modell.,* vol. 157, no. 2-3, pp. 101-118, 2002.
[http://dx.doi.org/10.1016/S0304-3800(02)00205-3]

[8] J. Elith, and J.R. Leathwick, "Species distribution models: ecological explanation and prediction across space and time", *Annu. Rev. Ecol. Evol. Syst.,* vol. 40, no. 1, pp. 677-697, 2009.
[http://dx.doi.org/10.1146/annurev.ecolsys.110308.120159]

[9] S.J. Phillips, R.P. Anderson, and R.E. Schapire, "Maximum entropy modeling of species geographic distributions", *Ecol. Modell.,* vol. 190, no. 3-4, pp. 231-259, 2006.
[http://dx.doi.org/10.1016/j.ecolmodel.2005.03.026]

[10] D.R. Cutler, T.C. Edwards Jr, K.H. Beard, A. Cutler, K.T. Hess, J. Gibson, and J.J. Lawler, "Random forests for classification in ecology", *Ecology,* vol. 88, no. 11, pp. 2783-2792, 2007.
[http://dx.doi.org/10.1890/07-0539.1] [PMID: 18051647]

[11] S. Christin, É. Hervet, and N. Lecomte, "Applications for deep learning in ecology", *Methods Ecol. Evol.,* vol. 10, no. 10, pp. 1632-1644, 2019.
[http://dx.doi.org/10.1111/2041-210X.13256]

[12] M. Araújo, and M. New, "Ensemble forecasting of species distributions", *Trends Ecol. Evol.,* vol. 22, no. 1, pp. 42-47, 2007.
[http://dx.doi.org/10.1016/j.tree.2006.09.010] [PMID: 17011070]

[13] F. Martínez-Plumed, L. Contreras-Ochando, C. Ferri, J. Hernández-Orallo, M. Kull, N. Lachiche, M.J. Ramirez-Quintana, and P. Flach, "CRISP-DM twenty years later: From data mining processes to data science trajectories", *IEEE Trans. Knowl. Data Eng.,* vol. 33, no. 8, pp. 3048-3061, 2021.
[http://dx.doi.org/10.1109/TKDE.2019.2962680]

[14] N. Pettorelli, W.F. Laurance, T.G. O'Brien, M. Wegmann, H. Nagendra, and W. Turner, "Satellite remote sensing for applied ecologists: opportunities and challenges", *J. Appl. Ecol.,* vol. 51, no. 4, pp. 839-848, 2014.
[http://dx.doi.org/10.1111/1365-2664.12261]

[15] D.P. Roy, M.A. Wulder, T.R. Loveland, C.E. Woodcock, R.G. Allen, M.C. Anderson, and Z. Zhu, "Landsat-8: Science and product vision for terrestrial global change research", *Remote Sens. Environ.,* vol. 145, pp. 154-172, 2014.
[http://dx.doi.org/10.1016/j.rse.2014.02.001]

[16] G.P. Asner, R.E. Martin, D.E. Knapp, R. Tupayachi, C.B. Anderson, F. Sinca, N.R. Vaughn, and W. Llactayo, "Airborne laser-guided imaging spectroscopy to map forest trait diversity and guide conservation", *Science,* vol. 355, no. 6323, pp. 385-389, 2017.
[http://dx.doi.org/10.1126/science.aaj1987] [PMID: 28126815]

[17] A.B. Davies, and G.P. Asner, "Advances in animal ecology from 3D-LiDAR ecosystem mapping", *Trends Ecol. Evol.,* vol. 29, no. 12, pp. 681-691, 2014.
[http://dx.doi.org/10.1016/j.tree.2014.10.005] [PMID: 25457158]

[18] N. Joshi, M. Baumann, A. Ehammer, R. Fensholt, K. Grogan, P. Hostert, M. Jepsen, T. Kuemmerle, P. Meyfroidt, E. Mitchard, J. Reiche, C. Ryan, and B. Waske, "A review of the application of optical and radar remote sensing data fusion to land use mapping and monitoring", *Remote Sens. (Basel),* vol. 8, no. 1, p. 70, 2016.
[http://dx.doi.org/10.3390/rs8010070]

[19] J. Paneque-Gálvez, M. McCall, B. Napoletano, S. Wich, and L. Koh, "Small drones for community-based forest monitoring: An assessment of their feasibility and potential in tropical areas", *Forests,* vol. 5, no. 6, pp. 1481-1507, 2014.
[http://dx.doi.org/10.3390/f5061481]

[20] R.E. Kennedy, S. Andréfouët, W.B. Cohen, C. Gómez, P. Griffiths, M. Hais, S.P. Healey, E.H. Helmer, P. Hostert, M.B. Lyons, G.W. Meigs, D. Pflugmacher, S.R. Phinn, S.L. Powell, P. Scarth, S. Sen, T.A. Schroeder, A. Schneider, R. Sonnenschein, J.E. Vogelmann, M.A. Wulder, and Z. Zhu, "Bringing an ecological view of change to Landsat-based remote sensing", *Front. Ecol. Environ.,* vol. 12, no. 6, pp. 339-346, 2014.
[http://dx.doi.org/10.1890/130066]

[21] Y. Cui, K. M. Eccles, R. K. Kwok, B. R. Joubert, K. P. Messier, and D. M. Balshaw, "Integrating multiscale geospatial environmental data into large population health studies: Challenges and opportunities," *Toxics*, vol. 10, no. 7, p. 403, 2022.
[http://dx.doi.org/10.3390/toxics10070403]

[22] S.L. Zeigler, W.F. Fagan, R. DeFries, and B.E. Raboy, "Identifying important forest patches for the long-term persistence of the endangered golden-headed lion tamarin (Leontopithecus chrysomelas)", *Trop. Conserv. Sci.,* vol. 3, no. 1, pp. 63-77, 2010.
[http://dx.doi.org/10.1177/194008291000300106]

[23] M.C. Ribeiro, J.P. Metzger, A.C. Martensen, F.J. Ponzoni, and M.M. Hirota, "The Brazilian Atlantic Forest: How much is left, and how is the remaining forest distributed? Implications for conservation", *Biol. Conserv.,* vol. 142, no. 6, pp. 1141-1153, 2009.
[http://dx.doi.org/10.1016/j.biocon.2009.02.021]

[24] C. Bellard, C. Bertelsmeier, P. Leadley, W. Thuiller, and F. Courchamp, "Impacts of climate change on the future of biodiversity", *Ecol. Lett.,* vol. 15, no. 4, pp. 365-377, 2012.
[http://dx.doi.org/10.1111/j.1461-0248.2011.01736.x] [PMID: 22257223]

[25] I.C. Chen, J.K. Hill, R. Ohlemüller, D.B. Roy, and C.D. Thomas, "Rapid range shifts of species associated with high levels of climate warming", *Science,* vol. 333, no. 6045, pp. 1024-1026, 2011.
[http://dx.doi.org/10.1126/science.1206432] [PMID: 21852500]

[26] S.J. Thackeray, P.A. Henrys, D. Hemming, J.R. Bell, M.S. Botham, S. Burthe, P. Helaouet, D.G.

Johns, I.D. Jones, D.I. Leech, E.B. Mackay, D. Massimino, S. Atkinson, P.J. Bacon, T.M. Brereton, L. Carvalho, T.H. Clutton-Brock, C. Duck, M. Edwards, J.M. Elliott, S.J.G. Hall, R. Harrington, J.W. Pearce-Higgins, T.T. Høye, L.E.B. Kruuk, J.M. Pemberton, T.H. Sparks, P.M. Thompson, I. White, I.J. Winfield, and S. Wanless, "Phenological sensitivity to climate across taxa and trophic levels", *Nature,* vol. 535, no. 7611, pp. 241-245, 2016. [http://dx.doi.org/10.1038/nature18608] [PMID: 27362222]

[27] C.A. Deutsch, J.J. Tewksbury, R.B. Huey, K.S. Sheldon, C.K. Ghalambor, D.C. Haak, and P.R. Martin, "Impacts of climate warming on terrestrial ectotherms across latitude", *Proc. Natl. Acad. Sci. USA,* vol. 105, no. 18, pp. 6668-6672, 2008. [http://dx.doi.org/10.1073/pnas.0709472105] [PMID: 18458348]

[28] R. Seidl, D. Thom, M. Kautz, D. Martin-Benito, M. Peltoniemi, G. Vacchiano, J. Wild, D. Ascoli, M. Petr, J. Honkaniemi, M.J. Lexer, V. Trotsiuk, P. Mairota, M. Svoboda, M. Fabrika, T.A. Nagel, and C.P.O. Reyer, "Forest disturbances under climate change", *Nat. Clim. Chang.,* vol. 7, no. 6, pp. 395-402, 2017. [http://dx.doi.org/10.1038/nclimate3303] [PMID: 28861124]

[29] R.J. Hobbs, E. Higgs, and J.A. Harris, "Novel ecosystems: implications for conservation and restoration", *Trends Ecol. Evol.,* vol. 24, no. 11, pp. 599-605, 2009. [http://dx.doi.org/10.1016/j.tree.2009.05.012] [PMID: 19683830]

[30] M.B. Araújo, and A.T. Peterson, "Uses and misuses of bioclimatic envelope modeling", *Ecology,* vol. 93, no. 7, pp. 1527-1539, 2012. [http://dx.doi.org/10.1890/11-1930.1] [PMID: 22919900]

[31] D.N. Karger, O. Conrad, J. Böhner, T. Kawohl, H. Kreft, R.W. Soria-Auza, N.E. Zimmermann, H.P. Linder, and M. Kessler, "Climatologies at high resolution for the earth's land surface areas", *Sci. Data,* vol. 4, no. 1, p. 170122, 2017. [http://dx.doi.org/10.1038/sdata.2017.122] [PMID: 28872642]

[32] A.J. Cannon, "Multivariate quantile mapping bias correction: an N-dimensional probability density function transform for climate model simulations of multiple variables", *Clim. Dyn.,* vol. 50, no. 1-2, pp. 31-49, 2018. [http://dx.doi.org/10.1007/s00382-017-3580-6]

[33] M. Marmion, M. Parviainen, M. Luoto, R.K. Heikkinen, and W. Thuiller, "Evaluation of consensus methods in predictive species distribution modelling", *Divers. Distrib.,* vol. 15, no. 1, pp. 59-69, 2009. [http://dx.doi.org/10.1111/j.1472-4642.2008.00491.x]

[34] L.L. Porfirio, R.M.B. Harris, E.C. Lefroy, S. Hugh, S.F. Gould, G. Lee, N.L. Bindoff, and B. Mackey, "Improving the use of species distribution models in conservation planning and management under climate change", *PLoS One,* vol. 9, no. 11, p. e113749, 2014. [http://dx.doi.org/10.1371/journal.pone.0113749] [PMID: 25420020]

[35] A. Guisan, and N.E. Zimmermann, "Predictive habitat distribution models in ecology", *Ecological Modelling,* no. 2-3, pp. 147-186, 2000. [http://dx.doi.org/10.1016/S0304-3800(00)00354-9]

[36] C.A. Schloss, T.A. Nuñez, and J.J. Lawler, "Dispersal will limit ability of mammals to track climate change in the Western Hemisphere", *Proc. Natl. Acad. Sci. USA,* vol. 109, no. 22, pp. 8606-8611, 2012. [http://dx.doi.org/10.1073/pnas.1116791109] [PMID: 22586104]

[37] M.B. Araújo, and M. Luoto, "The importance of biotic interactions for modelling species distributions under climate change", *Glob. Ecol. Biogeogr.,* vol. 16, no. 6, pp. 743-753, 2007. [http://dx.doi.org/10.1111/j.1466-8238.2007.00359.x]

[38] D. Zurell, L.J. Pollock, and W. Thuiller, "Do joint species distribution models reliably detect interspecific interactions from co-occurrence data in homogenous environments?", *Ecography,* vol. 41, no. 11, pp. 1812-1819, 2018.

[http://dx.doi.org/10.1111/ecog.03315]

[39] A. Bush, K. Mokany, R. Catullo, A. Hoffmann, V. Kellermann, C. Sgrò, S. McEvey, and S. Ferrier, "Incorporating evolutionary adaptation in species distribution modelling reduces projected vulnerability to climate change", *Ecol. Lett.,* vol. 19, no. 12, pp. 1468-1478, 2016. [http://dx.doi.org/10.1111/ele.12696] [PMID: 27873482]

[40] T.D. Ainsworth, S.F. Heron, J.C. Ortiz, P.J. Mumby, A. Grech, D. Ogawa, C.M. Eakin, and W. Leggat, "Climate change disables coral bleaching protection on the Great Barrier Reef", *Science,* vol. 352, no. 6283, pp. 338-342, 2016. [http://dx.doi.org/10.1126/science.aac7125] [PMID: 27081069]

[41] K. Oberhauser, R. Wiederholt, J. Diffendorfer, D. Semmens, L. Ries, W. Thogmartin, L. Lopez-Hoffman, and B. Semmens, "A trans-national monarch butterfly population model and implications for regional conservation priorities", *Ecol. Entomol.,* vol. 42, no. 1, pp. 51-60, 2017. [http://dx.doi.org/10.1111/een.12351]

[42] E. Kaky, V. Nolan, A. Alatawi, and F. Gilbert, "A comparison between Ensemble and MaxEnt species distribution modelling approaches for conservation: A case study with Egyptian medicinal plants", *Ecol. Inform.,* vol. 60, p. 101150, 2020. [http://dx.doi.org/10.1016/j.ecoinf.2020.101150]

[43] W. Thuiller, T. Münkemüller, K.H. Schiffers, D. Georges, S. Dullinger, V.M. Eckhart, T.C. Edwards Jr, D. Gravel, G. Kunstler, C. Merow, K. Moore, C. Piedallu, S. Vissault, N.E. Zimmermann, D. Zurell, and F.M. Schurr, "Does probability of occurrence relate to population dynamics?", *Ecography,* vol. 37, no. 12, pp. 1155-1166, 2014. [http://dx.doi.org/10.1111/ecog.00836] [PMID: 25722536]

[44] M.W. Tingley, W.B. Monahan, S.R. Beissinger, and C. Moritz, "Birds track their Grinnellian niche through a century of climate change", *Proceedings of the National Academy of Sciences,* vol. 106, pp. 19637-19643, 2009. [http://dx.doi.org/10.1073/pnas.0901562106]

[45] M.C. Fitzpatrick, J.F. Weltzin, N.J. Sanders, and R.R. Dunn, "The biogeography of prediction error: why does the introduced range of the fire ant over-predict its native range?", *Glob. Ecol. Biogeogr.,* vol. 16, no. 1, pp. 24-33, 2007. [http://dx.doi.org/10.1111/j.1466-8238.2006.00258.x]

[46] A. Guisan, R. Tingley, J.B. Baumgartner, I. Naujokaitis-Lewis, P.R. Sutcliffe, A.I.T. Tulloch, T.J. Regan, L. Brotons, E. McDonald-Madden, C. Mantyka-Pringle, T.G. Martin, J.R. Rhodes, R. Maggini, S.A. Setterfield, J. Elith, M.W. Schwartz, B.A. Wintle, O. Broennimann, M. Austin, S. Ferrier, M.R. Kearney, H.P. Possingham, and Y.M. Buckley, "Predicting species distributions for conservation decisions", *Ecol. Lett.,* vol. 16, no. 12, pp. 1424-1435, 2013. [http://dx.doi.org/10.1111/ele.12189] [PMID: 24134332]

[47] M. Bakkenes, J.R.M. Alkemade, F. Ihle, R. Leemans, and J.B. Latour, "Assessing effects of forecasted climate change on the diversity and distribution of European higher plants for 2050", *Glob. Change Biol.,* vol. 8, no. 4, pp. 390-407, 2002. [http://dx.doi.org/10.1046/j.1354-1013.2001.00467.x]

[48] N. Golding, and B.V. Purse, "Fast and flexible Bayesian species distribution modelling using Gaussian processes", *Methods Ecol. Evol.,* vol. 7, no. 5, pp. 598-608, 2016. [http://dx.doi.org/10.1111/2041-210X.12523]

[49] L. Buisson, W. Thuiller, N. Casajus, S. Lek, and G. Grenouillet, "Uncertainty in ensemble forecasting of species distribution", *Glob. Change Biol.,* vol. 16, no. 4, pp. 1145-1157, 2010. [http://dx.doi.org/10.1111/j.1365-2486.2009.02000.x]

[50] I.R. Naujokaitis-Lewis, J.M. Curtis, P. Arcese, and J. Rosenfeld, "Sensitivity analyses of spatial population viability analysis models for species at risk and habitat conservation planning", *Conserv. Biol.,* vol. 32, no. 6, pp. 1329-1341, 2018.

[PMID: 18798856]

[51] L. Poggio, A. Gimona, and I. Brown, "Spatio-temporal MODIS EVI gap filling under cloud cover: An example in Scotland", *ISPRS J. Photogramm. Remote Sens.,* vol. 72, pp. 56-72, 2012. [http://dx.doi.org/10.1016/j.isprsjprs.2012.06.003]

[52] M. Reichstein, G. Camps-Valls, B. Stevens, M. Jung, J. Denzler, N. Carvalhais, and P. Prabhat, "Deep learning and process understanding for data-driven Earth system science", *Nature,* vol. 566, no. 7743, pp. 195-204, 2019. [http://dx.doi.org/10.1038/s41586-019-0912-1] [PMID: 30760912]

[53] A. M. Ukkola, M. G. De Kauwe, M. L. Roderick, G. Abramowitz, and A. J. Pitman, "Robust future changes in meteorological drought in CMIP6 projections despite uncertainty in precipitation," *Geophys. Res. Lett.*, vol. 46, p. e2020GL087820, 2020. [http://dx.doi.org/10.1029/2020GL087820]

[54] W.B. Foden, B.E. Young, H.R. Akçakaya, R.A. Garcia, A.A. Hoffmann, B.A. Stein, C.D. Thomas, C.J. Wheatley, D. Bickford, J.A. Carr, D.G. Hole, T.G. Martin, M. Pacifici, J.W. Pearce-Higgins, P.J. Platts, P. Visconti, J.E.M. Watson, and B. Huntley, "Climate change vulnerability assessment of species", *Wiley Interdiscip. Rev. Clim. Change,* vol. 10, no. 1, p. e551, 2019. [http://dx.doi.org/10.1002/wcc.551]

[55] L.M. Bland, J.A. Rowland, T.J. Regan, D.A. Keith, N.J. Murray, R.E. Lester, M. Linn, J.P. Rodríguez, and E. Nicholson, "Developing a standardized definition of ecosystem collapse for risk assessment", *Front. Ecol. Environ.,* vol. 16, no. 1, pp. 29-36, 2018. [http://dx.doi.org/10.1002/fee.1747]

[56T] T. Iwamura, A. Guisan, K.A. Wilson, and H.P. Possingham, "How robust are global conservation priorities to climate change?", *Glob. Environ. Change,* vol. 23, no. 5, pp. 1277-1284, 2013. [http://dx.doi.org/10.1016/j.gloenvcha.2013.07.016]

[57] T.L. Morelli, C. Daly, S.Z. Dobrowski, D.M. Dulen, J.L. Ebersole, S.T. Jackson, J.D. Lundquist, C.I. Millar, S.P. Maher, W.B. Monahan, K.R. Nydick, K.T. Redmond, S.C. Sawyer, S. Stock, and S.R. Beissinger, "Managing climate change refugia for climate adaptation", *PLoS One,* vol. 11, no. 8, p. e0159909, 2016. [http://dx.doi.org/10.1371/journal.pone.0159909] [PMID: 27509088]

[58] J.L. McGuire, J.J. Lawler, B.H. McRae, T.A. Nuñez, and D.M. Theobald, "Achieving climate connectivity in a fragmented landscape", *Proc. Natl. Acad. Sci. USA,* vol. 113, no. 26, pp. 7195-7200, 2016. [http://dx.doi.org/10.1073/pnas.1602817113] [PMID: 27298349]

[59] L.P. Shoo, A.A. Hoffmann, S. Garnett, R.L. Pressey, Y.M. Williams, M. Taylor, L. Falconi, C.J. Yates, J.K. Scott, D. Alagador, and S.E. Williams, "Making decisions to conserve species under climate change", *Clim. Change,* vol. 119, no. 2, pp. 239-246, 2013. [http://dx.doi.org/10.1007/s10584-013-0699-2]

[60] A.E. Reside, N. Butt, and V.M. Adams, "Adapting systematic conservation planning for climate change", *Biodivers. Conserv.,* vol. 27, no. 1, pp. 1-29, 2018. [http://dx.doi.org/10.1007/s10531-017-1442-5]

[61] D.S. Wilcove, and M. Wikelski, "Going, going, gone: is animal migration disappearing", *PLoS Biol.,* vol. 6, no. 7, p. e188, 2008. [http://dx.doi.org/10.1371/journal.pbio.0060188] [PMID: 18666834]

[62] S.J. Mayor, R.P. Guralnick, M.W. Tingley, J. Otegui, J.C. Withey, S.C. Elmendorf, M.E. Andrew, S. Leyk, I.S. Pearse, and D.C. Schneider, "Increasing phenological asynchrony between spring green-up and arrival of migratory birds", *Sci. Rep.,* vol. 7, no. 1, p. 1902, 2017. [http://dx.doi.org/10.1038/s41598-017-02045-z] [PMID: 28507323]

[63] C. Both, C.A. Van Turnhout, R.G. Bijlsma, H. Siepel, A.J. Van Strien, and R.P. Foppen, "Avian population consequences of climate change are most severe for long-distance migrants in seasonal

habitats", *Proceedings of the Royal Society B: Biological Sciences,* vol. 277, no. 1685, pp. 1259-1266, 2010.
[http://dx.doi.org/10.1098/rspb.2009.1525]

[64] K.G. Horton, B.M. Van Doren, F.A. La Sorte, E.B. Cohen, H.L. Clipp, J.J. Buler, D. Fink, J.F. Kelly, and A. Farnsworth, "Holding steady: Little change in intensity or timing of bird migration over the Gulf of Mexico", *Glob. Change Biol.,* vol. 25, no. 3, pp. 1106-1118, 2019.
[http://dx.doi.org/10.1111/gcb.14540] [PMID: 30623528]

[65] H. Jachmann, "Monitoring law-enforcement performance in nine protected areas in Ghana", *Biol. Conserv.,* vol. 141, no. 1, pp. 89-99, 2008.
[http://dx.doi.org/10.1016/j.biocon.2007.09.012]

[66] J. Nichols, and B. Williams, "Monitoring for conservation", *Trends Ecol. Evol.,* vol. 21, no. 12, pp. 668-673, 2006.
[http://dx.doi.org/10.1016/j.tree.2006.08.007] [PMID: 16919361]

[67] A.C. Burton, E. Neilson, D. Moreira, A. Ladle, R. Steenweg, J.T. Fisher, E. Bayne, and S. Boutin, "REVIEW: Wildlife camera trapping: a review and recommendations for linking surveys to ecological processes", *J. Appl. Ecol.,* vol. 52, no. 3, pp. 675-685, 2015.
[http://dx.doi.org/10.1111/1365-2664.12432]

[68] L.P. Koh, and S.A. Wich, "Dawn of drone ecology: low-cost autonomous aerial vehicles for conservation", *Trop. Conserv. Sci.,* vol. 5, no. 2, pp. 121-132, 2012.
[http://dx.doi.org/10.1177/194008291200500202]

[69] S. Nazir, S. Newey, R.J. Irvine, F. Verdicchio, P. Davidson, G. Fairhurst, and R. Wal, "WiseEye: Next generation expandable and programmable camera trap platform for wildlife research", *PLoS One,* vol. 12, no. 1, p. e0169758, 2017.
[http://dx.doi.org/10.1371/journal.pone.0169758] [PMID: 28076444]

[70] R. Critchlow, A.J. Plumptre, M. Driciru, A. Rwetsiba, E.J. Stokes, C. Tumwesigye, F. Wanyama, and C.M. Beale, "Spatiotemporal trends of illegal activities from ranger-collected data in a Ugandan national park", *Conserv. Biol.,* vol. 29, no. 5, pp. 1458-1470, 2015.
[http://dx.doi.org/10.1111/cobi.12538] [PMID: 25996571]

[71] G. Wang, G.Z. Gertner, and A.B. Anderson, "Spatial-pattern analysis of monitoring data using a modified standard normal deviate", *Environmetrics,* vol. 15, no. 8, pp. 751-767, 2004.

[72] F. Fang, T. Nguyen, R. Pickles, W. Lam, G. Clements, B. An, A. Singh, M. Tambe, and A. Lemieux, "Deploying PAWS: Field optimization of the Protection Assistant for Wildlife Security," *Proc. AAAI Conf. Artif. Intell.*, vol. 30, no. 2, pp. 3966–3973, 2016.
[http://dx.doi.org/10.1609/aaai.v30i2.19070]

[73] P. Juang, H. Oki, Y. Wang, M. Martonosi, L.S. Peh, and D. Rubenstein, "Energy-efficient computing for wildlife tracking", *Oper. Syst. Rev.,* vol. 36, no. 5, pp. 96-107, 2002.
[http://dx.doi.org/10.1145/635508.605408]

[74] J. Zhu, Z. Jiang, and C. Li, "Optimization of power edge computing for delay minimization in mobile edge computing", *IEEE Syst. J.,* vol. 14, no. 3, pp. 4252-4265, 2020.

[75] N. Sornin, M. Luis, T. Eirich, T. Kramp, and O. Hersent, *LoRaWAN Specification*, V1.0, LoRa™ Alliance, 2015, pp. 1–82.

[76] U. Raza, P. Kulkarni, and M. Sooriyabandara, "Low power wide area networks: An overview", *IEEE Commun. Surv. Tutor.,* vol. 19, no. 2, pp. 855-873, 2017.
[http://dx.doi.org/10.1109/COMST.2017.2652320]

[77] S.L. Pimm, S. Alibhai, R. Bergl, A. Dehgan, C. Giri, Z. Jewell, L. Joppa, R. Kays, and S. Loarie, "Emerging technologies to conserve biodiversity", *Trends Ecol. Evol.,* vol. 30, no. 11, pp. 685-696, 2015.
[http://dx.doi.org/10.1016/j.tree.2015.08.008] [PMID: 26437636]

[78] C. Sandbrook, D. Clark, T. Toivonen, T. Simlai, S. O'Donnell, J. Cobbe, and W. Adams, "Principles for the socially responsible use of conservation monitoring technology and data", *Conserv. Sci. Pract.,* vol. 3, no. 5, p. e374, 2021.
[http://dx.doi.org/10.1111/csp2.374]

[79] D. Tuia, B. Kellenberger, S. Beery, B.R. Costelloe, S. Zuffi, B. Risse, A. Mathis, M.W. Mathis, F. van Langevelde, T. Burghardt, R. Kays, H. Klinck, M. Wikelski, I.D. Couzin, G. van Horn, M.C. Crofoot, C.V. Stewart, and T. Berger-Wolf, "Perspectives in machine learning for wildlife conservation", *Nat. Commun.,* vol. 13, no. 1, p. 792, 2022.
[http://dx.doi.org/10.1038/s41467-022-27980-y] [PMID: 35140206]

[80] M.A. Tabak, M.S. Norouzzadeh, D.W. Wolfson, S.J. Sweeney, K.C. Vercauteren, N.P. Snow, J.M. Halseth, P.A. Di Salvo, J.S. Lewis, M.D. White, B. Teton, J.C. Beasley, P.E. Schlichting, R.K. Boughton, B. Wight, E.S. Newkirk, J.S. Ivan, E.A. Odell, R.K. Brook, P.M. Lukacs, A.K. Moeller, E.G. Mandeville, J. Clune, and R.S. Miller, "Machine learning to classify animal species in camera trap images: Applications in ecology", *Methods Ecol. Evol.,* vol. 10, no. 4, pp. 585-590, 2019.
[http://dx.doi.org/10.1111/2041-210X.13120]

[81] J. LeBien, M. Zhong, M. Campos-Cerqueira, J.P. Velev, R. Dodhia, J.L. Ferres, and T.M. Aide, "A pipeline for identification of bird and frog species in tropical soundscape recordings using a convolutional neural network", *Ecol. Inform.,* vol. 59, p. 101113, 2020.
[http://dx.doi.org/10.1016/j.ecoinf.2020.101113]

[82] B. Kellenberger, D. Marcos, and D. Tuia, "Detecting mammals in UAV images: Best practices to address a substantially imbalanced dataset with deep learning", *Remote Sens. Environ.,* vol. 216, pp. 139-153, 2018.
[http://dx.doi.org/10.1016/j.rse.2018.06.028]

[83] J.F. Moore, F. Mulindahabi, M.K. Masozera, J.D. Nichols, J.E. Hines, E. Turikunkiko, and M.K. Oli, "Are ranger patrols effective in reducing poaching-related threats within protected areas?", *J. Appl. Ecol.,* vol. 55, no. 1, pp. 99-107, 2018.
[http://dx.doi.org/10.1111/1365-2664.12965]

[84] E. Di Minin, R. Slotow, L.T.B. Hunter, F. Montesino Pouzols, T. Toivonen, P.H. Verburg, N. Leader-Williams, L. Petracca, and A. Moilanen, "Global priorities for national carnivore conservation under land use change", *Sci. Rep.,* vol. 6, no. 1, p. 23814, 2016.
[http://dx.doi.org/10.1038/srep23814] [PMID: 27034197]

[85] C. Meyer, H. Kreft, R. Guralnick, and W. Jetz, "Global priorities for an effective information basis of biodiversity distributions", *Nat. Commun.,* vol. 6, no. 1, p. 8221, 2015.
[http://dx.doi.org/10.1038/ncomms9221] [PMID: 26348291]

[86] S.J. Phillips, M. Dudík, J. Elith, C.H. Graham, A. Lehmann, J. Leathwick, and S. Ferrier, "Sample selection bias and presence-only distribution models: implications for background and pseudo-absence data", *Ecol. Appl.,* vol. 19, no. 1, pp. 181-197, 2009.
[http://dx.doi.org/10.1890/07-2153.1] [PMID: 19323182]

[87] C. Maldonado, C.I. Molina, A. Zizka, C. Persson, C.M. Taylor, J. Albán, E. Chilquillo, N. Rønsted, and A. Antonelli, "Estimating species diversity and distribution in the era of Big Data: to what extent can we trust public databases?", *Glob. Ecol. Biogeogr.,* vol. 24, no. 8, pp. 973-984, 2015.
[http://dx.doi.org/10.1111/geb.12326] [PMID: 27656106]

[88] R.L. Walls, J. Deck, R. Guralnick, S. Baskauf, R. Beaman, S. Blum, S. Bowers, P.L. Buttigieg, N. Davies, D. Endresen, M.A. Gandolfo, R. Hanner, A. Janning, L. Krishtalka, A. Matsunaga, P. Midford, N. Morrison, É.Ó. Tuama, M. Schildhauer, B. Smith, B.J. Stucky, A. Thomer, J. Wieczorek, J. Whitacre, and J. Wooley, "Semantics in support of biodiversity knowledge discovery: an introduction to the biological collections ontology and related ontologies", *PLoS One,* vol. 9, no. 3, p. e89606, 2014.
[http://dx.doi.org/10.1371/journal.pone.0089606] [PMID: 24595056]

[89] O.J. Reichman, M.B. Jones, and M.P. Schildhauer, "Challenges and opportunities of open data in ecology", *Science,* vol. 331, no. 6018, pp. 703-705, 2011. [http://dx.doi.org/10.1126/science.1197962] [PMID: 21311007]

[90] M.D. Wilkinson, M. Dumontier, I.J.J. Aalbersberg, G. Appleton, M. Axton, A. Baak, N. Blomberg, J.W. Boiten, L.B. da Silva Santos, P.E. Bourne, J. Bouwman, A.J. Brookes, T. Clark, M. Crosas, I. Dillo, O. Dumon, S. Edmunds, C.T. Evelo, R. Finkers, A. Gonzalez-Beltran, A.J.G. Gray, P. Groth, C. Goble, J.S. Grethe, J. Heringa, P.A.C. 't Hoen, R. Hooft, T. Kuhn, R. Kok, J. Kok, S.J. Lusher, M.E. Martone, A. Mons, A.L. Packer, B. Persson, P. Rocca-Serra, M. Roos, R. van Schaik, S.A. Sansone, E. Schultes, T. Sengstag, T. Slater, G. Strawn, M.A. Swertz, M. Thompson, J. van der Lei, E. van Mulligen, J. Velterop, A. Waagmeester, P. Wittenburg, K. Wolstencroft, J. Zhao, and B. Mons, "The FAIR Guiding Principles for scientific data management and stewardship", *Sci. Data,* vol. 3, no. 1, p. 160018, 2016. [http://dx.doi.org/10.1038/sdata.2016.18] [PMID: 26978244]

[91] C.F. Dormann, J.M. Calabrese, G. Guillera-Arroita, E. Matechou, V. Bahn, K. Bartoń, C.M. Beale, S. Ciuti, J. Elith, K. Gerstner, J. Guelat, P. Keil, J.J. Lahoz-Monfort, L.J. Pollock, B. Reineking, D.R. Roberts, B. Schröder, W. Thuiller, D.I. Warton, B.A. Wintle, S.N. Wood, R.O. Wüest, and F. Hartig, "Model averaging in ecology: a review of Bayesian, information-theoretic, and tactical approaches for predictive inference", *Ecol. Monogr.,* vol. 88, no. 4, pp. 485-504, 2018. [http://dx.doi.org/10.1002/ecm.1309]

[92] D.R. Roberts, V. Bahn, S. Ciuti, M.S. Boyce, J. Elith, G. Guillera-Arroita, S. Hauenstein, J.J. Lahoz-Monfort, B. Schröder, W. Thuiller, D.I. Warton, B.A. Wintle, F. Hartig, and C.F. Dormann, "Cross-validation strategies for data with temporal, spatial, hierarchical, or phylogenetic structure", *Ecography,* vol. 40, no. 8, pp. 913-929, 2017. [http://dx.doi.org/10.1111/ecog.02881]

CHAPTER 7

Application of Machine Learning in Long-Term Trend Prediction of Surface Water Quality

Akhilesh Nautiyal[1,2,*], **Ravinder Kumar**[2], **Mukul Bajpai**[3] and **Rahul Shakya**[4]

[1] *Department of Civil Engineering, National Institute of Technology (NIT) Uttarakhand, Srinagar, Uttarakhand, India*

[2] *Department of Electrical Engineering, National Institute of Technology (NIT) Uttarakhand, Srinagar, Uttarakhand, India*

[3] *CSIR–National Institute of Science Communication and Policy Research, New Delhi, Delhi, India*

[4] *Department of Civil Engineering, Institute of Engineering and Technology Lucknow, Lucknow, Uttar Pradesh, India*

Abstract: Urbanization and land use changes have a significant impact on surface water quality, altering hydrological and ecological processes through increased pollutant runoff, sedimentation, and chemical contamination. Traditional water quality assessment methods often face challenges due to limited data, high costs, and the need for continuous monitoring. The integration of machine learning (ML) with Geographic Information Systems (GIS) and remote sensing offers a powerful approach for analysing, predicting, and managing water quality by leveraging large-scale environmental datasets. This chapter explores the application of ML techniques, including supervised, unsupervised, deep learning, and hybrid approaches in assessing the effects of land use and urbanization on water quality. It highlights key data sources such as satellite imagery, hydrological and meteorological data, and in-situ water quality measurements while discussing preprocessing techniques, feature selection, and spatial modelling. Additionally, challenges related to data availability, computational complexity, and model interpretability are examined, along with potential solutions such as explainable AI, multi-source data fusion, and cloud-based GIS integration.

Keywords: Machine learning, Surface water quality, Land use change, Urbanization, Remote sensing, Gis, Predictive modelling, Water pollution.

[*] **Corresponding author Akhilesh Nautiyal:** Department of Civil Engineering, National Institute of Technology (NIT) Uttarakhand, Srinagar, Uttarakhand, India and Department of Electrical Engineering, National Institute of Technology (NIT) Uttarakhand, Srinagar, Uttarakhand, India; E-mail: akhilesh.nautiyal@nituk.ac.in

Kanwarpreet Singh, Arundhati, Manmeet Kaur, Abhishek Sharma, Aditya Kumar Tiwary & Sahil Sharma (Eds.)
All rights reserved-© 2026 Bentham Science Publishers

INTRODUCTION

Increased impermeable surfaces, industrial discharges, and agricultural runoff resulting from land-use changes and urbanization significantly affect surface water quality. Cities' growth sometimes comes with the loss of wetlands, which naturally filter water pollution and flora. Growing demand for water resources as metropolitan areas expand drives over-extraction and contamination of surface water bodies. Although physical and chemical monitoring is the foundation of conventional water quality evaluation techniques, these can be expensive and time-consuming. Large-scale assessments are challenging with these techniques since they often require frequent sampling, laboratory analysis, and manual interpretation [1].

By leveraging large datasets from remote sensing, GIS, and environmental monitoring systems, machine learning (ML) approaches offer a quick alternative for overcoming these challenges [2]. ML techniques can spot trends in water quality, offer environmental managers and legislators decision-support tools, and help them recognize patterns. Based on land-use changes and pollution sources, recent research has demonstrated that ML models can efficiently forecast fundamental water quality indicators, including pH, turbidity, biochemical oxygen demand (BOD), and dissolved oxygen (DO) [3]. A general framework for ML-based water quality assessment is highlighted in Fig. (**1**). To provide a complete understanding of water quality dynamics, these models can combine hydrological, and meteorological datasets. With an emphasis on how various algorithms are used to examine the effects of urbanization and land-use changes, this chapter investigates the potential of machine learning for water quality assessment.

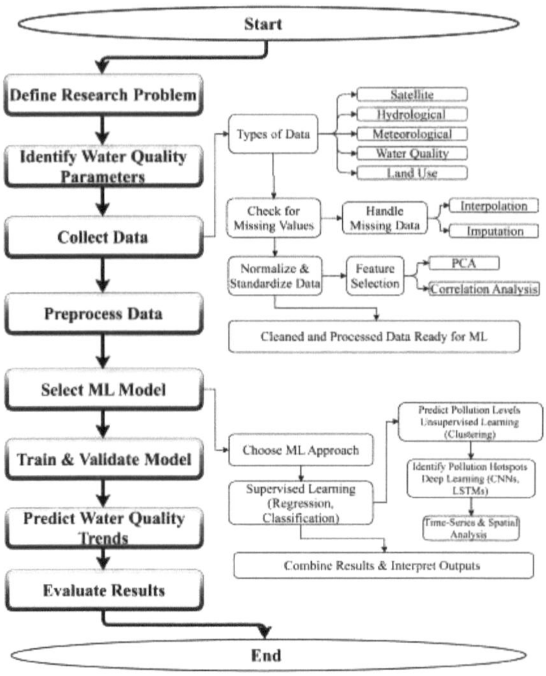

Fig. (1). General framework for ML-based water quality assessment.

ASSESSING THE IMPACT OF LAND USE AND URBANIZATION ON SURFACE WATER QUALITY USING MACHINE LEARNING

Urban areas' explosive growth results in increased stormwater runoff, which transports pollutants such as heavy metals, fertilizers, and sediments into aquatic bodies. Roads, pavements, and buildings' impervious surfaces stop natural water absorption, therefore increasing peak flow rates and causing flash floods that compromise water quality [4]. Moreover, urbanization aggravates water contamination by helping untreated sewage and industrial effluents to be released.

Urban heat island effects and climate change accentuate how urbanization influences water quality. Rising temperatures hasten metabolic activity in water bodies, leading to oxygen loss and algal blooms. Furthermore, often lacking appropriate treatment technologies, urban stormwater drainage systems let pollutants infiltrate rivers and lakes directly. Real-time monitoring of these changes in ML allows one to propose mitigating solutions [5].

Role of Land Use Changes

Surface water quality is substantially influenced by land use changes, including industrialization, agricultural development, and deforestation. Deforestation reduces the capacity for natural filtration, increasing sedimentation and nutrient loads in water bodies. Through fertilizers and pesticides, which promote eutrophication and harm aquatic life, agriculture, especially in highly cultivated regions, contributes to nutrient pollution [6].

Urban development and industrialization replace natural settings with engineered ecosystems, thereby increasing pollution loads in surrounding rivers and lakes. Changes in land use also affect hydrological cycles, thereby altering surface runoff patterns and groundwater recharge rates. Better urban design and environmental management are enabled by machine learning models' ability to analyze historical land-use data and predict future impacts on water quality.

Integration of ML models with GIS and remote sensing helps academics and legislators create predictive models to evaluate long-term impacts of land use modifications on water supplies [7]. These realizations can help apply sustainable urban design ideas, reduce pollution levels, and enhance water-saving campaigns.

DATA COLLECTION AND PREPROCESSING

Since water quality is affected by several environmental, hydrological, meteorological, and land use factors, accurate and dependable assessment of water quality calls for a complete strategy for data collection and preprocessing. Different dataset integration guarantees a comprehensive study of surface water conditions and helps machine learning (ML) models to generate more exact forecasts. Training strong ML models depends on high-quality data sources since erroneous predictions result from dataset mistakes or inconsistencies [8]. Combining satellite remote sensing data, hydrological observations, meteorological data, water quality metrics, and land-use data enables water quality assessment. Before being fed into ML models, the gathered data undergoes several preprocessing steps, including handling missing values, normalization, feature selection, and cleaning, to ensure consistency and accuracy. Using satellite images and remote sensing, which offer vast-scale, high-resolution data with continuous spatial and temporal coverage, is among the most important developments in water quality monitoring [3, 9].

Satellite Imagery and Remote Sensing Data

Offering large-scale, real-time, historical data on many water bodies, remote sensing technology has transformed water quality evaluation. Researchers and environmental organizations can study changes in aquatic ecosystems, monitor pollution levels, and detect toxins usinghis technology [10]. By recording optical, thermal, and multispectral data—which may be processed to yield water quality indicators—Satellite images offer insightful analysis of surface water conditions.

Monitoring variables, including turbidity, chlorophyll content, total suspended solids (TSS), and temperature fluctuations over large geographic areas, depend especially on remote sensing [11]. Several satellite missions have greatly aided high-resolution data for water quality evaluation.

Operating under NASA and the United States Geological Survey (USGS), the Landsat series has been a pillar of environmental monitoring. Landsat images are widely used to evaluate suspended sediments, track changes in land cover, and quantify chlorophyll concentration in surface water using sensors that detect several spectral bands [12]. These markers evaluate the ecological condition of water bodies over time and help to estimate the degree of pollution.

Managed by the European Space Agency (ESA), the Sentinel satellites offer high-resolution optical and radar images vital for identifying changes in aquatic environments. Particularly, Sentinel-2 has multispectral sensors that enable tracking of algal blooms, identification of pollution sources, and evaluation of water quality changes. Sentinel-3 captures ocean and inland water surface temperatures—necessary for understanding thermal pollution—providing water quality monitoring [13]. For long-term environmental monitoring, spectroradiometers (MODIS) offer daily global coverage of land and ocean surfaces, thereby offering great value. Large-scale water temperature fluctuations, seasonal pollution trends, and climate-induced changes in water quality are routinely analyzed using MODIS data. Its capacity to record algal bloom dynamics and chlorophyll concentration further improves water quality studies [12].

Hydrological and Meteorological Data

By influencing pollution movement, dilution, and biological reactions, hydrological and meteorological factors greatly impact surface water quality. The development of machine learning models that predict variations in water quality in response to environmental changes depends on these datasets. Rainfall frequency and intensity directly affect runoff, which brings heavy metals, nutrients, and sediments straight into water bodies. While extended dry periods can result in concentrated pollution due to decreased diffusion, high rainfall raises the risk of contamination [14]. Temperature Data: Algal blooms are encouraged, and dissolved oxygen (DO) levels are affected by temperature variations in water bodies, influencing biological reactions. Warmer temperatures hasten the breakdown of organic materials, therefore raising the biochemical oxygen demand (BOD) and causing oxygen depletion, a process that can endanger aquatic life.

Water flow dynamics control pollution transport and dispersion in streamflow and discharge data. While low-flow conditions cause stagnation, greater turbidity, and higher concentrations of pollutants like heavy metals and nutrients, high streamflow conditions improve dilution and lower pollution concentrations [15].

Water Quality Parameters

Crucially, for the training and validation of machine learning models, water quality measurements serve as basic indicators of the condition of aquatic ecosystems. These criteria provide insight into pollution levels, ecological balance, and overall water resource sustainability [16]. PH Levels: Directly affecting aquatic life, the pH value defines the acidity or alkalinity of water. Extreme pH levels affect the solubility of metals and minerals, but they can also damage fish and other aquatic life. Dissolved Oxygen: The survival of aquatic life depends critically on DO. Low DO levels can result from pollution, high temperatures, or excessive organic matter, indicating poor water quality. Fish kills and ecosystem imbalances can result from hypoxic conditions [17]. Biochemical Oxygen Demand (BOD): BOD gauges the oxygen required to break down organic waste. Often originating from wastewater discharges, agricultural runoff, and industrial effluents, high BOD levels indicate greater organic contamination. Total Suspended Solids (TSS) and turbidity evaluate sediment concentration and water clarity. While suspended particles can clog fish gills and disturb aquatic ecosystems, high turbidity reduces light penetration, thereby harming aquatic plant growth [18]. Nutrient Levels: Mostly from agricultural runoff and wastewater discharge, elevated nutrient concentrations can lead to eutrophication, resulting in excessive algal blooms, oxygen depletion, and degraded water quality. Lead, Mercury, Arsenic, etc., are heavy metals. Toxic contaminants come from urban runoff, mining, and industrial operations. These pollutants can seriously endanger human health and aquatic life, even at low levels.

Land Use and Land Cover Data

By affecting runoff patterns, pollution loads, and ecosystem stability, land use and land cover (LULC) changes significantly influence surface water quality. Deforestation, urbanization, and intensive farming, among other human activities, cause sedimentation, nutrient loading, and waterbody contamination. Predicting changes in water quality and applying effective management techniques depend on awareness of these land-use dynamics [19]. Data from Geographic Information Systems (GIS) provide spatial depictions of several land cover categories, including industrial, agricultural, forested, and urban areas. These maps examine land-use-related changes in water quality over time and help pinpoint pollution sources. Corine Land Cover (CLC) data is widely applied in European environmental research and scales land use patterns. It helps scientists evaluate how land-use changes affect surface water pollution and hydrological processes

[20]. By assessing population density, impervious surface expansion, and infrastructure development, the indices gauge the degree of human influence on landscapes. Higher levels of urbanization are usually associated with increased stormwater runoff, reduced natural filtration, and greater pollution loads in surrounding aquatic bodies [21,22].

Socioeconomic and Anthropogenic Data

Surface water quality is strongly influenced by human activities, as socioeconomic and anthropogenic factors directly affect pollution levels. Societal data must be included in water quality assessment models, as rapid urbanization, industrialization, and agricultural development have increased pollutant loads in water bodies. Knowing these factors helps one to locate pollution hotspots, project long-term trends, and create sensible mitigation plans. Population density and growth patterns: Water quality management depends much on the effectiveness of sewage infrastructure and wastewater treatment plants. Inappropriate or antiquated sewage systems may cause direct discharge of untreated wastewater, thereby increasing nutrient, organic contaminant, and pathogen loads in surface water. Reducing anthropogenic pollution requires effective wastewater management and investments in improved treatment technologies [23, 24].

Data Cleaning and Feature Selection

Machine learning-based water quality assessment depends critically on the preparation of gathered data. Missing values, irregularities, and redundant features abound in raw datasets, all of which can compromise model correctness and dependability. Correct feature selection and data cleaning guarantee that machine learning models are trained on high-quality, relevant data, therefore producing better forecasts and enhanced decision-making in environmental monitoring. Handling missing data, normalizing, standardizing, and feature selection comprise the main stages in this procedure [25, 26].

Handling Missing Data

Environmental events, uneven data collection, and sensor failures cause missing values in datasets. Maintaining dataset integrity and avoiding biased model training depend on proper management of missing data. Usually applied are the following methods:

- Based on spatial correlations between known data points, techniques such as Kriging and Inverse Distance Weighting (IDW) can estimate missing values. Many times utilized for filling in hydrological and water quality information are these geostatistical methods.

- By learning patterns from the given dataset, machine learning imputation models such as K-Nearest Neighbours (KNN) can impute missing values, and autoencoders can forecast missing values. These methods guarantee more accurate reconstruction of missing data, thereby preserving important trends.

Normalization and Standardization

Numerical variables must be converted to a common scale to guarantee consistency acrossatasets [27, 28]. This enhances model performance and helps some variables from controlling the learning process to be less dominant:

- Min-Max Normalization: Scaling preserves relationships among values by converting variables to a fixed range (*e.g*,., 0 to 1), thereby preventing the dominance of larger values.
- Z-score normalization standardizes data by centering it around zero with unit variance, thereby ensuring comparability across many measurement scales.

Feature Selection and Engineering

By lowering redundancy and improving model interpretability, feature selection and engineering help to optimize datasets. These methods are rather popular: Principal Component Analysis (PCA) is a dimensionality reduction method that improves computing efficiency by removing redundant or less important elements while preserving fundamental information. Strong data cleaning and feature selection methods help machine learning models analyze high-quality datasets, producing more accurate and reliable water quality evaluations. Effective decision-making in environmental management depends on higher generality, efficiency, and interpretability, which are ensured by these preprocessing actions [29].

MACHINE LEARNING AND AI TECHNIQUES FOR WATER QUALITY, CLIMATE, AND ENVIRONMENTAL FORECASTING

By leveraging large datasets and uncovering complex interactions among environmental variables, machine learning (ML) approaches provide powerful tools for assessing and predicting surface water quality. These methods support sustainable water resource management, aid in monitoring pollution trends, and forecast contamination events. From traditional statistical techniques to advanced deep learning algorithms, each with specific advantages for particular types of data and prediction tasks, ML models used in water quality evaluation are diverse.

Supervised Learning Methods

Supervised learning methods are widely applied in water quality assessment, in which models are trained on labelled datasets to build relationships between input variables (*e.g.*, land use patterns, pollution levels, hydrological conditions) and output predictions (*e.g.*, water quality classification, contaminant concentration forecasting). These models allow consistent, statistically backed forecasts [30 - 32].

Regression Models

Regression models, such as linear regression, are commonly used to predict continuous water quality indicators—including dissolved oxygen (DO), biochemical oxygen demand (BOD), turbidity, and nutrient concentrations. Linear regression establishes direct relationships between these water quality indicators and independent variables, such as land use changes or rainfall intensity [33, 34]. For time-series trend analysis, even a basic approach is efficient. Random Forest Regression is an ensemble learning method that combines several decision trees to improve predictive performance. For managing complex environmental datasets, especially non-linear interactions, it is quite helpful. Support Vector Regression (SVR): A machine learning model that effectively captures non-linear relationships between water quality measurements and land-use variables. It increases predictive accuracy and performs effectively across scenarios, including high-dimensional data.

Classification Models

Based on established classes such as clean, moderately contaminated, and badly polluted water bodies, classification models group water quality conditions.Simple yet powerful decision-tree models classify water bodies based on pollution levels. Widely applicable and interpretable, these models support environmental decision-making. Support Vector machines (SVMs) are a powerful classification method that excels at separating clean water samples from contaminated ones. SVMs are particularly helpful for binary classification challenges and are well-known for their effective generalization on unprocessed data. Predictive water quality assessment depends critically on supervised learning techniques, which enable scientists and legislators to create early warning systems, track pollution sources, and implement data-driven water management plans. Combining these models with geographical and remote sensing data helps to produce more thorough and accurate evaluations [35].

Unsupervised Learning Methods

Without labelled training data, unsupervised learning methods are helpful in identifying trends, grouping similar data points, and detecting anomalies in water quality datasets. These techniques expose latent correlations and structures in environmental data, therefore supporting exploratory data analysis. K-Means Clustering: Based on pH, dissolved oxygen (DO), and turbidity levels, this widely used clustering method groups water samples. K-Means facilitates the identification of pollution hotspots and classification of water bodies depending on pollution degree by separating data into several clusters. Large-scale water quality assessments where predefined contamination categories may not exist benefit especially from this approach. Density-Based Spatial Clustering of Applications with Noise, or DBSCAN, is useful for identifying anomalies and outliers in water quality databases. DBSCAN groups data points based on density, unlike K-Means, which requires a fixed number of clusters, thereby helping spot irregular pollution patterns, such as unexpected rises in heavy metal concentrations or algal bloom events.

Deep Learning Approaches

Because they can process vast, complex datasets—especially those incorporating spatial and temporal patterns—deep learning models are becoming increasingly important in water quality monitoring. These models are quite good at identifying complex interactions between water quality parameters and environmental elements. CNNs are extensively applied to evaluate surface water quality by means of remote sensing photos and satellite data. CNNs can identify variances in turbidity, chlorophyll concentration, and other pollution indicators by processing multispectral and hyperspectral images. This method helps improve large-scale water quality monitoring and provides real-time capability for assessing environmental change [36].

Applied to estimate future water quality changes based on past data, recurrent neural networks (RNNs) and long short-term memory (LSTM) networks are particularly tailored for time-series forecasting. Advanced versions of RNNs, such as LSTMs, efficiently capture long-term dependencies, which enable forecasting of parameters including dissolved oxygen levels, biochemical oxygen demand, and seasonal fluctuations in pollutant concentrations [37]. Several studies have explored the impact of road infrastructure, traffic patterns, and urbanization on environmental parameters, including water quality and land use changes [38 - 41]. Deep learning methods improve predictive modeling capacity, therefore enabling more accurate, automated, scalable assessments of water quality over many spatial and temporal scales. Combining these models with GIS data and remote sensing helps researchers create strong systems for environmental preservation and water resource management.

Hybrid Approaches

In machine learning (ML), hybrid methods integrate several methods to increase predicted accuracy, model performance, and offer a more complete study of water quality. Hybrid models can more effectively capture complex relationships between environmental factors and water quality metrics by integrating ML algorithms with physical hydrological models and GIS data [42 - 44]. Fig. (**2**) provides insight into the integration of GIS, RS, and ML.

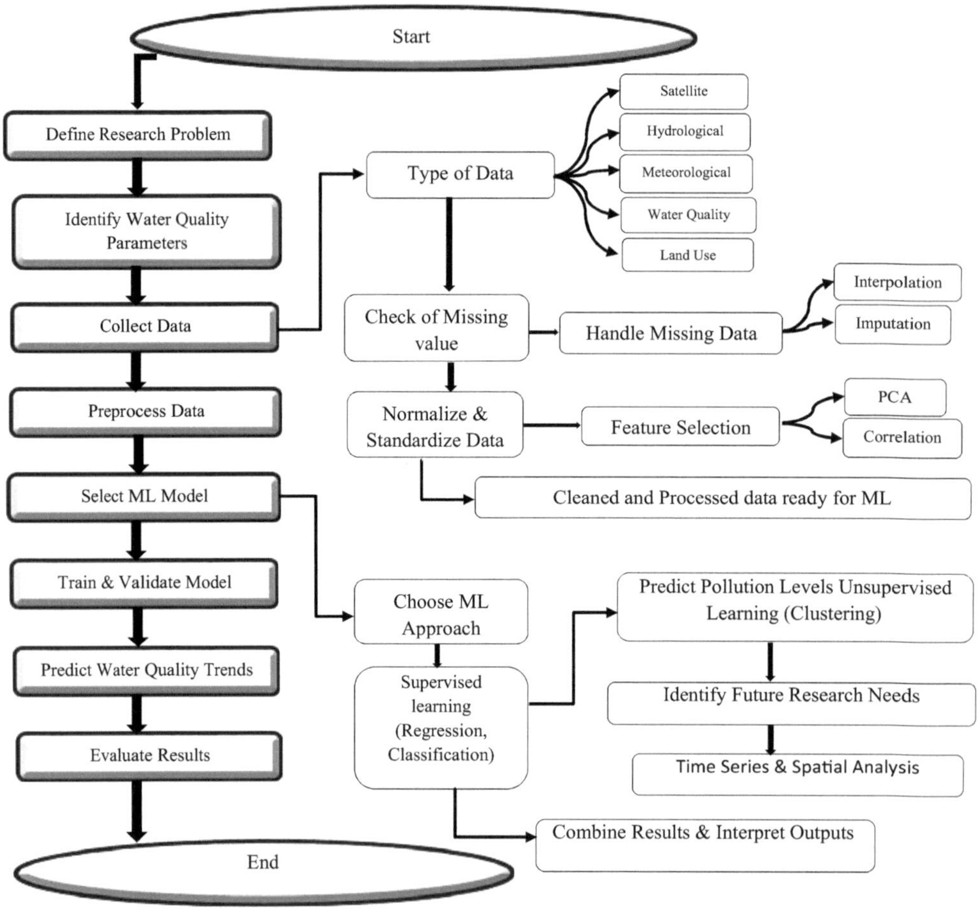

Fig. (2). Integration of GIS, Remote Sensing, and ML.

INTEGRATING MACHINE LEARNING WITH GIS AND REMOTE SENSING FOR BUILDING REAL-TIME ENVIRONMENTAL MONITORING AND EARLY WARNING SYSTEMS

Large-scale, automated evaluations made possible by the combination of machine learning (ML) with Geographic Information Systems (GIS) and remote sensing improve the spatial study of water quality. Remote sensing and GIS provide geospatial data; ML methods support pattern detection and predictive analytics. This section examines how remote sensing, GIS, and machine learning are combined to assessurface water quality [45, 46].

Spatial Interpolation Techniques

Spatial interpolation techniques play a crucial role in predicting water quality at unsampled locations by estimating values from nearby known data points. These methods help create continuous spatial distributions of water-quality indicators, aiding large-scale environmental assessments and decision-making.

The most commonly used interpolation techniques include:

Kriging: A geostatistical interpolation method that provides optimal predictions by considering spatial autocorrelation. Kriging generates smooth, accurate estimates of water quality parameters such as dissolved oxygen (DO) and turbidity by analysing the spatial relationships among observed data points. **Inverse Distance Weighting (IDW):** This deterministic technique estimates values at unsampled locations based on the proximity of known data points. Closer points exert greater influence on the prediction, making IDW useful for localized water-quality assessments. **Spline Interpolation:** This method generates smooth surfaces to analyse gradual variations in water quality parameters. It is particularly effective for modelling temperature changes, nutrient concentration gradients, and other continuous environmental variables [47, 48].

Nearest Neighbor (Thiessen/Voronoi Polygons) - this assignment method will take the value of the nearest sampled point and give this value to every unsampled location. This is a simple, easy approach to applying the original value of sampled data; however, it creates abrupt spatial edge definitions and therefore, will not be the best method for continuous areas, such as water quality, where you would expect gradual differences in values.

Trend Surface Analysis - this interpolation method fits a global polynomial to the data to represent broad, general trends across a study region. As a result of the regional gradients, it can be a useful nonparametric method, although it generally represents a simple explanation of localized features and is susceptible to outliers.

Natural Neighbor Interpolation - Natural Neighbor interpolation uses a weighted average of the nearest surrounding points. It is an interpolation method that produces a smooth and natural transition and is effective for irregularly spaced datasets. Natural neighbor interpolation may be less robust in areas with few data points or sectional distributions of data. Each interpolation method has unique benefits and downsides relative to the spatial structure of the dataset, density of sampling points, and the water quality parameter being evaluated. In any case, you must select the method that is appropriate to the application, and, where applicable, cross-validate your selected method to build confidence in the reliability of spatial prediction, outcomes, and environmental decisions.

Remote Sensing Indices for Water Quality Assessment

Remote sensing technologies provide spectral data that help assess various water quality parameters over large spatial scales. These indices enhance water quality monitoring by detecting pollutants, measuring algal blooms, and evaluating temperature variations. Commonly used indices include:

Normalized Difference Water Index (NDWI): This index is used to detect and delineate water bodies, helping evaluate surface water extent and changes over time. NDWI is particularly useful for identifying reductions in water levels due to climate change or excessive extraction. **Chlorophyll-a Concentration Analysis:** By analysing hyperspectral imagery, remote sensing techniques can estimate chlorophyll-a levels, which are indicators of algal blooms and eutrophication. Monitoring chlorophyll a concentrations helps in detecting harmful algal blooms (HABs) that can impact aquatic ecosystems and drinking water supplies. **Turbidity Index:** This index uses spectral reflectance data to estimate suspended sediment concentrations in water bodies. **Water Surface Temperature (WST):** Satellite-derived thermal imagery is used to measure surface water temperatures, which are crucial for detecting thermal pollution from industrial activities, power plants, and climate-induced warming effects. Changes in water temperature affect dissolved oxygen levels and aquatic biodiversity.

The integration of remote sensing indices with machine learning models enhances water quality assessment by enabling continuous, real-time monitoring. These indices help identify pollution trends, assess ecological health, and guide effective water resource management strategies [44].

Feature Engineering from GIS Data

Geographic Information Systems (GIS) play a crucial role in water quality assessment by enabling the extraction of spatial features that influence water pollution. Feature engineering from GIS data enhances machine learning (ML) models by providing relevant environmental and spatial attributes. Common GIS-based feature engineering techniques include:

Proximity Analysis: This method evaluates the distance between water bodies and potential pollution sources, such as urban settlements, industrial areas, and agricultural lands. By analyzing proximity, researchers can estimate the influence of human activities on water quality deterioration. *Watershed Delineation:* Watershed analysis helps identify drainage basins, stream networks, and pollutant flow patterns. Understanding how water moves through a landscape allows for better predictions of contamination spread and pollutant accumulation points. *Land Cover Classification:* Using supervised and unsupervised classification techniques, GIS data can categorize land use types such as forests, urban areas, agricultural fields, and wetlands. These classifications provide insights into how different land uses contribute to water pollution through runoff, deforestation, and industrial waste discharge.

Machine Learning Models for Spatial Water Quality Prediction

Machine learning models, when combined with GIS and remote sensing data, provide robust tools for spatially predicting water quality. These models analyze spatial patterns, classify land use, and forecast pollution levels with high accuracy. Commonly used ML models include:

Random Forest and Gradient Boosting: These ensemble learning techniques are highly effective in classifying land cover, detecting pollution sources, and predicting water quality parameters. They handle complex, non-linear relationships between spatial features and pollution levels. *Support Vector Machines (SVM):* SVMs are commonly used for spatial classification tasks, such as distinguishing between clean and polluted water zones. They are particularly effective in handling high-dimensional datasets and separating water quality categories based on GIS-derived features. *Deep Learning with Convolutional Neural Networks (CNNs):* CNNs process remote sensing images to detect patterns of water pollution, such as turbidity levels, algal blooms, and sediment concentrations [37]. By analyzing satellite imagery, CNNs enhance large-scale water quality monitoring and trend prediction.

CHALLENGES

Although machine learning (ML) is increasingly used in water quality evaluation, various issues limit its efficiency and general acceptance. Data availability and quality, computational complexity, and model generalization define these difficulties. Training strong models depends on consistent, high-quality datasets; however, data gaps, inconsistencies, and sensor errors often reduce predictive accuracy. Different spatial and temporal resolutions make integrating several sources—including remote sensing, in-situ measurements, and meteorological data—more difficult. Dealing with these constraints requires better data validation methods, sensor calibration, and ML-based approaches to handle inconsistent or missingata [36].

Another major obstacle is computational requirements, especially for deep learning models that handle vast amounts of water-quality data. Large-scale machine learning deployment is difficult, in part, due to real-time prediction constraints, high processing costs, and cloud computing costs. Overcoming these challenges depends on effective algorithms, hardware acceleration—that of GPUs, TPUs—and distributed computing solutions. Furthermore, site-specific environmental changes may make ML models trained on certain datasets difficult to generalize across different geographic areas. Often serving as "black boxes," deep learning models hinder interpretability and trust in artificial intelligence-driven decision-making. By developing explainable AI (XAI) techniques, integrating transfer learning, and applying uncertainty quantification approaches, model transparency, adaptability, and dependability will be improved.

FUTURE DIRECTIONS

Surface water quality evaluation is poised to be transformed by the combination of machine learning (ML), Geographic Information Systems (GIS), and remote sensing. Improving data integration, extending ML methods, enabling real-time applications, and enhancing policy frameworks to increase predictive accuracy and scalability should be the main priorities of future studies. Higher geographical and temporal precision will come from improving data integration via multi-source fusion involving satellites, drones, and IoT sensors. Dataset reliability will be improved through automated data cleansing methods, including ML-based imputation and anomaly detection. Furthermore, sophisticated ML techniques such as explainable artificial intelligence (XAI) and hybrid modeling will improve interpretability and model adaptability across multiple environmental contexts. Further improving the responsiveness of water quality monitoring will be the acceptance of real-time processing via edge computing, cloud-based platforms, and automated early warning systems.

Policy and regulatory systems must change to support AI-driven environmental management through standardized rules, public-private cooperation, and the resolution of ethical issues such as data privacy and bias. Integration of these future developments will help researchers and legislators create intelligent, scalable, and transparent water-quality monitoring systems, thereby guaranteeing sustainable global water resource management and active pollution control.

CONCLUDING REMARKS

By combining Geographic Information Systems (GIS) and remote sensing with machine learning (ML), surface water quality assessment has been revolutionized, providing data-driven insights for pollution monitoring, trend prediction, and supporting sustainable water resource management. This work emphasizes the importance of advanced ML methods—including supervised and unsupervised learning, deep learning, and hybrid approaches—in improving spatial analysis capacity and predictive accuracy. Notwithstanding challenges with data availability, computational complexity, and model interpretability, ongoing developments in multi-source data integration, explainable artificial intelligence, and real-time monitoring systems are enhancing the reliability and scalability of ML-based water quality assessments. To enable artificial intelligence-driven environmental decision-making, future studies should focus on improving ML models, maximizing computational efficiency, and developing uniform regulatory systems. Researchers and legislators can use cloud-based platforms, IoT-enabled sensor networks, and automated early warning systems to apply more proactive, data-driven water quality management plans. Ensuring the sustainable use and protection of global water resources depends critically on the ongoing development of ML, as well as on technical advances in GIS and remote sensing.

LIST OF ABBREVATIONS

ML	Machine Learning
GIS	Geographic Information Systems
DO	Dissolved Oxygen
BOD	Biochemical Oxygen Demand
TSS	Total Suspended Solids
MODIS	Moderate Resolution Imaging Spectroradiometer
USGS	United States Geological Survey
ESA	European Space Agency
AI	Artificial Intelligence
AIoT	Artificial Intelligence of Things
ANN	Artificial Neural Network
ARIMA	Autoregressive Integrated Moving Average
BOD	Biochemical Oxygen Demand
BRT	Boosted Regression Trees
CNN	Convolutional Neural Network
COD	Chemical Oxygen Demand
DO	Dissolved Oxygen

DT	Decision Tree
ESA	European Space Agency
EVI2	Enhanced Vegetation Index 2
EWS	Early Warning Systems
GAM	Generalized Additive Model
GIS	Geographic Information Systems
GLM	Generalized Linear Model
HSI	Habitat Suitability Index
ICT	Information and Communication Technologies
IDW	Inverse Distance Weighting
IoT	Internet of Things
LiDAR	Light Detection and Ranging
LSTM	Long Short-Term Memory
MAE	Mean Absolute Error
MaxEnt	Maximum Entropy (Model)
ML	Machine Learning
MNDWI	Modified Normalized Difference Water Index
MODIS	Moderate Resolution Imaging Spectroradiometer
NDVI	Normalized Difference Vegetation Index
NDWI	Normalized Difference Water Index
NbS	Nature-Based Solutions
NN	Neural Network
PCA	Principal Component Analysis
PINN	Physics-Informed Neural Network
RF	Random Forest
RL	Reinforcement Learning
RMSE	Root Mean Square Error
R^2	Coefficient of Determination
SAR	Synthetic Aperture Radar
SVM	Support Vector Machine
SWAT	Soil and Water Assessment Tool
SWMM	Storm Water Management Model
TSS	Total Suspended Solids
UAV	Unmanned Aerial Vehicles
UHI	Urban Heat Island

UNEP United Nations Environment Programme

USGS United States Geological Survey

WSN Wireless Sensor Network

XAI Explainable Artificial Intelligence

t-SNE t-distributed Stochastic Neighbor Embedding

REFERENCES

[1] H. M. Nazif, "Groundwater quality analysis by integrating water quality index, GIS techniques and supervised machine learning: A case study in Duhok Province, Iraq", *Passer J Basic Appl Sci,* vol. 6, no. Special Issue, pp. 28-40, 2024. [http://dx.doi.org/10.24271/PSR.2024.188474]

[2] G.S. Solangi, Z. Ali, M. Bilal, M. Junaid, S. Panhwar, H.A. Keerio, I.H. Sohu, S.G. Shahani, and N. Zaman, "Machine learning, Water Quality Index, and GIS-based analysis of groundwater quality", *Water Practice & Technology,* vol. 19, no. 2, pp. 384-400, 2024. [http://dx.doi.org/10.2166/wpt.2024.014]

[3] P. Jayaraman, K.K. Nagarajan, P. Partheeban, and V. Krishnamurthy, "Critical review on water quality analysis using IoT and machine learning models", *Int. J. Inf. Manag. Data Insights,* vol. 4, no. 1, p. 100210, 2024. [http://dx.doi.org/10.1016/j.jjimei.2023.100210]

[4] M.E. Omeka, O. Igwe, O.S. Onwuka, O.M. Nwodo, S.I. Ugar, P.A. Undiandeye, and I.E. Anyanwu, "Efficacy of GIS-based AHP and data-driven intelligent machine learning algorithms for irrigation water quality prediction in an agricultural-mine district within the lower benue trough, nigeria", *Environ. Sci. Pollut. Res. Int.,* vol. 31, no. 41, pp. 54204-54233, 2023. [http://dx.doi.org/10.1007/s11356-023-25291-3] [PMID: 36723836]

[5] M. Hossain, B. Wiegand, A. Reza, H. Chaudhuri, A. Mukhopadhyay, A. Yadav, and P.K. Patra, "A machine learning approach to investigate the impact of land use land cover (LULC) changes on groundwater quality, health risks and ecological risks through GIS and response surface methodology (RSM)", *J. Environ. Manage.,* vol. 366, p. 121911, 2024. [http://dx.doi.org/10.1016/j.jenvman.2024.121911] [PMID: 39032255]

[6] A. A, and V. v, "Effective monitoring of Noyyal River surface water quality using remote sensing and machine learning and GIS techniques", *Desalination Water Treat.,* vol. 320, p. 100630, 2024. [http://dx.doi.org/10.1016/j.dwt.2024.100630]

[7] H. Raheja, A. Goel, and M. Pal, "Evaluation of groundwater quality for drinking purposes based on machine learning algorithms and GIS", *Sustain. Water Resour. Manag.,* vol. 10, no. 1, p. 11, 2024. [http://dx.doi.org/10.1007/s40899-023-00990-4]

[8] D.T. Bui, K. Khosravi, J. Tiefenbacher, H. Nguyen, and N. Kazakis, "Improving prediction of water quality indices using novel hybrid machine-learning algorithms", *Sci. Total Environ.,* vol. 721, p. 137612, 2020. [http://dx.doi.org/10.1016/j.scitotenv.2020.137612] [PMID: 32169637]

[9] M. Ayyad, M.R. Hajj, and R. Marsooli, "Machine learning-based assessment of storm surge in the New York metropolitan area", *Sci. Rep.,* vol. 12, no. 1, p. 19215, 2022. [http://dx.doi.org/10.1038/s41598-022-23627-6] [PMID: 36357413]

[10] D.A. Alamri, S.G. Al-Solaimani, R.A. Abohassan, J. Rinklebe, and S.M. Shaheen, "Assessment of water contamination by potentially toxic elements in mangrove lagoons of the Red Sea, Saudi Arabia", *Environ. Geochem. Health,* vol. 43, no. 11, pp. 4819-4830, 2021. [http://dx.doi.org/10.1007/s10653-021-00956-5] [PMID: 34041655]

[11] C.W. Dawson, and R.L. Wilby, "Hydrological modelling using artificial neural networks", *Progress in Physical Geography,* no. 1, pp. 80-108, 2001.
[http://dx.doi.org/10.1177/030913330102500104]

[12] A. Kc, A. Chalise, D. Parajuli, N. Dhital, S. Shrestha, and T. Kandel, "Surface water quality assessment using remote sensing, gis and artificial intelligence", *Technical Journal,* vol. 1, no. 1, pp. 113-122, 2019.
[http://dx.doi.org/10.3126/tj.v1i1.27709]

[13] M. El-Rawy, M. Wahba, H. Fathi, F. Alshehri, F. Abdalla, and R.M. El Attar, "Assessment of groundwater quality in arid regions utilizing principal component analysis, GIS, and machine learning techniques", *Mar. Pollut. Bull.,* vol. 205, p. 116645, 2024.
[http://dx.doi.org/10.1016/j.marpolbul.2024.116645] [PMID: 38925024]

[14] C.O. Akinbile, and M.S. Yusoff, "Environmental impact of leachate pollution on groundwater supplies in Akure, Nigeria", *Int. J. Environ. Sci. Dev.,* vol. 2, no. 1, pp. 81-86, 2011.
[http://dx.doi.org/10.7763/IJESD.2011.V2.101]

[15] F. Abdalla, A. Al-Turki, and A. Al Amri, "Evaluation of groundwater resources in the Southern Tihama plain, Saudi Arabia", *Arab. J. Geosci.,* vol. 8, no. 5, pp. 3299-3310, 2015.
[http://dx.doi.org/10.1007/s12517-014-1401-3]

[16] M. El-Rawy, O. Batelaan, F. Alshehri, S. Almadani, M. S. Ahmed, and A. Elbeltagi, "An integrated GIS and machine-learning technique for groundwater quality assessment and prediction in southern Saudi Arabia", *Water,* vol. 15, no. 13, pp. 2448-2448, 2023.
[http://dx.doi.org/10.3390/W15132448]

[17] B. Helena, R. Pardo, M. Vega, E. Barrado, J.M. Fernandez, and L. Fernandez, "Temporal evolution of groundwater composition using multivariate statistical techniques", *Water Research,* no. 3, pp. 807-816, 2000.
[http://dx.doi.org/10.1016/S0043-1354(99)00225-0]

[18] A.K.A. Ahmed, M. El-Rawy, A.M. Ibraheem, N. Al-Arifi, and M.K. Abd-Ellah, "Forecasting of groundwater quality by using deep learning time series techniques in an arid region", *Sustainability (Basel),* vol. 15, no. 8, p. 6529, 2023.
[http://dx.doi.org/10.3390/su15086529]

[19] X. Chen, and H. Ishwaran, "Random forests for genomic data analysis", *Genomics,* vol. 99, no. 6, pp. 323-329, 2012.
[http://dx.doi.org/10.1016/j.ygeno.2012.04.003] [PMID: 22546560]

[20] F.S. Simões, A.B. Moreira, M.C. Bisinoti, S.M.N. Gimenez, and M.J.S. Yabe, "Water quality index as a simple indicator of aquaculture effects on aquatic bodies", *Ecol. Indic.,* vol. 8, no. 5, pp. 476-484, 2008.
[http://dx.doi.org/10.1016/j.ecolind.2007.05.002]

[21] J. Wang, Z. Fu, H. Qiao, and F. Liu, "Assessment of eutrophication and water quality in the estuarine area of Lake Wuli, Lake Taihu, China", *Sci. Total Environ.,* vol. 650, no. Pt 1, pp. 1392-1402, 2019.
[http://dx.doi.org/10.1016/j.scitotenv.2018.09.137] [PMID: 30308826]

[22] M. Zhu, J. Wang, X. Yang, Y. Zhang, L. Zhang, H. Ren, B. Wu, and L. Ye, "A review of the application of machine learning in water quality evaluation", *Eco-Environment & Health,* vol. 1, no. 2, pp. 107-116, 2022.
[http://dx.doi.org/10.1016/j.eehl.2022.06.001] [PMID: 38075524]

[23] R. Alam, Z. Ahmed, S.M. Seefat, and K.T.K. Nahin, "Assessment of surface water quality around a landfill using multivariate statistical method, Sylhet, Bangladesh", *Environ. Nanotechnol. Monit. Manag.,* vol. 15, p. 100422, 2021.
[http://dx.doi.org/10.1016/j.enmm.2020.100422]

[24] C. Escobar, E. Becerra-Agudelo, T. Hernández, M. Stiven, Y.A. Londoño, D.C. Rodríguez, and G.A.

Peñuela, "Seasonal and spatial variations in the presence of Giardia and cryptosporidium in rural drinking water supply systems in different municipalities of Antioquia, Colombia", *Water Air Soil Pollut.,* vol. 233, no. 9, p. 389, 2022.
[http://dx.doi.org/10.1007/s11270-022-05760-0]

[25] M. Hameed, S.S. Sharqi, Z.M. Yaseen, H.A. Afan, A. Hussain, and A. Elshafie, "Application of artificial intelligence (AI) techniques in water quality index prediction: a case study in tropical region, Malaysia", *Neural Comput. Appl.,* vol. 28, no. S1, pp. 893-905, 2017.
[http://dx.doi.org/10.1007/s00521-016-2404-7]

[26] L. Grbčić, I. Lučin, L. Kranjčević, and S. Družeta, "Water supply network pollution source identification by random forest algorithm", *J. Hydroinform.,* vol. 22, no. 6, pp. 1521-1535, 2020.
[http://dx.doi.org/10.2166/hydro.2020.042]

[27] N. Gupta, P. Pandey, and J. Hussain, "Effect of physicochemical and biological parameters on the quality of river water of Narmada, Madhya Pradesh, India", *Water Science,* vol. 31, no. 1, pp. 11-23, 2017.
[http://dx.doi.org/10.1016/j.wsj.2017.03.002]

[28] S. He, and J. Wu, "Relationships of groundwater quality and associated health risks with land use/land cover patterns: A case study in a loess area, Northwest China", *Hum. Ecol. Risk Assess.,* vol. 25, no. 1-2, pp. 354-373, 2019.
[http://dx.doi.org/10.1080/10807039.2019.1570463]

[29] D. Hammoumi, "Seasonal variations and assessment of surface water quality using water quality index (WQI) and principal component analysis (PCA): A case study", *Sustainability,* vol. 16, no. 13, pp. 5644-5644, 2024.
[http://dx.doi.org/10.3390/SU16135644]

[30] D. Valadkhan, R. Moghaddasi, and A. Mohammadinejad, "Groundwater quality prediction based on LSTM RNN: An Iranian experience," *Int. J. Environ. Sci. Technol.*, vol. 19, pp. 11397–11408, 2022.
[http://dx.doi.org/10.1007/s13762-022-04356-9]

[31] M. Zhu, J. Wang, X. Yang, Y. Zhang, L. Zhang, H. Ren, B. Wu, and L. Ye, "A review of the application of machine learning in water quality evaluation," *Eco-Environment & Health*, vol. 1, no. 2, pp. 107–116, Jun. 2022.

[32] M.E. Omeka, "Evaluation and prediction of irrigation water quality of an agricultural district, SE Nigeria: an integrated heuristic GIS-based and machine learning approach", *Environ. Sci. Pollut. Res. Int.,* vol. 31, no. 41, pp. 54178-54203, 2023.
[http://dx.doi.org/10.1007/s11356-022-25119-6] [PMID: 36622603]

[33] A. Das, "Investigation and comparative assessment of surface water quality for drinking purposes by using relief algorithm, GIS, and Machine learning: A case study of mahanadi river basin, odisha (India)", *MATEC Web of Conferences*. 2024, vol. 400, p. 02006
[http://dx.doi.org/10.1051/matecconf/202440002006]

[34] A. Gaagai, H. Aouissi, S. Bencedira, G. Hinge, A. Athamena, S. Heddam, M. Gad, O. Elsherbiny, S. Elsayed, M. Eid, and H. Ibrahim, "Application of water quality indices, machine learning approaches, and gis to identify groundwater quality for irrigation purposes: A case study of sahara aquifer, doucen plain, algeria", *Water,* vol. 15, no. 2, p. 289, 2023.
[http://dx.doi.org/10.3390/w15020289]

[35] M.L. Calijuri, J.S. Castro, L.S. Costa, P.P. Assemany, and J.E.M. Alves, "Impact of land use/land cover changes on water quality and hydrological behavior of an agricultural subwatershed", *Environ. Earth Sci.,* vol. 74, no. 6, pp. 5373-5382, 2015.
[http://dx.doi.org/10.1007/s12665-015-4550-0]

[36] S. Dutta, A. Dwivedi, and M. Suresh Kumar, "Use of water quality index and multivariate statistical techniques for the assessment of spatial variations in water quality of a small river", *Environ. Monit. Assess.,* vol. 190, no. 12, p. 718, 2018.

[http://dx.doi.org/10.1007/s10661-018-7100-x] [PMID: 30426242]

[37] S. Bedi, A. Samal, C. Ray, and D. Snow, "Comparative evaluation of machine learning models for groundwater quality assessment", *Environ. Monit. Assess.,* vol. 192, no. 12, p. 776, 2020. [http://dx.doi.org/10.1007/s10661-020-08695-3] [PMID: 33219864]

[38] A. Nautiyal, and S. Sharma, "A model to compute service life of rural roads using present pavement condition and pavement age", *COMPUSOFT: An Int. J. Adv. Comput. Technol.,* vol. 8, no. 7, pp. 3261-3268, 2024.

[39] A. Nautiyal, and S. Sharma, "Cost-optimized approach for pavement maintenance planning of low volume rural roads: a case study in himalayan region", *Int. J. Pavement Res. Technol.,* vol. 17, no. 2, pp. 335-352, 2024.
[http://dx.doi.org/10.1007/s42947-022-00239-x]

[40] A. Arora, and A. Nautiyal, "Road safety audit of Suratgarh bypass link road in Rajasthan, India", *AIP Conf. Proc.,* vol. 3146, no. 1, p. 030005, 2024.
[http://dx.doi.org/10.1063/5.0224970]

[41] A. Verma, and A. Nautiyal, "Sustainable approach for geometric design of highway using openroads: A case study of NH-05", *J. Min. Environ.,* vol. 14, no. 3, pp. 825-837, 2023.
[http://dx.doi.org/10.22044/JME.2023.12924.2346]

[42] S. Baidya Roy, and R. Avissar, "Impact of land use/land cover change on regional hydrometeorology in Amazonia", *J. Geophys. Res.,* vol. 107, no. D20, pp. LBA 4-1-LBA 4-12, 2002.
[http://dx.doi.org/10.1029/2000JD000266]

[43] N. Akhtar, M.I.S. Ishak, M.I. Ahmad, K. Umar, M.S. Md Yusuff, M.T. Anees, A. Qadir, and Y.K. Ali Almanasir, "Modification of the water quality index (WQI) process for simple calculation using the multi-criteria decision-making (MCDM) method: a review", *Water,* vol. 13, no. 7, p. 905, 2021.
[http://dx.doi.org/10.3390/w13070905]

[44] S.M. Avvannavar, and S. Shrihari, "Evaluation of water quality index for drinking purposes for river Netravathi, Mangalore, South India", *Environ. Monit. Assess.,* vol. 143, no. 1-3, pp. 279-290, 2008.
[http://dx.doi.org/10.1007/s10661-007-9977-7] [PMID: 17912597]

[45] W. Ahmad, J. Iqbal, M.J. Nasir, B. Ahmad, M.T. Khan, S.N. Khan, and S. Adnan, "Impact of land use/land cover changes on water quality and human health in district Peshawar Pakistan", *Sci. Rep.,* vol. 11, no. 1, p. 16526, 2021.
[http://dx.doi.org/10.1038/s41598-021-96075-3] [PMID: 34400746]

[46] K. Anwar, and V. Aggarwal, "Analysis of groundwater quality of Aligarh City,(India): using water quality index", *Curr. World Environ.,* vol. 9, no. 3, pp. 851-857, 2014.
[http://dx.doi.org/10.12944/CWE.9.3.36]

[47] R. Anjum, S.A. Ali, and M.A. Siddiqui, "Assessing the impact of land cover on groundwater quality in a smart city using GIS and machine learning algorithms", *Water Air Soil Pollut.,* vol. 234, no. 3, p. 182, 2023.
[http://dx.doi.org/10.1007/s11270-023-06198-8]

[48] S.-P. Shin, K. Kim, T. Ho, and M. Le, "Feasibility of advanced reflective cracking prediction and detection for pavement management systems using machine learning and image detection", *Buildings,* vol. 14, no. 6, pp. 1808-1808, 2024.
[http://dx.doi.org/10.3390/BUILDINGS14061808]

CHAPTER 8

Conclusion

Kanwarpreet Singh[1,*], **Abhishek Sharma**[1], **Arundhati**[2], **Manmeet Kaur**[2], **Aditya Kumar Tiwari**[1], **Sahil Sharma**[1], **Gagandeep Singh**[3] and **Preetpal Singh**[4]

[1] *University Centre for Research and Development (UCRD) Chandigarh University, Mohali, Punjab, India*

[2] *Department of Civil Engineering, Chandigarh University, Mohali, Punjab, India*

[3] *Department of Computer Science and Engineering, Chandigarh University, Mohali, Punjab, India*

[4] *Department of Civil Engineering, Rayat Bahra University, Kharar, Punjab, India*

SUMMARY OF THE BOOK

This book, titled "Machine Learning and Spatial Optimization" provides a thorough exploration of the evolving field of environmental observation, with a strong focus on analytical and geographic methods. The content is carefully organized to guide readers from identifying worldwide environmental challenges to applying sophisticated spatial and statistical techniques for effective environmental resource management and informed decision-making. The initial chapters delineate critical global environmental issues, including the deterioration of water quality, air pollution, climate change, loss of natural habitats, and the increasing occurrence of natural disasters. These sections establish the essential groundwork and context for appreciating the urgency of employing advanced analytical tools within the environmental sciences.

Following this, the book introduces a range of methodologies applicable to environmental monitoring. Particular emphasis is placed on techniques that enhance the ability to observe, analyze, and interpret environmental data. Chapters on predictive modeling, pattern recognition, and learning from data outline different strategies used to extract meaningful information from datasets, presented within a framework of statistical and predictive analysis. A diverse array of algorithmic approaches is presented, encompassing regression models, rule-based systems, and classification techniques. The text then transitions into a

* **Corresponding author Kanwarpreet Singh:** University Centre for Research and Development (UCRD) Chandigarh University, Mohali, Punjab, India; E-mail: singhkanwarpreetnit@gmail.com

Kanwarpreet Singh, Arundhati, Manmeet Kaur, Abhishek Sharma, Aditya Kumar Tiwary & Sahil Sharma (Eds.)
All rights reserved-© 2026 Bentham Science Publishers

detailed explanation of spatial analysis methods. Readers are introduced to fundamental concepts such as spatial estimation, Kriging, cluster identification, and high-risk area detection. These methodologies are vital for understanding geographic distribution patterns and making location-specific environmental decisions. The integration of satellite imagery and mapping tools is also highlighted as a significant advantage for acquiring up-to-date data across extensive, often inaccessible regions.

Water resource management is given substantial attention, with dedicated chapters on evaluating surface water quality, preserving spring water sources, and hydrological mapping. Various statistical methods and illustrative examples demonstrate how data can be utilized to assess pollution levels, track seasonal variations, and support the sustainable use of freshwater resources. Air quality studies form another key theme. The book covers various predictive modeling techniques for understanding pollution levels, tracking atmospheric patterns, and designing alert systems for public safety. Trend analysis tools and time-series evaluation methods are discussed in the context of identifying both seasonal and long-term changes in air pollutant concentrations. Disaster management constitutes a significant portion of the book. The application of geospatial mapping for identifying flood-prone zones, landslide-prone areas, and earthquake-prone regions is comprehensively examined. The importance of planning for emergency response and of optimizing resource allocation based on spatial data is emphasized through detailed case studies.

The book also addresses ecological themes, with chapters dedicated to mapping wildlife habitats and assessing the impact of environmental stress on species. Conservation strategies are discussed within the broader context of land-use changes and adaptation to climate change. Urban environmental planning is covered in a section that addresses the concept of climate-resilient cities. Topics include managing urban heat islands, reducing carbon emissions through land-use planning, and optimizing infrastructure development through geographic modeling.

In the concluding chapters, the book emphasizes the necessity of ethical data use, awareness of biases in data collection, and the potential of collaborative platforms that foster transparency and shared learning in environmental research. The conclusion reflects on the importance of policy interventions, stakeholder involvement, and continued investment in monitoring technologies. This volume offers readers a practical understanding of how environmental data can be effectively utilized for sustainable development, disaster preparedness, and the conservation of natural resources. By integrating theoretical insights with real-world applications, the book serves as a valuable resource for researchers, planners, environmental managers, and policymakers engaged in the planning of ecosystems and infrastructure.

AI ETHICS, DATA BIASES, AND THE ROLE OF OPEN-SOURCE PLATFORMS

Introduction

The role of artificial intelligence (AI) and machine learning (ML) has become integral in solving optimization challenges, resulting in the high importance of integrating soft computing with ethical fundamentals [1]. This integration is no longer optional; it is essential in today's evolving world. The confluence of these techniques has increased manifold across both old and emerging technologies. Societal infrastructure, environmental management, and resource planning require rigorous scrutiny of how models are trained, how data is curated, and who benefits from the resulting decisions. The chapter here highlights the importance of AI ethics, data biases, and the role of open-source platforms in democratizing access to AI tools [2].

The role of AI Ethics in Spatial Optimization

The importance of ethics in AI is enormous and is primarily concerned with ensuring that intelligent systems act in ways that are fair, transparent, and aligned with human values. In terms of spatial optimization, smooth integration will result in dynamic decisions that will impact urban development, reduce the timings of disaster response, and assist in agricultural planning. Thus displaying an amplified importance in the field of spatial optimization [3]. However, this integration is accompanied by numerous ethical challenges, which include:

- **Accountability and Transparency:** The models we talk about in artificial intelligence, deep learning, and machine learning used for spatial and geospatial analysis are often lacking boxes [4]. Explainability techniques (*e.g.*, SHAP, LIME) must be incorporated to justify decisions affecting real-world outcomes.
- **Consent and Privacy:** Spatial data may contain sensitive information, such as land ownership, migration patterns, or health indicators. Ensuring that data collection and model deployment comply with data protection regulations (*e.g.*, GDPR, DPDP Act) is critical [5].
- **Sustainability and Equity:** Optimizations should not reinforce inequalities like urban-rural divides or infrastructural disparities. Ethical AI must be proactive in promoting inclusive growth and sustainable resource allocation.

Data Biases and Their Implications

The performance of the machine learning models is as good as the amount of data associated with learning. The study pertaining to spatial domains can lead to data biases in the input, resulting in uncertainty in the outputs [6]. This can be due to inconsistent sampling, historical inequalities, or missing data from marginalized areas.

- **Sampling Bias:** This form of bias occurs due to training on one form of data and evaluation on another form of data. This means that the over-representation of urban or developed regions in training datasets may result in poorly performing models in rural or low-resource contexts [7].
- **Historical Bias:** Past policy decisions, mapping practices, or old land-use practices impact the dataset's quality, leading to an inclination away from the current real-world scenario, wrongly reflecting the contemporary realities [8].
- **Labelling and Annotation Bias:** In supervised learning, the subjectivity in labeling (*e.g.*, land-use classification by different experts) can embed inconsistencies and personal judgments into models [9].

To mitigate these biases:

- Making use of comprehensive datasets collected during the sampling campaigns.
- The algorithms and evaluation strategies should be incorporated so that they apply fairly to every region and space.
- The educated practice involves using an ensemble approach, which combines the evaluation designs of different performance models, thereby reducing underfitting and overfitting.

What Role Does Open-source Platform Play in Today's World

Open-source platforms are the need of the hour, enhancing transparency, reproducibility, and equity in deploying ML tools for spatial optimization [10].

- **Transparency and Peer Review:** By making codebases and workflows publicly available (*e.g., via* GitHub, Zenodo), researchers can ensure that their methods withstand external scrutiny.
- **Community Contribution:** Collaborative open-source ecosystems, such as TensorFlow, PyTorch, ARCGIS< QGIS, and Google Earth Engine, foster innovation and enable contributions from a diverse, global talent pool [11].
- **Bridging Gaps in Access:** Open-source tools reduce the barrier to entry for

low-resource institutions and researchers from developing regions, enabling them to contribute to and benefit from the latest advances in spatial AI [12].

However, coupling open-source platforms with well-documented scripts and policy will lead to user-friendly, accessible end products.

Conclusion

In the growing world of artificial intelligence, deep learning, and machine learning models, we must be aware of and equipped with the knowledge and responsibility to scientifically harness these tools for spatial optimization. Adequate focus should be given to guiding ethical principles, selecting representative datasets, and leveraging the strengths of open-source platforms in a fair, resilient, and inclusive manner. By integrating artificial intelligence with spatial datasets, the developed culture can ensure the applications are true, just, viable, and sustainable for a good today and a better tomorrow.

POLICY IMPLICATIONS OF USING MACHINE LEARNING IN ENVIRONMENTAL MONITORING

Introduction

The growing use of machine learning (ML) in environmental monitoring is changing the way we track and respond to environmental changes. With their advanced capabilities, ML tools are unlocking new opportunities, but they also bring a range of challenges that policymakers must carefully consider. In the past, environmental monitoring often faced limitations such as slow data collection, limited analytical tools, and tight budgets. ML is helping overcome these hurdles by identifying patterns in large, complex datasets, making accurate predictions, and automating processes that once required significant time and effort. This means we can now get faster, deeper insights into environmental trends and threats. However, the integration of these technologies is not without complications. Major key concerns include how reliable these systems are, whether their decision-making processes are transparent, who has access to the data, and how these tools fit into existing environmental goals and laws. There is also the issue of fairness, ensuring that vulnerable communities aren't left behind as digital tools become more central to environmental decision making.

This chapter takes a closer look at the policies needed to guide the use of ML in this space. It outlines how governments and international organizations can adapt existing rules or create new ones to keep pace with technological advances. It also explores how to ensure ethical data use, support international cooperation, and encourage inclusive access to the benefits of machine learning. In short, as ML continues to shape the future of environmental science and policy, it is important that we build thoughtful, forward-looking frameworks to guide its use, balancing innovation with responsibility.

- The changing landscape of environmental monitoring
- Evolution of environmental monitoring systems
- The role of machine learning in modern environmental monitoring

Over the past hundred years, the way we monitor the environment has changed dramatically. In the early days, it mostly involved scientists going out into the field, collecting samples by hand, and analyzing them in the lab. This approach, while valuable, was often slow, limited in coverage, and didn't capture rapid, widespread changes. Things began to shift in the mid-20th century with the introduction of remote sensing. For the first time, satellites could regularly scan large areas of Earth's surface, giving scientists a much broader view of environmental changes. Today, your monitoring systems are even more advanced. We now rely on a wide range of tools and data sources from Ground-based sensors and satellite images to inputs from everyday people and smart devices connected through the Internet of Things (IOT). The latest step in this evaluation is the use of machine learning. These advanced computer algorithms can analyze huge amounts of data, spot hidden patterns, and make accurate predictions, something that would take humans far more time or might not even be possible using traditional methods. As a result, machine learning is changing every stage of environmental monitoring, from how we collect data to how we make sense of it and communicate the findings.

- How Machine learning is being used today
- Machine learning is already making a difference across many areas of environmental science.
  Here are a few examples.
- Air Quality monitoring
- Water Quality Analysis
- Tracking Biodiversity
- Climate Science
- Land Use and Land Cover Monitoring
- Natural Disaster Management

Machine learning forecasts pollution levels, traces where harmful emissions are coming from, and designs better sensor networks to keep communities informed.

These tools can quickly process chemical and biological data to flag potential contamination events and even predict future water conditions. Using images and sound recordings, machine learning can identify different animal and plant species, allowing researchers to carry out large-scale biodiversity studies with minimal manual effort. Machine learning also improves climate models and helps in detecting extreme weather events sooner, making it easier to apply global climate projections to specific local areas. Machine learning can automatically analyse satellite images to detect changes like deforestation, new construction or shifts in farmland use. From floods to wildfires, machine learning systems analyse real-time and historical data to provide faster and more accurate early warnings.

Such examples show how powerful and adaptable Machine learning is in tackling various environmental challenges. But they also point to an important truth: different environmental issues have different needs. That's why thoughtful, well-crafted policies are essential to guide how we use machine learning in each area. The goal should be to support innovation while making sure the tools are accurate and aligned with our broader environmental goals.

- Data Governance and Access
- Data Ownership and Rights

The question of who owns environmental monitoring data generated through ML systems is fundamental to policy development. Various entities, including government agencies, private companies, research institutions, and citizen scientists, may collect environmental data. When this data is processed using ML algorithms—which may themselves be proprietary—the resulting insights raise complex questions of ownership and intellectual property rights.

Policy frameworks must address:

- Rights and responsibilities of data collectors, processors, and users
- Intellectual property considerations for ML-derived environmental insights
- Balancing proprietary interests with public good considerations
- Legal frameworks for data sharing across jurisdictions and sectors

Clear data ownership policies are essential for fostering innovation while ensuring that environmental monitoring serves the public interest. Policymakers must navigate tensions between commercial incentives for developing ML technologies and the societal benefits of open access to environmental information. Regulatory frameworks are highlighted in Table **1**.

Table 1. Privacy risks and mitigation strategies in ML-enhanced environmental monitoring.

Monitoring Type	Privacy Risks	Policy Mitigation Strategies
High-resolution satellite imagery	Identification of individuals, observation of private property.	Resolution limits in sensitive areas, blurring techniques, and notification systems.
Urban sensor networks	Tracking of movement patterns, behavioral monitoring.	Data aggregation requirements, opt-out provisions, and purpose limitations.
Acoustic monitoring	Recording of conversations, identification of individuals by voice.	Filtering algorithms for human speech, clear signage in monitored areas.
Mobile air quality sensors	Location tracking of individuals carrying sensors.	Data anonymization protocols, separation of location and environmental data.
Water consumption monitoring	Inference of household activities and behaviours.	Aggregation at the neighbourhood level, restricted access to household-level data.

Integration into Existing Environmental Regulations

Most of the environmental laws and regulations we rely on today were written long before machine learning became part of the picture. Now that machine learning is playing a growing role in monitoring and analysing environmental data, we need to rethink how our regulatory system works. This means asking important questions about how to use machine learning-generated insights to guide policy decisions, ensure compliance, and take enforcement actions when necessary. Some key policy questions that need attention include:

- Can machine learning data be considered legally valid for regulatory use?
- What standards should apply if enforcement actions are based on machine learning analysis?
- How much human supervision is needed when using automated monitoring systems.
- How should permitting systems evolve to include Machine learning tools.
- Should regulations support real-time, continuous monitoring instead of periodic checks.

Some governments are already taking steps to modernize their environmental policies. For instance, the European Union's environmental monitoring program has begun recognizing the role of artificial intelligence in environmental monitoring. Similarly, the US Environmental Protection Agency has issued guidance on validating ML models for regulatory use.

Liability and Accountability

As the use of machine learning systems for environmental monitoring increases, it becomes essential to determine accountability in cases of failure, whether the cause lies in software errors, inaccurate data inputs, or implementation shortcomings. Any failure in the monitoring system could lead to serious environmental consequences. But in these complex systems, figuring out who is responsible can be tricky

- To address these concerns, policy frameworks should consider?
- Why are liable tech developers, system operators, or the agencies using the technology?
- Should there be formal certification processes for Machine learning?
- Do we need special insurance to cover risks linked to Machine learning systems' work?
- How do we handle and communicate the uncertainty that comes with Machine learning predictions?

A good liability framework should strike a balance. It needs to hold people accountable for mistakes, but it should not be so harsh that it discourages innovation. If we want to keep developing better technologies to protect the environment, we need rules that support both progress and responsibility. Table **2** provides an insight into liability allocation models for ML-enhanced environmental monitoring systems.

Table 2. Liability allocation models for ml-enhanced environmental monitoring systems.

Liability Model	Description	Advantages	Disadvantages	Policy Implementation Examples
Developer Liability	Primary responsibility with the algorithm creators.	Clear accountability for algorithmic failures	May discourage innovation	EU Product Liability Directive extension to AI
Operator Liability	Primary responsibility with system deployers.	Encourages careful implementation.	May lead to overly cautious deployment	Traditional operator liability regimes
Shared Liability	Proportional responsibility across the value chain.	Distributed responsibility matches distributed control.	Complex to adjudicate	Emerging ML-specific frameworks
Public Insurance	Government-backed compensation system.	Provides a remedy without assigning blame	May reduce incentives for care	Environmental damage funds

(Table 2) cont.....

Liability Model	Description	Advantages	Disadvantages	Policy Implementation Examples
Safe Harbor with Standards	Liability protection for adherence to standards.	Encourages best practices.	Standards may lag behind technology	FDA medical device regulation model

RECOMMENDATIONS

Incorporating spatial analysis and machine learning (ML) into environmental monitoring has shown great promise in tackling ecological issues worldwide. To increase the efficiency of these technologies in environmental sustainability initiatives, the following suggestions are put forth in light of the knowledge gained from the previous chapters.

1. **Strengthening Data Collection and Accessibility**
   - High-Resolution and Real-Time Data: To increase data accuracy and temporal resolution, governments and academic institutions should spend money on satellite imaging, IoT-based sensors, and sophisticated remote sensing technologies.
   - Open Data Platforms: To promote cooperative research and model training, support the creation of open-source repositories for environmental datasets.
   - Data Format Standardization: To guarantee compatibility across various machine learning and spatial analysis tools, set international standards for environmental data collection.
2. **Enhancing Machine Learning Models for Environmental Applications**
   - Hybrid and Explainable AI Models: To gain the trust of policymakers, encourage the adoption of hybrid machine learning models (such as mixing CNNs and LSTMs to predict water quality) while maintaining model openness.
   - Transfer Learning for Regional Adaptation: To save computational costs and increase prediction accuracy, use previously trained models and modify them for local environmental conditions.
   - Real-Time Processing Capabilities: Create lightweight AI models and edge computing for real-time environmental monitoring, especially for disaster relief and air quality monitoring.
3. **Improving Spatial Analysis Techniques**
   - GIS and Remote Sensing Integration: Increase the usage of geospatial technologies (such as QGIS and ArcGIS) with machine learning algorithms to improve biodiversity conservation, land-use planning, and disaster risk assessment.

- Advanced Interpolation Techniques: To increase the accuracy of pollution mapping and resource allocation, apply kriging, spatial clustering, and hot spot analysis.
- Participatory GIS (PGIS): Increase the accuracy and usefulness of environmental monitoring programs by involving local communities in the collection of spatial data.

4. **Policy and Governance Interventions**
   - AI-Driven Environmental Policies: Plans for addressing climate change, urban planning, and water resource management should all include ML-based predictive analytics.
   - AI Ethics Frameworks: By making sure that training data is inclusive and diverse, especially for disadvantaged locations, biases in environmental datasets can be addressed.
   - Public-Private Partnerships (PPPs): Encourage cooperation between academic institutions, technology companies, and environmental organizations to boost the development of intelligent monitoring systems.
5. **Capacity Building and Public Awareness**
   - Training Programs: To give researchers and policymakers the technological know-how they need, introduce specialist courses in AI for environmental science.
   - Citizen Science Initiatives: Use crowdsourcing websites and mobile applications to promote public involvement in the gathering of environmental data.
   - Awareness Campaigns: Make effective use of AI-generated insights to inform the public about environmental hazards (such as flood warnings and air pollution alerts).
6. **Future Research Directions**
   - Quantum Machine Learning for Environmental Modelling: Investigate quantum computing to improve the efficiency of handling massive environmental datasets.
   - AI for the Circular Economy: Examine machine learning applications in sustainable resource use, recycling optimization, and trash management.
   - Climate-Resilient Smart Cities: Use spatial optimization approaches to advance studies on carbon capture, urban heat island abatement, and green infrastructure development.

The integration of environmental science, machine learning, and spatial analysis offers a revolutionary chance to tackle climate change, preserve biodiversity, and create sustainable urban environments. However, interdisciplinary cooperation, strong data governance, and ongoing innovation are necessary for successful deployment. Stakeholders can fully leverage AI-driven environmental monitoring to ensure a resilient and sustainable future by implementing these suggestions.

REFERENCES

[1] A. B. Rashid and M. D. A. K. Kausik, "AI revolutionizing industries worldwide: A comprehensive overview of its diverse applications", *Hybrid Advances*. vol. 7, 2024. [http://dx.doi.org/10.1016/j.hybadv.2024.100277]

[2] L. Zhang, S. Banihashemi, L. Zhu, H. Molavi, E. Odacioglu, and M. Shan, "A scientometric analysis of knowledge transfer partnerships in digital transformation", *J. Open Innov.,* vol. 10, no. 3, p. 100325, 2024. [http://dx.doi.org/10.1016/j.joitmc.2024.100325]

[3] N. Díaz-Rodríguez, J. Del Ser, M. Coeckelbergh, M. López de Prado, E. Herrera-Viedma, and F. Herrera, "Connecting the dots in trustworthy Artificial Intelligence: From AI principles, ethics, and key requirements to responsible AI systems and regulation," *Information Fusion*, vol. 99, Art. 101896, 2023. [http://dx.doi.org/10.1016/j.inffus.2023.101896]

[4] Y. Xu, X. Liu, X. Cao, C. Huang, E. Liu, S. Qian, X. Liu, Y. Wu, F. Dong, C.W. Qiu, J. Qiu, K. Hua, W. Su, J. Wu, H. Xu, Y. Han, C. Fu, Z. Yin, M. Liu, R. Roepman, S. Dietmann, M. Virta, F. Kengara, Z. Zhang, L. Zhang, T. Zhao, J. Dai, J. Yang, L. Lan, M. Luo, Z. Liu, T. An, B. Zhang, X. He, S. Cong, X. Liu, W. Zhang, J.P. Lewis, J.M. Tiedje, Q. Wang, Z. An, F. Wang, L. Zhang, T. Huang, C. Lu, Z. Cai, F. Wang, and J. Zhang, "Artificial intelligence: A powerful paradigm for scientific research", *Innovation,* vol. 2, no. 4, p. 100179, 2021. [http://dx.doi.org/10.1016/j.xinn.2021.100179] [PMID: 34877560]

[5] E. M. Delmelle, M. R. Desjardins, P. Jung, C. Owusu, Y. Lan, A. Hohl, and C. Dony, "Uncertainty in geospatial health: challenges and opportunities ahead," *Ann. Epidemiol.*, vol. 65, pp. 15–30, 2022. [http://dx.doi.org/10.1016/j.annepidem.2021.10.002]

[6] M. Z. Naser, "From failure to fusion: A survey on learning from bad machine learning models," *Information Fusion*, vol. 120, p. 103122, 2025. [http://dx.doi.org/10.1016/j.inffus.2025.103122]

[7] M.G. Hanna, L. Pantanowitz, B. Jackson, O. Palmer, S. Visweswaran, J. Pantanowitz, M. Deebajah, and H.H. Rashidi, "Ethical and bias considerations in artificial intelligence/machine learning", *Mod. Pathol.,* vol. 38, no. 3, p. 100686, 2025. [http://dx.doi.org/10.1016/j.modpat.2024.100686] [PMID: 39694331]

[8] Y. K. Dwivedi, L. Hughes, A. M. Baabdullah, S. Ribeiro-Navarrete, M. Giannakis, M. M. Al-Debei, D. Dennehy, B. Metri, D. Buhalis, C. M. K. Cheung, K. Conboy, R. Doyle, R. Dubey, V. Dutot, R. Felix, D. P. Goyal, A. Gustafsson, C. Hinsch, I. Jebabli, and S. F. Wamba, "Metaverse beyond the hype: Multidisciplinary perspectives on emerging challenges, opportunities, and agenda for research, practice and policy," *Int. J. Inf. Manag.*, vol. 66, Art. 102542, Oct. 2022. [http://dx.doi.org/10.1016/j.ijinfomgt.2022.102542]

[9] C. Cipriano, S. Noce, S. Mereu, and M. Santini, "Algorithms going wild – A review of machine learning techniques for terrestrial ecology," *Ecol. Model.*, vol. 506, Art. 111164, Jul. 2025. [http://dx.doi.org/10.1016/j.ecolmodel.2025.111164]

[10] T. Zhao, S. Wang, C. Ouyang, M. Chen, C. Liu, J. Zhang, L. Yu, F. Wang, Y. Xie, J. Li, F. Wang, S. Grunwald, B.M. Wong, F. Zhang, Z. Qian, Y. Xu, C. Yu, W. Han, T. Sun, Z. Shao, T. Qian, Z. Chen, J. Zeng, H. Zhang, H. Letu, B. Zhang, L. Wang, L. Luo, C. Shi, H. Su, H. Zhang, S. Yin, N. Huang, W. Zhao, N. Li, C. Zheng, Y. Zhou, C. Huang, D. Feng, Q. Xu, Y. Wu, D. Hong, Z. Wang, Y. Lin, T. Zhang, P. Kumar, A. Plaza, J. Chanussot, J. Zhang, J. Shi, and L. Wang, "Artificial intelligence for geoscience: Progress, challenges, and perspectives", *Innovation,* vol. 5, no. 5, p. 100691, 2024. [http://dx.doi.org/10.1016/j.xinn.2024.100691] [PMID: 39285902]

[11] A. Velastegui-Montoya, N. Montalván-Burbano, P. Carrión-Mero, H. Rivera-Torres, L. Sadeck, and M. Adami, "Google Earth Engine: A global analysis and future trends," *Remote Sens.*, vol. 15, no. 14, Art. 3675, 2023. [http://dx.doi.org/10.3390/rs15143675]

[12] D.G. Silva, C. Coutinho, and C.J. Costa, "Factors influencing free and open-source software adoption in developing countries—an empirical study", *J. Open Innov.,* vol. 9, no. 1, p. 100002, 2023. [http://dx.doi.org/10.1016/j.joitmc.2023.01.002]

SUBJECT INDEX

A

B

C

D

E

F

G

H

Kanwarpreet Singh, Arundhati, Manmeet Kaur, Abhishek Sharma, Aditya Kumar Tiwary & Sahil Sharma (Eds.)
All rights reserved-© 2026 Bentham Science Publishers

I

K

L

M

N

O

P

Q

R

S

T

U

V

W

X

www.ingramcontent.com/pod-product-compliance
Lightning Source LLC
LaVergne TN
LVHW070948210926
848482LV00002B/134
* 9 7 9 8 8 9 8 8 1 3 8 0 2 *